Lecture Notes in Computer Science 1146

Edited by G. Goos, J. Hartmanis and J. van Leeuwen

Advisory Board: W. Brauer   D. Gries   J. Stoer

Springer
Berlin
Heidelberg
New York
Barcelona
Budapest
Hong Kong
London
Milan
Paris
Santa Clara
Singapore
Tokyo

Elisa Bertino   Helmut Kurth
Giancarlo Martella   Emilio Montolivo (Eds.)

Computer Security – ESORICS 96

4th European Symposium
on Research in Computer Security
Rome, Italy, September 25-27, 1996
Proceedings

Springer

Series Editors

Gerhard Goos, Karlsruhe University, Germany

Juris Hartmanis, Cornell University, NY, USA

Jan van Leeuwen, Utrecht University, The Netherlands

Volume Editors

Elisa Bertino
Giancarlo Martella
Università degli Studi di Milano, Dipartimento di Scienze dell'Informazione
Via Comelico 39/41, I-20135 Milano, Italy
E-mail: (bertino/martella)@disi.unige.it

Helmut Kurth
IABG, Dep. CC33
Einsteinstraße 20, D-85521 Ottobrunn, Germany
E-mail: kurth@iabg.de

Emilio Montolivo
Fondazione Ugo Bordoni
Via B. Castiglione 59, I-00142 Rome, Italy
E-mail: montoliv@fub.it

Cataloging-in-Publication data applied for

Die Deutsche Bibliothek - CIP-Einheitsaufnahme

Computer security : proceedings / ESORICS 96, 4th European
Symposium on Research in Computer Security, Rome, Italy,
September 25 - 27, 1996. Elisa Bertino ... (ed.). - Berlin ;
Heidelberg ; New York ; Barcelona ; Budapest ; Hong Kong ;
London ; Milan ; Paris ; Santa Clara ; Singapore ; Tokyo :
Springer, 1996
  (Lecture notes in computer science ; Vol. 1146)
  ISBN 3-540-61770-1
NE: Bertino, Elisa [Hrsg.]; ESORICS <4, 1996, Roma>; GT

CR Subject Classification (1991): D.4.6, E.3, C.2.0, H.2.0, K.6.5

ISSN 0302-9743
ISBN 3-540-61770-1 Springer-Verlag Berlin Heidelberg New York

© Springer-Verlag Berlin Heidelberg 1996
Printed in Germany

Typesetting: Camera-ready by author
SPIN 10513746   06/3142 – 5 4 3 2 1 0   Printed on acid-free paper

Foreword

Developments in computer technology and telecommunications today provide means for efficient storage, processing, retrieval, transmission, and distribution of information. This situation has been a necessary condition for the development of information systems. However, the availability of integrated databases to a large number of users and the widespread use of interconnecting networks, such as Internet, have increased the need for data protection.

Techniques, tools, and procedures must therefore be provided to ensure information availability and integrity as well as its protection against unauthorized or improper modification and leakage. In network environments, protection must be provided to ensure integrity and privacy of the messages being transmitted and the authenticity of the messages' senders and receivers. The peculiarity of Internet, the unpredictable and uncontrollable consequences of information alteration and loss, the heterogeneity of users, and the wide area distribution of interconnections at both national and international level, are among the factors that require security to be tackled with adequate competence and resources.

To this end, we need to: clarify the fundamental concepts of security and computer crime; develop methods and techniques to analyze, detect, evaluate, prevent, and neutralize computer crime; develop suitable security systems; and set criteria to plan and control the introduction of security systems in companies, taking into consideration their effects on how the information systems work. In other words, we must introduce companies to real "information security engineering".

Technological and organizational techniques are today available for the development of security systems. Microtechnology and smartcards provide sophisticated identification and authentication techniques. Logical and physical access to the system can be controlled by software and hardware mechanisms. Cryptography techniques can be used to ensure data privacy and authenticity in networks. Finally, digital signature techniques are successfully applied in electronic fund transfer. Organizational measures available today include: security key management (e.g., passwords, cryptographic keys), emergency plans (e.g., back-up, recovery plan), program development and maintenance, and personnel management.

It is most important today that all users of a system, from the operative to the top management level, be aware of the security problem. This widely distributed consciousness for the security problem would bring a twofold advantage. First, it allows users to concretely understand and put into effect security policies. Second, it allows them to suggest security system requirements. This is not happening today.

As we all can imagine, it is difficult to point out the reasons why companies do not sufficiently consider the data protection problem. Computer security, even if the discipline is still far from mature, should be tied into information systems development and evolution. It is widely known that security measures have often been applied as a response to security violations, mostly by management moved by emotional feelings. As a result, the security measures adopted are often limited in scope. Moreover, the security problem is not well understood. Security systems, where in place, are often inadequate for the real needs of the information systems.

Factors contributing to the inadequacy of security systems include: (i) the lack of interest among top management; (ii) the chronic limited availability of security experts; (iii) the insufficient demand for security systems, too low to justify considerable investments by suppliers; (iv) research activity insufficiently distributed and funded.

The response from research is at present inadequate with respect to the requirements and the dimension of the problem. Moreover, very few research groups are investigating the security problem and up to few years ago there was no funding allocated within UE and ESPRIT projects for research on security. Industry products do not well meet the different protection requirements. On top of all these critical factors there is also insufficient training and teaching activity in the security field.

To overcome those problems it is important to exchange information and experience at the international level. In my view, this cannot be reached without the establishment, in each country, of a "national security reference point", to create a world-wide security network like that of the World Health Organization. In this framework, Internet and Internet-like systems today represent an excellent means for circulating security information.

I hope this conference will be a step towards undertaking synergistic initiatives in this direction.

Giancarlo Martella
General Chair

July 1996

Preface

The series of European Symposium on Research in Computer Security (ESORICS) represents an important international event in the computer security area. The symposium started in 1990 in Toulouse (France) and is now held every two years in different European countries. It attracts an audience from both the academic and industrial communities. Previous ESORICS meetings were held in Toulouse, France (1990 and 1992), and Brighton, United Kingdom (1994).

In response to the call for papers of ESORICS'96, 58 papers were received from different countries in Europe, America, and Far East. All papers were reviewed by at least three members of the program committee. The program committee was selective and only 21 papers were accepted for inclusion in the symposium program. We are very pleased with the overall quality of the program, covering a wide spectrum of topics, from theoretical issues, to database access control, to networks. Among application areas, electronic commerce has received special attention in ESORICS'96. We gratefully acknowledge all our colleagues who committed their time by submitting papers. The program is well complemented by two panels, the first on firewalls and the second on the protection of authors' rights and copyright. Finally, we are very happy that Peter Landrock, a well-known expert in computer security, has agreed to give the invited talk.

We greatly appreciate the help we received from the members of our cooperative and responsible program committee. Special thanks go to Elena Ferrari, who helped us with the preparation of the PC meeting, and to Maria Grazia Baggi from AICA, who handled the publicity for the symposium.

Elisa Bertino
Program Chair

Helmut Kurth   **Emilio Montolivo**
Program Vice-Chair   Program Vice-Chair

July 1996

ESORICS'96 Organization

General Chair

Giancarlo Martella, Universita' di Milano, Italy

Program Chair
Elisa Bertino, Universita' di Milano, Italy

Program Vice-Chairs
Helmut Kurth, IABG, Germany
Emilio Montolivo, Fondazione Ugo Bordoni, Italy

Program Committee

Bruno d'Ausbourg (CERT-ONERA, France)
Joachim Biskup (U.of Dortmund, Germany)
Martha Branstad (TIS, USA)
Yves Deswarte (LAAS-CNRS, France)
Gerard Eizenberg (CERT-ONERA, France)
Ed Fernandez (Florida Atlantic U., USA)
Simon Foley (U. College, Cork, Ireland)
Walter Fumy (Siemens ZFE, Germany)
Dieter Gollmann (U. of London, UK)
Li Gong (SRI, USA)
Mike Walker (Vodafone, UK)
Jeremy Jacob (U. of York, UK)

Sushil Jajodia (USA)
John McLean (NRL, USA)
Roger Needham (U. of Cambridge, UK)
Pierre Paradinas (RD2P/Gemplus,France)
Andreas Pfitzmann (U. of Dresden,Germany)
Jean-Jacques Quisquater (UCL, Belgium)
Pierangela Samarati (U. of Milan, Italy)
Einar Snekkenes (NDRE, Norway)
Bhavani Thuraisingham (MITRE, USA)
V. Varadharajan (U. of West Sydney, Australia)
Simon Wiseman (DRA, UK)

Local Arrangements Chair
Francesco Gentile, Fondazione Ugo Bordoni, Italy

Steering Committee Chair
Yves Deswarte (LAAS-CNRS, France)

Sponsor
AICA (Associazione Italiana per l'Informatica ed il Calcolo Automatico)

Cooperating Organizations
Fondazione Ugo Bordoni (Italy)
AFCET (France)
the Norwegian Computer Society (Norway)
Gesellschaft fuer Informatik (Germany)

Additional Referees
Vijay Atluri, Barbara Catania, Elena Ferrari, Marc Dacier, Guenter Karjoth, Stewart Lee
Volkmar Lotz, Vincent Nicomette, Rodolphe Ortalo, Mike Roe, Jie Wu

Table of Contents

Development of a
Secure Electronic Marketplace for Europe

Michael Waidner

IBM Zurich Research Laboratory
CH 8803 Rüschlikon, Switzerland
e-mail <wmi@zurich.ibm.com>

Abstract: Backed by the European Commission, a consortium of partners from European industry, financial institutions, and academia has embarked on a research project to develop the fundamentals of secure electronic commerce. The goal of Project *SEMPER* (Secure Electronic Marketplace for Europe) is to provide the first open and comprehensive solutions for secure commerce over the Internet and other public information networks. We describe the objectives and summarise the initial architecture of *SEMPER*.

1 Introduction

Backed by the European Commission, a consortium from European industry and academia has embarked on a research project to develop the fundamentals of secure electronic commerce. The goal of the 9-million ECU project, *SEMPER* (Secure Electronic Marketplace for Europe), is to provide the first open and comprehensive solutions for secure commerce over the Internet and other public information networks.

A wide range of businesses are rapidly moving to explore the huge potential of networked information systems, especially with the Internet-based WWW (World-wide Web). The Internet, which already connects more than 3 million computers and a substantially larger number of users, is growing at a breathtaking pace with thousands of newcomers every day. Although the Internet has its roots in academia and is still dominated by free-of-charge information, dramatic changes are expected in the near future. For instance, the WWW will be used for a wide variety of electronic commerce such as on-line trade or delivery of advanced multimedia information services. The evolution of broadband networks and "information highways" will intensify this trend.

The need for secure transactions in this new business environment, which involves networks available to the general public, has triggered a number of related efforts. These initial developments are based almost exclusively in the US and most of them are limited to proprietary, or otherwise closed solutions, involving only electronic payment issues. In contrast, *SEMPER* is directed towards a comprehensive solution for secure electronic commerce, considering legal, commercial, social, and technical requirements as well as different options for an electronic marketplace.

SEMPER started on September 1st, 1995. The first of the three project phases addresses a coherent security model and a generic, open security architecture for the electronic marketplace. This architecture is independent of specific hardware, software, or network architectures. The most fundamental electronic commerce services, such as secure offering, order, payment and information delivery, are also integrated in the first phase.

Subsequent phases will concentrate on more advanced services. These will include fair exchange of documents, credentials, advanced document processing, notary services and multimedia-specific security services, such as protection of intellectual property rights. Multi-party security and protection of users' privacy receive prime attention. *SEMPER* uses and integrates existing architectures, tools, and services where appropriate.

Trials will be provided for WWW and ATM-based broadband networks. They will demonstrate the broad applicability of *SEMPER*'s architecture and services.

The *SEMPER* project is part of the Advanced Communication Technologies and Services (ACTS) research program established by the European Commission Directorate General XIII for 1994-1998 [http://www.analysys.co.uk/acts/cec/].

The members of the *SEMPER* consortium are *Cryptomathic* (DK), *DigiCash* (NL), *EUROCOM EXPERTISE* (GR), *Europay International* (B), *FOGRA Forschungsgesellschaft Druck* (D), *GMD - German National Research Center for Information Technology* (D), *IBM* (CH, D, F), *INTRACOM* (GR), *KPN Research* (NL), *Otto-Versand* (D), *r3 security engineering* (CH), *SEPT* (F), *Stichting Mathematisch Centrum / CWI* (NL), *University of Freiburg* (D), *University of Hildesheim* (D). *Banksys* (B), *Banque Générale du Luxembourg* (L) and *Telekurs* (CH) are associated with *SEMPER*. *IBM Zurich Research Laboratory* provides the technical leadership for the project.

2 Electronic Commerce

Like on a physical marketplace, the main purpose of an electronic marketplace is to bring potential *sellers* and *buyers* together:

- Sellers *offer* their goods and buyers *order* these goods; together this is a two-party *negotiation*, sometimes ending with a *contract*.

- Both seller and buyer might need certain *certificates* for such a contract. For instance, a buyer might only want to buy from sellers that are accredited with a well-known payment system provider, so that they can use a certain payment instrument, or they may only trust them if a consumer organisation has declared them trustworthy, or a seller might be allowed to deliver certain goods only to residents of the European Union.

- Sellers *deliver* their goods and buyers make *payments*; together this is a two-party *(fair) exchange*.

- Instead of goods, the buyer might receive a specific certificate that subsequently enables *conditional access* to certain services, e.g., like a subscription to a journal.

- Buyers or sellers might be dissatisfied with what has happened so far, i.e., several *exception handlers* and *dispute handlers* are necessary.

- Some services require third parties to co-operate, e.g., *notaries* and *financial institutions*.

- Many services require that buyer and seller have some relations already established, e.g., to banks or government agencies. This requires *registration* and *certification*, and in most cases also *directory* authorities.

In all these actions, the parties have specific *security requirements,* namely integrity, confidentiality, and availability. Confidentiality includes anonymity which is often a requirement for browsing catalogues or purchases for small amounts.

Several typical scenarios of electronic commerce are to be covered by *SEMPER*:

- *Mail-order Retailing:* A retailer accepts electronic orders and payments, based on digital or conventional catalogues, and delivers physical goods.

- *On-line Purchase of Information:* Like mail-order retailing, but with digital, maybe copyright-protected goods that are delivered on-line.

- *Electronic Mall:* An organisation offers services for several service providers, ranging from directory services ("index") over content hosting to billing services.

- *Subscriptions:* An organisation offers services on a subscription basis, e.g., subscription to news services, database services, or journals. The subscription might be valid only for some time, and it might be transferable or not.

- *Statements:* Transfer of electronic documents, supporting all kinds of security requirements, such as confidentiality and non-repudiation of delivery. A statement might be based on a pre-defined statement template certified by a third party.

- *Contract Signing:* Two or more parties exchange signed copies of the same *statement.*

- *Insurance:* Subscription to an insurance, payment of fees, regulation of damages.

- *Auctioning:* Users participate in an auction, maybe anonymously, and with the usual fairness requirements.

- *Ticketing:* A user buys a ticket that can be used to access a certain service for some time or exactly once, etc., and for that user or for the user's family, etc.

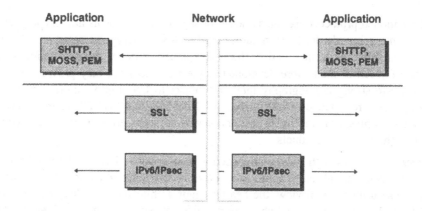

Application	Network	Application

Fig. 1. Proposed Internet security enhancements

3 Existing Technology

The development of electronic commerce on the Internet has come about in a very fast but highly disorganised manner. Currently, there is only a limited understanding of the functionality and security properties of services that are required by merchants and their potential customers. Coherent strategies for marketing, advertising, accounting, and payment are missing. Neither a comprehensive model of an electronic marketplace nor a generic functional and security architecture exists.

Most proposals for electronic commerce originated from one of the following three classes:

Communication security protocols: Most proposals for secure electronic commerce are based on techniques for classical end-to-end security. The currently best known protocols are the following:

- SHTTP [ReSc 95], PEM [Linn93], and MOSS [CFGM95] are extensions to HTTP, electronic mail, and MIME, respectively. In order to use them one has to modify the applications, e.g., one needs security enhanced browsers and servers in order to use SHTTP. They work on individual application layer messages, which is an advantage for electronic commerce because digital messages are used like paper documents: for disputes one needs individually signed messages. *CommerceNet* [http://www.commerce.net] has developed some examples of how SHTTP can be used to simulate paper forms that must be filled-in and signed (e.g., cheques).

- SSL [HiEl 95] and IPv6/IPsec [Atki95] offer secure communication *below* the application layer. Therefore they can be used almost transparently. Their main problem with respect to electronic commerce is that they do not work on documents, i.e., the user does not receive something like a signature that can be stored and used in case of disputes.

All mentioned protocols use the same set of security mechanisms and cryptographic algorithms, primarily digital signatures based on RSA, encryption based on DES and RSA, and MD5 as hash function (for an explanation of all these techniques, see [Schn 96]). All of them were developed in the US, and since they provide an open interface to strong cryptography they are subject to US crypto export regulations. They all require a public-key infrastructure. Both SSL and SHTTP are integrated in commercial products, and most vendors of web browsers and servers announced to support them in their products.

Merchant servers with support for secure transactions: The best known example of such a commercial server comes from *OpenMarket* [http://www.openmarket. com]. From a security point of view, the heart of their architecture is a "payment switch" [GSPT 95]. The payment switch supports different types of customer identification (e.g., password, some secure tokens), collects payments (supporting different payment systems; *OpenMarket* announced to support *CyberCash* [http://www.cybercash. com]), and grants access to information (i.e., specific URL's of short life time) after successful payment. The server supports *SSL* and *SHTTP*. Obviously the architecture is highly centralised and considers the server side only.

Electronic on–line payment systems: Most of the existing work on electronic commerce services concentrates on the development of electronic payment systems. The spectrum of systems includes (see [JaWa 96] for more details):

- systems that do not use any strong protection methods and require prior registration of user accounts, and may be considered as insufficiently secure;
- systems that implement a credit card model, processing customer authentication and payment information by specific security protocols, e.g., *iKP* [BGHH 95] and the proposed Mastercard/VISA standard *SET* [SET 96]);
- one system (*ecash*, from DigiCash, see also [Chau 89]) that implements an anonymous electronic cash model.

Outside the Internet, some interesting, smartcard-based off-line payment systems were developed, which could be used on-line as well. The spectrum ranges from classical electronic wallets and purses to systems that provide strong multi-party security and anonymity (e.g., the system developed by the ESPRIT Project CAFE [BBCM 94]). The leading payment system companies, Europay/Mastercard/VISA intend to support transactions based on smartcards (they published joint specifications), and the US Financial Services Technology Consortium (FSTC) initiated a project that will use a PCMCIA card as "Electronic Checkbook," also via Internet. All these approaches share the problem that the customer's stations need an interface to smartcards or PCMCIA cards, which is not the case in general, yet. Probably this will change in the near future.

None of the different existing or proposed on-line payment systems are interoperable. Most of them do not provide strong multi-party security or user privacy.

Public–key infrastructure: There are mechanisms and standards for key certification, e.g., CCITT X509. Up to now, there is no sufficient certification infrastructure for public keys, but several projects aim at this. Examples are the TEDIS Project FAST, and activities within RARE and TERENA, based on the results of the EU VALUE Project PASSWORD. Several national post offices (e.g., the USPO) plan to provide such services.

Miscellaneous: In addition there are several initiatives that primarily aim at co-ordination and consensus forming, like *CommerceNet*. Similar initiatives exist or are proposed in Japan and Europe.

Beyond these systems, few other services are available for electronic commerce. The experimental *NetBill* [SiTy 95] system supports accounting and billing based on central billing servers. Several companies offer technology for secure metering or copyright protection based on superdistribution (or variant thereof) [MoKa 90]. Some companies offer tools for using EDI messages in electronic commerce over the Internet.

What is missing? Some aspects of secure electronic commerce are not covered by any of the mentioned projects, or at least not in a sufficient form:

- All listed technical projects deal with partial aspects of secure electronic commerce only. No project aims at the complete picture, i.e., at defining a complete model and architecture for secure electronic commerce.

- Although some systems are supposed to become standards, only few standardised API's exist. Defining generic API's and gateways between protocols is absolutely required for an open marketplace.

- Most electronic commerce systems are closed: They use proprietary technology, or support only a specific set of protocols and mechanisms. Often they are based on one central server that acts as a trusted third party for all participants, per marketplace. Often they require specific browsers and servers to be used.

- Although most proposals use public-key cryptography, only little attention is paid to multi-party security. No decision procedures for disputes are defined, which would be necessary for non-repudiation of origin. Usually no security requirements are explicitly formulated, and often no systematic security evaluation is performed.

- The aspects of customer anonymity and privacy are not sufficiently considered yet. Neither are the requirements completely clear, nor are the technologies completely available. Several payment systems, with *ecash* as the most advanced, provide some sort of anonymity, but anonymous payments without anonymous communication does not make much sense. No project deals with the more general problems like anonymous credentials.

- Most systems assume a master-slave relation between seller's server and buyer's browser. The resulting asymmetry limits the complexity of protocols that can be performed in this model, and does not allow protocols between users (i.e., between two slaves without master).

- Most systems are limited to 2 parties. For instance, SSL supports a secure session between browser and server only. Integrating a secure connection to a third party like a "bank" in a payment system would be difficult.

- All projects that aim at prototype or product developments consider just on-line purchases, i.e., offer, order, payment and delivery. Multi-party problems (like auctioning) and fairness aspects (like contract signing, certified mail) are not considered yet.

- Most projects are US based. This means that their results are subject to US export control, i.e., they are not necessarily available outside the US. For instance, an SSL or SHTTP enabled browser developed in the US must not be exported unless the cryptographic algorithms are replaced by weak, i.e., breakable "export versions." Additionally, the law of some countries (e.g., France) does not allow to use products that support strong encryption of arbitrary data.

4 Objectives of *SEMPER*

The list of scenarios, actions, and security requirements in Section 2 already describe the working area of *SEMPER*. Within this area, the main objective of *SEMPER* is

> to develop, implement, trial and evaluate an open architecture for secure electronic commerce, especially taking into account multi-party security and privacy requirements.

Open Architecture for Electronic Commerce: *SEMPER* defines an *open* and *system independent* architecture for electronic commerce:

- The architecture is *independent* of specific hardware, operating systems, or networks.

- The architecture supports "plug-in" of new components, i.e., it is *independent* of specific service implementations, e.g., independent of the specific payment systems used in the trials; most payment systems can be "plugged-in."

- The architecture is *independent* of specific business applications. It supports any business application of electronic commerce that can be expressed in our model, i.e., as sequence of exchanges.

- The design process is *open* for public review. The *SEMPER* consortium has committed to publish all specifications, and appreciates security evaluations by third parties. The results of *SEMPER* will be used as input for standardisation.

Security: As in the physical marketplace, all participants have specific security requirements:

- Buyers often require to reliably authenticate the sellers they are dealing with. Note that it is easy to set up a WWW server and attach the name of a well known seller to it; even names that are already in use can be assigned; the highly fault-tolerant Internet tolerates such inconsistencies;

- Buyers might wish to browse anonymously through the catalogues of sellers, and if money and goods are exchanged fairly, identification of the buyer is not necessary at all.

- A seller does not want to deliver on-line goods without some guarantee of payment.

- In some scenarios, a seller might require specific credentials from a buyer.

- Buyer and seller might wish means for secure on-line payments, but certainly all parties — payer, payee and the financial services providers — do not want an increased risk compared to the physical marketplace.

Multi-party security means that the security requirements of all parties are considered individually, and that all security requirements of a party are guaranteed without forcing this party to trust other parties unreasonably. In particular, mutual trust between parties with conflicting interests like payer and payee in a payment is not assumed. Ideally, a party only has to trust itself and the jurisdiction and even the decision of a court may be verified.

In order to support the necessary degree of security, several cryptographic mechanisms must be applied. The architecture of *SEMPER* has to support

- for authentication: certification; credentials; non-repudiation of origin, submission, delivery; contract signing; fair exchange;

- electronic payment systems following different payment models, e.g., pre-paid cash like, credit card like, cheque like, money transfers;

- anonymous communication;

- copyright protection.

The Internet poses the strongest security challenges: It is completely open, without a central network security management, without any provisions for communication integrity, authenticity, or confidentiality. Even worse, the structure and openness of Internet makes life for attackers as easy as possible. For instance, it is a trivial task to check the traffic routed through a node controlled by an attacker for *telnet* or *ftp* passwords, or to send electronic mail under an arbitrary sender address via *smtp*. See, e.g., [ChBe 94] for a description of the most common security problems of the Internet. Thus, showing the feasibility of a secure and advanced electronic marketplace on the Internet proves feasibility for almost all other types of networks.

Trials: The architecture and services developed by the *SEMPER* consortium will be evaluated by means of trials. The first trial will be based on the Internet only, while later trials will use ATM-broadband networks.

The initial trials will be based on the minimum set of services that are necessary to secure the existing services of the 3 trial partners in *SEMPER*, namely

- EUROCOM (Athens), offering on-line multi-media training courses;
- FOGRA (Munich), offering several publications and on-line consulting;
- Otto-Versand (Hamburg), offering a small part of their mail-order catalogue.

Transfer / Exchange *of* → *for* ↓	Money	Signed document	Information
nothing (i.e., Transfer)	Payment	Certificate transfer etc.	Information transfer
Money	Fair money exchange	Fair payment with receipt	Fair purchase
Signed document	*Same as* ...	Fair Contract Signing	Fair conditional access
Information	*... in upper ...*	*... right half*	Fair information exchange

Fig. 2. Transfers and exchanges of primitive types

5 Initial Architecture

Model: The model of *SEMPER* describes business sessions in terms of sequences of *transfers* and *exchanges* similar to the *dialogues* of interactive EDI.

A *container* is the general data structure for what can be transferred and exchanged. It contains several *primitive types* together with their security attributes in a tree-like structure, namely

- signed documents, such as certificates, receipts, and signed statements;

- information, such as digital goods, information necessary to access a service (e.g., an address and password or a cryptographic key that protects a video stream), and information necessary to access physical goods;

- money.

A container can be structured according to a *template* which also defines the semantics of its contents, and which might be certified by a third party (e.g., like today's standard contracts for apartment rentals with fields to fill in). The concept of templates is similar to the concept of messages in EDI. Each template clearly defines the meaning of the data contained in the fields of the template.

In a *transfer*, one party sends a container to one or more other parties. The sending party can define certain security requirements, such as confidentiality, anonymity, non-repudiation of origin. The sender receives an acknowledgement for each transfer, but this acknowledgement does not necessarily prove successful submission.

A *fair exchange* is an exchange of containers where two or more parties have the *assurance* that if they transfer something specific to the others, they will also receive something specific. Note that we require a *guarantee* of fairness. If no such guarantee is required, we can model such a conversation by several transfers.

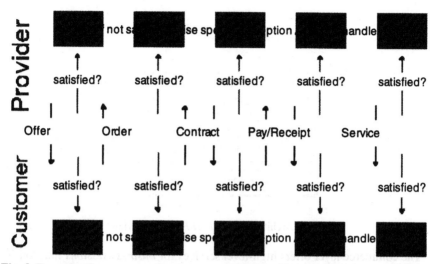

Fig. 3. Example of a sequence of exchanges and transfers The protocol might enable other sequences as well, e.g., after "Contract" "Payment without Receipt" might also be enabled.

The actual sequence of transfers and exchanges in a business session can either be determined directly by the users, or it can be described by a protocol for such business sessions. Of course, a protocol may branch, i.e., allow more than one sequence.

Fig. 2 gives an overview of the possible exchanges of primitive types. Transfers are included as exchanges of "something" for "nothing."

Obviously, the matrix of Fig. 2 is complete with respect to pairs, but there may be different security requirements in detail. The initial architecture of *SEMPER* is two-party centred. The same considerations can be applied to the multi-party case. For instance, more than two parties might wish to sign a joint contract, or one sender might want to send a certified mail to several recipients.

In the course of an ongoing business session, after each transfer or exchange, the parties are either

- *satisfied* and thus willing to proceed with a certain number of other transfers or exchanges or

- *dissatisfied*, in which case an *exception* or *dispute* handler is raised which might end up at a real court if all else fails.

Layers of *SEMPER*: The main activity of *SEMPER* during its first 6 months was the definition of an initial model and architecture, and the specification of a basic set of services.

The security architecture of *SEMPER* describes a layered structure in which the business applications are on the upper layer and services for secure commerce on the lower layers (see Fig. 4).

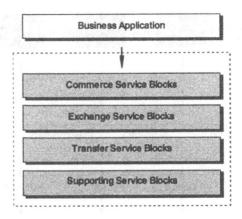

Fig. 4. Architecture of *SEMPER* — Overview

- The commerce layer offers high-level services for *business sessions* like "on-line purchase of information" or "registration with service provider", and template management.

- The exchange layer supports *fair exchange* services.

- The transfer layer provides the *transfer* services for sending information.

- The supporting services are the usual cryptographic services, communication, archiving of data (keys, non-repudiation tokens, templates, audit), setting preferences and handling access-control, a trusted user interface which the user can enter or be shown sensitive information (TINGUIN: Trusted INteractive Graphical User INterface).

The architecture supports, but does not prescribe, the use of trusted hardware, like smartcards or electronic wallets. Commerce services, i.e., new scripts for business sessions, can be downloaded and added dynamically.

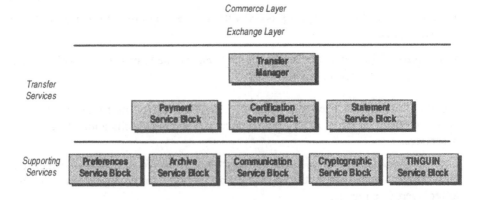

Fig. 5. Initial design of *SEMPER*

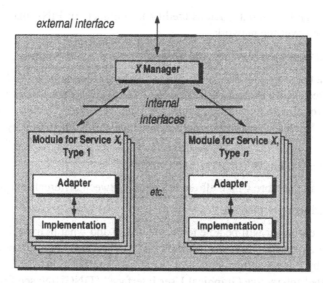

Fig. 6. Integration of different service modules in *SEMPER*. A payment manager, for example, may manage different payment systems like SET/iKP and e-cash.

The first actual design based on this architecture is summarised in Fig. 5. It supports transfer services and a fixed set of commerce services only. The functionality of the transfer layer is divided into the 3 fundamental blocks electronic payments, certification, and general statements which includes digital signatures.

Each service block in Fig. 5 provides a generic interface and allows to integrate different service modules that actually provide the service (see Fig. 6). For instance, the payment service block provides a generic "external" payment API that is independent of specific payment systems [APAW 96]. A concrete payment system can be integrated by providing an "adapter" mapping the concrete system's API to an "internal" API of the payment service block. Currently one internal API for account based systems (like *SET* or *iKP*) and one for cash-like payment systems (like *ecash)* are being designed.

The basic trials will use IBM's *iKP* and DigiCash's *ecash* for electronic payments, GMD's *SecuDE* toolkit for X.509 certificates, and crypto toolkits developed by *Cryptomathic* and *GMD* for statements. The system will be implemented in software only. Later versions might use *SET* instead of *iKP* (both implementing the same payment model).

Trust in Components: Naturally, without correctly working components, no security can be achieved:

- Software components may not behave as specified and, e.g., sign fake statements.
- The user-interface may display wrong amounts to pay, or questions to decide, so called masquerade attacks.

- Confidential user-input, such as credit-card numbers or PINs, may be stored and distributed over the network.

- Secret keys may be retrieved and misused.

Therefore, a user of *SEMPER* has to *believe* that their components and user-interface behave correctly and protect their security. We call this *trust* in components. Since *SEMPER* provides an open architecture, we cannot assume that all parties trust every component. However, trust of the parties involved can be increased by several measures:

- public design, implementation, and evaluation.

- an open architecture which allows to choose between different manufacturers;

- dedicated security modules.

In addition, each user will be able to decide whom and what to trust. If some components, such as specific payment systems, are not trusted, these components will be moderated by trusted components. For trusted user-interaction, *SEMPER* provides a local "Trusted Interactive Graphical User Interface" (TINGUIN; see Fig. 5) which is unambiguously distinguishable from the user-interface of the business application, and should be ideally implemented on a separate security module, e.g., a secure electronic wallet.

6 Summary

SEMPER is the first open architecture for multi-party secure electronic commerce. We described our view of electronic commerce, the existing technologies, the objectives of *SEMPER*, and the initial architecture. For more information see <http://www.semper.org>.

This work was partially supported by the ACTS Project AC026, *SEMPER*. However, it represents the view of the author. *SEMPER* is part of the Advanced Communication Technologies and Services (ACTS) research program established by the European Commission, DG XIII. This description is based on joint work of all partners of the consortium. It is a pleasure to thank all of them for their co-operation.

7 References

APAW 96   *J. Abad Peiro, N. Asokan, M. Waidner:* **Payment Manager;** SEMPER Activity Paper 212ZR054 <http://www.semper.org/info/>.

Atki 95   *R. Atkinson:* **Security Architecture for the Internet Protocol;** Internet RFC 1825, August 1995.

BBCM 94   *J.-P. Boly, A. Bosselaers, R. Cramer, R. Michelsen, S. Mjølsnes, F. Muller, T. Pedersen, B. Pfitzmann, P. de Rooij, B. Schoenmakers, M. Schunter, L. Vallée, M. Waidner:* **The ESPRIT Project CAFE – High Security Digital Payment Systems;** ESORICS '94, LNCS 875, Springer-Verlag, Berlin 1994, 217-230.

BGHH 95   *M. Bellare, J. A. Garay, R. Hauser, A. Herzberg, H. Krawczyk, M. Steiner, G. Tsudik, M. Waidner:* **iKP — A Family of Secure Electronic Payment Protocols; First** Usenix Workshop on Electronic Commerce, New York 1995.

CFGM95   *S. Crocker, N. Freed, J. Galvin, S. Murphy:* **MIME Object Security Services;** Internet RFC 1848, October 1995.

Chau 89   *D. Chaum:* **Privacy Protected Payments;** SMART CARD 2000, North-Holland, Amsterdam 1989, 69-93.

ChBe 94   *W. R. Cheswick, S. M. Bellovin:* **Firewalls and Internet Security — Repelling the Wily Hacker;** Addison-Wesley, Reading 1994.

GSPT 95   *D. K. Gifford, L. C. Stewart, A. C. Payne, G. W. Treese:* **Payment Switches for Open Networks;** IEEE COMPCON, March 1995.

HiEl 95   *K. Hickman, T. ElGamal:* **The SSL Protocol;** Internet Draft, June 1995.

JaWa 96   *P. Janson, M. Waidner:* **Electronic Payment Systems;** SI Informatik /Informatique 3/ (1995) 10-15; extended version accepted for: Datenschutz und Datensicherung DuD (1996).

Linn93   *J. Linn:* **Privacy Enhancement for Internet Electronic Mail;** Internet RFC 1421-24; February 1993.

MoKa 90   *R. Mori, M. Kawahara:* **Superdistribution — The Concept and the Architecture;** The Transactions of the IEICE; 73/7 (1990).

ReSc 95   *E. Rescorla, A. Schiffman:* **The Secure HyperText Transfer Protocol;** Internet Draft, July 1995.

Schn 96   *B. Schneier:* **Applied Cryptography;** John Wiley & Sons, 1994, 1995.

SET 96   *Mastercard, VISA:* **Secure Electronic Transactions;** Draft, June 26, 1996. (available from <http://www.mastercard.com/set/set.htm>)

SiTy 95   *M. Sirbu, J. D. Tygar:* **NetBill: An Internet Commerce System;** IEEE COMPCON, March 1995.

Lightweight Micro-cash for the Internet

Wenbo Mao

Hewlett-Packard Laboratories
Bristol BS12 6QZ
United Kingdom

Abstract. We propose a micro-cash technique based on a one-time signature scheme: signing a message more than once leads to disclosure of the signer's private key. In addition to usual cash properties such as off-line bank for payment and spender's anonymity, the technique also provides a number of useful features. These include: identifying double spender with strong proof, cash revocable for identified double spender, independent of using tamper-resistant devices, coin sub-divisible to smaller denominations, and system simplicity in terms of small-sized data for cash representation as well as simple protocols for cash withdrawal, payment and deposit. We reason that these features support a lightweight cash system suitable for handling very low value payment transactions, such as information purchases on the Internet.

Keywords: Revocable cash for double spender, Internet electronic commerce.

1 Introduction

Today, the business potential of the Internet, particularly, of the world-wide-web applications, forms a new dimension in electronic commerce. It is believed that information purchases will form a big part of the activities in the Internet electronic commerce [33]. A typical nature of this form of commerce is to deal with large volume of low-value transactions. Usual price for a few information pages can be as low as several cents. Various techniques proposed for macro payments, e.g., [26, 33], are not suitable to be used here, as transaction fees may well exceed the value of payments. Furthermore, these techniques (including [33]) do not serve a proper purchaser's anonymity which can be an essentially important feature in information purchases. On the other hand, the vast diversity nature of the Internet information services means that the subscription-based services may not be very attractive to a large number of one-off viewers.

It is thus reasonable to consider facilitating information purchases on the Internet with a cash-like payment instrument.

Chaum's invention of blind signature techniques [7, 9] sets an important milestone for electronic commerce in cash-like transactions. After Chaum's original idea, the subject of electronic cash has widely been studied and many schemes proposed to tackle various unsolved problems (see e.g., [2, 3, 4, 5, 6, 8, 10, 11, 12, 13, 14, 17, 18, 19, 20, 22, 27, 28, 34]). Early schemes for off-line cash (e.g., Chaum, Fiat and Naor [14], Hayes [22], Okamoto and Ohta [28]) are notoriously inefficient as a result of using "cut-and-choose" techniques in cash withdrawal as well as in payment phases in order to thwart cheating. (Though the method of Okamoto and Ohta [28] includes a binary-tree technique for an efficient representation of coin division into smaller denominations.) Franklin and Yung first introduced a "line method" [19, 20] based on the Diffie-Hellman problem and set off a promising approach to avoidance of cut-and-choose (their scheme still uses cut-and-choose in withdrawal phase). More efficient "single-term" coins using no cut-and-choose were subsequently achieved by Brands [3] and by Ferguson [18]. Brands further generalised the line method into a "representation of Diffie-Hellman problem in groups of prime orders" [5] which can be used to design an electronic wallet with an observer nested in. Eng and Okamoto combined the Brands' representation problem with the binary-tree method for an improved efficiency of divisible coins [17].

Considering off-line cash with a decent anonymity service, an evident limitation in various previous schemes is the high degree of system complexity. Some of the above schemes, e.g., [14, 19, 20, 22, 28], require handling too large amount of data to be economically usable. Others, e.g., [3, 4, 5, 15, 17], critically rely on using a tamper-resistant device (a smartcard "observer" co-working with an electronic wallet) to protect the system secret. If we regard that the former kind of schemes have a high complexity in data processing, then the latter ones should be regarded to be expensive in hardware configuration: considering ubiquitous use of cash including on point sale, two co-working devices are necessary, a wallet to protect the personal secret and an observer to protect the system secret; further, the observer should meet a high standard of tamper-resistance as the holder has an incentive to open it.

In this paper we propose a micro-cash technique based on a new technique to solve the high cost problem. In addition to usual cash properties such as off-line bank for payment and spender's anonymity, the technique also provides a number of useful features. These include: identifying double spender with strong proof, cash revocable for identified double spender, independent of using tamper-resistant devices, coin sub-divisible to smaller denominations, and system simplicity in terms of small-sized data for cash representation as well as simple protocols for cash withdrawal, payment and deposit. We will reason that these features support a lightweight cash system suitable for handling very low value payment transactions.

Similar to all other off-line cash techniques, a double spender will be identified after a double spending has occurred. However, a unique and new feature in our after-the-fact identification method is that the identification is in terms of discovering the double spender's private key by the bank. Such a result of identification is effective to stop double spending: the bank can simply show the double spender's private key to the appropriate public-key certification authority (CA); the associated public-key certificate and the public key (needed for making payment) will be revoked instantly and unconditionally. Thus, double spending will be stopped within the cash mechanism itself rather than resorting to external forces. It is our understanding that every previous off-line cash scheme including those relying on tamper-resistant devices uses some unspecified external mechanisms to stop double spending (a tamper-resistant device only adds difficulty to double spending, once it is opened, double spending must be stopped by other mechanisms). Typically, the external mechanisms are police and the law court which are likely to be ineffective and too expensive for micro-cash payment systems.

The method proposed here also strongly deters double spending in the first place: a new certificate for an identified double spender can be made sufficiently expensive so that the price far outweighs the benefit of double spending low-value coins. Notice that the use of public key and certificate for payment does not mean that the spender's anonymity has to be compromised, as a certificate can be devised not to denote its holder's identity provided it is not abused.

The remainder of this paper is organised as follows. In Section 2 we introduce a one-time signature technique based on Schnorr's signature scheme. The special use of Schnorr's scheme forms the main security basis of our cash technique. In Section 3 the signature scheme will be applied to demonstrate the working principle of a simple cash coin. In Section 4 we analyse the security of the basic scheme. In Section 5 the basic scheme will be extended into one in which a coin unit can be divided into smaller denominations without adding space complexity. Using the extended scheme, a given payment amount can be made in one transaction without increasing the quantity of data flow. Finally, Section 6 summarizes the features of the electronic cash technique.

2 Schnorr's Digital Signature as a One-Time Signature Scheme

We use Schnorr's digital signature scheme [30, 31, 32] to describe a one-time signature scheme to be applied in our cash technique. We start by presenting Schnorr's original scheme[1]

In Schnorr's scheme, users in the whole system can share some public values as part of their public keys. First, choose two large primes, p and q where p is sufficiently large (512-1024 bits) such that the discrete logarithm problem in Z_p is intractable; q is also large (160 bits) and $q|(p-1)$. Then, choose a number $a \in Z_p$ of order q; namely, q is the smallest positive integer satisfying $a^q \equiv 1 \pmod{p}$. The number a can be computed as the $(p-1)/q$th power of a primitive element modulo p. It will be assumed that all parties in the system share these numbers. To generate a particular private/public key pair, Alice chooses a random number s for $0 < s < q$. This is her private key. Then she calculates

$$v := (a^{-s} \bmod p) \tag{1}$$

The result v is Alice's public key. Schnorr's scheme uses a secure one-way hash function. Let $h(.)$ denote such a function which maps from the integer space to

---

[1] The use of Schnorr's scheme is not necessary. Other schemes, such as ElGamal [16] and DSS [1], can also be used.

Z_q^* and symbol $\|$ be bit-string concatenation. To sign a message m, Alice picks a random number $r \in Z_q^*$ and does the following computations:

$$x := (a^r \bmod p) \tag{2}$$

$$e := h(m \| x) \tag{3}$$

$$y := ((r + se) \bmod q) \tag{4}$$

The signature on the message m is the pair (e, y). We will call the other two quantities r and x, *secret* and *public signature generators* (or SSG, PSG for short), respectively. To verify the signature, Bob computes:

$$z := (a^y v^e \bmod p) \tag{5}$$

and tests if e is equal to $h(m \| z)$. If the testing is true, Bob accepts the signature as valid.

Schnorr's signature scheme gets its security from the difficulty of calculating discrete logarithm. The difficulty means that the private key s cannot be easily derived from the public key v from their relation in (1). Similarly, the SSG r cannot be easily derived from the non-secret number x from their relation in (2) (x is equal to z available to the verifier). If SSG r can easily be discovered, then the private key s can easily be derived from (4).

Besides relying on the difficulty of discrete logarithm, the security of the one-way hash function $h(.)$ also plays an important role. The security is in terms of the infeasibility of inverting the function, and of finding two input values $x \neq x'$ such that $h(x) = h(x')$. When Bob verifies the signature, he knows from the property of the hash function that, without knowing Alice's private key, it is computationally infeasible to create the consistency among the numbers e, z and m which are related under the hash function used.

Note that the SSG r must be treated as one-time material. It must not be used more than once to generate different signatures. Assume that Alice has used an SSG r before to sign a message m and now she re-uses it to sign a different message m'. Let (e, y) and (e', y') be the respective signatures. Now that $m' \neq m$, from (3) and the property of the hash function we know with an overwhelming probability that $e' \neq e \pmod q$. With these two signatures, Bob can compute Alice's private key s by subtracting two instances of (4) and obtain

$$s = (\frac{y - y'}{e - e'} \bmod q) \tag{6}$$

When creating a new signature, as long as Alice always choose a new SSG at uniformly random from Z_q^*, then subtraction of (4) will only result in

$$y - y' \equiv r - r' + s(e - e') \pmod q$$

Here the value $r - r' \neq 0 \pmod q$ remains to be a secret that protects the private key s just in the same way as in Schnorr's scheme. More precisely, Alice should not use an SSG which is related to old SSG's in any known algorithmic way. As long as this precaution measure is taken, no computationally feasible method is known to derive the private key from different instances of signatures. In fact, the digital signature standard (DSS) proposed by NIST [1] uses essentially the same principle to protect the signer's private key.

We can employ the property illustrated in (6) to prevent a user from using certain data more than once. The idea is to let the user sign the data as a condition of using the data and the signature must be generated in such a way that the verifier can check whether the user has correctly complied with the signing procedure: to have used a specified PSG. If the signature is generated under challenge (e.g., to include time/location information), then the user cannot sign (use) the data more than once without disclosing her/his private key.

Electronic cash forms a good example of such data. A coin can be constructed to contain a PSG x. During the payment time Alice must sign the coin for the merchant to verify. The coin will not be accepted if Alice's signature is generated with using a wrong PSG (when the merchant sees z in (5) to be different from x in the coin) even if the signature is valid in the sense of the original Schnorr's scheme. If the signature also includes a timestamp and a merchant identity, then Alice cannot double spend a coin without identify herself since she cannot sign the coin more than once without disclosing her private key.

Theorem 1 *Let $a > 1$ and $a^q = 1 \pmod p$. Then $r \not\equiv r' \pmod q$ implies $(a^r \bmod p) \neq (a^{r'} \bmod p)$.*

Proof Assume $a^r = a^{r'} \pmod p$. We have $a^{r-r'} = 1 \pmod p$. Conjuncting this with $a^q = 1 \pmod p$, we reach $r \equiv r' \pmod q$. $\qquad\qquad\square$

Theorem 1 insures that it is impossible for Alice to find two different SSG's $r \not\equiv r' \pmod q$ that map to the same PSG x. Being able to do so would allow Alice to cheat the bank since using (6) will not correctly reveal her private key, and also to cheat the merchant as if a "correct" PSG has been used.

Finally, we should point out that a digital signature can be produced without identifying the signer. In fact, a public-key can be certified to an anonymous holder in such a manner that even the key certification authority cannot link a certificate to its holder. Such a technique is reported in [25]. In the rest of this paper, we will always assume that Alice uses an anonymous public key certificate which does not contain her identity, even though the certificate will be denoted by $Cert_A$.

3   A Simple Cash Coin

We now devise a simple off-line electronic cash scheme. The scheme consists of three protocols: withdrawal, payment and deposit.

3.1 Withdrawal

Alice can withdraw a coin by running a withdrawal protocol with a bank. The bank need not be one in which she keeps an account.[2] The coin will be blindly signed by the bank to worth a specified value and this can be validated by any receiver if the signature is supported with a public-key certificate. Let B denote the bank; (K_B, N_B) be the bank's RSA public key; $f(.)$ be a secure one-way hash function, $x = (a^r \bmod p)$ be a PSG pre-computed by Alice and v be Alice's public key in Schnorr's scheme. Further, let b be a blinding factor in Chaum's blind signature technique that is chosen by Alice at uniformly random from Z_{N_B} (In RSA, there is no need to differentiate $Z_{N_B}^*$ and Z_{N_B} because the chance to have chosen a number in $Z_{N_B} \setminus Z_{N_B}^*$ is equivalent to have factorised N_B). The withdrawal protocol can be as follows.

Step 1. $A \rightarrow B :$ $request$, $(b^{K_B} * f(x \parallel v)) \bmod N_B$

Step 2. $B \rightarrow A :$ $(b^{K_B} * f(x \parallel v))^{K_B^{-1}} \bmod N_B$, $Cert_B$

The message "$request$" in Step 1 represents a (credit or debit) transaction request. It instructs the bank how to obtain money from Alice. For instance, it is a result of another fund transfer protocol (e.g., SET [26]). Let $L(x)$ be the length of bit string x. Considering that usually $L(f(.)) < L(N_B)$, in implementation $f(x \parallel v)$ can be replaced with a concatenation of itself for $\lfloor L(N_B)/L(f(.)) \rfloor$ times.

Upon receipt of the replied message from the bank, Alice can obtain her coin by dividing the blinding factor b into the first chunk. We will use $Coin$ to denote the coin which has been blindly signed by the bank:

$$Coin = f(x \parallel v)^{K_B^{-1}} \bmod N_B$$

Notice that the withdrawal protocol does not go through any cut-and-choose style of cheating detection procedure because there is no need to do so. It is computationally infeasible for Alice to make more than one different coins out of one withdrawal transaction. Also in her own interest, Alice will not construct an invalid coin, such as one which encodes an invalid PSG x (replayed, or the matching SSG is not known by Alice), or an invalid public key v (uncertified, or not knowing the matching private key); or else the money is wasted.

3.2 Payment

When paying $Coin$ to a merchant, Alice must sign a spending signature. The signature should include the merchant's identity and a timestamp stating the spending time. Let M be the merchant's identity, and $DateTime$ be a timestamp.

---

[2] This is a useful feature not available in any previous cash scheme: cash can be withdrawn when the spender's bank is off-line (e.g., in a foreign country), or even the spender need not be any bank account holder (e.g., a child).

The message to be signed should be *"Coin, M, DateTime"*. Following (3) and (4), the spending signature is a pair (e, y) where

$$e := h(Coin \parallel M \parallel DateTime \parallel x) \tag{7}$$

$$y := ((r + se) \bmod q) \tag{8}$$

and $x := (a^r \bmod p)$ as the PSG integrated in $Coin$. It suffices to use the following single step to specify the payment protocol:

$$A \rightarrow M : Coin, M, DateTime, e, y, v, Cert_A, Cert_B$$

Upon receipt of the payment, the merchant will validate the coin by verifying the bank's blind signature on $Coin$, and verify the spending signature. The verification of the spending signature goes as follows. The merchant should first validate the public key v and the supporting anonymous certificate $Cert_A$. In addition to the standard way of checking certificate, the merchant should also check if the public key has been revoked. A revoked key should appear in his local certificate revocation list (CRL) as a result of being periodically fed with a shorter CRL called Δ-CRL from the network directory services to update his local copy of CRL (see Section 12.6 of [23]). If v is properly backed by the anonymous certificate $Cert_A$ and is not in the CRL, the merchant will carry on to verify the spending signature. This is to compute z from a, v, e, y as in (5), and test if $h(Coin \parallel M \parallel DateTime \parallel z)$ is equal to e. If the testing passes, he should also check the correct use of the PSG x and the public key v. The correct use of these values is witnessed by hashing z and v into $f(x \parallel v)$ in $Coin$. Permitting the use of a wrong PSG or an invalid public key will put the merchant in trouble if Alice later double spends $Coin$ (see section 4.3).

The payment protocol has a trivially low computational complexity for Alice since to make a payment is merely to compute a hash function (7) and to give a dot on the line (8). Considering that in real application cash should be usable ubiquitously and in some environment (e.g., point of sale), a smartcard-like device should be used to protect trapdoor information for how to use cash (in this technique, this consists of the SSG r and the private key s). In a point-of-sale environment, payment should only be made by using such devices which in general have very limited computing capacity. The extremely low computational complexity for the customer to make payment is evidently desirable.

3.3 Deposit

In some time later, the merchant will redeem $Coin$ by depositing it to the bank:

$$M \rightarrow B : Sign_M(Coin, M, DateTime, e, y, E_M(z)), Cert_M$$

We call these data *coin-deposit*. Here, $Sign_M(.)$ denotes a digital signature of the merchant and $E_M(z)$ means that the merchant encrypts z using his own public key. (Usual implementations of digital signatures use a one-way hash function and so $Sign_M(\cdots, E_M(m))$ will not reveal the encrypted message m.) The merchant's signature on the coin-deposit means that the merchant has properly dealt with the data in the payment protocol and in the deposit protocol. The bank cannot alter the coin-deposit (e.g., to frame the merchant).

4   Analysis

Now we examine the security of the electronic cash scheme.

4.1   Anonymity

First, we assume that Alice does not double spend her coins. Her anonymity of using the coins will be protected. This is because no data in the payment and in the deposit protocols contains any information about her identity. In this paper we only assume that the public-key certification authority (CA) is a trusted anonymity server; it issues the anonymous certificate $Cert_A$ to Alice and is trusted not to identify Alice without a good reason. However, this trusted service is not necessary. A blind certification technique is reported in [25]. Using the technique, a certificate can be blindly issued to Alice such that after the issuing, the CA loses the linkage between Alice and $Cert_A$.

With the trusted anonymity service, collusion among all banks and all merchants will not identify the spender of a coin. If the blind certification technique [25] is used, then even adding a collusive CA will not be able to identify an honest spender.

4.2   Practical Unlinkability

A pragmatic unlinkability service is supplied. The service means that it is impractical for any party in the system to determine an anonymous spender's spending pattern. We will reason that in order to determine the spending pattern of an anonymous spender, there would have to be a large scale collusion between the bank and merchants in the system. Note that because money will eventually converge to the bank, the bank is in a better position than any merchant to partition a large number of coins. Our analyses in unlinkability will therefore be focused on the bank, with and without the help from merchants.

First of all, it is obvious that if public keys and/or the supporting anonymous certificates are deposited together with coins, then coins can be partitioned by public keys and/or anonymous certificates; all coins in the same partition are spent by the same person. Depositing public keys or anonymous certificates together with coins is regarded as collusion. Slightly less obvious is that the value z, if deposited, can also be used to derive the public key v. This is because of the following congruence:

$$v^e \equiv z/a^y \pmod{p} \tag{9}$$

Once v^e is known, it is easy to reveal v as

$$v := (v^{ed} \bmod p) \quad \text{where} \quad ed \equiv 1 \pmod{p-1} \tag{10}$$

Without giving these values to the bank, it is computationally infeasible for the bank to partition coins that have deposited. It suffices for a merchant to be non-collusive if he simply forgets the anonymous spender's public key, the anonymous certificate and the value z once the coin has been accepted. Each coin is a function of a one-time random PSG, so is each spending signature. Thus, in the absence of double-spending, no set of coin-deposit will give any information whatsoever about its relationship with other sets of coin-deposits. Brute-force searching through the public-key space, e.g., using a candidate public key v and (5) to get a candidate value z followed by checking if they can be hashed to $f(x \parallel v)$ in $Coin$ (since $z = x$), is intractable as the searching has to go through the vast space Z_p, unless the bank has acquired a sufficiently large number of public keys of the users in the system (which form a trivially small subset of the whole public-key space). However to collect public keys requires a large scale collusion among the banks and the merchants. Brute-force searching z for a matching $E_M(z)$, which would allow the computation of the associated public key using (7) and (8), is as infeasible as searching the public-key space, and the searching can also be thwarted by using randomised encryption in the coding of $E_M(z)$.

Finally we point out that even the bank has successfully collected data needed to investigate an anonymous person's spending pattern, the data are only good for knowing the person's spending *history*. Linking future coins requires further collusion. The necessity for maintaining a long-term collusion forms the foundation for us to claim the impracticability of the collusion, or in other words, that our technique gives unlinkability in practice.

4.3 Correctness

Now we look at the difficulty for various parties to defraud. Assume that the bank sees duplicated copies of $Coin$. This may be resulted from either (i) Alice's double spending, or (ii) the merchant's replay or depositing of bad data, or (iii) a collusion between Alice and the merchant.

Case (i) Alice double spends. There will be difference either in M, or in $DateTime$, or in both, and any of these will result in two pairs of spending signatures (e, y) and (e', y') where $e \not\equiv e' \pmod{q}$ (and hence $y \neq y'$) with an overwhelming probability. These two pairs will suffice the bank to discover Alice's private key s using (6), and further obtain her public key v from (1).

The bank can see the correctness of the revealed keys by re-verifying the two spending signatures as the merchants have done. Any incorrectness in the re-verification indicates either a fraudulent merchant, or a collusion between Alice and the merchant(s). These will be dealt with in Cases (ii) or (iii), respectively. Assume that the re-verification of the spending signatures passes. Now the bank can identify Alice by showing the revealed private/public key pair (s, v) to the appropriate CA. (The private key s can contain a sub-string that points uniquely to the CA which has issued the anonymous certificate to Alice.) Upon seeing the revealed key pair, the CA will revoke the public key v by publishing it onto the Δ-CRL. Alice's identity will also be revealed.

Case (ii) The merchant replays data or deposits bad data. Because the merchant is unable to generate a valid spending signature using other people's coins, double depositing coins is confined to the following uninteresting scenario: the merchant simply replays all messages in the deposit protocol. It is easy for the bank to discover the replay and thereby only one instance of deposit will be redeemed.

Note that since the merchant is required to digitally sign each coin-deposit, depositing incorrect data containing gibberish as if they were "spending signatures" will lead to identifying the merchant as fraudulent. This is because, as long as a duplication of $Coin$ is detected, the bank will demand the merchant to prove his honesty in depositing by decrypting $E_M(z)$ in the deposit and the result of decryption, z, will suffice the bank to re-verify the spending signature (using (9) and (10) to recover the public key v needed). We will see more about this in Case (iii).

Case (iii) Alice and the merchant collude. A collusion will make sense only if it does not lead to identifying Alice. Feasible ways to achieve this include that the merchant permits using incorrect public keys (uncertified or not matching v in $Coin$), or incorrect PSG's (not matching x in $Coin$). For instance, in the case of permitting the use of incorrect keys, a coin can be double spent by different people, or by the same person who holds different public keys (certified or not).

Firstly, we assume that the merchant permits the use of an uncertified public key; namely, the public key used in spending signature verification is not supported by a valid anonymous certificate. This collusion will be discovered because the correctly revealed private key (assuming it is in a valid format pointing to a known CA) will not lead to identification of a certificate holder from the CA's database. Such a public key will also be revoked (published in the CRL) to stop any further collusion. The merchant responsible will be identified (see below).

In other scenarios of collusion listed above, upon seeing duplication of $Coin$, the bank's computation using (6) will not reveal a correct private key, either. For instance, assume that two spending signatures (e_1, y_1) and (e_2, y_2) have been generated by two different key pairs where the private keys are s_1 and s_2, respectively. Then, using (6) will result in the following value:

$$s' = \left(\frac{s_1 e_1 - s_2 e_2}{e_1 - e_2} \bmod q\right)$$

Similarly, assume a merchant permits Alice to use an incorrect PSG which is mapped from a wrong SSG $r \not\equiv r'$ (mod q) where r' may or may not be a valid

SSG. Then (6) will disclose the following value:

$$s' = (\frac{s(e_1 - e_2) \pm (r - r')}{e_1 - e_2} \bmod q)$$

Other wrong forms of "private keys" can also be derived by mixed uses of wrong/good keys and wrong/good PSG's. Let v' be the matching "public key" computed from s' using (1). The bank will always re-verify the two spending signatures using the revealed public key v' as the merchant(s) have supposedly done during the two runs of the payment protocol. The re-verification will result in inconsistency; e.g., either s' is in an invalid format (does not point to a correct CA), or the two spending signatures $(e_{1,2}, y_{1,2})$ are incorrect regarding the verification key v' used, or the hashed value $f(z' \| v')$ does not match $f(x \| v)$ in Coin. (N.B. the re-verification excludes any possibility of mistakenly identifying an innocent user whose private key coincides with s' because even in such an extremely unlikely case, the "spending signatures" $(e_{1,2}, y_{1,2})$ will be found to be incorrect when verified using v' as the "signatures" were not created by s' at all.)

In these situations, the two merchants (let them be M_1 and M_2) will be asked to decrypt $E_{M_1}(z)$ and $E_{M_2}(z)$, respectively, in order to prove their honesty. An honest merchant will be indicated by a z which can derive a public key v using (9) and (10) such that v is not in CRL, and using it the spending signature deposited by him can be re-verified as correct (using the same way as he has done during the payment time). The other merchant will be identified as fraudulent.

To this end, we see that Alice and the merchant cannot help each other to achieve double spending without identification. It is however interesting to point out that, as long as a coin is not to be double spent or double deposited, using invalid public keys or incorrect PSG's or even depositing gibberish spending signatures will not be detected since the bank will not and cannot verify the fake spending signature. Indeed, the bank need not be concerned with anything other than double spending.

Finally we point out that since each payment is signed by the merchant, the bank cannot frame the merchant by forging data.

5   Divisible Coin

In this section we will extend the basic scheme to one with which Alice can pay varied amount of moneies to various merchants who will be denoted as M_1, M_2, $\cdots$. The basic idea of the extension follows the Payword technique of Rivest and Shamir [29], or in a different topic, attributes to Lamport's original password identification technique [24] (also known as the S/Key technique [21]). It is to apply a secure one-way hash function, recursively, on a secret for a specified number of times. In the following three subsections we provide revised protocols for cash withdrawal, payment and deposit.

5.1 Withdrawal

To prepare withdrawal, Alice constructs a stick of n coins $C_0, C_1, C_2, \cdots, C_{n-1}$ by applying the hash function $f(.)$ recursively:

$$C_i = f(C_{i+1}) \text{ for } i = 0, 1, 2, \cdots, n - 1 \tag{11}$$

where C_{n+1} is a secret random number (it is not a coin) chosen by Alice. She also chooses the first SSG r_1 and computes the respective PSG $x_1 := (a^{r_1} \bmod p)$, and creates

$$Top := C_0 \parallel f(x_1 \parallel v) \parallel n \tag{12}$$

The withdrawal protocol is similar to that for a single coin:

Step 1. $A \rightarrow B :$ $request,$ $(b^{K_B} * Top) \bmod N_B$

Step 2. $B \rightarrow A :$ $(b^{K_B} * Top)^{K_B^{-1}} \bmod N_B,$ $Cert_B$

Upon receipt of the replied message from the bank, Alice can obtain her coin stick by dividing the blinding factor b into the first chunk. We will use $Stick(n)$ to denote the coin stick blindly signed by the bank containing n coins:

$$Stick(n) = Top^{K_B^{-1}} \bmod N_B \tag{13}$$

Due to the one-way-ness of the hash function, the signature means that the bank has actually signed all of the n coins. The system can stipulate the bank's public key (K_B, N_B) to be only good for supporting a stick containing n coins. There will be no point for Alice to construct a longer stick $Stick(m)$ for $m > n$ since upon using (K_B, N_B) the merchant will not accept more than n coins from the stick. Thus, no cheating detection is needed still.

5.2 Payment

We begin with an informal description on the basic idea of how Alice pays coins to the first merchant M_1. After the informal description on the special case, we will specify the payment protocol in a general setting.

Assume that Alice is to pay i coins $(1 \leq i \leq n)$ to the first merchant M_1. The idea is that in addition to sending a signed payment (on $Stick(n)$), Alice should also disclose C_i in the stick to the merchant. The merchant can verify the validity of the i coins between the C_0 and C_i by recursively applying the hash function for i times, starting from C_i and finishing at C_0. To this end, the bank's blind signature on $Stick(n)$ can be verified (see (11, 12, 13)). However, this only tells the merchant the good structure of the coins. The merchant will only accept the coins provided that Alice has also correctly signed the spending signature on $Stick(n)$.

If $i \neq n$, then the coins in $Stick(n)$ has not been used up, and the merchant should make change. To let change be made, Alice should generate a second pair of SSG and PSG. Let them be r_2 and $x_2 := (a^{r_2} \bmod p)$ respectively. She sends the hashed value $f(x_2 \| v)$ to the merchant (can be sent together with the payment). These values together with C_i will allow the merchant to return change. To return change, the merchant M_1 generates and send back the following value which we will denote by $Stick(n-1)$:

$$Stick(n-i) := Sign_{M_1}(C_i, f(x_2 \| v), n-i)$$

A nice feature in Schnorr's scheme is that, the SSG, PSG pairs can be pre-computed before the signing time. Thus, there will be no problem for Alice to prepare these pairs for future use.

Now we describe the general setting. Assume Alice has spent j $(j < n)$ coins with $k-1$ previous merchants $M_1, M_2, \cdots, M_{k-1}$ (some or all of them may be the same merchant) and she now holds

$$Stick(n-j) = Sign_{M_{k-1}}(C_j, f(x_k \| v), n-j), \ Cert_{M_{k-1}}$$

which have been returned as change from the merchant M_{k-1} with whom Alice has shopped most recently. Under the general setting, we specify the payment protocol with which Alice pays i coins to the next merchant M_k for $k > 0$. These i coins are in $Stick(n-j)$. Note that in the above, we have informally described a special case where $j = 0$, $k = 1$ and $M_0 = B$.

Payment step

$$A \to M_k : \ Stick(n), \ Stick(n-j), \ DateTime, \ e_k, \ y_k$$
$$i, \ C_{j+i}, \ f(x_{k+1} \| v), \ v, \ Cert_A, \ Cert_B, \ Cert_{M_{k-1}}$$

Here

$$e_k = h(Stick(n-j) \| M_k \| DateTime \| x_k)$$

and

$$y_k = (r_k + se_k \bmod q)$$

Upon receipt of the message in **Payment step**, the merchant M_k will first validate the coins by applying the hash function for i times to see if he can start from C_{j+i} and reach C_j. Then after having checked the previous merchant's signature on $Stick(n-j)$, he can further apply the hash for another j times to reach C_0 followed by verifying the bank's blind signature on $Stick(n)$.

Assume the coins pass the validation, the merchant will verify the spending signature on $Stick(n-j)$. Analogous to (5), this is by computing z_k as follows:

$$z_k = (a^{y_k} v^{e_k} \bmod p)$$

and checking if the following equation holds:

$$e_k = h(Stick(n-j) \| M_k \| DateTime \| z_k)$$

Besides this, he must also check the spending signature has been generated using correct PSG x_k and public key v. If everything goes well, these i coins will be accepted.

If there are still unspent coins left (i.e., $n - j - i > 0$), there is a need to make change. In such a case, the merchant M_k should send the following message back to Alice:

Change step:

$$M_k \rightarrow A : Stick(n - j - i), Cert_{M_k}$$

where

$$Stick(n - j - i) = Sign_{M_k}(C_{j+i}, f(x_{k+1} \| v), n - j - i)$$

Note that although the scheme requires a merchant generate the integral combination between remaining coins and the (PSG, public-key) pair, this does *not* mean that the next merchant who is to be paid with the remaining coins has to trust the previous merchant. The signature merely indicates that the merchant has followed the protocol. Alice has freedom to choose any PSG she likes. It is purely Alice's interest to let each merchant combine a good PSG and the correct public key with the remaining coins.

In the next subsection, we will analyse the impossibility for any merchant to help Alice to spend more than n coins from $Stick(n)$ without being identified.

5.3 Deposit

Later, the merchant M_k can redeem the i coins he has been paid from the bank B by depositing the following data:

$$M_k \rightarrow B : Stick(n), Stick(n - j), Stick(n - j - i),$$
$$Sign_{M_k}(M_k, DateTime, e_k, y_k, E_{M_k}(x_k)), Cert_{M_k}, Cert_{M_{k-1}}$$

The certificate of the previous merchant M_{k-1} is needed in order to allow verification of his signature on $Stick(n - j)$ and thereby allow the current merchant M_k to correctly redeem i coins between $Stick(n - j)$ and $Stick(n - j - i)$.

Upon receipt of the coin-deposit message, the bank will check duplication of the coins. If any coin C_l for $j \leq l \leq j + i$ is found in the database, a fraud has been detected. The bank can differentiate double spending from double depositing, and deal with these frauds accordingly (see below). If everything is OK, it will credit the merchant the value of i coins. Data $Stick(n - j)$, $Stick(n - j - i)$, together with the signature and certificate of the merchant will be archived.

Property 2 *The merchant M_k can only get paid for coins between $Stick(n - j)$ and $Stick(n - j - i)$.*

Reasoning Firstly, M_k cannot get paid for coins above $Stick(n - j)$ because the previous merchants M_l for $l < k$ will claim them and whenever disputes occur between M_k and M_l, it can easily be checked that M_k does not have correct spending signatures from Alice. Secondly, M_k cannot claim any coins below $Stick(n - j - i)$ because the next merchant will claim them using the signature of M_k on the top of that stick. Similarly, no other merchants can claim coins between $Stick(n-j)$ and $Stick(n-j-i)$. $\square$

Property 3 *No merchant is able to help Alice to spend more than n coins out of Stick(n).*

Reasoning Assume that the merchant M_k helps Alice by making two different coin sticks which will be viewed by subsequent merchants as:

$$Stick(n-j-l) = Sign_{M_k}(C_{j+l}, f(x \parallel v), n-j-l)$$

$$Stick(n-j-m) = Sign_{M_k}(C_{j+m}, f(x' \parallel v), n-j-m)$$

where $x \neq x'$ and l may or may not be equal to m. The intention of this help is to let Alice use these different coin sticks and so she can spend more than n coins from $Stick(n)$. The collusion must not demand Alice make two different spending signatures on $Stick(n-j)$, otherwise it is a simple double spending of $Stick(n-j)$. The collusive merchant can only deposit either coins between $SticK(n-j)$ and $Stick(n-j-l)$, or those between $SticK(n-j)$ and $Stick(n-j-m)$, but not coins in both of the cases. In the first case of depositing, Alice cannot use $Stick(n-j-m)$ because the next merchant who deposits it will turn in the collusive merchant M_k. Samely, Alice cannot use $Stick(n-j-l)$ in the alternative case of depositing. Even if the collusive merchant does not deposit any coins, he will still be turned in as long as Alice uses the both sticks made by him. $\square$

6 Conclusion

Finally we conclude the paper with a summary of the features of the electronic cash scheme.

An effective way to stop double spending. Double spending can be stopped within the cash mechanism. This is a unique feature that is not available in any previous off-line electronic cash schemes. After detection of a double spending, all the bank need to do is to revoke the double spender's public key. Since the identification of double spender is a strong proof, it is simple to achieve. This method of stopping double spending is cost effective.

Strong anonymity for the spender. The spender enjoys a decent anonymity service as long as she does not double spend. Collusion among banks and merchants will not lead to any computationally feasible way to compromise the anonymity. If the anonymous certificate is issued blindly, then even adding collusive CA's will not be able to identify an honest spender.

Independent of using tamper-resistant devices. It is not necessary to use tamper-resistant devices because there is no system secret need to be protected. Of course, in a point-of-sale environment, using tamper-resistant devices (e.g., smartcards) by the spender will undoubtedly be helpful in protecting the private key and in preventing accidental human errors. However, cheap devices suffice because there is no need to prevent the device holders from extracting data in the devices. (In fact, they should keep safe backup of the data.)

Coin sub-divisible to variant denominations. For instance, a typical coin stick can be $Stick(1,000)$ to worth 10 dollars with each coin in it to worth 1 cent. During spending, after having released a top coin with spending signature, Alice can then continuously release coins down to 1-cent refinement, no further signature on these subsequent coins is needed, until she feels enough services have been purchased. This why of payment is particularly suitable for web-based interactive information page purchase.

System simplicity. The protocols for cash withdrawal, payment and deposit are simple and the data size for coin representation is small. The payment protocol has an exceptionally low computational complexity for the spender because to compute hash function is efficient and to generate a spending signature is merely to release a dot in a line. These are attractive features for making point-of-sale payment using smartcards. Further, cash can easily be withdrawn from a foreign bank and usable by a non-bank-account holder.

We believe that the proposed electronic cash technique is readily workable and has potential to lead to a full-fledged electronic commerce for Internet information purchases.

Acknowledgements

Part of the work was completed when the author was participating in the research programme in Computer Security, Cryptography and Coding (the CCC Programme) at the Newton Institute, Cambridge University, April, 1996. Discussions with Tatsuaki Okamoto and Claus Schnorr during the CCC Programme were very interesting and helpful. The author would also like to thank Dipankar Gupta, Miranda Mowbray and anonymous reviewers for their helpful comments on an early version of this paper.

References

1. Proposed Federal Information Processing Standard for Digital Signature Standard (DSS). Federal Register, v.56, n.169, August 1991.
2. J.-P. Boly et al. The ESPRIT Project CAFE — High Security Digital Payment Systems. In *Computer Security — ESORICS'94 (LNCS 875)*, pages 217–230. Springer-Verlag, 1994.
3. S. Brands. Untraceable off-line cash in wallet with observers. In *Advances in Cryptology — Proceedings of CRYPTO'93 (LNCS 773)*, pages 302–318. Springer-Verlag, 1993.

4. S. Brands. Electronic cash on the internet. In *Proceedings of the Internet Society 1995 Symposium on Network and Distributed System Security*, 1995.

5. S. Brands. Off-line electronic cash based on secret-key certificates. Technical Report: CS-R9506, 1995.

6. J. Camenisch, J-M. Piveteau, and Stadler M. An efficient electronic payment system protecting privacy. In *Computer Security — ESORICS'94, (LNCS 875)*, pages 207–215. Springer-Verlag, 1994.

7. D. Chaum. Blind signatures for untraceable payments. In *Advances in Cryptology — Proceedings of Crypto'82*, pages 199–203. Plenum Press, 1983.

8. D. Chaum. Security without identification: Transaction systems to make big brother obsolete. *Communications of the ACM*, 28(10):1030–1044, October 1985.

9. D. Chaum. Blind signatures systems. U.S. Patent No 4,759,063, July 1988.

10. D. Chaum. Privacy protected payments: Unconditional payer and/or payee untraceability. In *Smartcard 2000*. North Holland, 1989.

11. D. Chaum. Online cash checks. In *Advances in Cryptology — Proceedings of EUROCRYPT'89 (LNCS 434)*, pages 288–293. Springer-Verlag, 1990.

12. D. Chaum. Achieving electronic privacy. *Scientific American*, pages 96–101, August 1992.

13. D. Chaum, B. den Boer, E. van Heyst, S. Mjolsnes, and A. Steenbeek. Efficient offline electronic checks. In *Advances in Cryptology — Proceedings of EUROCRYPT'89 (LNCS 434)*, pages 294–301. Springer-Verlag, 1990.

14. D. Chaum, A. Fiat, and M. Naor. Untraceable electronic cash. In *Advances in Cryptology — Proceedings of CRYPTO'88 (LNCS 403)*, pages 319–327. Springer-Verlag, 1990.

15. D. Chaum and T. Pedersen. Wallet databases with observers. In *Advances in Cryptology — Proceedings of CRYPTO'92 (LNCS 740)*, pages 89–105. Springer-Verlag, 1992.

16. T. ElGamal. A public-key Cryptosystem and a signature scheme based on discrete logarithms. In *Advances in Cryptology — Proceedings of CRYPTO'84 (LNCS 196)*, pages 10–18. Springer-Verlag, 1985.

17. T. Eng and T. Okamoto. Single-term divisible electronic coins. In *Advances in Cryptology — Proceedings of EUEOCRYPT'94 (LNCS 950)*, pages 306–319. Springer-Verlag, 1995.

18. N. Ferguson. Single term off-line coins. In *Advances in Cryptology — Proceedings of EUROCRYPT'93 (LNCS 765)*, pages 318–328. Springer-Verlag, 1994.

19. M. Franklin and M. Yung. Towards provably secure efficient electronic cash. Technical Report: TR CUCS-018-92, April 1992.

20. M. Franklin and M. Yung. Secure and efficient off-line digital money. In *Proceedings of ICALP'93, (LNCS 700)*, pages 265–276. Springer-Verlag, 1993.

21. N.M. Haller. The S/Key one-time password system. http://ftp.cert.dfn.de/pub/tools/password/SKey/.

22. B.. Hayes. Anonymous one-time signatures and flexible untraceable electronic cash. In *Advances in Cryptology — Proceedings of AUSCRYPT'90 (LNCS 453)*, pages 294–305. Springer-Verlag, 1990.

23. ITU/ISO/IEC. Draft Amendment 1 to ITU Rec. X.509 (1993) — ISO/IEC 9594-8: Information Technology — Open Systems Interconnection — The Directory: Authentication Framework, Amendment 1: Certificate Extensions. ISO/IEC JTC 1/SC 21/WG 4 and ITU-T Q 15/7 Collaborative Editing Meeting on the Directory, Ottawa, Canada, July 1995.

24. L. Lamport. Password identification with insecure communications. *Communications of the ACM*, 24(11):770–772, 1981.

25. W. Mao. Blind Certification of Public Keys and Off-Line Electronic Cash. HP Laboratories Technical Report, HPL-96-71, May 1996.

26. MasterCard and Visa Secure Electronic Transaction (SET) (see, e.g., http://www.visa.com/), February 1996.

27. G. Medvinsky and B.C. Neuman. NetCash: A design for practical electronic currency on the Internet. In *Proceedings of First ACM Conference on Computer and Communications Security*, pages 102–196. ACM Press, 1993.

28. T. Okamoto and K. Ohta. Universal electronic cash. In *Advances in Cryptology — Proceedings of CRYPTO'91 (LNCS 576)*, pages 324–337. Springer-Verlag, 1992.

29. R.L. Rivest and A. Shamir. Payword and micromint: Two simple micropayment schemes. http://theory.lcs.mit.edu/~rivest/publications.html, December 1995.

30. C.P. Schnorr. Efficient signature generation for smart cards. In *Advances in Cryptology — Proceedings of CRYPTO'89 (LNCS 435)*, pages 239–252. Springer-Verlag, 1990.

31. C.P. Schnorr. Efficient signature generation for smart cards. *Journal of Cryptology*, 4(3):161–174, 1991.

32. C.P. Schnorr. A method for identifying subscribers and for generating and verifying electronic signatures in a data exchange system. U.S. Patent No. 4,995,082, February 1991.

33. M. Sirbu and J.D. Tygar. NetBill: An Internet Commerce System. http://www.ini.cmu.edu/netbill/CompCon.html.

34. UK banks introduce Mondex, the cashless cash card. Newsbytes News Network (also see http://www.mondex.com/), January 1993.

Digital Payment Systems with Passive Anonymity-Revoking Trustees

Jan Camenisch[1]*   Ueli Maurer[1]   Markus Stadler[2]

[1] Department of Computer Science
ETH Zurich
CH-8092 Zurich, Switzerland
Email: {camenisch|maurer}@inf.ethz.ch

[2] UBILAB
Union Bank of Switzerland
Bahnhofstrasse 45
CH-8021 Zurich, Switzerland
Email: stadler@ubilab.ubs.ch

Abstract. Anonymity of the participants is an important requirement for some applications in electronic commerce, in particular for payment systems. Because anonymity could be in conflict with law enforcement, for instance in cases of blackmailing or money laundering, it has been proposed to design systems in which a trustee or a set of trustees can selectively revoke the anonymity of the participants involved in suspicious transactions. From an operational point of view, it can be an important requirement that such trustees are neither involved in payment transactions nor in the opening of an account, but only in case of a justified suspicion. In this paper we propose the first efficient anonymous digital payment systems satisfying this requirement. The described basic protocol for anonymity revocation can be used in on-line or off-line payment systems.

Keywords: Digital payment systems, electronic money, cryptography, privacy, anonymity revocation.

1 Introduction

In most presently-used payment systems the protection of the user's privacy relies exclusively on administrative and legal measures. Using cryptographic tools, in particular blind signature schemes [9], it is possible to design electronic payment systems that allow the customers to remain anonymous, without affecting the other security requirements of the system (e.g. [2, 6, 10, 11]). However, while protecting the honest customers' privacy, the anonymity also opens the door for misuse by criminals, for instance for perfect blackmailing [19] or for money laundering.

* Supported by the Swiss Commission for Technology and Innovation (KTI), and by the Union Bank of Switzerland.

Therefore, in order to make anonymous payment systems acceptable to governments and banks, they must provide mechanisms for revoking a participant's anonymity under certain well-defined conditions. Such anonymity revocation must be possible only for an authorised trusted third party or a set of such parties. In this paper we refer to trusted third parties as *trustees*. In a concrete scenario a trustee could be a judge or a law enforcement agency.

The concept of *anonymity-revocable payment systems*, sometimes called fair payment systems, was introduced independently in [4] and [18]. The customer's privacy cannot be compromised by the bank nor by the payee, even if they collaborate, but the trustee or a specified set of trustees can (in cooperation with the bank) revoke a customer's anonymity. It is understood that the trustee(s) answer a request only if there exists sufficient evidence that a transaction is not lawful.

All previously proposed anonymity-revocable systems [4, 7, 8, 13, 18] are either inefficient because they are based on the cut-and-choose paradigm, or they require the trustee's participation in the opening of accounts or even in withdrawal transactions.

From an operational point of view, it is an important requirement that a trustee can be passive, i.e., that he need not be involved in regular transactions nor when a customer opens a new account. The goal of this paper is the design of the first efficient anonymous digital payment systems satisfying this requirement.

2 Digital payment systems

An electronic payment system consists of a set of protocols between three interacting parties: a bank, a customer (the payer), and a shop (the payee). The customer and the shop have accounts with the bank. The goal of the system is to transfer money in a secure way from the customer's account to the shop's account. It is possible to identify three different phases: a *withdrawal phase* involving the bank and the customer, a *payment phase* involving the customer and the shop, and a *deposit phase* involving the shop and the bank. In an *off-line* system, each phase occurs in a separate transaction, whereas in an *on-line* system, payment and deposit take place in a single transaction involving all three parties.

The bank, the shop and the customer have different security requirements. The bank must ensure that money can be deposited only if it has previously been withdrawn. In particular, double-spending of digital money must be impossible. The shop, upon receiving a payment in an off-line system, must be assured that the bank will accept the payment. Finally, the customer must be assured that the withdrawn money will later be accepted for a payment and that the bank is not able to claim that the money has already been spent (framing), i.e., falsely accuse him of double-spending. Furthermore, the customer may require that his privacy be protected. We refer to [6] for a detailed discussion of security requirements for payment systems.

Anonymous electronic payment systems (e.g. [2, 6, 10, 11]) are based on a cryptographic mechanism called a blind signature scheme [5, 9]. Such a signature scheme allows a signer (the bank) to sign a message without seeing its content. Furthermore, while anyone, including a shop or the bank, is able to verify such a signature, even the bank is not able to link a particular signature with a particular instance of signing a message. In order to implement an anonymous payment system based on a blind signature scheme, any message signed (blindly) by the bank with the secret key corresponding to a particular public key is agreed to have a certain value (e.g. $10).

An obvious problem with such a scheme is that money can in principle be spent more than once. In an on-line system, double-spending can be prevented by checking for multiple deposits. This requires that all deposit transactions (at least within the validity period of the bank's public key) are stored by the bank. In an off-line system, double-spending cannot be prevented, but it is possible to design systems that allow to revoke a customer's anonymity when the money is spent more than once. This can be achieved by assuring that the customer's identity is properly encoded in the signed message and by having the customer answer a challenge message during the payment such that the identity can be computed from the answers to two different challenges. Alternatively, the anonymity revoking mechanism of this paper can be used.

3 Anonymity revocation by a trustee

Anonymity revocation by a trustee means that, when the need arises, the trustee can link a withdrawal transaction with the corresponding deposit transaction. There are two types of anonymity revocation, depending on which kind of information is available to the trustee:

- *Withdrawal-based* anonymity revocation: Based on the bank's view of a withdrawal transaction, the trustee can compute a piece of information that can be used (by the bank or a payee) to recognize the money when it is spent later. This type of anonymity revocation can for instance be used in case of blackmailing. When the owner of an account is forced to withdraw money and to transfer it to an anonymous criminal, the account owner could secretly inform the bank and the trustee could be asked to compute a value that can be put on a black list and linked with the money when it is deposited.
- *Payment-based* anonymity revocation: Based on the bank's view of a deposit transaction, the trustee determines the identity of the person who had withdrawn the money. This may for instance be needed when the suspicion of money laundering arises.

One of the security requirements of such a payment system is that the trustee must be capable only of anonymity revocation but that he cannot play a different role in the system. In particular, the trustee must be unable to forge money.

It it possible to distinguish three different approaches to achieving the above goals according to the type of the trustee's involvement.

1. The trustee is involved in every withdrawal. In such systems [7, 13] the trustee plays the role of an intermediary during the withdrawal protocol and performes the blinding operation on behalf of the customer. The trustee can then trivially revoke the anonymity if needed.

2. The trustee is involved in the opening of accounts, but not in transactions (e.g. [8]). Such systems are potentially more efficient because normally an account is used for more than a single transaction.

3. The trustee is not involed in any protocols of the payment system but is needed only for anonymity-revocation. In such systems the customer proves the bank in the withdrawal protocol that the coin and the exchanged messages contain information, encrypted under the public key of a trustee, that allow revoking the anonymity. This can in principle be achieved by application of the well-known cut-and-choose paradigm, as described independently in [4] and [18]. However, such a system would be inefficient as explained in the following rough description of the scheme of [18]. A more efficient scheme is proposed in this paper.

We now describe the scheme of [18]. In order to obtain a blind signature on a message m, the customer prepares $2K$ blinded messages, each of which contains m encrypted with the trustee's public key as well as a session identifier encrypted with the trustee's public key. K is a security parameter. These encryptions are probabilistic (i.e. the text is padded with a random string of at least 64 bits before encryption) in order to prevent decryption by an exhaustive search over a small set of possible values. To check that these messages are properly formed, the bank chooses a random subset of K blinded messages and asks the customer to open all of them, where "open" means presenting the random padding used for encrypting the session identifier. For the purpose of possible later anonymity revocation, the bank stores the corresponding K encryptions of m. Then it blindly signs the remaining K messages that were not opened. The verification of such a coin (a blind signature for the message m) consists of the verification of the bank's signature as well as the verification that m had correctly been encrypted for the trustee.

In the described system, withdrawal-based revocation can be achieved by asking the trustee to open the encryptions of m the bank obtained during the withdrawal protocol. Payment-based anonymity revocation can be achieved by asking the trustee to decrypt the encrypted session ID contained in each of the K components of the signature. The probability that a dishonest customer manages to escape payment-based anonymity revocation is $1/\binom{2K}{K} \approx 2^{-2K}/\sqrt{\pi K}$. The same holds for withdrawal-based revocation. To achieve a reasonable security, K should be at least 20; hence both signatures and the revocation information stored by the bank are long.

The goal of this paper is to propose an efficient anonymity-revocable payment system that allows both types of anonymity revocation and in which, in contrast to the previously proposed efficient systems, the trustee is completely passive unless he is asked to revoke the anonymity of a person. In particular, after initially publishing a public key, the trustee need neither be involved in the opening of an account nor in any withdrawal or deposit transaction.

4   Building blocks

We briefly describe a few well-known cryptographic building blocks based on the computational difficulty of the discrete logarithm problem and then describe our main building block (protocol $\mathbf{P}$). Variations of this protocol $\mathbf{P}$ have previously been proposed in [2] and [12].

Let G be a finite cyclic group of order q and let $g \in G$ be a generator of G, such that computing discrete logarithms to the base g is infeasible. Let $\mathcal{H}_\ell : \{0,1\}^* \rightarrow \{0,1\}^\ell$ ($\ell \approx 128$) denote a cryptographically strong hash function. For a number of different cryptographic schemes, a public key is constructed by computing $y = g^x$ for a secret key x chosen at random from $\mathbb{Z}_q$.

We will make use of extensions of the Schnorr signature scheme [16]. A Schnorr signature for a message m is a pair (c, s) with $c \in \{0,1\}^\ell$ and $s \in \mathbb{Z}_q$, satisfying the verification equation

$$c = \mathcal{H}_\ell(m\|g^s y^c).$$

Such a signature can be generated only if one knows the secret key x, by choosing r at random from $\mathbb{Z}_q$ and computing c and s according to

$$c = \mathcal{H}_\ell(m\|g^r)$$

and

$$s \equiv r - cx \quad (\text{mod } q).$$

Basically, a Schnorr signature with respect to a public-key (g, y) is a proof (depending on the message m to be signed) that the signer knows the discrete logarithm of his public key y to the base g.

We now give definitions for two cryptographic primitives for proving knowledge and equality of discrete logarithms, respectively. A proof of knowledge of the discrete logarithm of a group element h to the base g, denoted $PKLOG(g, h)$ consists of a Schnorr signature with respect to a public-key (g, h) for the message $g\|h$, i.e.,

$$PKLOG(g, h) = (c, s)$$

with

$$c = \mathcal{H}_\ell(g\|h\|g^s h^c).$$

A (message-dependent) proof of equality of the discrete logarithm of h_1 to the base g_1 and the discrete logarithm of h_2 to the base g_2, denoted $PLOGEQ(m, g_1, h_1, g_2, h_2)$, is a pair (c, s) satisfying the following condition:

$$PLOGEQ(m, g_1, h_1, g_2, h_2) = (c, s)$$

with

$$c = \mathcal{H}_\ell(m\|g_1\|g_2\|h_1\|h_2\|g_1^s h_1^c\|g_2^s h_2^c).$$

Such a proof can be obtained if and only if one knows the discrete logarithms $\log_{g_1} h_1$ and $\log_{g_2} h_2$ and if they are both equal to some value x. One first chooses r at random from $\mathbb{Z}_q$ and computes $c = \mathcal{H}_\ell(m\|g_1\|g_2\|h_1\|h_2\|g_1^r\|g_2^r)$ and $s \equiv r - cx \pmod{q}$. Note that the message m can be the empty string.

The following protocol is a blind Schnorr signature protocol [15]. When a message m is signed by this protocol, the signer $\mathcal{B}$ learns neither m nor the resulting signature (c, s).

$\mathcal{C}(m, g, y)$ $\qquad\qquad\qquad\qquad\qquad\qquad\qquad$ $\mathcal{B}(g, x)$

$$
\begin{array}{ll}
 & \tilde{r} \in_R \mathbb{Z}_q \\
 & \tilde{t} := g^{\tilde{r}} \\
 \xleftarrow{\qquad \tilde{t} \qquad} & \\
\gamma, \delta \in_R \mathbb{Z}_q & \\
t := \tilde{t} g^\gamma y^\delta & \\
c := \mathcal{H}_\ell(m\|t) & \\
\tilde{c} := c - \delta \pmod{q} & \\
\xrightarrow{\qquad \tilde{c} \qquad} & \\
 & \tilde{s} := \tilde{r} - \tilde{c}x \pmod{q} \\
\xleftarrow{\qquad \tilde{s} \qquad} & \\
s := \tilde{s} + \gamma \pmod{q} & \\
\downarrow & \downarrow \\
(c, s) & (\tilde{r}, \tilde{t}, \tilde{c}, \tilde{s})
\end{array}
$$

If both $\mathcal{C}$ and $\mathcal{B}$ follow the protocol, $\mathcal{C}$ obtains a valid Schnorr signature (c, s) of the message m:

$$g^s y^c = g^{\tilde{s}+\gamma} y^{\tilde{c}+\delta} = g^{\tilde{r}-\tilde{c}x+\gamma+\tilde{c}x} y^\delta = \tilde{t} g^\gamma y^\delta = t .$$

The signature is valid because $c = \mathcal{H}_\ell(m\|t)$ holds. $\mathcal{B}$'s output of the protocol is the entire view consisting of $\tilde{r}$, $\tilde{t}$, $\tilde{c}$, and $\tilde{s}$. Note that the pair (c, s) is statistically independent of the pair $(\tilde{c}, \tilde{s})$ because γ and δ are randomly and uniformly chosen from $\mathbb{Z}_q$, and that therefore the message-signature pair and $\mathcal{B}$'s view are unlinkable.

This basic blind issuing protocol for Schnorr signatures is now extended to a protocol that not only proves $\mathcal{B}$'s knowledge of the secret key x, but simultaneously that the discrete logarithm of a value z_w to the base h_w is equal to x. $\mathcal{C}$ can then modify this proof in order to obtain a message-dependent proof of equality of $\mathcal{B}$'s secret key and the logarithm of a value z_p to a base h_p, with $h_p = h_w^\alpha g^\beta$, and $z_p = z_w^\alpha y^\beta$ for some $\alpha, \beta \in \mathbb{Z}_q$.

Protocol P:

$\mathcal{C}(m, g, y, h_w, \alpha, \beta)$ $\qquad\qquad\qquad\qquad\qquad\qquad$ $\mathcal{B}(g, x, h_w)$

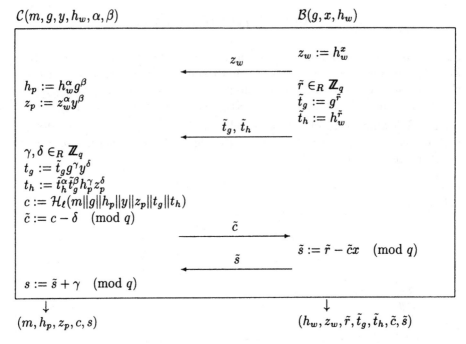

Note that (c, s) is a valid message-dependent $PLOGEQ(m, g, y, h_p, z_p)$ for message m. It can easily be proved that $\mathcal{B}$'s view of protocol **P** is unlinkable to (i.e., statistical independent of) $\mathcal{C}$'s output (m, h_p, z_p, c, s).

An important property of protocol **P** is that $\mathcal{C}$ can obtain a valid output only if he computes h_p as $h_w^\alpha g^\beta$ for some $\alpha, \beta \in \mathbb{Z}_q$. The following payment system will make use of this property to construct an anonymity-revocation mechanism.

5 An efficient anonymous payment system with a passive anonymity-revoking trustee

For simplicity, we describe only a simple on-line payment scheme with a single denomination of coins. An extension to multiple denominations is trivial. The scheme can also be extended to off-line payments, as described in Section 6. The withdrawal protocol described in this section is based on a fair blind signature scheme proposed in [17].

System setup:

1. The bank chooses a finite group G of prime order $q > 2^{170}$, such that computing discrete logarithms in G is infeasible. Note that such a group is cyclic and every element (except the neutral element) is a generator of the group. Three elements g, g_1 and g_2 are chosen by a publicly verifiable pseudo-random mechanism which guarantees that the discrete logarithms of none of these elements with respect to another one is known. Finally, the bank

chooses a secret key $x \in_R \mathbb{Z}_q$ and computes the public key $y = g^x$. The bank publishes G, g, g_1, g_2, and y.

2. The trustee randomly chooses his secret key $\omega \in \mathbb{Z}_q^*$ and computes his public key $g_T = g_2^\omega$. He publishes g_T.

The withdrawal protocol, which makes use of our building block (protocol **P**), is described below (ϵ denotes the empty string).

Customer(g, y, g_1, g_2, g_T) Bank(g, x, g_1, g_2, g_T)

Identification $\longrightarrow$

choose a random coin number $c\#$
$\alpha \in_R \mathbb{Z}_q^*$
$h_w := g_1^{\alpha^{-1}} g_2$
$d := g_T^\alpha$
$U := PLOGEQ(\epsilon, g_1, (h_w/g_2), d, g_T)$

$\xrightarrow{\quad h_w, d, U \quad}$ verify U and stop if verification fails

$\mathcal{C}(c\#, g, y, h_w, \alpha, 0)$ $\mathcal{B}(g, x, h_w)$

Protocol P

$\downarrow$ $\downarrow$

$(c\#, h_p, z_p, c, s)$ $(h_w, z_w, \tilde{r}, \tilde{t}_g, \tilde{t}_h, \tilde{c}, \tilde{s})$

$V := PKLOG(g_2, h_p/g_1)$ debit customer's account
$W := (c, s) = PLOGEQ(c\#, g, y, h_p, z_p)$

$\downarrow$ $\downarrow$

$(c\#, h_p, z_p, V, W)$ $(h_w, z_w, U, d, \tilde{r}, \tilde{t}_g, \tilde{t}_h, \tilde{c}, \tilde{s})$

The withdrawn coin consists of the coin number $c\#$ and the values h_p, z_p, V, and W and can be verified by checking the two proofs V and W. For the purpose of later anonymity revocation, the bank keeps the value d.

Note that (in contrast to protocol **P**) now the bank's view and the generated signature (coin) are only computationally unlinkable: i.e., the bank could link by testing whether $\log_{g_T} d = \log_{g_2}(h_p/g_1)$. However, this is intractable because the bank does not know $\log_{g_2} g_T$ (see [2] for a discussion about the so called decision-Diffie-Hellman problem).

In the computation of U we have made use of the fact that by exchanging base and input element of a discrete logarithm computation, the resulting discrete logarithm is inverted modulo the group order:

$$\log_g h \equiv (\log_h g)^{-1} \quad (\text{mod } q).$$

Therefore, the proof $U = PLOGEQ(\epsilon, g_1, (h_w/g_2), d, g_T)$ in the withdrawal protocol proves that the discrete logarithm $\log_{g_1}(h_w/g_2)$ is inverse to $\log_{g_T} d$.

We now discuss the anonymity-revocation mechanism. The facts that the customer

- knows $\log_{g_1}(h_w/g_2)$ as can be verified by checking U,
- knows $\log_{g_2}(h_p/g_1)$ as can be verified by checking V,
- neither knows $\log_{g_1} g$, $\log_{g_2} g$, nor $\log_{g_1} g_2$ (which is guaranteed by the way these elements were generated),

imply that the customer has executed protocol $\mathbf{P}$ with

$$\alpha = (\log_{g_1}(h_w/g_2))^{-1} = \log_{g_T} d = \log_{g_2}(h_p/g_1)$$

and $\beta = 0$. This relationship can now be used for anonymity revocation.

Withdrawal-based anonymity revocation is achieved as follows. Given the value d observed in a withdrawal transaction, the trustee computes

$$g_1 d^{\omega^{-1}} = g_1 g_2^\alpha = h_p.$$

This value can be put on a black list and recognised when the coin is spent.

Payment-based revocation is achieved as follows. Given the component h_p observed in a payment transaction, the trustee can compute the value

$$(h_p/g_1)^\omega = (g_2^\alpha)^\omega = d$$

which can be compared with the corresponding value in the revocation database obtained from the withdrawal transactions.

6 Efficiency considerations and extensions

We now compare the efficiency of the proposed scheme with the previously proposed schemes based on the cut-and-choose paradigm. In a scheme of the latter type, a blind signature consists of $K \approx 20$ components, each of which consists of a random padding string and a public-key encrypted value. In order to achieve a reasonable security level, the lengths of these two values must be at least 64 and 512 bits, respectively, resulting in a total signature length of close to 12,000 bits. The value stored by the bank for each withdrawal transaction is of a comparable size. The withdrawal transaction requires $4K$ public-key encryption operations, which in general is quite inefficient, but could be as fast as our scheme if RSA with small exponents is used.

In contrast, the signature in the proposed scheme consists of two group elements, two hash values, and two numbers smaller than q. When the group allows for a compact representation of its elements, the signatures can be quite short. For instance, elements of an elliptic curve with order q over a field of cardinality close to q can be represented by two field elements. Hence for $q \approx 2^{170}$, the total signature length is roughly $6 \log_2 q + 256 \approx 1300$ bits. This could even be reduced to about 1000 bits if the representation of group-elements is compressed and the challenges for the proofs V and W are chosen to be the same. The signature length compares favourably with a cut-and-choose based scheme.

To achieve higher security against fraudulent anonymity revocation, the protocol described in the previous section can be extended to incorporate several trustees who can only in cooperation revoke a customer's anonymity. This is achieved by letting each trustee choose a secret key ω_i and defining ω to be the product of the ω_i. Raising a value to the power ω or ω^{-1} during anonymity revocation is achieved by asking all trustees to consecutively compute the ω_i-th or ω_i^{-1}-th powers, respectively.

To extend our scheme to off-line payments, the customer replaces the coin number $c\#$ by $t = g_2^r$ for r chosen at random from $\mathbb{Z}_q$. To spend a coin the customer must provide a Schnorr-signature (c, s), where c must be $\mathcal{H}(m\|t)$, and the public key is h_p/g_1. The message m must depend on (or be chosen by) the shop. This signature is a message-dependent proof of knowledge with t as commitment. If the customer spends a coin twice the bank can, upon receiving both signatures, calculate α and thereby identify the double-spender.

Another method for extending our scheme to off-line payments would be that the customer replaces the coin number $c\#$ by a randomly chosen public key of any (fixed) signature scheme. To spend the coin he signs a message containing some shop-dependent data. Thus double-spending can be detected by the fact that more than one message was signed with respect to the same public-key. However the offender can be identified only by invoking the anonymity-revocation mechanism which is acceptable if it happens rarely. This could be guaranteed by so-called observers (as proposed in [3] and [12]) which would imply that double-spending required breaking a tamper-proof component. This method has the advantage that an arbitrary and hence very efficient signature scheme could be used (e.g. [1, 14]).

As is the case with most complex cryptographic protocols, the proposed protocol can quite convincingly be argued to be secure if computing discrete logarithms in the underlying group is infeasible, but the security cannot be proved rigorously. It is an open problem to prove that the protocol is as secure as the discrete logarithm problem.

Acknowledgements

Some ideas of this paper are based on results of a previous cooperation with Jean-Marc Piveteau.

References

1. D. Bleichenbacher and U. Maurer. Directed acyclic graphs, one-way functions and digital signature. In Y. Desmedt, editor, *Advances in Cryptology — CRYPTO '94*, volume 839 of *Lecture Notes in Computer Science*, pages 75–82. Springer Verlag Berlin, 1994.
2. S. Brands. An efficient off-line electronic cash system based on the representation problem. Technical Report CS-R9323, CWI, Apr. 1993.

3. S. Brands. Untraceable off-line cash in wallets with observers. In D. R. Stinson, editor, *Advances in Cryptology — CRYPTO '93*, volume 773 of *Lecture Notes in Computer Science*, pages 302–318, 1993.

4. E. Brickell, P. Gemmel, and D. Kravitz. Trustee-based tracing extensions to anonymous cash and the making of anonymous change. In *Proceedings of the 6th Annual Symposium on Discrete Algorithms*, pages pp 457–466, Jan. 1995.

5. J. Camenisch, J.-M. Piveteau, and M. Stadler. Blind signatures based on the discrete logaritm problem. In A. D. Santis, editor, *Advances in Cryptology — EUROCRYPT '94*, volume 950 of *Lecture Notes in Computer Science*, pages 428–432. Springer Verlag Berlin, 1994.

6. J. Camenisch, J.-M. Piveteau, and M. Stadler. An efficient payment system protecting privacy. In D. Gollmann, editor, *Computer Security — ESORICS 94*, volume 875 of *Lecture Notes in Computer Science*, pages 207–215. Springer Verlag, 1994.

7. J. Camenisch, J.-M. Piveteau, and M. Stadler. Faire Anonyme Zahlungssysteme. In F. Huber-Wäschle, H. Schauer, and P. Widmayer, editors, *GISI 95*, Informatik aktuell, pages 254–265. Springer Verlag Berlin, Sept. 1995.

8. J. Camenisch, J.-M. Piveteau, and M. Stadler. An efficient fair payment system. In *3rd ACM Conference on Computer and Communicatons Security*, pages 88–94, New Delhi, Mar. 1996. acm press.

9. D. Chaum. Blind signature systems. In D. Chaum, editor, *Advances in Cryptology — CRYPTO '83*, page 153. Plenum, 1983.

10. D. Chaum. Security without identification: Transaction systems to make big brother obsolete. *Communications of the ACM*, 28(10):1030–1044, Oct. 1985.

11. D. Chaum, A. Fiat, and M. Naor. Untraceable electronic cash. In S. Goldwasser, editor, *Advances in Cryptology — CRYPTO '88*, volume 403 of *Lecture Notes in Computer Science*, pages 319–327. Springer Verlag, 1990.

12. D. Chaum and T. Pedersen. Wallet databases with observers. In E. F. Brickell, editor, *Advances in Cryptology — CRYPTO '92*, volume 740 of *Lecture Notes in Computer Science*, pages 89–105. Springer-Verlag, 1993.

13. M. Jakobsson and M. Yung. Revokable and versatile electronic money. In *3rd ACM Conference on Computer and Communicatons Security*, pages 76–87, New Delhi, Mar. 1996. acm press.

14. R. Merkle. A certified digital signature. In G. Brassard, editor, *Advances in Cryptology — CRYPTO '89*, volume 435 of *Lecture Notes in Computer Science*, pages 218–238. Springer Verlag Berlin, 1990.

15. T. Okamoto. Provable secure and practical identification schemes and corresponding signature schemes. In E. F. Brickell, editor, *Advances in Cryptology — CRYPTO '92*, volume 740 of *Lecture Notes in Computer Science*, pages 31–53. Springer-Verlag, 1993.

16. C. P. Schnorr. Efficient signature generation for smart cards. *Journal of Cryptology*, 4(3):239–252, 1991.

17. M. Stadler. *Cryptographic Protocols for Revocable Privacy*. PhD Thesis, ETH Zürich, 1996. Diss. ETH No. 11651.

18. M. Stadler, J.-M. Piveteau, and J. Camenisch. Fair blind signatures. In L. C. Guillou and J.-J. Quisquater, editors, *Advances in Cryptology — EUROCRYPT '95*, volume 921 of *Lecture Notes in Computer Science*, pages 209–219. Springer Verlag, 1995.

19. S. von Solms and D. Naccache. On blind signatures and perfect crimes. *Computer & Security*, 11(6):581–583, 1992.

An Authorization Model for Workflows*

Vijayalakshmi Atluri and Wei-Kuang Huang

Center for Information Management, Integration, and Connectivity (CIMIC)
and
MS/CIS Department
Rutgers University
180 University Avenue, Newark, NJ 07102
{atluri,waynexh@andromeda.rutgers.edu}

Abstract. Workflows represent processes in manufacturing and office environments that typically consist of several well-defined activities (known as tasks). To ensure that these tasks are executed by authorized users or processes (subjects), proper authorization mechanisms must be in place. Moreover, to make sure that authorized subjects gain access on the required objects only during the execution of the specific task, granting and revoking of privileges need to be synchronized with the progression of the workflow. A predefined specification of the privileges often allows access for more than the time required, thus, though a subject completes the task or have not yet begun the task, it may still possess privileges to access the objects, resulting in compromising security.

In this paper, we propose a *Workflow Authorization Model* (WAM) that is capable of specifying authorizations in such a way that subjects gain access to required objects only during the execution of the task, thus synchronizing the *authorization flow* with the workflow. To achieve this synchronization, we associate an *Authorization Template* (AT) with each task, which allows appropriate authorizations to be granted only when the task starts and to revoke them when the task finishes. In this paper, we also present a model of implementation based on *Petri nets* and show how this synchronization can be implemented. Because the theoretical aspects of Petri nets have been extensively studied and due to their strong mathematical foundation, a Petri net representation of an authorization model serves as a good tool for conducting safety analysis since the safety problem in the authorization model is equivalent to the reachability problem in Petri nets.

Key Words: Security, Authorization, Workflow, Petri nets

1 Introduction

Workflows typically represent processes involved in manufacturing and office environments and heterogeneous database management systems. The various activities in a workflow can usually be separated into well defined tasks. These tasks in turn are related and dependent on one another, and therefore need to

---

* This work was supported in part by the National Science Foundation grant IRI-9624222.

be executed in a coordinated manner. Execution of these separate tasks can either be carried out by humans, processes such as an application program, or a database management system.

To ensure that these tasks are executed by authorized subjects (users or processes), appropriate authorization mechanisms must be in place. A suitable authorization model for workflows must ensure that authorization is granted only when the task starts and revoked as soon as the task finishes. Otherwise, a subject may possess authorization for time periods longer than required, which may compromise security.

For example, consider a workflow that represents document release process in an organization. Assume this workflow consists of the following two tasks: A scientist prepares a document (task 1) and then prior to releasing this document gets approval from the patent-officer of his organization (task 2). During execution of task 1, the scientist will have all the rights on the document (read, write etc.). When he submits it to the patent-officer, a read authorization on the document has to be granted to the patent-officer. Since the scientist should not be allowed to modify the document during or after the approval process, the write privilege of the scientist on the document must be revoked as soon as he submits it for approval. This is required to ensure that the scientist is not able to alter the document during or after the approval. (Such non-monotonic authorization models can be found, for example, in [22].) In the paper world, since the patent-officer receives a hard copy of the document, and therefore it is no longer with the scientist, the revocation of the write privilege from the scientist will be automatically accomplished. In case of electronic documents, a proper authorization model should mimic such a scenario. In order to ensure authorized subjects are granted privileges on required objects only while the task is being executed, propagation of authorization (i.e. *authorization flow*) has to be synchronized with the workflow.

To our knowledge, no authorization model can be found in the literature that addresses this issue of achieving synchronization between authorization flow and workflow. Recently, several extensions to the basic authorization model can be seen in number of directions. One direction deals with increasing the expressive power of the authorization models and developing appropriate tools and mechanisms to support these models. These include introducing negative authorization [3, 17], role-based and task-based authorizations and separation of duties [6, 19, 20], and temporal authorization [2]. Other direction deals with extending authorization models for advanced DBMSs such as object-oriented [8, 17, 4] and distributed [25, 18, 11] DBMSs.

However, in these models, authorizations are in general specified with respect to object, right, subject granting right, subject receiving right, etc. These models study the propagation of authorization but do not tie it with any activity in the system. However, as seen from the above example, authorization flow need to be tightly coupled to the workflow in order to ensure subjects possess authorizations only when required. [21] also recognizes that more sophisticated approaches than the conventional access control techniques are required when dealing with situations that control operation sequences.

Although models exist that allow specification of authorizations associated with a time interval, they are not suitable for workflow environments. For example, recently, an authorization model to represent temporal privileges has been proposed by Bertino et al. [2]. It allows authorizations to be specified on objects for specified time intervals. In this model a temporal authorization is specified as (time, auth), where time $= [t_b, t_e]$ is a time interval, and auth $= (s, o, m, pn, g)$ is an authorization. Here t_b and t_e represent the beginning and ending time during which auth is valid, s represents the subject, o the object, m the privilege, pn whether negative or positive authorization, and g the grantor of the authorization.

Since in this model authorization is granted during a predefined and fixed time interval, it is not suitable when dealing with workflows because appropriate authorizations should be granted or revoked synchronously with the starting and ending of a task. This is because it is difficult to predict the actual execution time of each task in many workflow situations and therefore not possible to determine their time interval in advance.

For example, imagine the following scenario: Suppose the authorization for relevant subjects on required object to execute a task has been specified with time interval $[t_b, t_e]$. Also assume the task actually starts at t_s and finishes by t_f. Consider the following three cases: (1) if $[t_b, t_e]$ is same as $[t_s, t_f]$, then authorization is valid exactly during the execution of the task (2) if $[t_s, t_f]$ is within $[t_b, t_e]$ then authorization is valid for a longer duration than required (3) if $[t_b, t_e]$ is within $[t_f, t_s]$ or $[t_b, t_e]$ overlaps $[t_f, t_s]$, then either the authorization is not valid when needed or valid for a longer period than required.

Even if one can determine the temporal interval during which a task has to be executed, delays experienced by one task may propagate to subsequent tasks thereby delaying their execution. Thus by the time the task actually starts, the required authorization may expire. On the other hand, it is not practical for a security administrator to monitor the workflow and grant (or revoke) authorizations accordingly. Although no formal authorization models exist that can synchronize authorization flow with the workflow, in some commercial Workflow Management Systems (WFMSs) such as Lotus Notes, this can be simulated by embedding scripts that test for the completion of the task and thereby revoke authorizations for individuals who have performed the task.

Bertino et al.'s model also allows operations such as WHENEVER, ASLONGAS, WHENEVERNOT and UNLESS to be specified on authorizations, where WHENEVER states that a subject s_i can gain a privilege on object o WHENEVER subject s_j has the same privilege on o. (ASLONGAS, WHENEVERNOT and UNLESS can also be interpreted similarly.) Since specification of authorizations is not based on the tasks this model is not completely suitable for workflow environments.

In addition to synchronizing the authorization flow with the workflow, there are several other desirable features that a suitable workflow authorization model must possess. We take a concrete example to illustrate these features.

Example 1. Consider a workflow that represents the selection process of research papers for a conference. This workflow consists of a number of tasks including collection of papers from the authors, distribution of papers to selected reviewers, generation of the reviews, summarizing all the reviews, forwarding the summary and decision of the conference chair to the authors and then finally announcing the list of selected papers to the research community. Assume that three individuals are required to review each paper. Authors are given privileges to create objects thereby anybody can submit a paper to the conference by creating an object. Authors will have read and write privileges on their paper although the write privilege is associated with a time limit since it has to be revoked after the deadline for submission of the papers. The conference chair then selects the reviewers. Though anyone among the set of reviewers may play the role of a reviewer, for any given paper, the three reviewers have to be different individuals and they must not be the authors of the paper. Reviewers send their responses by creating an object on which only read privilege has to be given to the conference chair. The conference chair then produces a summary of all the three reviews which is accessible only to the chair and the authors of the paper at which point authors are given back the write privileges on the paper. The final decision as to whether the paper has been accepted or rejected is produced and the list of accepted papers will be created by the conference chair, and this object is public and anyone can gain read privileges on this object. This workflow has been depicted in figure 1.

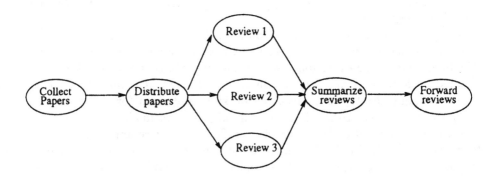

Fig. 1. Workflow Representing the Paper Reviewing Process

As seen from the example above, a workflow authorization model should support the following features. We explain below why these are required with the above example.

1. Authorizations have to be granted to subjects only during the execution of the task and must be revoked immediately after the completion of the task. This is required to guarantee that an author cannot modify the paper after submitting it to the conference chair.

2. Capability to handle temporal constraints is required to express conditions such as a reviewer must return the reviews by May 1996.

3. A role-based authorization is required to express an authorization such as "anyone in the program committee may act as a reviewer."

4. Separation of duties, which is necessary to prevent a single person providing all the three reviews on a paper, or an author of the paper reviewing his/her own paper.

5. Event-based authorization is required because the paper has to be made public and anyone can gain read access on the paper only if it is accepted for publication. Otherwise, the author(s) gain all the privileges on the paper. In other words, authorizations on objects and tasks may depend on the outcome of a task (such as its success or failure, or even the value of the outcome of the task).

In this paper, we propose a *Workflow Authorization Model* (WAM) that can *dynamically* change the time interval that specifies during which the authorization is valid. By the term dynamic, we mean that the time interval associated with the required authorization to perform a task changes according to the time during which the task actually executes. Our model addresses the first two issues enumerated above, i.e., synchronization of authorization flow with the workflow and specification of temporal constraints. In WAM, we introduce the notion of *Authorization Template* (AT) which specifies the static parameters of the authorization that can be defined during the design of the workflow and can be attached to the task. When the task actually starts execution, AT is used to derive the actual authorization. Section 2 presents WAM and shows how synchronization of authorization flow and workflow can be achieved.

We have presented a model of implementation of WAM using Petri nets, in which we show how synchronization of authorization flow and workflow can be achieved. Petri nets have been widely used for modeling synchronous activities. Their graphical nature and ability to model concurrent processes in a natural manner make them excellent tools for modeling workflow authorization. Moreover, because of their strong mathematical foundation, Petri nets are good tools for analysis of the authorization models. The main reason for adapting Petri nets is that *the safety problem[2] in authorization models is equivalent to the reachability problem in Petri nets.* Since Petri nets have been extensively studied with respect to this issue, representation of WAM allows us to adapt the existing reachability analysis techniques of Petri nets to conducting the safety analysis of WAM. (Similar representations such as finite state automata for the enforcement of security specifications [5] do not possess the aforementioned advantages of Petri nets.) We use a combination of two extended Petri net models – colored and timed Petri nets – to represent WAM as a Petri net. The Petri net representation of WAM is presented in section 3.

In section 4, we have presented a brief discussion of how WAM can be extended to specify role-based authorizations and separation of duties.

---

[2] The safety problem can be stated as the following question: "Is there a reachable state in which a particular subject possesses a particular privilege for a specific object?"

2 Workflow Authorization Model (WAM)

In this section, we propose a workflow authorization model (WAM) and show how required authorizations can be assigned to subjects so that the time interval during which an authorization is valid can be synchronized with workflow execution.

A workflow W can be represented as a *partially ordered* set of tasks $\{w_1, w_2, \ldots w_n\}$, where each task w_i in turn can be defined as a set OP_i of a partial or total order of operations $\{op_1, op_2 \ldots op_n\}$ that involve manipulation of objects [9].

Most workflows can be perceived as coordinated execution of tasks that involve processing of relevant objects by subjects (either humans or programs). Thus one can imagine every task starts when one or more objects arrive to the task for processing, and when the task finishes these objects leave. For example, consider the workflow of check processing consisting of three tasks: (1) preparation, (2) approval and (3) issue of the check. For the second task, i.e., check approval, to start, the object (check) has to be sent from the previous task (i.e., check preparation). When the approval task finishes, the approved check has to be sent to the following task, i.e., check issuing. Therefore, we assume a task starts only when one or more objects arrive to the task and when it finishes one or more objects leave the task. If there exists no such object moving from one task to the other, then one can assume the signal which acts as an input to trigger the starting of the task as an object.

Processing of a task involves accessing certain objects by certain subjects with certain privileges. To execute a task w_i, relevant privileges on required objects have to be granted to appropriate subjects. In this section, we develop several definitions to construct WAM.

Let $S = \{s_1, s_2 \ldots\}$ denote the set of subjects, $O = \{o_1, o_2 \ldots\}$ the set of objects $\Gamma = \{\gamma_1, \gamma_2 \ldots\}$ a finite set of objects types. The function $Y : O \to \Gamma$. That is, if $Y(o_i) = \gamma_j$, then o_i is of type γ_j. Let PR denote a finite set of privileges.

The following defines a time set and a time interval.

Definition 1.

1. Time set $\mathcal{T} = \{\tau \in \mathcal{R}^3 \mid \tau \geq 0\}$, and
2. a time interval $\{[\tau_l, \tau_u] \in \mathcal{T} \times \mathcal{T} \mid \tau_l \leq \tau_u\}$ represents the set of all closed intervals. $\quad\square$

The above definition dictates that the interval is guided by an lower and a upper boundary, τ_l and τ_u, respectively. We say an interval $[\tau_1, \tau_2]$ is within $[\tau_3, \tau_4]$ iff $\tau_3 \leq \tau_1$ and $\tau_4 \geq \tau_2$ and a time τ_1 is within $[\tau_3, \tau_4]$ iff $\tau_3 \leq \tau_1 \leq \tau_4$.

Definition 2. We define a *task* w_i as: $(OP_i, \Gamma_{IN_i}, \Gamma_{OUT_i}, [\tau_{l_i}, \tau_{u_i}])$, where OP_i is the set of operations to be performed in w_i, $\Gamma_{IN_i} \subseteq \Gamma$ is the set of object types

---

[3] $\mathcal{R}$ represents the set of all real numbers.

allowed as inputs, $\Gamma_{OUT_i} \subseteq \Gamma$ is the set of object types expected as outputs, and $[\eta_i, \tau_{u_i}]$ is the time interval during which w_i must be executed. □

Here $[\eta_i, \tau_{u_i}]$ specify temporal constraints stating the lower and upper bounds of the time interval during which a task is allowed to be executed. As an example, a temporal constraint may be specified as follows: "a task for preparing a check must be started after time $= 10$ and finished by time $= 20$."

Definition 3. We define a *task-instance*, $w\text{-}inst_i$ as: $(OPER_i, IN_i, OUT_i, [\tau_{s_i}, \tau_{f_i}])$ where $OPER_i$ is the set of operations performed during the execution of w_i, IN_i is the set of input objects to w_i such that $IN_i = \{x \in O | Y(x) \in \Gamma_{IN_i}\}$, OUT_i is the set of output objects from w_i such that $OUT_i = \{x \in O | \gamma(x) \in \Gamma_{OUT_i}\}$, and $[\tau_{s_i}, \tau_{f_i}]$ is the time interval during which w_i has been executed. □

Whenever a task is executed, a task-instance will be generated. Thus, a task w_i may generate several $w\text{-}inst_i$'s. τ_{s_i} and τ_{f_i} in the above definition indicate the time at which that particular task-instance has started and finished execution, respectively, whereas $[\eta_i, \tau_{u_i}]$ represent the time during which the task must be executed. Note that $[\eta_i, \tau_{u_i}]$ may differ from $[\tau_{s_i}, \tau_{f_i}]$, however, to ensure the temporal constraints, $[\tau_{s_i}, \tau_{f_i}]$ must be within $[\eta_i, \tau_{u_i}]$. To guarantee the above requirement, we use a model based on Petri nets.

Definition 4. We define an authorization as a 4-tuple $A = (s, o, pr, [\tau_b, \tau_e])$, where subject s is granted access on object o with privilege pr at time τ_b and is revoked at time τ_e. □

Definition 5. Given a task w_i, we define an authorization template $AT(w_i)$ as a 3-tuple $AT(w_i) = (s_i, (\gamma_i, -), pr_i)$ where
(i) $s_i \in S$,
(ii) $(\gamma_i, -)$ is an *object hole* which can be filled by an object o_i of type γ_i, and
(iii) pr_i is the privilege to be granted to s_i on object o_i when $(\gamma_i, -)$ is filled by o_i. □

In the definition for $AT(w_i)$ (i) says that only subject s_i is allowed to execute task w_i, (ii) dictates that only objects of type γ_i can be processed by w_i thus the object hole $(\gamma_i, -)$ allows objects of only type γ_i to be filled in, and (iii) says that s_i requires a privilege pr_i on the objects that arrive at w_i for processing.

Authorization templates are attached to the tasks in a workflow.[4] A task w_i may have more than one authorization template attached to it. More ATs are required in cases where there are more than one type of object to be processed, or more than one subject is required to perform the processing.

---

[4] The notion of templates can also be found in systems such as Hydra [26] where a template is defined as (type, required-rights). This is used to generate a new capability for an object by checking the type and rights specified in the template with its type and existing capability. Our notion of authorization template is different from that is Hydra in the sense that it grants a new authorization to a subject on the specified object if the object's type is same as that specified in the template.

To distinguish the subjects and privileges in AT from those in A, we often use $s(AT)$ and $pr(AT)$.

An authorization template allows us to specify rules such as "A subject John is allowed to perform check preparation." These can actually be stated during the design process by the workflow designer. However, the authorization to prepare the check is granted to John only when the task of check preparation actually starts. And this privilege will be revoked when this task is completed. The following authorization derivation rule ensures this.

Definition 6 Authorization Derivation Rule. Given an authorization template $AT(w_i) = (s_i, (\gamma_i, -), pr_i)$ of task $w_i = (OP_i, \Gamma_{IN_i}, \Gamma_{OUT_i}, [\eta_i, \tau_{u_i}])$, an authorization $A_i = (s_i, o_i, pr_i, [\tau_{b_i}, \tau_{e_i}])$ is derived as follows:

Grant Rule: Suppose object $o_i \in \Gamma_{IN_i}$ is sent to w_i at τ_{a_i} to start w_i. Let the starting time of w_i be τ_{s_i}.

If $\tau_{a_i} \leq \tau_{u_i}$, then $s_i \leftarrow s(AT)$, $pr_i \leftarrow pr(AT)$, $\tau_{e_i} \leftarrow \tau_{u_i}$, and (if $\tau_{a_i} \leq \eta_i$ then $\tau_{b_i} \leftarrow \eta_i$; otherwise $\tau_{b_i} \leftarrow \tau_{a_i}$)

Revoke Rule: Suppose w_i ends at τ_{f_i} at which point o_i leaves w_i.
If $\tau_{f_i} \leq \tau_{u_i}$, then $\tau_{e_i} \leftarrow \tau_{f_i}$. $\qquad\qquad\square$

We explain below how authorizations are derived from the authorization templates. Suppose a workflow consists of two tasks w_i and w_j. Also suppose there exists a temporal constraint on w_i which states that w_i must be executed only during the time interval $[\eta_i, \tau_{u_i}]$. Assume executing w_i involves processing and therefore accessing object o which is of type γ_i. To start w_i, an object o of type γ_i is first sent as an input to w_i.[5] After completing the execution, w_i passes the object o to the next task w_j. The authorization templates associated with w_i and w_j are: $AT(w_i) = (s_i, (\gamma_i, -), pr_i)$ and $AT(w_j) = (s_j, (\gamma_j, -), pr_j)$ (in this case γ_i may equal γ_j).

Execution of w_i starts when o arrives to w_i. Let this time be τ_{a_i}. If τ_{a_i} is within the specified time interval $[\eta_i, \tau_{u_i}]$ then w_i will be started, and the object hole in the authorization template is filled with o. At this point, the corresponding authorization A_i is derived according to the authorization derivation rule as follows: If $\tau_{a_i} \geq \eta_i$, then the time at which the object arrives (τ_{a_i}) is assigned to τ_{b_i}, and the specified time before which the task must complete (τ_{u_i}) is assigned to τ_{e_i}. Assigning τ_{u_i} as τ_{e_i} is required to ensure that A_i is not valid after the specified interval even if the task is still executing beyond the upper bound specified in the time constraint of w_i. However, if $\tau_{a_i} < \eta_i$, then η_i is assigned to both τ_{b_i}. That is, even if the object arrives earlier than the specified time interval, authorization is valid only from η_i but not from the time at which the object arrives. If $\tau_{a_i} > \tau_{u_i}$ then the object is rejected. Thus s_i is given privilege pr_i on o only when w_i starts execution.

When w_i finishes its execution (say at τ_{f_i}), o is passed on to w_j. Now, the object hole in the authorization template $AT(w_j)$ is filled with o, while that in $AT(w_i)$ becomes empty. If $\tau_{f_i} < \tau_{u_i}$ then τ_{e_i} in A_i is modified such that $\tau_{e_i} =$

---

[5] If there are no input objects to be sent to w_i, one can imagine that the input to start a task can be treated as an object or a dummy object can be assumed.

τ_{f_i}. Otherwise, τ_{e_i} is not modified. Thus s_i has privilege pr_i on o only until τ_{f_i}, i.e., only during the execution of w_i and is taken away from it as soon as w_i is completed. Even if w_i does not complete by time τ_{u_i}, A_i is valid only until τ_{u_i}. The validity of authorization is therefore guided by the specified duration. The authorization thus created showing the duration that the authorization has been granted for a particular task can be used for auditing purposes. In the following, we explain the process of deriving authorizations by taking a real example.

Example 2. Consider once again the check processing workflow, which involves the following three tasks, w_1, w_2 and w_3 denoting prepare check, approve check and issue check, respectively. They can be expressed as follows:

$w_1 = (\{\text{read request, prepare check}\}, \{\text{request, check}\}, \{\text{check}\}, [10,50])$
$w_2 = (\{\text{approve check}\}, \{ \text{check}\}, \{ \text{check}\}, [20,60])$
$w_3 = (\{\text{issue check}\}, \{ \text{check}\}, \{ \text{check}\}, [40,80])$

Suppose the associated subjects for performing these processes are John, Mary, and Ken, respectively. Now, instead of granting all the required privileges for every involved staff in advance, we first create the following authorization templates. (Appropriate authorizations to perform these tasks are not enforced until the tasks are actually processed.)

$AT_1(w_1) = (\text{John, (request,-), read})$
$AT_2(w_1) = (\text{John, (check,-), prepare})$
$AT(w_2) = (\text{Mary, (check,-), approve})$
$AT(w_3) = (\text{Ken, (check,-), issue})$

Now suppose the requests for payment arrive as follows.

Request $rq1$ at 40
Request $rq2$ at 55.

Before any task starts, no one in the workflow has been granted any valid authorization. At 40, the object $rq1$ arrives to w_1. This object is filled into the authorization template $AT_1(w_1) = (\text{John, (request,-), read})$, thereby generating an authorization $(\text{John}, rq1, \text{read}, [40,50])$. According to w_1, a new object check, say $ck023$ is created at w_1. Thus $AT_2(w_1) = (\text{John, check(-), prepare})$ is filled with $ck023$ thus generating another authorization $(\text{John}, ck023, \text{prepare}, [40,50])$.

Suppose John finishes w_1 at 47, then the authorizations on $rq1$ and $ck023$ are revoked for John by replacing the upper bound with 47, thus forming the authorizations as $(\text{John}, rq1, \text{read}, [40,47])$, and $(\text{John}, ck023, \text{prepare}, [40,47])$. Also note that, at this point, a task-instance $w\text{-}inst_1 = (\{\text{read } rq1, \text{ prepare } ck023\}, \{rq1\}, \{ck023\}, [40,47])$ will also be generated.

Suppose at 47, $check_1$ is sent to w_2. Then the authorization template $AT(w_2) = (\text{Mary, (check,-),approve})$ would be filled, thus generating the authorization $(\text{Mary}, ck023, \text{approve}, [47, 60])$. Assume w_2 completes at 54. Then the authorization is changed to (Mary, ($ck023$, approve, [47,54]). At this point the object $ck023$ is sent to w_3 which fills $AT(w_3)=$ (Ken, (check,-), issue) and generates an authorization (Ken, $ck023$, issue, [54,80]). After the completion of this task (say at 60) this authorization changes to (Ken, $ck023$, issue, [54,60]).

However, in case of $rq2$, since the upper limit in $w_1 = (\{$read request, prepare check$\}$, $\{$request$\}$, $\{$check$\}$, [10,50]) is lower than the time at which $rq2$ arrives at w_1 (55) the authorization template does not generate an authorization. Thus the workflow cannot be started for $rq2$, and therefore, there will not be a task-instance for $rq2$.

For the sake of simplicity, indeed, in this example we have omitted details such as when a check is issued, it has to be assigned to an account and appropriate authorizations such as read, write (to perform debit) have to be granted on this account.

3   A Petri net representation of the Workflow Authorization Model

In this section, we present a model of implementation of WAM, which is based on Petri nets (PN). PNs are a graphical as well as a mathematical modeling tool. As a graphical tool PNs provide visualization (similar to flow charts, block diagrams, and the like) of the workflow process, and as a mathematical tool PNs enable analysis of the behavior of the workflow. Petri net representation of the Workflow Authorization Model provides us with good analysis tools for safety because the safety problem in the workflow authorization models can be made equivalent (with an appropriate PN representation) to the reachability problem in Petri nets. Thus, existing reachability analysis techniques, methods and results can be directly adapted to WAM. Therefore, in this section, we first provide a brief review of Petri nets. Then we show how Petri nets can be used as a modeling tool to represent WAM. We use a combination of two extended Petri net models – *colored* and *timed* Petri nets – to represent WAM as a Petri net.

3.1   Overview of Petri Nets

A *Petri Net* (PN) is a bipartite directed graph consisting of two kinds of nodes called *places* and *transitions* where arcs (edges) are either from a place to a transition or from a transition to a place. While drawing a PN, places are represented by circles and transitions by bars. A *marking* may be assigned to places. If a place p is marked with a value k, we say that p is marked with k *tokens*. Weights may be assigned to the edges of PN, however, in this paper we use only the ordinary PN where weights of the arcs are always equal to 1.

Definition 7. [16] A Petri net (PN) is a 5-tuple, $PN = (P, T, F, H, M)$ where
$P = \{p_1, p_2, \ldots, p_n\}$ is a finite set of places,
$T = \{t_1, t_2, \ldots, t_n\}$ is a finite set of transitions,

$F \subseteq (P \times T) \cup (T \times P)$ is a set of arcs, and
$P \cap T = \emptyset$ and $P \cup T \neq \emptyset$.
$H = F \to \{1, 2, 3, \ldots\}$ is the weight of each arc,
$M = P \to \{0, 1, 2, 3, \ldots\}$ is the marking. $\square$

We use $m(p)$ to denote the marking of place p (or number of tokens in p), $f(p, t)$ to denote an arc from p to t and $f(t, p)$ to denote an arc from t to p.
A transition (place) has a certain number (possibly zero) of input and output places (transitions).

Definition 8. [16] Given a PN, the input and output set of transitions (places) for each place p_i (t_i) are defined as,
the set of input transitions of p_i, denoted $\bullet p_i = \{t_j | f(t_j, p_i) \in F\}$
the set of output transitions of p_i, denoted $p_i \bullet = \{t_j | f(p_i, t_j) \in F\}$, and
the input and output set of places for each transition t_i are defined as,
the set of input places of t_i, denoted $\bullet t_i = \{p_j | f(p_j, t_i) \in F\}$
the set of output places of t_i, denoted $t_i \bullet = \{p_j | f(t_i, p_j) \in F\}$. $\square$

At any time a transition is either *enabled* or *disabled*. A transition t_i is enabled if each place in its input set $\bullet t_i$ has at least one token. An enabled transition can fire. In order to simulate the dynamic behavior of a system, a marking in a PN is changed when a transition fires. Firing of t_i removes the token from each place in $\bullet t_i$, and deposits one into each place in $t_i \bullet$. The consequence of firing a transition results in a change from original marking M to a new marking M'. For the sake of simplicity, we assume firing of a transition is an instantaneous event. The firing rules can be formally stated as follows:

Definition 9.

1. A transition t_i is said to be enabled if $\forall p_j \in \bullet t_i$, $(m(p_j) > 0)$. An enabled transition may fire.
2. Firing a transition t_i results in a new marking M' as follows: $\forall p_j \in \bullet t_i$, and $\forall p_k \in t_i \bullet$, $m'(p_j) = m(p_j) - 1 \wedge m'(p_k) = m(p_k) + 1$ $\square$

Example 3. Figure 2 shows an example of a simple PN in which more than one firing sequence can be generated. It comprises of four places p_1, p_2, p_3, and p_4, and two transitions t_1 and t_2. The input and output sets of the places and transitions are as follows: $\bullet t_1 = \{p_1, p_2\}$, $\bullet t_2 = \{p_2\}$, $t_1 \bullet = \{p_3\}$, $t_2 \bullet = \{p_4\}$, $\bullet p_3 = \{t_1\}$, $\bullet p_4 = \{t_2\}$, $p_1 \bullet = \{t_1\}$, and $p_2 \bullet = \{t_1, t_2\}$.
The initial state of the PN is shown in figure 2(a) where p_1 and p_2 are both marked with one token each. Since both places in the input set of t_1 are marked (i.e., both $m(p_1)$, $m(p_2) > 0$), t_1 is enabled. Similarly, t_2 is also enabled as $m(p_2) > 0$. Although both t_1 and t_2 are enabled, firing one of them will disable the other. Thus, this net will result in two different firing sequences. Suppose t_1 fires first, it results in a new marking where the tokens from p_1 and p_2 are removed and a token is placed in p_3, as shown in figure 2(b). Since p_2 becomes empty, this disables t_2. The second firing sequence would result in by firing t_2

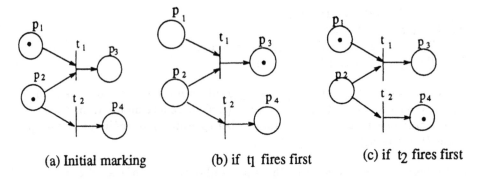

(a) Initial marking   (b) if t_1 fires first   (c) if t_2 fires first

Fig. 2. An example PN

first. It removes one token from p_2 and deposits one into p_4 thus resulting in a marking as depicted in figure 2(c). Since p_2 is empty, t_1 is disabled. Because there are no more transitions to fire after firing either t_1 or t_2, the PN stops (said to be *not live*).

Definition 10. A marking M is said to be *reachable* from a marking M_0 if there exists a sequence of firings that transforms M_0 to M.   □

Reachability is a fundamental property for studying the dynamic properties of any system. It has been shown [12] that the reachability problem is decidable although it takes at least exponential space and time.

3.2   Petri Net Representation of WAM

We use a combination of timed and colored Petri nets [23, 15, 24] for representing WAM. The definition for colored and timed Petri nets is as follows:

Definition 11. A Colored + Timed Petri Net (CTPN) [10, 7][6] is a tuple $CTPN = (PN, \Sigma, C, E, D, IN)$ where
(i) $PN = (P, T, F, M)$ is an ordinary Petri net.
(ii) A finite set of colors or types, called color sets $\Sigma = \{\sigma_1, \sigma_2, \ldots\}$
(iii) C is a color function such that $C(p) \in \Sigma_{MS}$,[7] and $\forall y \in m(p), C(y) \in \Sigma$
(iv) E, the arc set, defined from F into a set such that:
$\forall f(p, t), f(t, p) \in F, E_f \in C(p)_{MS}$
(v) D is a delay function, $D : P \to T$
(vi) IN is an interval function such that $IN(t) = [\eta(t), \tau_u(t)] \in \{T \times T | \eta(t) \leq \tau_u(t)\}$.   □

---

[6] Although we use the term "timed," our timed PN is different from the traditional timed PN.
[7] Σ_{MS} represents a multi-set or a bag over Σ. For example, given a set $\Sigma = \{a, b, \ldots\}$, the multi-sets $a, a + b, a + 2b$ are members of Σ_{MS}.

We represent a token in place p as (v, x) where $v \in C(m(p))$ represents the color of the token and x represents its timestamp such that $x \in T$. Whenever a token moves from one place to another through a fired transition, its timestamp is modified as the firing time of the transition.

The above definition dictates that each token has a color (or type) which is defined in the color set Σ. Each place has a color set (i.e., denoted as $C(p)$) attached to it which specifies the set of allowable colors of the tokens to enter the place. For a token to reside in a place, it must satisfy that the color of token is a member in the color set of the place. Each arc $f(p, t)$ or $f(t, p)$ is associated with a color set such that this set is contained in the multi-set of $C(p)$.

A transition t is enabled only if all of its input places p contain at least as many tokens of the type as that specified in the arc set $E_{f(p,t)}$ of the corresponding $f(p, t)$. An enabled transition fires after the delay $D(p) = d$ specified in its input place. t fires only if this time falls within the specified time interval $IN(t)$. Both the time interval and delay can be specified as variables instead of fixed values. When more than one input place exists, the transition fires after the maximum delay of all the input places has elapsed.[8] Upon firing, a transition t consumes as many tokens of colors from each of its input places p as those specified in the corresponding $E_{f(p,t)}$ and deposits as many tokens with specified colors into each output place p as those specified in the corresponding $E_{f(t,p)}$. That is, the arc set of $f(p, t)$ specifies the number of tokens of specified colors to be removed from p when t fires, and the arc set $f(t, p)$ specifies the number of tokens of specified colors to be inserted into p when t fires.

Marking of a place $m(p)$ is expressed as a list of tokens with respect to distinctive colors (e.g., $m(p) = 3\langle g \rangle, 2\langle r \rangle$). A transformation of colors may occur during firing of a transition. The firing of a transition is determined by the firing rules and the transformation by the arc set E.

The firing rules can be formally stated as follows:

Definition 12. Given a transition t_i such that $IN(t_i) = [\tau_l(t), \tau_u(t)]$, $\forall p_j \in \bullet t_i$ and $\forall p_k \in t_i \bullet$,

1. t_i is said to be *enabled* if $E_{(p_j, t_i)} \subseteq m(p_j)$ and $\max\{x + D(p_j)$ where $x = \max\{x_j | x_j$ is the timestamp of all $m(p_j)\}\}$ is within $IN(t_i)$. An enabled transition may fire.
2. Suppose t_i fires at τ_i. Firing of t_i results in a new marking M' as follows: $m'(p_k) = m(p_k) + E_{f(t_i, p_k)}$[9] and the timestamp of each element in $m'(p_k)$ is τ_i. □

We now illustrate the working of CTPN with a simple example. Assume there are two places p_1 and p_2 and a transition t_1 as shown in figure 3(a) such that the color sets of p_1 and p_2 are $C(p_1) = \{\langle a \rangle, \langle b \rangle, \langle c \rangle\}$ and $C(p_2) = \{\langle a \rangle, \langle c \rangle, \langle d \rangle\}$,

---

[8] If two or more transitions have the same input set, then more than one transition is enabled. In that case, only one transition fires. Selection of the firing transition among the many enabled transitions is determined non-deterministically.

[9] Note that these two are bags but not sets.

(a) before t_1 fires   (b) after t_1 fires

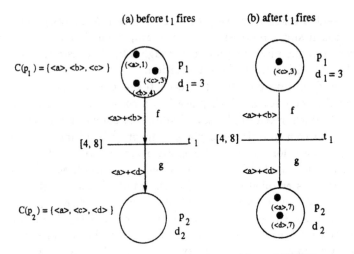

Fig. 3. An example showing the working of CTPN

respectively. The delay associated with p_1, i.e., $d_1 = 3$. The time interval of t_1, $IN(t_1) = [4, 8]$. Suppose p_1 is initially marked with three tokens: one of each color $(\langle a \rangle, 1), (\langle b \rangle, 3)$ and $(\langle c \rangle, 4)$. The arc set associated with the two arcs f and g are $E_f = \langle a \rangle + \langle b \rangle$ and $E_g = \langle a \rangle + \langle d \rangle$. The corresponding CTPN is shown in figure 3(a). Transition t_1 is enabled at time 7 because the maximum timestamp of all the tokens in p_1 is 4 and the time delay of p_1 is 3. Since $E_f \subset C(p_1)$ and and the enabled time is within $IN(t_i)$, t_1 is enabled. When t_1 fires, one token of each color $\langle a \rangle$ and $\langle b \rangle$ are removed from p_1, and according to E_g one token of each color $\langle a \rangle$ and $\langle d \rangle$ with timestamp $= 7$ are deposited in p_2. The resulting CTPN is shown in figure 3(b).

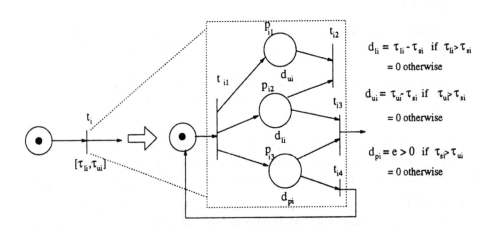

Fig. 4. A CTPN with temporal constraints

We have represented the temporal constraint by attaching t with the time interval $[\eta(t), \tau_u(t)]$ in the constraint as a gate on transition t. This means, t is enabled only during this time interval and is disabled during all other times even if tokens are present in its input places. A detailed implementation of the temporal constraint for each transition t is shown in figure 4. Note that the delays d_{l_i} and d_{u_i} are not predefined constants but vary depending on the enabled time (or token arrival time) τ_{a_i} as follows: If $\eta_i > \tau_{a_i}$, then $d_{l_i} = \eta_i - \tau_{a_i}$, otherwise $d_{l_i} = 0$. If $\tau_{u_i} > \tau_{a_i}$, then $d_{u_i} = \tau_{u_i} - \tau_{a_i}$, otherwise $d_{u_i} = 0$. If $\tau_{a_i} > \tau_{u_i}$, then $d_{p_i} = \epsilon$ (where ϵ is a small positive value). It works as follows: when t_{i_1} fires, p_{i_1}, p_{i_2} and p_{i_3} are all marked. If $\tau_{a_i} \leq \eta_i$, delay d_{l_i} ensures that t_{i_2} can be enabled no sooner than η_i thereby guaranteeing the lower boundary of the constraint. If $\eta_i \leq \tau_{a_i} \leq \tau_{u_i}$, d_{l_i} becomes 0 which allows t_{i_2} to be enabled and therefore fire immediately. When $\tau_{a_i} > \tau_{u_i}$, both d_{l_i}, d_{u_i} are 0 and $d_{p_i} = \epsilon$. Thus t_{i_2} is enabled and therefore fires, disabling t_{i_3}. Since p_{i_2} is no longer marked, t_{i_3} cannot fire, thus ensuring that authorizations are never granted if the object arrives after the upper bound on the constraint has elapsed.

3.3 CTPN representation of WAM

In the Petri net representation of WAM, we use two distinct color sets Ω and Λ such that $\Omega \cup \Lambda = \Sigma$ and $\Omega \cap \Lambda = \emptyset$, where we use Ω to denote the types of objects and Λ to denote the different privileges.

To represent WAM as a CTPN, we use the following mapping:

1. Two transitions t_s and t_f to represent the beginning and ending of a task, and the time at which they fire denote τ_s and τ_f, respectively.
2. A time interval $IN(t)$ at each t_s and t_f to represent the specified time constraint of the task ($[\eta, \tau_u]$).
3. A place to represent the execution state of the task w (depicted as a circle)
4. Different colored tokens to represent different types of objects ($\omega_1, \omega_2 \ldots$), i.e., $\Omega = \Gamma$.
5. A place to represent each subject (denoted as a square in the diagram), i.e., s in $AT(w)$.[10]
6. Different colored tokens to represent different types of object-privilege pairs ($\lambda_1, \lambda_2 \ldots$), i.e., $\Lambda = \Gamma \times PR$.
7. A color set associated with circles (squares) to denote the allowed type of objects (object-privilege pairs)
8. An arc set of $f(p, t)$ (where p is a circle) to represent the type of input objects to be sent to a task for execution.
9. An arc set of $f(t, p)$ (where p is a circle) to represent the type of output objects of the task.

---

[10] If a task is associated with multiple AT's with different subjects, then each subject has to be represented as a different square. On the other hand, if a single subject is involved in number of AT's for that task, then the arc function of the input arc reflects this.

10. An arc set of $f(p, t)$ (where p is a square) to represent the privileges (represented as object-privilege pairs) to be granted when a task starts.

11. An arc set of $f(t, p)$ (where p is a square) to represent the privileges to be revoked when a task completes its execution.

12. A delay (d) associated with the place to represent the execution time of the task. Note that d is associated with only places representing tasks (circles) but not subjects (squares).

13. A token (v, x) to represent the movement of objects (privileges) to and from the tasks (subjects) where v is the color of the token representing the type of the object (object-privilege pair), and x the timestamp representing the arrival time of the object τ_a.

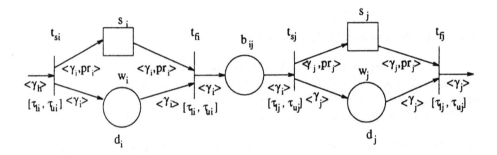

Fig. 5. A CTPN representation of WAM for a Workflow with two tasks

Figure 5 shows a CTPN representation of the authorization model for a workflow consisting of two tasks w_i and w_j. The execution state of w_i and w_j are represented as two places (circles), and the subjects authorized to execute these two tasks s_i and s_j are represented as another two places (squares). t_{s_i} fires when an object of type γ_i arrives, thus starting w_i. A token of color γ_i is placed in w_i and another token $\langle \gamma_i, pr_i \rangle$ is placed in s_i. Thus privilege is granted to s_i on the object only at this point. After d_i, the task completes its execution thus firing t_{f_i}. This removes the objects from w_i and place them in another place b_{ij} since both $E_{f(w_i, t_{f_i})}$ and $E_{f(t_{f_i}, b_{ij})}$ is $\{\langle \gamma_i \rangle\}$. Here b_{ij} represents the state after w_i finishes but before w_j starts. Firing of t_{f_i} also removes the privilege $\langle \gamma_i, pr_i \rangle$ from s_i, but does not deposit any token in b_{ij}.

The CTPN of the WAM for the workflow in example 2 is shown in figure 6. Figure 7 shows the state when w_1 starts execution. It shows objects and the privileges as tokens in w_i and "John," respectively. The two tokens in each place correspond to request and check. Figures 8 and 9 depict the states when w_1 finishes execution and w_2 starts execution, respectively.

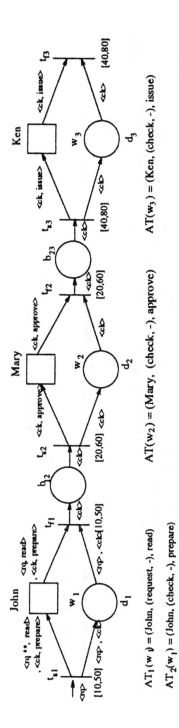

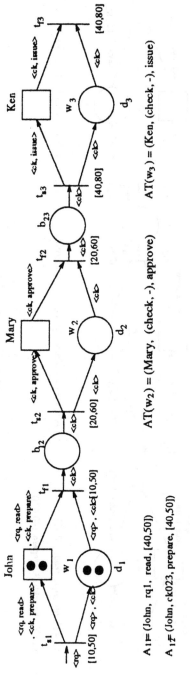

Fig. 6. CTPN for the WAM of the Check Processing workflow

$AT_1(w_1)$ = (John, (request, -), read)

$AT_2(w_1)$ = (John, (check, -), prepare)

$AT(w_2)$ = (Mary, (check, -), approve)

$AT(w_3)$ = (Ken, (check, -), issue)

** Remark: For simplicity of notation, the <request> and <check> types are substituted with <rq> and <ck>, respectively

A_1 = (John, rq1, read, [40,50])

A_1 = (John, ck023, prepare, [40,50])

Fig. 7. When w_1 starts

61

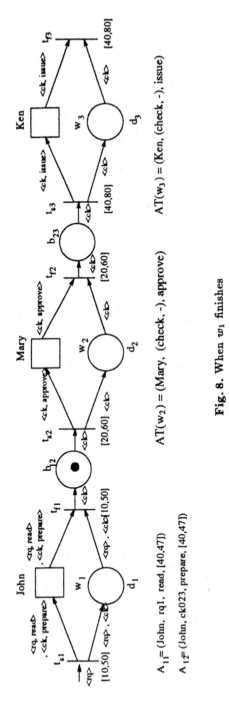

Fig. 8. When w_1 finishes

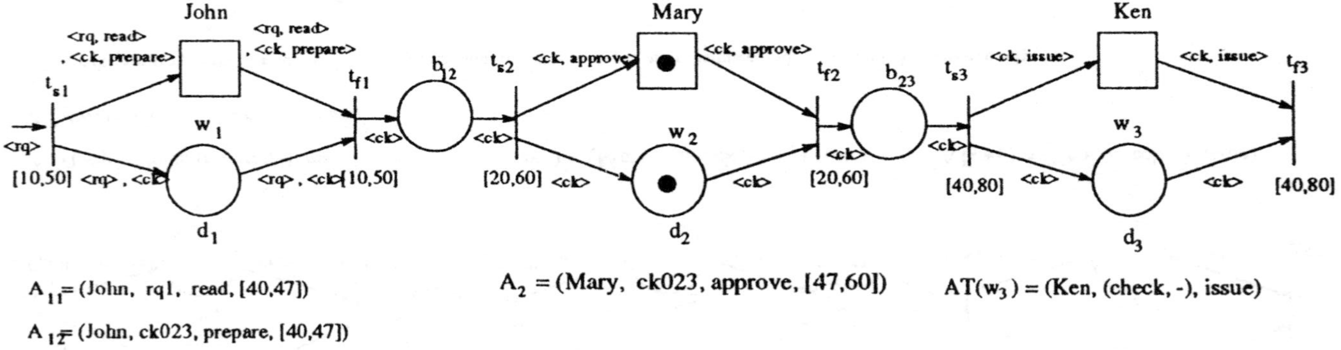

$AT(w_2) = $ (Mary, (check, -), approve)

$AT(w_3) = $ (Ken, (check, -), issue)

$A_{11} = $ (John, rq1, read, [40,47])

$A_{12} = $ (John, ck023, prepare, [40,47])

Fig. 9. When w_2 starts

$A_2 = $ (Mary, ck023, approve, [47,60])

$AT(w_3) = $ (Ken, (check, -), issue)

$A_{11} = $ (John, rq1, read, [40,47])

$A_{12} = $ (John, ck023, prepare, [40,47])

4 Extensions to the Workflow Authorization Model

In the WAM proposed in section 2 and its Petri net representation presented in section 3, we have not incorporated all the desirable features of WAM described in section 1. In this section, we will provide a brief explanation of how role-based authorizations and separation of duties can be incorporated into our model.

Most commercial Workflow Management Systems (WFMSs) such as Lotus Notes and Action Workflow enforce security based on organizational roles [14, 13, 9]. Privilege to perform a task is assigned to an organizational role rather than to human users, and human users in turn are authorized to assume prespecified roles. It is particularly beneficial in workflow environments to facilitate dynamic load balancing when a task can be performed by several individuals.

Note that the subject in the AT's can be specified in terms of roles [19, 21] by replacing s with R in AT as follows:

$$AT = ((R, -)(\gamma, -), pr, [\eta, \tau_u])^{11}$$

For example, considering example 2 once again, the corresponding $AT's$ are modified as:

$AT_1(w_1) =$ (clerk, (request,-),read)
$AT_2(w_1) =$ (clerk, (check,-), prepare)
$AT(w_2) =$ (supervisor, (check,-), approve)
$AT(w_3) =$ (clerk, (check,-), issue)

The authorization derivation rule to derive A from AT need to be modified as follows.

Definition 13 Authorization Derivation Rule with Roles. Given an authorization template $AT(w_i) = (R_i, (\gamma_i, -), pr_i)$ of task $w_i = (OP_i, \Gamma_{IN_i}, \Gamma_{OUT_i}, [\eta_i, \tau_{u_i}])$, an authorization $A_i = (s_i, o_i, pr_i, [\tau_{b_i}, \tau_{e_i}])$ is derived as follows:
Grant Rule: Suppose object $o_i \in \Gamma_{IN_i}$ is sent to w_i at τ_{a_i} to start w_i. Let the starting time of w_i be τ_{s_i}.
If $\tau_{a_i} \leq \tau_{u_i}$, then $s_i \in R_i$, $pr_i \leftarrow pr(AT)$, $\tau_{e_i} \leftarrow \tau_{u_i}$, and
(if $\tau_{a_i} \leq \eta_i$ then $\tau_{b_i} \leftarrow \eta_i$; otherwise $\tau_{b_i} \leftarrow \tau_{a_i}$.
Revoke Rule: Suppose w_i ends at τ_{f_i} at which point o_i leaves w_i.
If $\tau_{f_i} \leq \tau_{u_i}$, then $\tau_{e_i} \leftarrow \tau_{f_i}$. ☐

This authorization rule is similar to that in definition 6 except that we select a subject from the set of subjects playing the specific role while assigning the authorizations.

Separation of duties can be incorporated by including the identity of the place (i.e. subject) to the token. That is, a token is of the form $((p, v), x)$ where p is the place v refers to the object type and x is the current timestamp.

---

[11] Here the notion of $(R, -)$ is similar to that of object hole. The actual authorization is derived when this is filled by a subject.

5 Conclusions and Future work

In this paper, we have presented an authorization model for workflow environments that is capable of synchronizing the authorization flow along with the workflow. Our model is also capable of ensuring temporal constraints on tasks. We have provided an implementation model based on Petri nets. We have also shown how to incorporate authorizations that can be assigned to organizational roles rather than to subjects and how separation of duties can be incorporated. As part of future work, we intend to implement WAM and conduct the safety analysis. Moreover, in this paper, we have not considered the various dependencies among the tasks within a workflow. A complete model should take into account these dependencies as well. We intend to combine the Petri net models developed in [1] into the proposed CTPN.

References

1. Vijayalakshmi Atluri and Wei-Kuang Huang. An extended petri net model for supporting workflows in a multilevel secure environment. In *Proc. of the 10th IFIP WG 11.3 Workshop on Database Security*, July 1996.

2. Elisa Bertino, Claudio Bettini, Elena Ferrari, and Pierangela Samarati. A temporal access control mechanism for database systems. *IEEE Transactions on Knowledge and Data Engineering*, 8(1):67–80, 1996.

3. Elisa Bertino, Pierangela Samarati, and Sushil Jajodia. Authorizations in relational database management systems. In *Proc. First ACM Conference on Computer and Communications Security*, Fairfax, VA, November 1993.

4. Elisa Bertino, Pierangela Samarati, and Sushil Jajodia. High assurance discretionary access control for object bases. In *Proc. First ACM Conference on Computer and Communications Security*, Fairfax, VA, November 1993.

5. J. Biskup and C. Eckert. About the enforcement of state dependent security specifications. In *Proc. of the 7th IFIP WG 11.3 Workshop on Database Security*, pages 3–17, August 1993.

6. David D. Clark and David R. Wilson. A comparison of commercial and military computer security policies. In *Proc. IEEE Symposium on Security and Privacy*, pages 184–194, Oakland, California, April 1987.

7. Rene David and Hassane Alla. *Petri Nets and Grafcet - Tools for modeling discrete event systems*. Prentice Hall, 1992.

8. E. B. Fernandez, E. Gudes, and H. Song. A security model for object-oriented databases. *Proc. IEEE Symposium on Security and Privacy*, pages 110–115, May 1989.

9. Dimitrios Georgakopoulos, Mark Hornick, and Amit Sheth. An overview of workflow management: From process modeling to workflow automation infrastructure. *Distributed and Parallel Databases*, pages 119–153, 1995.

10. K. Jensen. Colour petri nets: A high level language for system design and analysis. In K.Jensen and G. Rozenberg, editors, *High-level Petri Nets - Theory and Application*, pages 44–119. Springer-Verlag, Lecture Notes in Computer Science, 1991.

11. D. Johnscher and K.R. Dittrich. Argos - A configurable access control system for interoperable environments. In *Proc. of the 9th IFIP WG 11.3 Workshop on Database Security*, pages 39–63, August 1995.

12. S. R. Kosaraju. Decidability and reachability in vector addition systems. In *Proc. of the 14th ACM Symposium on Theory of Computing*, pages 267–281, May 1982.

13. Lotus Corporation. *Lotus Notes Administrator's Reference Manual, Release 4*, 1996.

14. Raul Medina-Mora, Harry K.T. Wong, and Pablo Flores. ActionWorkflow'm as the enterprise integration technology. *Bulletin of IEEE Technical Committee on Data Engineering*, 16(2):49–52, 1993.

15. S. Morasca, M.Pezzè, and M. Trubian. Timed high-level nets. *Journal of Real-Time Systems*, 3:165 – 189, 1991.

16. Tadao Murata. Petri nets: Properties, analysis and applications. *Proceedings of the IEEE*, 77(4):541–580, April 1989.

17. F. Rabitti, E. Bertino, W. Kim, and D. Woelk. A model of authorization for next-generation database systems. *ACM Trans. on Database Systems*, 16(1):88–131, March 1991.

18. Pierangela Samarati, Paul Ammann, and Sushil Jajodia. Propagation of authorizations in distributed database systems. In *Proc. Second ACM Conference on Computer and Communications Security*, Fairfax, VA, November 1994.

19. Ravi S. Sandhu. Transaction control expressions for separation of duties. In *Fourth Computer Security Applications Conference*, pages 282–286, 1988.

20. Ravi S. Sandhu. Separation of duties in computerized information systems. In Sushil Jajodia and Carl Landwehr, editors, *Database Security, IV: Status and Prospects*, pages 179–189. North Holland, 1991.

21. Ravi S. Sandhu. Role-based access control models. *IEEE Computer*, pages 38–47, February 1996.

22. Ravi S. Sandhu and Gurpreet S. Suri. Non-monotonic transformation of access rights. In *Proc. IEEE Symposium on Security and Privacy*, pages 148–161, Oakland, California, May 1992.

23. W.M.P van der Aalst. Interval timed coloured petri nets and their analysis. In *Application and Theory of Petri Nets 1993, Proc. 14th International Conference*, volume 691, pages 453–472, Chicago, (USA), 1993. Springer-Verlag, Lecture Notes in Computer Science.

24. K.M. van Hee, L.J. Somers, and M. Voorhoeve. Executable specifications for distributed information systems. In E.D. Falkenberg and P. Lindgreen, editors, *Proc. of the IFIP TC 8/WG 8.1 Working Conference on Information System Concepts: An In-depth Analysis*, volume 691, pages 139–156, Namur, (Belgium), 1989. Elsevier Science Publishers, Amsterdam.

25. Thomas Y.C. Woo and Simon S. Lam. Authorization in distributed systems: A formal approach. In *Proc. IEEE Symposium on Security and Privacy*, pages 33–50, Oakland, California, May 1992.

26. William A. Wulf, Roy Levin, and Samuel P. Harbison. *HYDRA/C.mmp, An Experimental Computer System*. McGraw-Hill, 1981.

Role Hierarchies and Constraints for Lattice-Based Access Controls

Ravi Sandhu*

George Mason University & SETA Corporation**

Abstract Role-based access control (RBAC) is a promising alternative to traditional discretionary and mandatory access controls. In RBAC permissions are associated with roles, and users are made members of appropriate roles thereby acquiring the roles' permissions. In this paper we formally show that lattice-based mandatory access controls can be enforced by appropriate configuration of RBAC components. Our constructions demonstrate that role hierarchies and constraints are required to effectively achieve this result. We show that variations of the lattice-based ⋆-property, such as write-up (liberal ⋆-property) and no-write-up (strict ⋆-property), can be easily accommodated in RBAC. Our results attest to the flexibility of RBAC and its ability to accommodate different policies by suitable configuration of role hierarchies and constraints.

1 INTRODUCTION

Role-based access control (RBAC) has recently received considerable attention as a promising alternative to traditional discretionary and mandatory access controls (see, for example, [FK92, SCY96, SCFY96]). In RBAC permissions are associated with roles, and users are made members of appropriate roles thereby acquiring the roles' permissions. This greatly simplifies management of permissions. Roles are created for the various job functions in an organization and users are assigned roles based on their responsibilities and qualifications. Users can be easily reassigned from one role to another. Roles can be granted new permissions as new applications and systems are incorporated, and permissions can be revoked from roles as needed.

An important characteristic of RBAC is that by itself it is policy neutral. RBAC is a means for articulating policy rather than embodying a particular security policy (such as one-directional information flow in a lattice). The policy enforced in a particular system is the net result of the precise configuration and interactions of various RBAC components as directed by the system owner. Moreover, the access

* This research is partly supported by contract 50-DKNB-5-00188 from the National Institute of Standards and Technology at SETA Corporation, and grant CCR-9503560 from the National Science Foundation at George Mason University.

** All correspondence should be addressed to Ravi Sandhu, ISSE Department, MS 4A4, George Mason University, Fairfax, VA 22030, USA. Email: sandhu@isse.gmu.edu, voice: +1 703 993 1659, fax: +1 703 993 1638, URL: http://www.isse.gmu.edu/faculty/sandhu.

control policy can evolve incrementally over the system life cycle, and in large systems it is almost certain to do so. The ability to modify policy to meet the changing needs of an organization is an important benefit of RBAC.

Classic lattice-based access control (LBAC) models [San93] on the other hand are specifically constructed to incorporate the policy of one-directional information flow in a lattice.[3] There is nonetheless strong similarity between the concept of a security label and a role. In particular, the same user cleared to say Secret can on different occasions login to a system at Secret and Unclassified levels. In a sense the user determines what role (Secret or Unclassified) should be activated in a particular session.

This leads us naturally to ask whether or not LBAC can be simulated using RBAC. If RBAC is policy neutral and has adequate generality it should indeed be able to do so. Particularly, because the notion of a role and the level of a login session are so similar. This question is theoretically significant because a positive answer would establish that LBAC is just one instance of RBAC thereby relating two distinct access control models that have been developed with different motivations. A positive answer is also practically significant, because it implies that the same Trusted Computing Base can be configured to enforce RBAC in general and LBAC in particular. This addresses the long held desire of multi-level security practitioners that technology which meets needs of the larger commercial marketplace be applicable to LBAC. The classical approach to fulfilling this desire has been to argue that LBAC has applications in the commercial sector. So far this argument has not been terribly productive. RBAC, on the other hand, is specifically motivated by needs of the commercial sector. Its customization to LBAC might be a more productive approach to dual-use technology.

In this paper we answer this question positively by demonstrating that several variations of LBAC can be easily accommodated in RBAC by configuring a few RBAC components.[4] We use the family of RBAC models recently developed by Sandhu et al [SCFY96] for this purpose. Our constructions show that the concepts of role hierarchies and constraints are critical to achieving this result. Changes in the role hierarchy and constraints lead to different variations of LBAC. A simulation of LBAC in RBAC has been earlier given by Nyanchama and Osborn [NO96], however, they do not exploit role hierarchies and constraints and cannot handle variations so easily as our constructions of this paper.

The rest of this paper is organized as follows. We review the family of RBAC models due to Sandhu et al [SCFY96] in section 2. This is followed by a quick review of LBAC in section 3. Our simulation of several LBAC variations in RBAC is described in section 4. Section 5 gives our conclusions.

---

[3] This one-directional information flow can be applied for confidentiality, integrity, confidentiality and integrity together, or for aggregation policies such as Chinese Walls [San93].

[4] It should be noted that RBAC will only prevent overt flows of information. This is true of any access control model, including LBAC. Information flow contrary to the one-directional requirement in a lattice by means of so-called covert channels is outside the purview of access control per se. Neither LBAC nor RBAC addresses the covert channel issue directly. Techniques used to deal with covert channels in LBAC can be used for the same purpose in RBAC.

2 RBAC MODELS

A general RBAC model was recently defined by Sandhu et al [SCFY96]. It is summarized in Figure 1.[5] The model is based on three sets of entities called users (U), roles (R), and permissions (P). Intuitively, a user is a human being or an autonomous agent, a role is a job function or job title within the organization with some associated semantics regarding the authority and responsibility conferred on a member of the role, and a permission is an approval of a particular mode of access to one or more objects in the system.

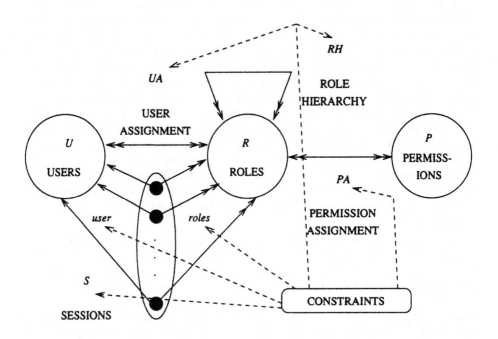

Fig. 1. The RBAC Model

The *user assignment* (UA) and *permission assignment* (PA) relations of Figure 1 are both many-to-many relations. A user can be a member of many roles, and a role

---

[5] Figure 1 shows the RBAC$_3$ model which is the most general among the family of models described in [SCFY96]. The administrative model of [SCFY96] is not relevant here. For our purpose we assume a single security officer is the only one who can configure various components of RBAC.

can have many users. Similarly, a role can have many permissions, and the same permission can be assigned to many roles. There is a partially ordered *role hierarchy* RH, also written as $\geq$, where $x \geq y$ signifies that role x inherits the permissions assigned to role y. Inheritance along the role hierarchy is transitive and multiple inheritance is allowed in partial orders.

Figure 1 shows a set of sessions S. Each session relates one user to possibly many roles. Intuitively, a user establishes a session during which the user activates some subset of roles that he or she is a member of (directly or indirectly by means of the role hierarchy). The double-headed arrow from a session to R indicates that multiple roles can be simultaneously activated. The permissions available to the user are the union of permissions from all roles activated in that session. Each session is associated with a single user, as indicated by the single-headed arrow from the session to U. This association remains constant for the life of a session. A user may have multiple sessions open at the same time, each in a different window on the workstation screen for instance. Each session may have a different combination of active roles. The concept of a session equates to the traditional notion of a *subject* in access control. A subject (or session) is a unit of access control, and a user may have multiple subjects (or sessions) with different permissions active at the same time.

Finally, Figure 1 shows a collection of *constraints*. Constraints can apply to any of the preceding components. An example of constraints is mutually disjoint roles, such as purchasing manager and accounts payable manager, where the same user is not permitted to be a member of both roles.

The following definition formalizes the above discussion.

Definition 1. (RBAC Model) The RBAC model has the following components:

- U, R, P, and S, sets of users, roles, permissions and sessions respectively,
- $PA \subseteq P \times R$, a many-to-many permission (to role) assignment relation,
- $UA \subseteq U \times R$, a many-to-many user (to role) assignment relation,
- $RH \subseteq R \times R$, a partially ordered role hierarchy (written as $\geq$ in infix notation),
- $user : S \to U$, a function mapping each session s_i to the single user $user(s_i)$ (constant for the session's lifetime),
- $roles : S \to 2^R$ a function mapping each session s_i to a set of roles $roles(s_i) \subseteq \{r \mid (\exists r' \geq r)[(user(s_i), r') \in UA]\}$ (which can change with time) so that session s_i has the permissions $\bigcup_{r \in roles(s_i)} \{p \mid (\exists r'' \leq r)[(p, r'') \in PA]\}$, and
- a collection of *constraints* that determine whether or not values of various components of the RBAC model are acceptable (only acceptable values will be permitted). $\qquad \square$

3 LBAC MODELS

Lattice based access control (LBAC) is concerned with enforcing one directional information flow in a lattice of security labels. LBAC is also known as mandatory access control (MAC) or multilevel security.[6] Depending upon the nature of the lattice the one-directional information flow enforced by LBAC can be applied for confidentiality, integrity, confidentiality and integrity together, or for aggregation policies such as Chinese Walls [San93]. There are also variations of LBAC where the one-directional information flow is partly relaxed to achieve selective downgrading of information or for integrity applications [Bel87, Lee88, Sch88].

The mandatory access control policy is expressed in terms of security labels attached to subjects and objects. A label on an object is called a *security classification*, while a label on a user is called a *security clearance*. It is important to understand that a Secret user may run the same program, such as a text editor, as a Secret subject or as an Unclassified subject. Even though both subjects run the same program on behalf of the same user, they obtain different privileges due to their security labels. It is usually assumed that the security labels on subjects and objects, once assigned, cannot be changed (except by the security officer). This last assumption, that security labels do not change, is known as *tranquility*.[7] The security labels form a lattice structure as defined below.

Definition 2. (Security Lattice) There is a finite lattice of security labels SC with a partially ordered dominance relation $\geq$ and a least upper bound operator.[8] □

An example of a security lattice is shown in Figure 2. Information is only permitted to flow upward in the lattice. In this example, H and L respectively denote high and low, and M1 and M2 are two incomparable labels intermediate to H and L. This is a typical confidentiality lattice where information can flow from low to high but not vice versa.

The specific mandatory access rules usually specified for a lattice are as follows, where λ signifies the security label of the indicated subject or object.

Definition 3. (Simple Security) Subject s can read object o only if $\lambda(s) \geq \lambda(o)$. □

Definition 4. (Liberal ⋆-property) Subject s can write object o only if $\lambda(s) \leq \lambda(o)$. □

The ⋆-property is pronounced as the star-property.

For integrity reasons sometimes a stricter form of the ⋆-property is stipulated. The liberal ⋆-property allows a low subject to write a high object. This means that high data may be maliciously destroyed or damaged by low subjects. To avoid this possibility we can employ the strict ⋆-property given below.

---

[6] LBAC is typically applied in addition to classical discretionary access controls (DAC) [SS94] but for our purpose we will focus only on the MAC component. DAC can be accommodated in RBAC as an independent access control policy just as it is done in LBAC.

[7] Non-tranquil LBAC can also be simulated in RBAC but is outside the scope of this paper.

[8] The least upper bound operator is not relevant to our constructions which apply to partially ordered security labels in general.

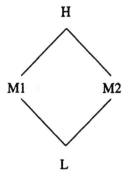

Fig. 2. A Partially Ordered Lattice

Definition 5. (Strict *-property) Subject s can write object o only if $\lambda(s) = \lambda(o)$. □

The liberal *-property is also referred to as write-up and the strict *-property as non-write-up or write-equal.

In variations of LBAC the simple-security property is usually left unchanged as we will do in all our examples. Variations of the *-property in LBAC whereby the one-directional information flow is partly relaxed to achieve selective downgrading of information or for integrity applications [Bel87, Lee88, Sch88] will be considered later.

4   CONFIGURING RBAC FOR LBAC

We now show how different variations of LBAC can be simulated in RBAC. It turns out that we can achieve this by suitably changing the role hierarchy and defining appropriate constraints. This suggests that role hierarchies and constraints are central to defining policy in RBAC.

4.1   A Basic Lattice

We begin by considering the example lattice of Figure 2 with the liberal *-property. Subjects with labels higher up in the lattice have more power with respect to read operations but have less power with respect to write operations. Thus this lattice has a dual character. In role hierarchies subjects (sessions) with roles higher in the hierarchy always have more power than those with roles lower in the hierarchy. To accommodate the dual character of a lattice for LBAC we will use two dual hierarchies in RBAC, one for read and one for write. These two role hierarchies for the lattice of Figure 2 are shown in Figure 3(a). Each lattice label x is modeled as

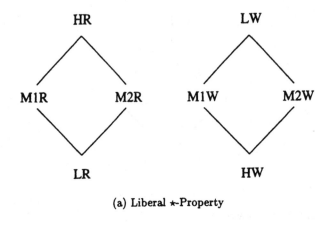

(a) Liberal ⋆-Property

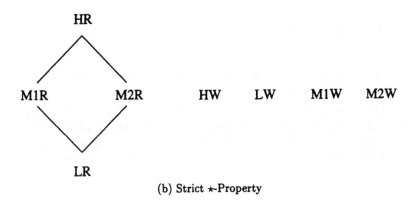

(b) Strict ⋆-Property

Fig. 3. Role Hierarchies for the Lattice of Figure 2

two roles xR and xW for read and write at label x respectively. The relationship among the four read roles and the four write roles is respectively shown on the left and right hand sides of Figure 3(a). The duality between the left and right lattices is obvious from the diagrams.

To complete the construction we need to enforce appropriate constraints to reflect the labels on subjects in LBAC. Each user in LBAC has a unique security clearance. This is enforced by requiring that each user in RBAC is assigned to exactly two matching roles xR and xW. An LBAC user can login at any label dominated by the user's clearance. This requirement is captured in RBAC by requiring that each session has exactly two matching roles yR and yW. The condition that $x \geq y$, that is the user's clearance dominates the label of any login session established by the user, is not explicitly required because it is directly imposed by the RBAC model anyway.

LBAC is enforced in terms of read and write operations. In RBAC this means our permissions are read and writes on individual objects written as (o,r) and (o,w) respectively. An LBAC object has a single sensitivity label associated with it. This is expressed in RBAC by requiring that each pair of permissions (o,r) and (o,w) be assigned to exactly one matching pair of xR and xW roles respectively. By assigning permissions (o,r) and (o,w) to roles xR and xW respectively, we are implicitly setting the sensitivity label of object o to x.

The above construction is formalized below.

*Example 1. (Liberal *-Property)*

- R = {HR, M1R, M2R, LR, HW, M1W, M2W, LW}
- RH as shown in Figure 3(a)
- P = {(o,r), (o,w) | o is an object in the system}
- Constraint on UA: Each user is assigned to exactly two roles xR and xW
- Constraint on sessions: Each session has exactly two roles yR and yW
- Constraints on PA:
    - (o,r) is assigned to xR iff (o,w) is assigned to xW
    - (o,r) is assigned to exactly one role xR   □

The set of permissions P remains the same in all our examples so we will omit its explicit definition in subsequent examples.

Variations in LBAC can be accommodated by modifying this basic construction in different ways. In particular, the strict *-property retains the hierarchy on read roles but treats write roles as incomparable to each other as shown in Figure 3(b).

*Example 2. (Strict *-Property)* Identical to example 1 except RH is as shown in Figure 3(b).   □

Now the permission (o,w) is no longer inherited by other roles as is the case in example 1.

4.2 Lattice with Trusted Write Range

Next we consider a version of LBAC in which subjects are given more power than allowed by the simple security and *-properties [Bel87]. The basic idea is to allow subjects to violate the *-property in a controlled manner. This is achieved by associating a pair of security labels λ_r and λ_w with each subject (objects still have a single security label). The simple security property is applied with respect to λ_r and the liberal *-property with respect to λ_w. In the LBAC model of [Bel87] it is required that λ_r should dominate λ_w. With this constraint the subject can read and write in the range of labels between λ_r and λ_w which is called the *trusted range*. If λ_r and λ_w are equal the model reduces to the usual LBAC model with the trusted range being a single label.

The preceding discussion is remarkably close to our RBAC constructions. The two labels λ_r and λ_w correspond directly to the two roles xR and yW we have introduced earlier. The dominance required between λ_r and λ_w is trivially recast as a dominance constraint between x and y. This leads to the following example.

Example 3. (Liberal ⋆-Property with Trusted Range) Identical to example 1 except

- Constraint on UA: Each user is assigned to exactly two roles xR and yW such that x ≥ y in the original lattice
- Constraint on sessions: Each session has exactly two roles xR and yW such that x ≥ y in the original lattice ☐

Lee [Lee88] and Schockley [Sch88] have argued that the Clark-Wilson integrity model [CW87] can be supported using LBAC. Their models are similar to the above except that no dominance relation is required between x and y. Thus the write range may be completely disjoint with the read range of a subject. This is easily expressed in RBAC as follows.

Example 4. (Liberal ⋆-Property with Independent Write Range) Identical to example 3 except x ≥ y is not required in the constraint on UA and the constraint on sessions. ☐

A variation of the above is to use the strict ⋆-property as follows.

Example 5. (Strict ⋆-Property with Designated Write) Identical to example 2 except

- Constraint on UA: Each user is assigned to exactly two roles xR and yW
- Constraint on sessions: Each session has exactly two roles xR and yW ☐

Example 5 can also be directly obtained from example 4 by requiring the strict ⋆-property instead of the liberal ⋆-property. Example 5 can accommodate Clark-Wilson transformation procedures as outlined by Lee and Schockley. (Lee and Schockley actually use the liberal ⋆-property in their construction, but their lattices are such that the construction is more directly expressed by example 5.)

4.3 Independent Confidentiality and Integrity Roles

Next we turn our attention to integrity lattices and their interaction with confidentiality lattices. LBAC was first formulated for confidentiality purposes. It was subsequently observed that if high integrity is at the top of the lattice and low integrity at the bottom then information flow should be downward rather than upward (as in confidentiality lattices). In [San93] it is argued that it is simpler to fix the direction of information flow and put high integrity at the bottom and low integrity at the top in integrity lattices. Because the confidentiality models were developed earlier we might as well stay with lattices in which information flow is always upwards.

Figure 3(a) shows two independent lattices. The one on the left has HS (high secrecy) on the top and LS (low secrecy) on the bottom. The one on the right

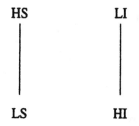

(a) Two Independent Lattices

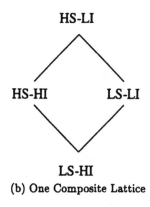

(b) One Composite Lattice

Fig. 4. Confidentiality and Integrity Lattices

has LI (low integrity) on the top and HI (high integrity) on the bottom. In both lattices information flow is upward. The two lattices can be combined into the single composite lattice shown in Figure 3(b).[9]

One complication in combining confidentiality and integrity lattices (or multiple lattices in general) is that these lattices may be using different versions of the ⋆-property. We have discussed earlier that the strict ⋆-property is often used in confidentiality lattices due to integrity considerations. In integrity lattices there is no similar need to use the strict ⋆-property, and one would expect to see the liberal ⋆-property instead.

In order to accommodate different versions of the ⋆-property for the two lattices we could keep two distinct lattices as shown in Figure 3(a). We know how to recast each lattice in RBAC with liberal or strict ⋆-properties as appropriate. Three of these combinations[10] are shown in Figure 5 and described formally below.

---

[9] It is always possible to mathematically combine multiple lattices into a single lattice.
[10] The fourth combination of liberal confidentiality and strict integrity could be easily constructed but is rather unlikely to be used in practice so is omitted.

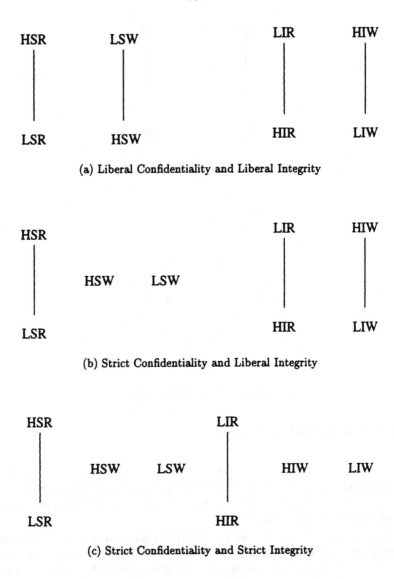

(a) Liberal Confidentiality and Liberal Integrity

(b) Strict Confidentiality and Liberal Integrity

(c) Strict Confidentiality and Strict Integrity

Fig. 5. Independent Confidentiality and Integrity Roles

Example 6. (Liberal Confidentiality and Liberal Integrity ⋆-Property)

- R = {HSR, LSR, LSW, HSW, LIR, HIR, HIW, LIW}
- RH as shown in Figure 5(a)
- Constraint on UA: Each user is assigned to exactly two pairs of roles xSR, xSW and yIR, yIW
- Constraint on sessions: Each session has exactly two pairs of roles xSR, xSW and yIR, yIW
- Constraints on PA:
    - (o,r) is assigned to xSR iff (o,w) is assigned to xSW
    - (o,r) is assigned to exactly one role xSR
    - (o,r) is assigned to yIR iff (o,w) is assigned to yIW
    - (o,r) is assigned to exactly one role yIR   □

Example 7. (Strict Confidentiality and Liberal Integrity ⋆-Property) Identical to example 6 except that RH is as shown in Figure 5(b).   □

Example 8. (Strict Confidentiality and Strict Integrity ⋆-Property) Identical to example 6 except that RH is as shown in Figure 5(c).   □

4.4   Composite Confidentiality and Integrity Roles

The preceding constructions require each user and session to have a pair of roles for each lattice. We now show how the same results can be achieved by a single pair of roles. Consider the composite lattice of Figure 3(b). Since the simple security property does not change we have a similar role hierarchy for the read roles shown on the left hand side of the three role hierarchies of Figures 6(a), (b) and (c). In each case the hierarchy for the write roles needs to be adjusted as shown on the right hand side of each of these figures. The constructions are formally described below.

Example 9. (Liberal Confidentiality and Liberal Integrity ⋆-Property)

- R = {HSR-LIR, HSR-HIR, LSR-LIR, LSR-HIR, HSW-LIW, HSW-HIW, LSW-LIW, LSW-HIW}
- RH as shown in Figure 6(a)
- Constraint on UA: Each user is assigned to exactly two roles xSR-yIR and xSW-yIW
- Constraint on sessions: Each session has exactly two roles uSR-vIR and uSW-vIW
- Constraints on PA:
    - (o,r) is assigned to xSR-yIR iff (o,w) is assigned to xSW-yIW
    - (o,r) is assigned to exactly one role xSR-yIR   □

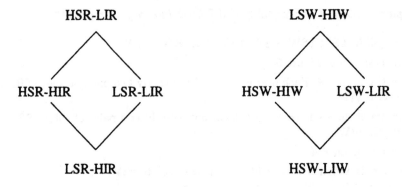

(a) Liberal Confidentiality and Liberal Integrity

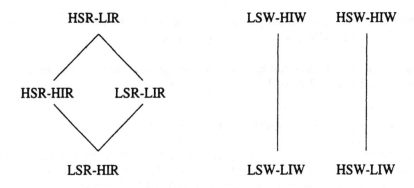

(b) Strict Confidentiality and Liberal Integrity

(c) Strict Confidentiality and Strict Integrity

Fig. 6. Composite Confidentiality and Integrity Roles

Example 10. (Strict Confidentiality and Liberal Integrity ⋆-Property) Identical to example 9 except that *RH* is as shown in Figure 6(b). □

Example 11. (Strict Confidentiality and Strict Integrity ⋆-Property) Identical to example 9 except that *RH* is as shown in Figure 6(c). □

The constructions indicate how a single pair of roles can accommodate lattices with different variations of the ⋆-property. The construction can clearly be generalized to more than two lattices.

5 CONCLUSION

In this paper we have shown how different variations of lattice based access controls (LBAC) can be simulated in role-based access control (RBAC), specifically using the models developed by Sandhu et al [SCFY96]. RBAC is itself policy neutral but can be easily configured to specify a variety of policies as we have shown. The main components of RBAC that need to be adjusted for different LBAC variations are the role hierarchy and constraints. This attests to the flexibility and power of RBAC.

A practical consequence of our results is that it might be better to develop systems that support general RBAC and specialize these to LBAC. RBAC has much broader applicability than LBAC, especially in the commercial sector. LBAC can be realized as a particular instance of RBAC. This approach provides the added benefit of greater flexibility for LBAC, for which we have seen there are a number of variations of practical interest. In LBAC systems these variations so far require the rules to be adjusted in the implementation. RBAC provides for adjustment by configuration of role hierarchies and constraints instead.

References

[Bel87]   D.E. Bell. Secure computer systems: A network interpretation. In *Third Annual Computer Security Application Conference*, pages 32–39, 1987.

[CW87]   D.D. Clark and D.R. Wilson. A comparison of commercial and military computer security policies. In *Proceedings IEEE Computer Society Symposium on Security and Privacy*, pages 184–194, Oakland, CA, May 1987.

[FK92]   David Ferraiolo and Richard Kuhn. Role-based access controls. In *15th NIST-NCSC National Computer Security Conference*, pages 554–563, Baltimore, MD, October 13-16 1992.

[Lee88]   T.M.P. Lee. Using mandatory integrity to enforce "commercial" security. In *Proceedings IEEE Computer Society Symposium on Security and Privacy*, pages 140–146, Oakland, CA, May 1988.

[NO96]   Matunda Nyanchama and Sylvia Osborn. Modeling mandatory access control in role-based security systems. In *Database Security VIII: Status and Prospects*. To appear, 1996.

[San93]   Ravi S. Sandhu. Lattice-based access control models. *IEEE Computer*, 26(11):9–19, November 1993.

[SCFY96] Ravi S. Sandhu, Edward J. Coyne, Hal L. Feinstein, and Charles E. Youman. Role-based access control models. *IEEE Computer*, 29(2):38–47, February 1996.

[Sch88] W.R. Schockley. Implementing the clark/wilson integrity policy using current technology. In *NIST-NCSC National Computer Security Conference*, pages 29–37, 1988.

[SCY96] Ravi Sandhu, Ed Coyne, and Charles Youman, editors. *Proceedings of the 1st ACM Workshop on Role-Based Access Control.* ACM, 1996.

[SS94] Ravi S. Sandhu and Pierangela Samarati. Access control: Principles and practice. *IEEE Communications*, 32(9):40–48, 1994.

A Multilevel Security Model
For Distributed Object Systems

Vincent Nicomette and Yves Deswarte

LAAS-CNRS & INRIA
7, Avenue du Colonel Roche
31077 Toulouse Cedex - France
Telephone: +33/61 33 62 88 - Fax: +33/61 33 64 11
(nicomett@laas.fr, deswarte@laas.fr)

Abstract. In this paper, the Bell-LaPadula model for multilevel secure computer systems is discussed. We describe the principles of this model and we try to show some of its limits. Then we present some possible extensions of this model, with their drawbacks and advantages. We finally present our own extension of the model for object-oriented systems. In this last section, we first explain the principles of our security policy, then we describe the rules of our authorization scheme and we give an example of a typical scenario in a distributed object-oriented system.

1   Introduction

During the last few years, object-oriented programming has been the most important issue of software engineering. Thanks to its power of abstraction and re-usability, the object model appears to be suitable to the development of nowadays systems which are increasingly complex. But this object model does not fit easily the usual protection models. As a matter of fact, most of these protection models are based on the notions of subjects and objects that do not correspond to the notion of object as defined in the object-oriented languages. Furthermore, the information flows in object systems have a very concrete and natural embodiment in the form of requests and corresponding replies. To prevent confidential information leakage through these information flows, we propose a multilevel security model.

As such, our model is similar to the well-known Bell-LaPadula model, which is promoted by the US Department of Defense. Bell-LaPadula 's rules do prevent illegal information flows but are often too restrictive. The purpose of this paper is thus to present a confidentiality model which has the same properties as the Bell-LaPadula model but which is less restrictive. Section 2 is dedicated to the presentation of the Bell-LaPadula model and its main drawbacks. Section 3 presents some extensions which have been proposed for this model. Section 4 introduces our protection model and gives an illustration of this model by means of a detailed example. Section 5 demonstrates how this model prevents illegal information flows. Section 6 compares this model to existing models and section 7 presents some perspectives for future work.

2 The Bell-LaPadula model

The Bell-LaPadula model [1] is a prominent model for mandatory access-control mechanisms enforcing a multilevel security policy in automated information-processing systems. The Bell-LaPadula model was adopted as the formal policy in the US Department of Defense's influential Trusted Computer System Evaluation Criteria (TCSEC), commonly known as the Orange Book [2]. In order to obtain the "B" classification of the Orange Book, a system must enforce a mandatory access-control mechanism based on the Bell-LaPadula model's formal security policy.

The Bell-LaPadula model is a state machine model that abstractly describes a system in terms of system *states*, and *rules* that enable transitions between states. The state of the system includes a set of triples that define the current access mode each *subject* has to each *object* in the system. A subject represents an active entity, such as a process. An object is a passive container of data, such as a file. The set of all modes in which a subject can access an object is (*execute*, *read*, *append*, *write*):

- *execute* corresponds to: neither observation nor alteration;
- *read* corresponds to: observation with no alteration;
- *append* corresponds to: alteration with no observation;
- *write* corresponds to: both observation and alteration.

Different security levels are defined and partially ordered. Each object is assigned one security level which is called the *classification* attribute of the object and each subject is assigned two security levels: the first one represents the *clearance* of the subject and is a static level, the second one is the *current security level* of the subject; it is required that the clearance of the subject dominates the current security level of the subject.

This model describes two access-control rules:

- **The simple security property:** A state is secure iff, for every subject in the system with the ability to observe an object, the subject's clearance is greater than or equal to the object's classification.
- **The *-property:** A state is secure iff no subject may observe the contents of an object O_1 and store information in an object O_2 unless O_2's classification is greater than or equal to O_1's classification.

  The definition of the *-property can be refined in terms of current security level:

  A state is secure iff for each access (subject, object, access mode) in the system :

    • the object classification dominates the subject current security level if the access mode is append;
    • the object classification equals the subject current security level if the access mode is write;
    • the object classification is dominated by the subject current security level if the access mode is read.

The simple security property prevents users from accessing information they are not cleared to access and the *-property prevents the information flow from a high level of classification to a lower level of classification in the system.

The main drawback of this model is that the *-property is too restrictive. For example, in a system which enforces a security policy based on the Bell-LaPadula model, let us consider a user, logged in as SECRET, who reads a CONFIDENTIAL file and then makes a copy of this file. The *-property requires the user to create the copy with a classification which is at least SECRET. But obviously the classification of the information which is contained in the copy is the same as the classification of the information of the original file, i.e., CONFIDENTIAL. Thus, the *-property requires the user to create a file with a label that does not correspond to the real classification of its content. This example puts the emphasis on one of the main drawback of the Bell-LaPadula model: the classification of the information in the system goes on increasing. This increasing leads to a degradation of the information in terms of accessibility. Thus, such a system needs the intervention of trusted subjects in order to periodically declassify the information. *Trusted subjects* are subjects that can be relied on not to compromise security. Thus their operations in the system are not submitted to the access control rules. They can declassify information, which is an illegal operation according to the access control rules of the model. In sum, the main problems with this model are not the things it allows but the things it disallows [3]. Many operations that are in fact secure will be disallowed by the model. The systems that choose to use the Bell-LaPadula model either strictly implement it and thus accept a degradation in the functionality of the system, or implement a lot of services as trusted subjects.

A second important drawback of the Bell-LaPadula model has been underlined in many papers: this model does not prevent the existence of covert channels. *Covert channels* are paths not normally intended for information transfer at all, but which could be used to signal some information towards lower levels. The problem of covert channels is directly connected to the sharing of different resources of the system (storage resources or timing resources). A covert channel may be used in two ways:

- directly by a malicious user with a high clearance who intentionally transmits information to a malicious user with a low clearance; in that case, the users both collaborate in order to realize illegal information flows;
- indirectly by a Trojan horse: a user with a high clearance involuntarily executes the Trojan horse which transmits information to the malicious user with a low clearance.

As originally formulated, some of the rules in Bell-LaPadula model allowed information to be transmitted improperly through control variables (storage channels). As reported by Landwehr in [3], Walter et al. established a final form of the model in which the rules of the model do not contain storage channels, but in which timing channels can exist. Unfortunately, timing channels can be implemented easily, if a resource is shared between high and low users. For example, a process p_1 might vary its paging rate in response to some sensitive data it observes. Another process p_2 (whose current security level is inferior to the current security level of p_1) may observe the variations in paging rate and "decipher" them to reveal the sensitive data. There is no rule in the Bell-LaPadula model that can prevent such an information flow. Further reading about the Bell-LaPadula model and its drawbacks can be found in [4], [5], [6].

3 Some extensions of the model

3.1 The floating labels method

In [7], John Woodward explains that the over-classification problem stems from the fact that, in traditional implementations of secure/trusted systems, such as SCOMP [8], subjects and objects inherit the sensitivity label of their creator. If we consider the example given in the previous section, when the user logs in at a SECRET level, the system creates a SECRET command interpreter to service him. When the user enters a copy file command, the command interpreter creates a SECRET process to run the command. This process is SECRET because it is created by a SECRET level command interpreter. The copy process creates a new file into which it intends to copy the CONFIDENTIAL file but this new file must be created SECRET thus over-classifying the data.

John Woodward proposes to associate two labels to each process and data in the system. The first label (called the sensitivity label) is a floating label that is intended to represent the *actual* sensitivity of the data stored in an object. Upon creation, each object must have the lowest sensitivity level of the system because it contains no data. In the same way, upon subject creation, the sensitivity label of the subject must represent the sensitivity of the data of its address space. Furthermore, if a subject executes a system call in such a way that its whole address space is reinitialized, then the sensitivity label of the subject must represent the sensitivity of this new address space even if this new sensitivity label is lower than the previous one. The second label that is associated with each object and subject of the system is a security label exclusively used for mandatory access control. This label is called MACL (Mandatory Access Control Level). It represents for an object the classification of the data that it contains and for a subject the clearance, i.e., the maximum level of data that it can read. The sensitivity level of a subject or object can never exceed its MACL. An example of such a labeling is detailed in Figure 1.

J. Woodward argues that this method allows to properly label a file which is to be exported from the system because the sensitivity label represents the actual level of information stored in the file. He also explains that any user in the system can set (using a trusted/privileged system command) a file's security level to the sensitivity level of this file when he wants to share this file with someone he trusts.

It seems to be interesting to keep this sensitivity label with each object and subject in the system. As a matter of fact, if we consider the declassification process, the sensitivity label allows to declassify the information at a level that

User logs in with SECRET clearance

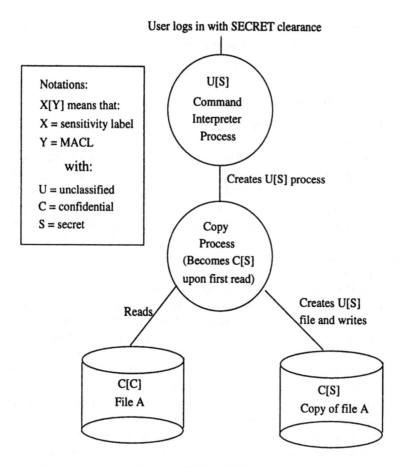

Fig. 1. Floating labels

is really the actual level of the information. Thus, there is no need for trusted users in order to estimate the information which is to be declassified.

The main drawback of this model is the creation of covert channels that do not exist in the Bell-LaPadula model, in particular storage channels. For example, let us imagine a user p with a SECRET clearance who wants to give information to a user q with a CONFIDENTIAL clearance. The user p declassifies several files from SECRET classification to CONFIDENTIAL classification (in order to be authorized to realize this declassification, the user p had taken care of not writing information with classification higher than CONFIDENTIAL in these files). When the declassification process is realized, the user q can read all these files and in particular their names. If the user q knows that a name which begins with a vowel means 0 and that a name which begins with a consonant means 1, there is an illegal information flow thanks to this covert channel.

There are also timing channels in this model. Let us imagine for example a user p who chooses to declassify some files at some very precise dates. If a user

q with a lower clearance can notice these precise dates (each date corresponds to the precise moment when he can read one more file), then he can use these dates to receive information from p.

3.2 Causal dependencies

Bruno d'Ausbourg [9] presents an original way to model the information flow in multilevel systems. He describes a system as a set of points. A point (o,t) references an object o at a time t. These points evolve with time and this evolving is due to elementary transitions made by the system. An elementary transition can modify a point: then, at instant t, it sets a new value v for the object o of the point. This instant t and the new value v functionally depend on previous points. This dependency on previous points is named *causal* dependency. The causal dependency of (o,t) on (o',t') with $t' < t$ is denoted by $(o',t') \rightarrow (o,t)$. The *causality cone* is defined as:

$$cone(o,t) = \{(o',t')/(o',t') \rightarrow^* (o,t)\}$$

where $\rightarrow^*$ is the transitive closure of the relation $\rightarrow$.

These causal dependencies makes up the structure of information flows inside the system. If a subject has any knowledge about the internal functioning of the system, then he is able to know the internal scheme of causal dependencies. So if a user has knowledge of the internal functioning of the system and if he can observe an output point x_0, then he is able to infer any information in $cone(x_0)$, i.e., he is able to observe all the points in $cone(x_0)$.

With respect to disclosure of information, a system is considered secure if a subject can observe only the objects he has the right to observe. If we note Obs_s the set of objects that a user s can observe and R_s the set of objects that this user is authorized to observe, we can say that the system is secure if: $Obs_s \subseteq R_s$.

In a system enforcing a multilevel security policy, d'Ausbourg explains that two conditions are sufficient to guarantee the security of the system. In such a system, a classification level $l(x)$ is assigned to points x and a clearance $l(s)$ is assigned to subjects s. The first condition is that the clearance of a user s dominates the set of output points O_s that he can observe:

$$\forall s, x_0 \in O_s \Rightarrow l(x_0) \leq l(s)$$

The second condition requires a monotonic increasing of levels over causal dependencies:

$$\forall x, \forall y, x \rightarrow y \Rightarrow l(x) \leq l(y).$$

This model is interesting because it contributes in a new way of formalizing the information flows in a system. Furthermore, what makes this formalization interesting is its minimal aspect: the notion of causal dependencies allows the information flows to be described in a minimal way. Thus, if we define a security policy and an authorization scheme based on this notion of causal dependencies, the rules of the authorization scheme can describe the minimum conditions that are to be enforced in a system in order to prevent the information flows. From this point of view, this model is better that the Bell-LaPadula model that controls the information flows with too severe measures. For example, in the model based on causal dependencies, a user SECRET can change the label of an object from

SECRET to UNCLASSIFIED if it is reinitialized. As a matter of fact, the dependencies that can be established for this operation do not lead to illegal information flows.

The main drawback of such a model seems to be the difficulty to enforce it in real systems. As a matter of fact, it seems to be difficult to very closely establish the causal dependencies in a system, just as the set of objects that may be observed by a subject. Furthermore, the author does not indicate any formal method which could help the administrators to precisely evaluate the causal dependencies in a system. And this evaluation even becomes more tricky in distributed systems where subjects and objects from multiple sites may cooperate.

4 A multilevel security model for distributed object systems

4.1 Secure entities

Our model is based on two main concepts: the notions of *objects* and *activities*. These entities are assigned labels as will be explained in the next paragraph.

The objects of our model are objects as defined in the object-oriented languages. Each object is made up of a private state information and a set of operations which represent the object interface. The operations defined on an object are called *methods* and are the only way to modify the state of the object or to get information from this state. The communication between objects consists in sending messages. An object O calls a method of an other object O' by sending O' a request. This message consists of a method selector and a list of arguments.

An activity in distributed object systems consists in a succession of method executions and requests through different objects of the system. This set of method executions and requests are dependent and collaborate to achieve a high-level task (e.g., printing a file on a printer). An activity exchanges information with the different objects it accesses. This notion is similar to the notion presented for the Chorus micro-kernel in [10]. In Figure 2, an activity is represented. This activity realizes a high-level task: recording a scene. This activity consists in:

1. Starting the execution of the method *Record-Scene* of the object *Client*,
2. Making a request to the method *Record* of the object *Recorder*,
3. Starting the execution of the method *Record* of the object *Recorder*,
4. Making a request to the method *Take* of the object *Movie-Camera*,
5. Executing the method *Take* of the object *Movie-Camera*,
6. Returning to the method *Record*,
7. Making a request to the method *Write* of the object *Video-Tape*,
8. Executing the method *Write* of the object *Video-Tape*,
9. Returning to the method *Record*.
10. Returning to the method *Record-Scene*.

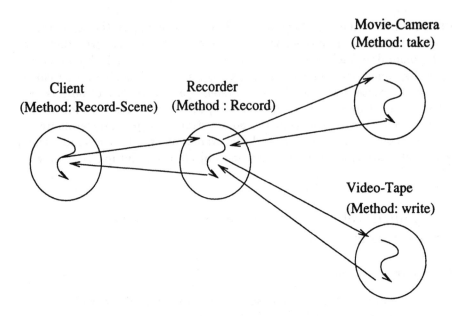

Fig. 2. An activity

The point in the notion of activity is the idea of dependence, of collaboration: an activity is made of a set of method executions that form parts of the same global operation from a user point of view.

One of the important features of our model is that we distinguish two object families: the *stateless objects* and the *stateful objects*. In the previous example, the activity flows information from the object *Movie-Camera* to the object *Video-Tape*. The object *Recorder* does not keep any memory of the information that it receives from the object *Movie-Camera*; it simply writes this information in the object *Video-Tape*. Yet, the object *Recorder* is accessed by the activity as the two other objects. We can generalize this idea: any object stores data but these data may be classified in two categories: the system data and the application data. The application data are the data which compose the state of the object from the application point of view, i.e., the data that are declared in the source code of the object by the programmer. The system data are data added by the system in the object to control the execution of the object (for example the process stack). A stateless object is an object which does not store application data: its state is initialized at each invocation. There is no information flow between two successive requests that access a stateless object. This notion of stateless object is analogous to the notion of "object reuse" of the Orange Book [2]. Conversely, a stateful object is an object which stores application data and whose methods consist in reading or writing these data. A lot of examples of stateless objects can be found in classical systems such as Unix. For instance, an NFS server is a stateless object. This server does not keep in memory any of the requests that it receives. Its state is initialized at each invocation. All object managers, in general, are stateless objects (browsers for example). We will see in the next section that this notion of stateless object will be useful to implement a less restrictive authorization policy than the Bell-LaPadula policy while preventing in the same way the illegal information flows.

The goal of a multilevel security policy is to prevent users to get information they are not cleared to access. As we suppose that each task realized in the system by a user is realized by means of an activity, we can prevent illegal information flows between users by preventing illegal information flows between activities. We must thus ensure that an activity with a high security level cannot transmit information to an activity with a lower security level (we will define in the next section how a security level is assigned to an activity). Yet, two activities may exchange information by accessing the same object (one activity writes an object and the other activity reads this object). Thus, we have to control in our system all interactions between activities and objects, i.e., to control each request accessing an object.

In order to realize these access controls, we have to assign security levels to the different entities of our model. We basically assign a security level to each user of the system. As the objects are the containers of information of the system, we have to assign them a security level (we will differently label stateless and stateful objects). In order to control each interaction between activities and objects, we have to assign security levels to the different requests of our system.

4.2 The different labels

We define a finite set of security levels partially ordered with respect to a binary relation "$\leq$".
Users:
    A label is associated to each user of the system. This label represents the user's clearance.
Objects:
    We label in a different way the stateless and the stateful objects. A label L_O is associated to each stateful object O. This label is the classification of the object. It represents the classification of the data that compose the state of the object. This classification is fixed and cannot be changed during the object lifetime.

Two labels $Llow_O$ and $Lhigh_O$ are associated to each stateless object O ($Llow_O \leq Lhigh_O$). $[Llow_O, Lhigh_O]$ is a *confidence interval* defining the trust one can put on the object. As a matter of fact, a stateless object does not store any application data, and thus cannot be assigned a classification as a stateful object. Nevertheless, each stateless object may be accessed by an activity like a stateful object. Each activity carries information with a particular security level. Each stateless object may thus potentially access this information. The labels we assign to a stateless object represent the trust one can put in this object, i.e., the trust that one can put on the actions that the object, as active entity, can execute. The high label represents the highest security level of data that can be read by the object. The low label represents the lowest security level of data that could be written by the object. Let us imagine, for example, that a stateless object is in fact a Trojan horse that keeps a local copy of all the data that are carried by all the requests accessing it. The low label of the object will guarantee that the copy will not be created with a label inferior to this label. This means that a future, malicious activity will need a clearance superior or equal to this low label to read the data. Conversely, the Trojan horse cannot read and then store data with a level highest than $Lhigh_O$. Let us imagine an administrator of a system who decides to use a new freeware NFS server that he gets from an anonymous ftp server. The administrator then estimates the trust that he can put in this NFS server (which is supposed to be a stateless object) and thus assigns it a confidence interval representing this trust.

Requests:

Just as we said in the previous paragraph, each activity in the system carries information and exchanges information with the objects it accesses. Thus, an activity must be labeled. We assign a *parenthesis* of labels (i.e., two labels) to each activity a. These labels are noted $Llow_a$ and $Lhigh_a$. These labels are floating labels and may change according to the type and the labels of the objects accessed by the activity. The low label represents the classification of the information carried by the activity, i.e., the highest level of the information that has been previously read by the activity. The high label represents the clearance of the activity. This clearance is initialized with the clearance of the user who started this activity. The parenthesis can then be noted: [*classification, clearance*]. The information carried by an activity is in fact carried by the different requests among the objects of the system it accesses. Thus, in order to make access controls in our model, we have to label these requests. We assign a *parenthesis* of fixed labels to each request r. These labels are noted $Llow_r$ and $Lhigh_r$. Let us imagine that an activity is composed of n requests $(r_1, r_2, ...r_n)$. The first request r_1 accesses an object in order to provoke the execution of one of its methods. This execution leads to the sending of a new message, the request r_2. The parenthesis of labels of r_2 will depend on the parenthesis of labels of r_1 and on the type and labels of the object accessed by r_1. Thus, the parenthesis of the different requests will be different according to the different objects accessed by the activity. The labels of the activity $[Llow_a, Lhigh_a]$ (which are floating labels) will successively be $[Llow_{r_1}, Lhigh_{r_1}]$ ... $[Llow_{r_n}, Lhigh_{r_n}]$.

4.3 The access rules

Our authorization scheme is composed of mandatory access rules based on the different labels we have just presented. These rules cannot be bypassed.

4.3.1 Notion of read access and write access

In the rest of the paper, the term of *read access* and *write access* must be understood in a very precise sense. We call read access on a stateful object O, any execution of a method of O which provokes an information flow from the internal state of O to the activity which executes the method. Reciprocally, we call write access any execution of a method of O which provokes an information flow from the activity which executes the method to the internal state of O. We will call read-write access any execution of a method of O which provokes an exchange of information between the activity which executes the method and the state of O (it is not worth considering "null access", i.e. methods which provoke no information flow between a stateful object and the request).

4.3.2 Access Rules

Access to stateless objects:

If a request r may access a stateless object O (through invoking any of its methods) then the intersection of $[Llow_O, Lhigh_O]$ and $[Llow_r, Lhigh_r]$ is not empty. (R1)

Access to stateful objects:

With respect to stateful objects, the security policy is enforcing the following rules (these rules derive from the Bell-LaPadula security policy rules):

simple security condition:

If a request r may read a stateful object O, then $L_O \leq Lhigh_r$. (R2)

*-property:

If a request r may write a stateful object O, then $Llow_r \leq L_O$. (R3)

To enforce these rules, each method of a stateful object is assigned an attribute indicating which kind of access is realized by the method: read, write or read-write.

4.4 The access control scheme

In this section we consider the current request r of an activity a which accesses an object O.

- If O is a stateless object:
  - If $Lhigh_r < Llow_O$ or $Lhigh_O < Llow_r$:
    the access is denied. (R4)
  - If $Llow_O \leq Lhigh_r$ and $Llow_r \leq Lhigh_O$:
    the access is authorized with restriction: $[Llow_a, Lhigh_a]$ is changed to $[Max(Llow_a, Llow_O), Min(Lhigh_a, Lhigh_O)]$. (R5)

    This restriction means that the next request r' of the activity a will be labeled $[Llow_{r'}, Lhigh_{r'}] = [Max(Llow_r, Llow_O), Min(Lhigh_r, Lhigh_O)]$. Note the particular case: if $[Llow_O, Lhigh_O] \subset [Llow_a, Lhigh_a]$, then the access is authorized without restriction since $Max(Llow_a, Llow_O) = Llow_a$ and $Min(Lhigh_a, Lhigh_O) = Lhigh_a$.

  Rule (R4) guarantees that the request may not access objects unless the intersection of the request's parenthesis and the object's confidence interval is not empty. Rule (R5) describes the evolution of the parenthesis of an activity accessing an object O by a request r. If an activity accesses a stateless object whose low label dominates the current classification of the information carried by the activity then this current classification has to be set to this label. If an activity accesses an object whose high label is dominated by the clearance of the activity then the clearance of the activity has to be set to the high label of the object.

- If O is a stateful object:

  - If method m is a read method and if $Lhigh_r < L_O$:
    the access is denied. $\qquad$ (R6)
  - If method m is a read method and if $L_O \leq Lhigh_r$:
    the access is authorized with restriction:
    $Llow_a$ is changed to $Max(Llow_a, L_O)$. $\qquad$ (R7)
    Note the particular case: if $Max(Llow_a, L_O) = Llow_a$, the access is authorized without restriction.
  - If method m is a write method and if $L_O < Llow_r$:
    the access is denied. $\qquad$ (R8)
  - If method m is a write method and if $Llow_r \leq L_O$:
    the access is authorized with no restriction. $\qquad$ (R9)
  - If method m is a read-write method and if L_O is not in the interval $[Llow_r, Lhigh_r]$:
    the access is denied. $\qquad$ (R10)
  - If method m is a read-write method and if L_O is in the interval $[Llow_r, Lhigh_r]$:
    the access is authorized with restriction:
    $Llow_a$ is changed to $Max(Llow_a, L_O)$. $\qquad$ (R11)
    Note the particular case: if $Max(Llow_a, L_O) = Llow_a$, the access is authorized without restriction.

Rules (R6) and (R7) describe the evolution of the parenthesis of an activity making a read access to a stateful object. An activity must not read a stateful object whose classification dominates the high label of the activity (R6). If an activity makes a read access to an object whose classification dominates the classification of the information carried by the activity (i.e., the low label), then this low label has to be set to the classification of the object (R7). There is no restriction to be applied to the activity's parenthesis when an activity makes a write access to a stateful object. As a matter of fact, the sensitivity of the information carried by the activity does not change during such an access: there is only an information flow from the activity to the object. So, whether the access is authorized, or it is denied, no restriction is to be applied. An activity can always make a write access to a stateful object whose classification dominates the classification of the information carried by the activity (R9) and an activity cannot make a write access to a stateful object whose classification is dominated by the classification of the information carried by the activity (this corresponds to the *-property of the Bell-LaPadula model) (R8).

4.5 An example of an authorization scheme

In the following example, we consider that a SECRET user U wants to print an UNCLASSIFIED file f_3 on printer p_4 whose confidence interval is [UNCLASSIFIED, CONFIDENTIAL]. The set of objects which take place in the execution of this action are represented in Figure 3. U is a user (a person) of the system, ps_1 a print server of class *PrintServer*, fs_2 a file server of class *FileServer*, f_3 a file of class *File*, p_4 a printer of class *Printer* and tf a transient file located on the site of ps_1.

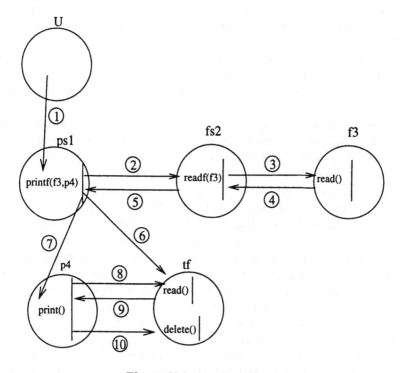

Fig. 3. Objects cooperation

The hierarchy of labels used in our example is represented below just as the labels of the different components of the system:

UNCLASSIFIED < CONFIDENTIAL < SECRET < TOPSECRET.

User U : SECRET
ps_1   : [CONFIDENTIAL, SECRET] (stateless object)
fs_2   : [UNCLASSIFIED, SECRET] (stateless object)
p_4   : [UNCLASSIFIED, CONFIDENTIAL] (stateless object)
f_3   : UNCLASSIFIED (stateful object with methods *read()*, *write()*, *update()*
                and *delete()*)

The scenario can be summarized as follows:

- User U logs in the system with a SECRET clearance. The activity a starts executing the first request for U. This request is the invocation of method *printf* of print server ps_1. This first request (**message 1**) is labeled [UNCLASSIFIED, SECRET]. The low label is UNCLASSIFIED because the activity does not hold any sensitive information. The high label represents the clearance of the user U.
- Print server ps_1 is a stateless object labeled [CONFIDENTIAL, SECRET]. The intersection between the parenthesis of labels of the request and the confidence interval of ps_1 is not empty, but as $Llow_r < Llow_{ps_1} \leq Lhigh_r \leq Lhigh_{ps_1}$, the access is authorized with restriction: $Llow_a$ is changed to CONFIDENTIAL, i.e., the parenthesis of the activity is changed to [CONFIDENTIAL, SECRET] (cf. R5).
- The activity goes on by invoking method *readf* of file server fs_2 (**message 2**). This request is labeled [CONFIDENTIAL, SECRET]. fs_2 is a stateless object labeled [UNCLASSIFIED, SECRET]. The access is thus authorized without restriction (cf. R5).
- The activity then makes an access to method *read* of f_3 (**message 3**). This request is labeled [CONFIDENTIAL, SECRET]. f_3 is a stateful object which is labeled UNCLASSIFIED and the access is a read access. The access is thus authorized without restriction (cf. R7).
- The activity then returns to fs_2 and then to ps_1 in two replies labeled [CONFIDENTIAL, SECRET] (**messages 4 and 5**). These two replies are authorized without restriction because their parenthesis of labels is respectively included in the confidence interval of fs_2 and ps_1 (particular case of R5).
- ps_1 creates a temporary file tf in which it copies f_3 (**messages 6**). This creation request is part of the same activity and thus must be labeled [CONFIDENTIAL, SECRET]. The file tf is a stateful object created with label $L_{tf} = Llow_r$ [1]. ps_1 makes a write access to tf with a [CONFIDENTIAL, SECRET] request. tf is a stateful object and $Llow_r \leq L_{tf}$, thus the access is authorized with no restriction (cf. R9).
- The activity then accesses printer p_4 through method *print* (**message 7**). The request is labeled [CONFIDENTIAL, SECRET], p_4 is a stateless object and the intersection between the parenthesis of labels of the request and the confidence interval of p_4 is not empty. But, as $Llow_{p_4} \leq Llow_r \leq Lhigh_{p_4} < Lhigh_r$, the access is authorized with restriction: $Lhigh_a$ is changed to CONFIDENTIAL (cf. R5).
- p_4 then invokes method *read* of tf (**message 8**). The request is now labeled [CONFIDENTIAL, CONFIDENTIAL] (because of the previous access to p_4), tf is a stateful object, the invoked method is a read method and $L_{tf} = Llow_r$, the access is thus authorized without restriction. The return of this request (**message 9**) is labeled [CONFIDENTIAL, CONFIDENTIAL] and is authorized because this parenthesis of labels is included in the confidence interval of ps_1. After printing, p_4 deletes file tf (**message 10**) in a [CONFIDENTIAL,

---

[1] The label of a transient stateful object is defined by a parameter of the creation request. Its level must be higher than or equal to the lower label of the request.

CONFIDENTIAL] request. The access is authorized with no restriction because $Llow_r = L_{tf}$ (delete is a write access).

5 Preventing the illegal information flows

5.1 Proof

This section is dedicated to the demonstration that our model prevents the illegal information flows. We describe here how we prevent these illegal information flows thanks to the set of rules that we have presented in the previous sections.

Preventing the illegal information flows consists in demonstrating that there does not exist a way for a user to infer information whose classification dominates the clearance of the user. This information inference might imply the collaboration of several users and the handling of several objects in the system. This can be expressed in the following way :

We want to verify that if s is a user, O a stateful object and $L_s < L_O$, then there do not exist series $\{i_1, i_2, ...i_l\}$ and $\{j_1, j_2, ...j_m\}$ such as:

$(s_{j_1}, O_{i_1}, read) \wedge (s_{j_1}, O_{i_2}, write) \wedge (s_{j_2}, O_{i_2}, read) \wedge \cdots \wedge (s_{j_m}, O_{i_l}, read)$.
with $s_{j_m} = s$ and $O_{i_1} = O$.

In the context of our model, this means that there do not exist series of activities and objects whose collaboration allow illegal information flows. Formally, this means, that there do not exist series $\{i_1, i_2, ...i_l\}$ and $\{k_1, k_2, ..., k_n\}$ such as:

$(a_{k_1}, O_{i_1}, read) \wedge (a_{k_1}, O_{i_2}, write) \wedge (a_{k_2}, O_{i_2}, read) \wedge (a_{k_2}, O_{i_3}, write) \wedge \cdots$
$\wedge (a_{k_n}, O_{i_l}, read)$ (a_{k_i} is an activity; the last one, a_{k_n} is started by user s_{j_m})

$(a_{k_1}, O_{i_1}, read)$ implies:
. $Lo_{i_1} \leq Lhigh_{a_{k_1}}$ (Rule R1)
. $Llow_{a_{k_1}}$ is changed to $Max(Llow_{a_{k_1}}, Lo_{i_1})$ (Rule R7)
$(a_{k_1}, O_{i_2}, write)$ implies:
. $Llow_{a_{k_1}} \leq Lo_{i_2}$ (Rule R9).
(with $Llow_{a_{k_1}}$ changed according to the access to O_{i_1}).

This leads to: $Lo_{i_1} \leq Lo_{i_2}$ and thus to: $Lo_{i_1} \leq Lo_{i_2} \cdots \leq Lo_{i_l}$

On the other hand, $(a_{k_n}, O_{i_l}, read)$ implies: $Lo_{i_l} \leq Lhigh_{a_{k_n}}$. Furthermore, as the activity a_{k_n} is started by the user s_{j_m}, we have the relation: $Lhigh_{a_{k_n}} \leq L_{s_{j_m}}$. This leads to: $Lo_{i_l} \leq L_{s_{j_m}}$.

We thus obtain: $Lo_{i_1} \leq Lo_{i_2} \cdots \leq Lo_{i_l} \leq L_{s_{j_m}}$ and thus $Lo_{i_1} \leq L_{s_{j_m}}$, i.e., $L_O \leq L_s$ which is contrary to the hypothesis ($L_s \leq L_O$).

5.2 Validation process and covert channels

We have presented in the previous sections some important notions of our model: the stateless objects and the attributes assigned to each method of a stateful object (read, write, read/write). The flexibility of our model and its interest with respect to the Bell-LaPadula security policy depend on the fact that we can or cannot validate such entities in the system. Given that, our model needs some validation processes in order to verify that an object which is supposed to be stateless is actually stateless (i.e., that it does not keep in local variables some information carried by the requests that access it). The confidence interval that we assign to a stateless object represents the trust we have for this object to be really a stateless object, thanks to the validation process. In the same way, we need to validate that each method of a stateful object which pretends to be a read (respectively write, read/write) method is actually a read (respectively write, read/write) method. We think that techniques like program proof, code analysis would quite easily allow to make such verifications. As a matter of fact, the properties that we want to check are quite simple. In order to check that a stateless object is actually a stateless object, we have to check that it does not keep in memory any information exchanged with the activities which access it. We can make this verification by checking that a stateless object reinitializes all its local variables after each method invocation. In order to check that a read method (for instance) is actually a read method, we have to check that the method only reads information from the activities which access it but does not give any information to these activities. If the messages are sent via sockets for example, we thus have to check all socket handlings in the source code of the method and check that all these handlings consist in reading information on the sockets.

In the same say, we must validate each object of the system to check that it cannot use a covert channel. A secure computer system ideally would not allow communication channels to exist. But eliminating all the covert channels in a secure system is in fact a quasi-impossible task: as soon as some resources of the system are shared, there are covert channels. Furthermore, eliminating all the covert channels in a system may lead to a non-responsive, non-reliable system. Given that, it is generally better to find ways to minimize illicit information leakage through such covert channels. That is the approach chosen in this paper. The model we present does not eliminate the existence of covert channels but aims at limiting the use of these covert channels: we consider that we can validate each object introduced in the system in a way that we can trust it not to try to transmit information using a covert channel. This validation is realized "off-line", i.e., before introducing the object in the system. This validation concerns all the objects of the system, stateless objects as well as stateful objects. One could pretend that this task seems quite difficult. We think it is not. As a matter of fact, it is commonly agreed that it is possible to identify all the covert channels that may exist on a system and that it is possible to measure their brandwidth. The B3 evaluation [2] of a system requires this identification and these measures, and B3 and even A1 systems do exist. So, if it is possible to identify the covert channels of a system, we assert that it is then possible to detect in a source code, the mechanisms that may try to exploit these covert channels (such analysis even seems easier that the analysis of the existence of covert channels).

If we consider that we cannot trust our validation process (i.e., methods to assign the confidence interval to stateless objects, mechanisms to check that a read (respectively write, read/write) method is really a read (respectively write, read/write) method and processes that verify that an new object introduced in the system does not try to transmit information through covert channels), a pessimistic solution is to consider that all objects are stateful (a single label is thus assigned to each object), that all the operations in the system are read/write and that all the activities have a parenthesis reduced to: $Llow_a = Lhigh_a$. This leads us to use the classical Bell-LaPadula model directly applied to distributed object systems.

6 Related work

One of the main characteristics of our model is that we always try to assign an activity the classification that actually represents the classification of the information carried by the activity. This allows to avoid the over-classification of the information because objects that are created are assigned a label that actually reflects the sensitivity of their state. The floating labels proposed by John Woodward (see Section 3.1) aim at implementing the same property even if this implementation does not address object systems.

This idea has also been exploited in object oriented databases. The SODA model [11] is based on the notions of object and method activation. In SODA, an object may have a label protecting the whole object or a set of labels protecting independently each attribute of the object and the whole object itself. Each method activation (the active entity in SODA) is assigned a clearance level and a current classification level. The clearance level is an upper bound for the current classification level and this current level can raise according to the objects accessed by the method activation. Just as in our model, the login method begins execution with classification level equal to SYSTEM LOW. The security policy in the SODA model is defined by rules that are similar to the rules we have presented here except one: a method may not modify an object unless the current classification level of the method is dominated by the level of the object and after the modification, the current classification level of the method becomes equal to the level of the object. We think that this modification of the current classification level of the method is not justified. As we said in the previous section, we think that it is possible to verify that some modifications are strictly write accesses (i.e., information flows from the method activation to the object) and that, in such cases, there is no reason to increase the current classification level of the method activation. Furthermore, the way of labeling the objects and particularly the attributes of the objects in SODA is only well suited to database systems and corresponds to a client/server model rather than a model based on cooperative objects. We think that this granularity of protection does not correspond to object oriented systems in which the protection rather addresses the whole state of the object. Thus, we think that it may be quite difficult to adapt SODA's model to distributed object systems.

In the message filter object-oriented model, Jajodia and Kogan [12] choose to assign one label to each object. Objects can exchange information only by sending messages. Thus, the principle of the model is to control all information flows by mediating the flow of messages. The message filter takes appropriate action upon intercepting a message and examining the classification of the sender and the receiver. Each method activation is assigned a level given by a variable *rlevel*. Jajodia and Kogan explain that the intuitive significance of *rlevel* is that it keeps track of the least upper bound of all objects encountered in a chain of method invocations, going back to the root of the chain (this *rlevel* corresponds to the classification of an activity of our model). This model has also some additional features in order to eliminate some timing channels. In [13], this model has also been proposed, in the context of a discretionary system. Even if this model is an interesting adaptation of the Bell-LaPadula model to object systems, we think that its main drawback is that it uniformly considers the objects of the system (and thus assigns a single label to stateless objects). This model is thus as restrictive as the Bell-LaPadula model in classical systems.

7 Conclusion and future work

The Bell-LaPadula security model prevents illegal information flows in a multi-level system but is too restrictive. We have proposed in that paper a multilevel security model that is derived from the Bell-LaPadula model but that is less restrictive (thanks to the notion of stateless objects) and that is adapted to the distributed object systems.

It should be interesting to study the adaptation of other security policies to distributed object systems. For example, we think it an interesting future work to study the adaptation of Biba's [14] integrity policy to object systems.

References

1. D. Bell and L. LaPadula, "Secure Computer Systems: unified Exposition and Multics Interpretation," Tech. Rep. MTR-2997, MITRE Co., July 1975.
2. "U.S. Departement of Defense Trusted Computer Security Evaluation Criteria (TCSEC)." 5200.28-STD, December 1985.
3. C. Landwehr, "Formal Models for Computer Security," *ACM Computing Surveys*, vol. 3, pp. 247–278, September 1981.
4. E. R. Lindgreen and I. Herschberg, "On the Validity of the Bell-LaPadula Model," *Computers and Security*, vol. 13, pp. 317–333, 1994.
5. J. McLean, "Reasoning about Security Models," in *Proc. of Symposium on Research in Security and Privacy, IEEE Computer Society Press*, (Oakland, California(USA)), pp. 123–131, 1987.
6. D. Bell, "Concerning 'Modeling' of Computer Security," in *Proc. of Symposium on Research in Security and Privacy, IEEE Computer Society Press*, (Oakland, California(USA)), pp. 8–13, 1988.
7. J. Woodward, "Exploiting the Dual Nature of Sensitivity Labels," in *Proc. of Symposium on Research in Security and Privacy, IEEE Computer Society Press*, (Oakland, California(USA)), pp. 23–30, 1987.

8. L. Fraim, "Scomp: A Solution to the Multilevel Security Problem," *IEEE Computer*, vol. 16, pp. 26–34, July 1983.

9. B. d'Ausbourg, "Implementing Secure Dependencies Over a Network by Designing a Distributed Security Subsystem," in *Proc. of European Symposium on Research in Computer Security*, (Brighton(UK)), pp. 249–266, November 1994.

10. J. Banino, J. Fabre, M. Guillemont, G. Morisset, and M. Rozier, "Some Fault-Tolerant Aspects of the Chorus Distributed System," in *Proc. of 5th International Conference on Distributed Computing Systems*, (Denver, Colorado), pp. 430–437, May 1985.

11. T. Keefe, W. Tsai, and M. Thuraisingham, "SODA: a Secure Object-oriented Database System," *Computers and Security*, vol. 8, no. 6, pp. 517–533, 1989.

12. S. Jajodia and B. Kogan, "Integrating an Object-Oriented Data Model with Multi-Level Security," in *Proc. of the 1990 IEEE Symposium on Security and Privacy*, (Oakland, CA), pp. 48–69, May 1990.

13. E. Bertino, P. Samarati, and S. Jajodia, "High Assurance Discretionary Access Control for Object Bases," in *Proc. of 1st ACM Conference on Computer and Communications Security*, (Fairfax, Virginia (USA)), pp. 140–150, November 1993.

14. K. Biba, "Integrity Considerations for Secure Computer Systems," Tech. Rep. ESD-TR 76-372, MITRE Co., April 1977.

An Authorization Model for Federated Systems

Sabrina De Capitani di Vimercati　　　　Pierangela Samarati

Dipartimento di Scienze dell'Informazione
Università di Milano
via Comelico 39/41 Milano 20135, Italy
Phone: (+39) 2-55006227
Fax: (+39) 2-55006253
{decapita,samarati}@dsi.unimi.it

Abstract. We present an authorization model for federated systems based on a tightly coupled architecture. The model supports authorizations to build and maintain the federation as well as authorizations to access the federated data. At each component site owners declare the objects they wish to export and the access modes executable on them by users of the federation. Inclusion of objects into the federation requires their subsequent import by the federation administrator. Different degrees of authorization autonomy are supported, whereby users can retain or delegate the federation administrator the task of specifying authorizations. A site can require to authenticate the user at each access or accept his identity as communicated by the federation. An access control algorithm describing controls to be enforced at the federation and at each local site under the different authentication and administrative options is presented.

Keywords: Federated systems, access control, authorization administration, authorization autonomy.

1   Introduction

A federated system is a collection of cooperating but autonomous component systems [17]. Autonomy of a component means that the local administrator maintains some form of control over its system. Four different kinds of autonomy can be supported: *design autonomy, communication autonomy, execution autonomy,* and *association autonomy.*

Enforcing protection of information in federated systems requires the investigation of several issues which traditional access control models, proposed for centralized or distributed systems [3, 15], do not address. A major issue that becomes very important in this context is the establishment of administrative policies regulating grant and revocation of authorizations on federated data. While in a centralized or distributed system ownership or centralized administration may be satisfactory solutions, federated systems call for more flexible approaches. On one side, enforcing ownership would require data owner to specify authorizations for federated users and therefore to maintain information of how the federation is composed. On the other side, applying a centralized administration approach may imply a loss of control, and therefore of autonomy of the data owner. Moreover, even traditional problems, such as authentication or user identities, require careful reconsideration in a federated context, where single components may specify accesses for federated subjects (users, groups, or whole sites).

Although recent research has addressed the problem of protecting federated systems [2, 7, 8, 12, 14, 20, 21, 22] and few federated systems, like Mermaid [18], Orion-2 [10], or the one proposed by Heimbigner and McLeod [5] support some form of authorization specification and access control, several issues still remain to be investigated. In this paper we investigate these issues and focus on two particular subtypes of association autonomy, meaning *authentication* and *authorization* autonomy. By authentication autonomy we mean the ability of a site to decide how the identity of each user accessing data stored at the site is established. By authorization autonomy we mean the ability of a site to specify which accesses are to be allowed or denied on objects stored at the site.[1]

We propose an authorization model for the protection of information in a tightly coupled federated system. The reason for considering a tightly coupled federation is to avoid the users the burden of explicitly maintaining the relationships with each single site participating in the federation. A tightly coupled architecture allows to rely on a central authority for defining and maintaining the federation. Even with this centralized administration we allow a good degree of autonomy to each single site participating in the federation. In particular, our model allows users to selectively share their objects by specifying, for each object, the access modes that are available to the federation. Different kinds of administrative policies are also supported whereby users can retain the privilege of specifying authorizations on objects, can delegate the federation administrator the task of specifying authorization, or can require that accesses be authorized by both the federation administrator and by them in order to be allowed. Access authorizations are specified at both the global level (on federated objects) and the local level (on exported objects). Local authorizations can also be negative. The possibility of specifying negative authorizations at the local level allows owners to retain control over their objects even when delegating administration to the federation administrator. Although in the paper we do not deal with authentication issues, the model assumes that two different authentication options are possible. A site can require to authenticate every user requiring access (even if the request comes through the federation) or can accept the identity of the user as communicated by the federation.

The remainder of the paper is organized as follows. Section 2 illustrates previous work on authorization models in federated systems. Section 3 presents the reference architecture of the federation and introducing some notations. Sec-

---

[1] The need to explicitly consider security issues in a separate category has been also pointed out in [8] where the notion of authorization autonomy is introduced. Note, however, that the notion introduced in [8] corresponds to our notion of authentication autonomy.

tion 4 illustrates authorizations and operations for constructing the federated data. Section 5 describes how authorizations can be specified at both the federation and the local level. Section 6 illustrates access controls enforced, globally and locally, upon submissions of access requests to the federation. Finally, Section 7 presents the conclusions and outlines future work.

2   Related work

Some federated database systems proposed in the literature present some form, often very limited, of authorization specification and access control.

Wang and Spooner [22] propose an approach to enforce content-dependent access control in a heterogeneous federated system where authorizations can be specified at both the local and the global level. The approach is based on views and ownership paradigm. Content-dependent access control is enforced by materializing views and treating them as protection objects.

In Mermaid [18], a front-end system to integrate multiple homogeneous DBMSs, an authorization model enforcing access control at both global and local level is presented. In order to use Mermaid a user must be registered for it. Access authorizations are specified both at the global level, in the Mermaid system, and at the local level, at each site. Access control at a site is always carried out with respect to the identity of the user at the site.

Another model allowing specification of authorizations at both the local and global level is proposed by Jonscher and Dittrich in [8]. In this model a global security administrator specifies the local identities corresponding to each global identifier. Authorizations can be positive or negative. The grantor of an authorization at the global level can require consistency of the authorizations. Consistency means that a request permitted according to the global authorizations cannot fail due to access rejection at the local level. Consistency is enforced by propagation of authorizations: every time a global authorization is granted, local sites are required to grant the corresponding necessary authorizations. The global authorization is inserted only if all the corresponding local grants can be enforced.

In the work of Heimbigner and McLeod [5] a loosely coupled federated architecture supporting a very primitive form of access control is presented. The data model is based on the concept of types and maps. Types are collections of objects that share common properties while maps are functions that map objects of some types into object instances. Authorizations on types and maps defined at a site are specified in terms of whole components and not to specific users identity. All types and maps defined at a given site s_1 for which another site s_2 is authorized constitute the export schema of s_1 for s_2. A site can import all types and maps contained in export schemas defined for it at other sites. Export and import operations are the result of negotiation between the two sites. Once types and maps are imported at a site no further negotiation is required for their access, which is completely analogous to access to a local type except that data is transferred over the network.

In ORION-2 [10], a federated loosely coupled object-oriented system is presented based on a shared database and a number of private databases. The shared database contains data accessible to all authorized users, while each private database can be accessed only by the user who owns it. Check in and check out operations allow users to get (copy) objects from the shared databse and returning them back. Updates to different copies checked out, which may be checked in again at a later time, are managed through the use of versions.

Blaustein et al. [2] propose an approach to control access in federated database systems based on agreements established among the different sites of the federation. Agreements are rules regulating the access by users at the different sites to the cooperating database systems. Two kinds of agreements are considered: action agreements and access agreements. Action agreements describe the action to be taken in response to database requests, while access agreements allow to enforce exceptions to prohibitions otherwise in effect. The identity of users at the remote site from which they submit the request is used in access control.

Other proposals have been presented based on the enforcement of mandatory policies [12, 14, 20, 21].

3 System's Architecture and Basic Concepts

In this section we illustrate the architecture of the federated system and give the basic assumptions on our model.

The system is essentially structured on two levels: at the global level there is the federation and at the local level the different sites participating in it. At the federation level a privileged user, called *federation administrator* is responsible for creating and maintaining the federated schema and establishing authorizations for users to access the objects in the federation.

At the local level there are the different sites taking part in the federation. We distinguish three categories of participants:

- *customers*. These are sites whose users can be authorized to connect to the federation and access its objects.
- *providers*. These are sites that take part in the construction of the federated data, i.e., that can export their local objects for the population of the federation.
- *customers-providers*. These are sites that fall in both the categories above.

At each site a privileged user, called *site administrator* is responsible for the relationship with the federations in which the site participates.[2] Registration of a site in a federation is the result of a negotiation between the administrator of the

---

[2] For the sake of simplicity we consider a single site administrator to be responsible for the relationship with all the federations in which a site can participate. The approach can be easily extended to the case where several administrators, each responsible for the relationship with a specific federation, exist at a site.

site and the administrator of the federation. In the following, given a federation f notation *providers(f)* and *customers(f)* indicate the sites registered as provider and customer of f, respectively. Sites in the third category belong to both sets.

A good user's authentication is a prerequisite for a successful access control. In this paper we do not deal with the problem of authenticating the users but assume different authentication options we allow the federation to support. Each site registered as a provider of a federation can, during the negotiation phase, choose between two different authentication policies according to which identity of federated users needing to access local objects through the federation can be established: *global* and *local* authentication. In the *global* authentication, federation's users do not need to identify themselves at the site, their identity as communicated to the site by the federation will be used for access control (of course the federation will have to authenticate itself). In the *local* authentication, before processing each access request coming by a user through the federation the participating site will require the user to identify himself at the site. This identity will be used in the access control process. Note that communication of identities between federation and sites requires some form of trust in both the federation/site that enforced the authentication and in the communication system. Different certification forms can be used to provide this, such as those illustrated in [1, 13, 23].

3.1 Subjects and Objects

At each site a set of local users is assumed and a set of local objects is stored. We do not make any assumption on the data model used at the federation or at each specific site. Given a site s, we will simply refer to the objects stored in it as O_s. Moreover, given an object $o \in O_s$, we denote with M_o the set of access modes executable on it. The specific data types and access modes applicable on the objects will depend on the data model considered. For instance, in a relational model, M_o will be composed of the elementary select, insert, and update operations plus all applications defined for a relation. In an object-oriented model, M_o will be composed of all methods, elementary and non, executable on object o. To make our model independent from the specific administrative policy applied at the local sites, we assume each object o is associated with a set of administrators. The set of administrators associated with an object o will contain: the object's owner, if ownership is applied; the system's administrator, if a centralized policy is applied; and all users owning an administrative authorization on the object if decentralized administration is applied.

At the federation site two kinds of subjects are considered: users and groups. Users are entities allowed to connect to the federation and submit requests on its data. Groups, which are sets of users, can be defined with reference to the users identities at the federation or at the site from which their connection originates (for instance a group can be defined as containing all users connecting to the federation from a specific site). Each user can belong to one or more groups.

At the federation level, three kinds of objects are supported:

- *Global* objects. These are objects created directly in the federation by the federation administrator or by users explicitly authorized for that.
- *Imported* objects. These are objects defined and stored at some site taking part in the federation and imported "as-is" by the federation.
- *Composite* objects. These are objects defined as aggregation of other global or imported objects.

3.2 Notations

Before proceeding further to illustrate our model we introduce some notations that will be used in the paper. In the following, we will use letters U, G, O, and A to denote respectively a set of users, groups, objects, and authorizations. Subscripts will be used to discriminate the site or federation to which they refer. For instance, O_s denotes the set of objects at site s and G_f denotes the set of user groups defined at federation f.

To take distribution into consideration we suppose each user/group identifier to have associated the site at which it has been defined. User identifiers at site s will therefore have the form **user@s**. Analogously, subject (i.e., user or group) identifiers at a federation f will have the form **subject@f**. We will omit the specification of the site when it is not needed in the explanation or it is clear from the text. For instance, the site specification in subjects of authorizations will be omitted when the site is the same as the one at which the authorization is stored.

In authorizations we will also allow subject patterns to be specified. Subject patterns can be specified by using the wild character in place of a specific identifier. We allow two kinds of pattern. Pattern "*@s*", which indicates any identifier at site s, and pattern "*", which indicates any identifier at any site. In the following, notation U_s will be used to indicate the set of all the identifiers of the form **user@s** together with *@s. Moreover, given a collection $s_1, \ldots, s_n$ of sites participating as customers in a federation f, we will use notation $U_{customers(f)}$ to indicate the set $U_{s_1} \cup \ldots \cup U_{s_n} \cup \{*\}$. A pattern satisfies all identifiers to which it can be reduced by appropriately instantiating the wild character. In other words, a patterns p *covers* an identifier **u@s**, denoted as $p \triangleright$ **u@s**, if either *i)* $p =$ **u@s**, *ii)* $p = $ *@s, or *iii)* $p = $ *.

Finally, given an object o, we will use notation *site(o)* to denote the site at which the object is stored.

3.3 Working of the System

Users of sites registered as customer of a federation and wishing to access the federation must explicitly open a working session by connecting to the federation site (see Figure 1). Connection requires identification of the user (1) and corresponding authentication of this identity by the federation. This identity will be used by the federation for enforcing access control. Note that this assumption does not rule out the possibility of anonymous connection. Anonymous connection may be treated with a special user identifier called **anonymous**. Besides the

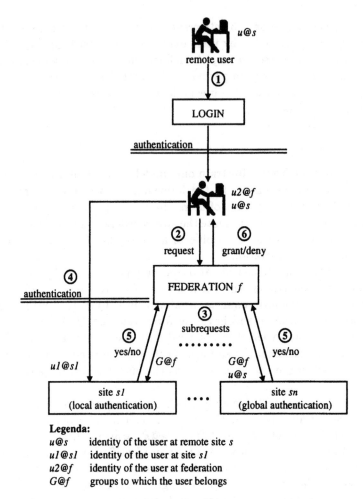

Fig. 1. Working of the system

identity with which he connected to the federation, a user has also associated an attribute containing his identity at the local site of origin.[3] Once the user has been authenticated by the federation he can submit requests to access the federated objects (2). Accessing a federated object may require to access the corresponding underlying local objects at the different sites. Each user request must therefore be split, for both access control and data retrieval in a set of requests on the underlying local objects (or a subset of them). Then, the federation sends each site storing a local object involved in the transaction an access request for the groups to which the user belongs together with the remote identity of the user (3). In case of local authentication the user will need to re-authenticate himself at the local site (4). Then, each local site controls whether the access

---

[3] Note that to allow non disclosure of identities, the case of attribute only partially specified, i.e., with indication only of the site, may be considered.

request is allowed and returns the result to the federation (5), which will take
the access decision (6) on the basis of the replies of the different sites.

Access control will be illustrated in details in Section 6.

4 Population of the Federation

Populating a federation means specifying the objects part of the federated
database. The federation can be populated directly, by explicitly creating global
objects in the federation or indirectly, by importing objects from the component
sites.

In the remainder of this section we discuss the authorizations required and
the operations that must be executed to populate the federation.

4.1 Authorizations for the Population

Creation of global objects can be done by any user explicitly authorized for that.
Authorizations allowing users to create objects in the federation, specified by the
federation administrator, have the following form.

Definition 1 Create authorization. Let f be a federation, a create autho-
rization $a \in A_f$ is a triple of the form $\langle fed\text{-}subject, \text{create}, remote\text{-}id \rangle$, with *fed-
subject* $\in U_f \cup G_f$ and *remote-id* $\in U_{customers(f)}$.

Authorization $\langle fed\text{-}subject, \text{create}, remote\text{-}id \rangle$ states that federation's user
fed-subject (its member in case *fed-subject* is a group), connected to the fed-
eration through some customer site with a login covered by *remote-id*, can cre-
ate objects in the federation. For instance, authorization $\langle \text{Tom}, \text{create}, * \rangle \in A_f$
states that federated user **Tom** can create objects in the federation **f**. Authoriza-
tion $\langle \text{senior-members}, \text{create}, *@\text{site1} \rangle \in A_f$ states that all users members of
group **senior-members** and which are connected to the federation from **site1**
can create objects in federation **f**.

Population of the federation by getting objects from sites participating in it
requires agreement of both the local object's administrator on one side and the
federation administrator on the other side. At the local site any of the object's
administrators must be willing to export their objects to the federation. At
the federation site, the federation administrator must be willing to import the
objects in the federation.

We allow objects to be exported with reference to specific access modes. For
instance, a user can decide to export one of his objects, i.e., allow access to the
federation's users, only for reading and another one of his objects for both reading
and writing. The set of objects stored at site s that can be exported to federation
f, together with the specification of access modes and additional administrative
information is called the export schema of the site for the federation, denoted as
$ES_{s,f}$. In order to export their objects, i.e., to include them in a given export
schema, users must be explicitly authorized for that by the site administrator.
Export authorizations are defined as follows.

Definition 2 Export authorization. Let s and f be a site and a federation respectively with $s \in providers(f)$. An export authorization $a \in A_s$ is a triple of the form $\langle loc\text{-}user, \textbf{export}, f \rangle$ with $loc\text{-}user \in U_s$.

Authorization $\langle loc\text{-}user, \textbf{export}, f \rangle$ states that user $loc\text{-}user$ can export to federation f the objects he administers.

Users can also delegate the site administrator to export their objects, with reference to specific access modes. Reasons for delegation can be various. On one hand, users may not want to worry about federations in which the site participates and about authorizations for users of the federation. On the other hand, the administrator himself may wish to not allow direct export of objects by users thus retaining the control of what the site exports (a kind of centralized administration). Authorizations that allow site administrators to export objects are as follows.

Definition 3 Del_export authorization. Let s be a site. An export delegation authorization $a \in A_s$ is a 4-tuple $\langle \textbf{lsa}, \textbf{del\_export}, loc\text{-}object, modes \rangle$ where **lsa** denotes the site administrator[4], $loc\text{-}object \in O_s$ is the object whose export is delegated, and $modes \subseteq M_{loc\text{-}object}$ is the set of access modes that can be exported.

Authorization $\langle \textbf{lsa}, \textbf{del\_export}, loc\text{-}object, modes \rangle \in A_s$ states that the administrator of site s can export object $loc\text{-}object$ with access modes $modes$ in any federations for which the site is registered as provider.

For instance, authorization $\langle \textbf{lsa}, \textbf{del\_export}, \textbf{myfile}, \{\textbf{read}\} \rangle$ granted by **Tom** at **site1** states that the local administrator of **site1** can make object **myfile** of **Tom** available for reading to all the federations in which the site participates.

4.2 Populating the Federation

In this section we discuss the operations to be executed in order to populate the federation with objects stored at the local sites.

When exporting an object, users must also decide the administrative policy establishing who can specify authorizations to access the object once imported in the federation. Three kinds of policies are supported:

- *site retained* - **SR** - Access authorizations can be specified only by the local administrators of the object;
- *federation controlled* - **FC** - The object is freely available to the federation. Access authorizations defined by the federation administrator establish who can access the object.
- *cooperative* - **C** - Access authorizations are granted by both the local administrator and the federation administrator.

---

[4] We note that, since the administrator is unique, its indication could have been omitted. However, to make the model easily extendable to the case of multiple administrators we prefer to explicitly indicate it.

The export operation, which can be executed by either any of the object's administrators or the site administrator, will be successful if the corresponding necessary authorization is present in A_s. Execution of the export operation for access modes *modes* on object *loc-object* with administrative policy *adm-policy* results in the addition of 4-tuple $\langle loc\text{-}object, modes, adm\text{-}policy, exporter \rangle$ in $ES_{s,f}$, where *exporter* is the user who required the operation. In the following, given an object *loc-object* and a federation f, notation $modes(loc\text{-}object, f)$ denotes the set of access modes exported for *loc-object* to federation f.

In order for an object to be accessible to the federated users, the object must then be imported by the federation administrator. The import operation in a federation can be executed only by the federation administrator. For the operation to be successful, the object must be contained in the export schema of the site for the federation. Upon import, the object is included in the federated schema and can therefore be made available, according to the access modes specified, to the federated users.

When an object is imported in a federation, the specification of the access modes with which it can be accessed and the administrative policy are also registered at the federation. For the purpose of this paper we consider the federated schema as a collection of triples of the form $\langle fed\text{-}object, modes, policy \rangle$ where *modes* is the set of access modes that can be exercised on the object and *policy* is the administrative policy to which *fed-object* is subject. In case of imported objects, *modes* and *policy* are exactly those indicated in the export schema. In case of global objects, *policy* has value **global (G)** and *modes* is equal to all the access modes that can be exercised according to the object type. In case of composite objects, the set of access modes is the set of all the access modes defined by the administrator according to the object type. The administrative policy is the one specified for the component objects, if all the component objects have the same administrative policy. It has value **undefined (U)** otherwise. We assume that composite objects are always defined on objects present in the federated schema. This implies that an object must be imported before being used in the definition of a composite object. In the following, given an imported object o we will denote with $loc(o)$ the corresponding local object.

4.3 Object's Withdrawal and Revocation of Authorizations for the Population

Objects exported by a site can be withdrawn. A user/administrator can withdraw only the objects he has exported. The withdrawal operation of an object from a federation has the effect of removing the object from the corresponding export schema. If the object had been imported in the federation, the withdraw operation will have effect on the federated schema, where it should also be deleted. Different strategies can be used for this, such as immediate propagation, periodic propagation, or propagation at access time. In the first strategy, whenever an object is withdrawn from an export schema a withdraw request is sent to the federation. In the second strategy, export schema changes are periodically sent to the federation. In the third strategy, no propagation of export schema changes is sent by the site to the federation. The fact that an object is not available anymore for the federation will be find out at the time the federation will try to access it. The specific strategy adopted depends on the underlying data model and is outside the scope of this paper.

We notice that the need may arise to temporarily suspend access to an object by users of the federation. If the only possibility of enforcing this were either revoking access authorizations or withdrawing the object, the need of re-specifying the authorizations and/or re-exporting the object would arise. To avoid this destructive effect, we allow users to temporarily isolate their objects from the federation. The *isolate* operation results in a temporarily suspension of accesses to the object through the federation but it does not affect in any way the export schema, the federated schema, or the authorizations specified on the objects.

During the life time of a federation, authorizations for exporting objects may change, i.e., new authorizations be granted and existing authorizations revoked. Revocation introduces the problem of dealing with objects exported thank you to the authorizations being revoked. Two different strategies, one destructive (i.e., with object withdrawal) and one more conservative (i.e., without object withdrawal), can be adopted with respect to this. In the destructive strategy, whenever a user is revoked the export authorization for a federation, all the objects exported by the user into that federation are removed from the export schema. Analogously, if the site administrator is revoked the del-export privilege on an object, the object will be removed from the export schemas in which it was included by the site administrator. In the conservative strategy, upon revocation of a export/del-export authorization, only this authorization is deleted and the export schema remains unchanged.

5 Access Authorizations

In our model we allow the specification of authorizations at both the global level, on the federated objects, and at the local level, on the objects stored at each site.

Authorizations at the global level can be specified only by the federation administrator in case of imported or composite objects. They can be specified by the federation administrator as well as by the creator in case of global objects.

Authorizations on federated objects can be granted to single users as well as to groups. Authorizations can also contain restrictions on the remote user's identity or on the remote site from which the user is connected. Subjects and remote identities can be specified completely by indicating user/group identifier and site, or by using subject patterns. Authorizations at the global level are defined as follows.

Definition 4 Global access authorization. Let f be a federation, an access authorization $a \in A_f$ is a 4-tuple $\langle fed\text{-}subject, mode, fed\text{-}object, remote\text{-}id \rangle$ where: $fed\text{-}subject \in U_f \cup G_f$, $mode \in M_{fed\text{-}object}$, $fed\text{-}object \in O_f$, $remote\text{-}id \in U_{customers(f)}$.

Authorization ⟨*fed-subject,mode,fed-object,remote-id*⟩ states that *fed-subject* (any of its members in case it is a group), connected to the federation through some customer site with a login covered by *remote-id*, can exercise privilege *mode* on *fed-object*. For instance, authorization ⟨Tom,read,object1,*⟩ states that federated user Tom can read object1. Authorization ⟨*,read,object2,*@site1⟩ states that all users connected from site1 can read object2.

At the local level, users can specify access authorizations over the objects they have exported. Subjects of authorizations at the local level are groups defined by the federation. The reason why groups are considered for authorizations at the local level is to avoid requiring each site to know about single users of the federation. Indeed, although it is reasonable to assume some knowledge of each site about global identifiers, it is quite improbable that each site can retain track of identifiers of each single user of the federation. The consideration of groups overcome this burden. Each federation declares a set of groups into which federated users are organized and for which users at local sites can specify authorizations. Changes to groups (i.e., addition or removal of members) will not therefore have any effect on authorizations specified at local sites.

Authorizations at the local level can also put constraints on the specific identity of the user requiring the access. In case of global authentication, the constraints will refer to the remote user's identity at the site from which the user connected to the federation. In case of local authentication, the constraints will refer to local identity of the user as authenticated by the site.

Access authorizations at local level can be positive or negative. Positive authorizations state accesses that must be granted, whereas negative authorizations state accesses that must be denied. Possible conflicts are solved according to the denials take precedence policy. Hence, if both a positive and a negative authorization applies for an access, the access is denied.

Local authorizations are defined as follows.

Definition 5 Local access authorization. Let s be a site in a federation f, an access authorization $a \in A_s$ is a 5-tuple ⟨*fed-group,mode,sign,loc-object,id*⟩ with *fed-group* $\in G_f$, *mode* $\in$ *modes(loc-object,f)*, *sign* $\in \{+,-\}$, *id* $\in U_s \cup U_{customers(f)}$.

Authorization ⟨*fed-group,mode,sign,loc-object,id*⟩ states that all members of *fed-group*, with a login (remote if authentication is global, and local otherwise) covered by *id*, can (cannot if *sign* = −) exercise privilege *mode* on *loc-object*.

For instance, authorization ⟨senior-members@fed3,read,+,object1,*⟩ $\in$ A_s states that group senior-members of federation fed3 can read object1 stored at site s.

Authorization ⟨senior-members@fed3,read,+,object2,*@site2⟩ $\in$ A_s states that the members of group senior-members who connected to federation fed3 from site2 can read object2 stored at site s.

Authorization ⟨*,read,−,object1,bob⟩ $\in A_s$ states that user bob@s cannot read object1 stored at site s.

The reason for considering both positive and negative authorizations at the local level is to give exporters a means of retaining control on accesses allowed on their objects. This characteristic is very important for two main reasons. First, authorizations are specified for groups of users. However, an exporter may wish to grant a whole group an access but at the same time make sure that a specific user will not be able to exercise it. Since user's groups are defined at the federation site, and therefore the exporter has no means of controlling their configuration (for instance by excluding the specific user), the specification of negative authorizations may be the only means to express this requirement. Second, in the case of federation controlled administration, the exporter delegates the federation administrator the task of specifying access authorizations on his object once imported. This means that federated users will not need to have local privileges in order to access the object. However, by specifying negative authorizations, the exporter can restrict the accesses that can be exercised on the object. As a matter of fact no access, even if authorized by the administrator, will be allowed if a negative authorization for it exists at the local level.

Subject patterns, together with positive and negative authorizations can be used to express different protection requirements, as illustrated by the following example.

Example 1. Consider a site s_1 enforcing local authentication and consider a user who exports an object o'_1 to federation f. Suppose the object is exported for the write access mode and under the **site retained** administrative policy. Suppose now that the user wishes to grant the write access to group **student** of the federation. However, he does not want local user **jimmy** to read the object, even in the case where **jimmy** is a member of **student**. This requirement can be expressed by specifying the following two local authorizations: $\langle$**student@f**,**read**,+,o'_1,*$\rangle$ and $\langle$*,**read**,−,o'_1,**jimmy**$\rangle$.

As another example consider a site s_2 enforcing global authentication. Suppose a user exports an object o'_2 to federation f. Suppose the object is exported for the read access mode and under the **federation controlled** policy. Since the policy is federation controlled, in order to access the object, users need to have the authorization for the access at the global level. By contrast, no authorization is necessary at the local level. Suppose now that the exporter wants to make sure that users from site $s1$ will not read the object. He can do so by specifying the following negative authorization: $\langle$*,**read**,−,o'_2,*@$s_1$$\rangle$. □

6 Access Control

Users connected to the federation can submit requests to access federated objects. In order to determine whether to grant or deny the access, authorizations specified at the federation as well as at the local sites involved in the access must be controlled. Specific controls and additional authentication processes required depend on: the type of object (global versus imported or composite), the kind of administrative policy of the component object(s), and the authentication policy required by each site involved. Each request on an imported or composite object is translated into a request, or a set of requests, on the corresponding

/* Input: Request (u, m, o, rid) of federated user u, remotely connected as rid, to exercise access mode m on federated object o */

At the federation site f
1. Determine the groups G_u to which the user belongs.
2. /* Access control at global level*/
   If $adm\text{-}policy(o) = \mathbf{G}$
   then if $\exists a \in A_f$ such that $a \triangleright \langle u, m, o, rid \rangle$ or $a \triangleright \langle G_u, m, o, rid \rangle$
         then *grant access*
         else *deny access*
   else if $adm\text{-}policy(o) \neq \mathbf{SR}$
         then if $\not\exists a \in A_f, a \triangleright \langle u, m, o, rid \rangle$ or $a \triangleright \langle G_u, m, o, rid \rangle$
              then *deny access*
3. /* Split into requests on component objects */
   Decompose access (m, o) into a set of accesses $S = \{(m_1, o_1), \ldots, (m_n, o_n)\}$.
4. /* Check locally all accesses for which component object is global */
   If there exists $(m_i, o_i) \in S$ such that $adm\text{-}policy(o_i) = \mathbf{G}$ and $\not\exists a \in A_f$,
   $a \triangleright \langle u, m, o, rid \rangle$ or $a \triangleright \langle G_u, m, o, rid \rangle$
     then *deny access*
     else if there do not exists $(m_i, o_i) \in S$ such that $adm\text{-}policy(o_i) \neq \mathbf{G}$
         then *grant access*
5. /* Send requests on imported objects to local */
   For each pair $(m_i, o_i) \in S$ such that $adm\text{-}policy(o_i) \neq \mathbf{G}$ do
       $o_i' = loc(o_i)$
       send request $r_i = (G_u, m_i, o_i', rid)$ to the site $site(o_i')$ from which o_i' was imported
6. /* Collect replies from site and return response to the user */
   Collect replies from all sites
   If the reply has value true for all requests r_i then *grant access* else *deny access*

At each local site $s = site(o_i')$
/* upon reception of request $r_i = (G_u, m_i, o_i', rid)$ from federation f */

1. if $\exists \langle o_i', modes, policy \rangle \in E_{s,f}$ with $m_i \in modes$
   then $adm\text{-}policy := policy$
   else $reply :=$ **false**, go to step 4
2. if authentication is global
   then $id = rid$
   else Authenticate user. Assign id the local user identity.
3. case $adm\text{-}policy$ of
       SR or **C**: if $\exists a \in A_s, a \triangleright \langle G_u, m_i, +, o_i', id \rangle$ and $\not\exists a \in A_s, a \triangleright \langle G_u, m_i, -, o_i', id \rangle$
                then $reply :=$ **true**
                else $reply :=$ **false**
       FC: if $\not\exists a \in A_s, a \triangleright \langle G_u, m_i, -, o_i', id \rangle$
                then $reply :=$ **true**
                else $reply :=$ **false**
4. Send $reply$ to f

Fig. 2. Access control algorithm

local object(s). Each of these requests must be communicated to the appropriate site for both access control, since local authorizations must be verified to determine whether access must be allowed or denied, and data retrieval, since the data stored at the different sites are not replicated at the federation. The mapping of access operations on federated objects onto access operations on the corresponding local objects is enforced by the data management system of the federation. It is outside of the scope of this paper to discuss this mapping. We therefore assume that each operation to access a federated object o with access mode m is mapped by the data management system onto a set of operations $\langle m_1, o_1 \rangle, \ldots, \langle m_k, o_k \rangle$, where $o_1, \ldots, o_k$ are local objects corresponding to o and $m_1, \ldots, m_k$ are the access modes to be exercised on these objects.

In the following, we say that a global authorization $a = \langle fed\text{-}subject, mode, fed\text{-}object, remote\text{-}id \rangle$ covers a tuple $t = \langle u, m, o, id \rangle$, written $a \triangleright t$ iff: $fed\text{-}subject \triangleright u$, $mode = m$, $fed\text{-}object = o$, and $remote\text{-}id \triangleright id$. The cover relationship for local authorizations requires in addition, the sign in the authorization and in the tuple to be the same.

Figure 2 illustrates the different controls to be executed at the federation site and at each local site involved. In the figure, given a group G_r, we use notation $\langle G_r, m, o, rid \rangle$ as an abbreviation for the set $\{\langle g_i, m, o, rid \rangle \mid g_i \in G_r\}$. Moreover we use $a \triangleright \langle G_r, m, o, rid \rangle$ as an abbreviation for $a \triangleright \langle g_1, m, o, rid \rangle \lor a \triangleright \langle g_2, m, o, rid \rangle \lor \ldots \lor a \triangleright \langle g_k, m, o, rid \rangle$. Let f be a federation and u be a federated user connected to the federation with some remote login rid. Consider the request submitted to the federation by this user to exercise access mode m on object o. In step 1, the set of groups G_u to which the user belongs are determined. In step 2, access control on global authorizations is enforced.

If the object is global (administrative policy **G**) this is the only control that must be executed. Then, access is granted or authorized according to whether an authorization covering the request exists or not. Otherwise, the controls to be executed depend on the administrative policy to which the object is subject. In particular, if the administrative policy is site retained, no authorization is needed for the access at the global level and therefore no authorization check is performed. In any other case (i.e., administrative policy equal to **FC**, **C**, or **U**), the system looks for an authorization covering the request. If no such authorization exists the access is denied, otherwise the process continues. Hence, the access on the federated object is split into the corresponding accesses on component objects. (Note that access splitting is meaningful only for accesses on composite objects, it has not effect otherwise). As a result a set of accesses to be controlled is obtained. If any of these accesses is on a global object and no authorization exists for it, the request is denied. Then, if no access to local objects is required the request is granted. Otherwise, the algorithm proceeds by sending, for each access on an imported object, a request to the corresponding site for the set of subjects G_u with remote identity rid. The access is granted if all local sites accept the request, it is denied otherwise.

Access control at each local site s works as follows. Upon reception of a request by a federation, the export schema of the site for the federation is con-

Constraints on authorizations	Administrative policy			
	Site retained	Federation Controlled	Cooperative	Global
At federation f (in A_f)		$\exists a: a \triangleright (u,m,o,rid)$ or $a \triangleright (G_u,m,o,rid)$	$\exists a: a \triangleright (u,m,o,rid)$ or $a \triangleright (G_u,m,o,rid)$	$\exists a: a \triangleright (u,m,o,rid)$ or $a \triangleright (G_u,m,o,rid)$
At site s of o (in A_s) global auth.	$\exists a: a \triangleright (G_u,m,+,o',rid)$ / $\nexists a: a \triangleright (G_u,m,-,o',rid)$	$\nexists a: a \triangleright (G_u,m,-,o',rid)$	$\exists a: a \triangleright (G_u,m,+,o',rid)$ / $\nexists a: a \triangleright (G_u,m,-,o',rid)$	
local auth.	$\exists a: a \triangleright (G_u,m,+,o',lid)$ / $\nexists a: a \triangleright (G_u,m,-,o',lid)$	$\nexists a: a \triangleright (G_u,m,-,o',lid)$	$\exists a: a \triangleright (G_u,m,+,o',lid)$ / $\nexists a: a \triangleright (G_u,m,-,o',lid)$	

Legenda: $o' = loc(o)$

rid remote identity of user u

lid identity of user u at site s

Table 1. Conditions necessary to grant request by user u of groups G_u with remote location rid to exercise mode m on federated object o

trolled. If there is no triple in the export schema for the object with access modes including the one required, a false reply is immediately returned to the federation. Otherwise the control proceeds. The identity to be considered in the access control depends on the authentication policy established for the site. If the authentication is global, the remote identity of the user as communicated by the federation is considered. If the authentication is local, the user will be asked to identify himself. This local identity, once authenticated, will be used in place of the remote identifier in the access control. Hence the local authorizations are checked. In case of **site-retained** or **cooperative** administrative policy a **true** is returned only if there exists a positive authorization and there does not exist any negative authorizations for the access. In case of **federation controlled** administrative policy a **true** is returned if no negative authorization exists for denying the access.

Table 1 summarizes the authorizations necessary at global and local level in order for a request on a global or imported object to be granted. In case of composite objects, at the local level the conditions must be satisfied, at the corresponding site, with reference to each access (m_i, o_i) in which the global operation is decomposed.

Example 2. Let s_1, s_2, s_3 be three sites in a federation **f**. Let the export schema and authorizations at sites s_1 and s_2 be as follows.

$$ES_{s_1,f} = \{\langle o'_1, \{read,write\}, SR, u_1 \rangle\}; \quad A_{s_1} = \{\langle student@f, read, +, o'_1, * \rangle,$$
$$\langle *, read, -, o'_1, jimmy \rangle\}$$
$$ES_{s_2,f} = \langle o'_2, \{read\}, FC, lsa \rangle; \quad A_{s_2} = \{\langle *, read, -, o'_2, *@s_1 \rangle\}$$

Suppose objects o'_1 and o'_2 have been imported in the federation as o_1 and o_2, respectively. Let the federated schema and the authorizations at the federation be as follows:

$$FS_f = \{\langle o_1, \{read,write\}, SR \rangle, \langle o_2, \{read\}, FC \rangle\}; \quad A_f = \{\langle jeremy, read, o_2, * \rangle\},$$

where **jeremy** is a user belonging to groups **student** and **us-citizens**.

Consider now user `jim@s₃`, connected to the federation as `jeremy`, that submits a request to `read o₁`. Since the administrative policy of o_1 is site retained no control is executed at the federation and the request for the set of groups {`student`, `us-citizens`} (the groups to which `jeremy` belongs) to read o_1' is sent to site s_1. Since s_1 enforces local authentication, `jeremy` will need to identify himself. Let `jimmy` be his identity at s_1. Access control for request ⟨{`student`, `us-citizens`}`@f`,`read`,o_1',`jimmy`⟩ returns false due to the negative authorization stored at s_1 and therefore the access will be denied.

Consider now a request by the same user to read o_2. Access control at the federation level is successful thank you to the authorization for `jeremy`. Since the administrative policy is federation controlled no authorization is needed at local level, however, local control must be executed to make sure that no negative authorizations exist for the access. Hence, a request for the set of groups {`student`, `us-citizens`} with remote login `jim@s₃` to access o_2 is sent to site s_2. Since site s_2 enforces global authentication, no further authentication is necessary. Since no negative authorization denying the access exists (the only negative authorization applies only to user remotely connected from s_1) the reply of site s_2 is positive and the access will be granted. □

7 Conclusions and Future Research

We have presented an authorization model for the protection of information in a tightly coupled federated system. The model allows users to decide which of their objects to share with the federation and how to share them. In particular they can specify the specific access modes allowed by federated users and the administrative policy establishing how authorizations on objects are to be specified. Inclusion of objects in the federated schema is a two step-process requiring agreement of both the administrator of the object at one side and the administrator of the federation at the other. Authorizations can be specified both at the global level, on federated objects, and at the local level on local objects exported to the federation. An algorithm describing the controls to be executed at the federation and at each local site to determine whether to grant or deny access to federated data has also been presented. The model results flexible and able to support different kinds of protection requirements users may have.

Our paper leaves space for further work. A first issue we plan to investigate is the relationship between global and local authorizations. In the paper we have assumed that global and local authorizations are specified independently. The approach could be extended to the consideration of different strategies for the specification of authorizations. A first possible strategy is that upon specification of a global authorization, the local authorizations needed for the access globally granted to be allowed are derived and inserted at the local sites. Another strategy could be that of deriving global authorizations on federated objects from the authorizations specified locally. A further issue to be investigated concerns the communication of identities or group memberships between the federation and the sites. In this paper we have assumed that local access control on requests by a federated user is always carried out with reference to the groups to which the user belongs, and that the federation communicates these groups to the local sites. Alternative approaches can be considered such as the use of a call back mechanism, where a site explicitly asks whether a user belongs to a group, or the use of credentials [6]. Moreover, our model could be made more precise by considering at the global level specific data model. In this case, all the issues related to the translation of the export schemas into this data model should be taken into consideration. Finally, a further issue that can be investigated concerns the consideration of component sites with heterogeneous data models or heterogeneous security policies, and of different cooperation rules that can be established among sites to regulate access to the shared data.

References

1. M. Abadi, M. Burrow, B. Lampson, and G. Plotkin. A Calculus for Access Control in Distributed Systems. Technical Report 70, DEC, System Research Center, Palo Alto, February 1991.
2. Barbara T. Blaustein, Catherine D. McCollum, Amon Rosenthal, and Kenneth P. Smith. Autonomy and Confidentiality: Secure Federated Data Management. In *Proceeding of the 2nd International Workshop on Next generation Information Technologies and Systems*, Naharia, Israel, June 1995.
3. S. Castano, M.G. Fugini, G. Martella, and P. Samarati. *Database Security*. Addison-Wesley, 1995.
4. M. L. Goyal and G. V. Singh. Access Control in Distributed Heterogeneous Database Management Systems. *Computers & Security*, 10:661–669, 1991.
5. D. Heimbigner and D. McLeod. A Federated Architecture for Information Management. *ACM Transactions on Office Information Systems*, 3(3):253–278, 1985.
6. V. E. Jones, N. Ching, and M. Winslett. Credentials for Privacy and Interoperation. In *Proc. New Security Paradigms Workshop*, pages 93–100, La Jolla, California, U.S.A, August 1995.
7. Dirk Jonscher and Klaus R. Dittrich. Access Control for Database Federations a discussion of the state-of-the-art. In *Proceeding DBTA Workshop on Interoperability of DBSs and DB Applications*, October 1993.
8. Dirk Jonscher and Klaus R. Dittrich. An Approach for Building Secure Database Federations. In *Proceedings of the 20th VLDB Conference, Santiago, Chile*, 1994.
9. Dirk Jonscher and Klaus R. Dittrich. Argos — A Configurable Access Control Subsystem Which Can Propagate Access Rights. In *Proc. 9th IFIP Working Conference on Database Security*, Rensselaerville, New York, U.S.A, August 1995.
10. Wom Kim, Nat Ballou, Jorge F. Garza, and Darrel Woelk. A Distributed Object-Oriented Database System Supporting Shared and Private Databases. *ACM Transactions on Office Information Systems*, 9(1):31–51, January 1991.
11. Witold Litwin, Leo Mark, and Nick Roussopoulos. Interoperability of Multiple Autonomous Databases. *ACM Computing Surveys*, 22(3):267–293, 1990.
12. J. McHugh and B. Thuraisingham. Multilevel Security Issues in Distributed Database Management Systems. *Computers & Security*, 7:387–396, 1988.
13. B. Clifford Neuman and Theodore Ts'o. Kerberos: An Authentication Service for Computer Networks. *IEEE Communications Magazine*, 32(9):33–38, 1994.

14. Martin S. Olivier. A Multilevel Secure Federated Database. In *Proc. 9th IFIP Working Conference on Database Security, Rensselaerville,* pages 23–38, New York, U.S.A, August 1995.

15. R.S. Sandhu and P. Samarati. Access Control: Principles and Practice. *IEEE Communications,* pages 2–10, September 1994.

16. M. Satyanarayanan. Integrating Security in a Large Distributed System. *ACM Transactions on Computer Systems,* 7(3):247–280, August 1989.

17. Amit P. Sheth and James A. Larson. Federated Database Systems for Managing Distributed, Heterogeneous, and Autonomous Databases. *ACM Computing Surveys,* 22(3):183–236, 1990.

18. M. Templeton, E. Lund, and P. Ward. Pragmatics of Access Control in Mermaid. In *IEEE-CS TC Data Engineering,* pages 33–38, September 1987.

19. Gomer Thomas, Glenn R. Thompson, Chin-Wan Chung, Edward Barkmeyer, Fred Carter, Marjorie Templeton, Stephen Fox, and Berl Hartman. Heterogeneous Distributed Database Systems for Production Use. *ACM Computing Surveys,* 22(3):237–266, 1990.

20. B. Thuraisingham. Multilevel Security Issues in Distributed Database Management Systems II. *Computers & Security,* 10:727–747, 1991.

21. B. Thuraisingham and Harvey H. Rubinovitz. Multilevel Security Issues in Distributed Database Management Systems III. *Computers & Security,* 11:661–674, 1992.

22. Ching-Yi Wang and David L. Spooner. Access Control in a Heterogeneous Distributed Database Management System. In *IEEE 6th Symp. on Reliability in Distributed Software and Database Systems, Williamsburg,* pages 84–92, 1987.

23. Edward Wobber, Martin Abadi, Michael Burrows, and Butler Lampson. Authentication in the Taos Operating System. *ACM Transactions on Computer Systems,* 12(1):3–32, 1994.

Security for Mobile Agents: Authentication and State Appraisal *

William M. Farmer, Joshua D. Guttman, and Vipin Swarup

The MITRE Corporation
202 Burlington Road
Bedford, MA 01730-1420
{farmer, guttman, swarup}@mitre.org

Abstract. Mobile agents are processes which can autonomously migrate to new hosts. Despite its many practical benefits, mobile agent technology results in significant new security threats from malicious agents and hosts. The primary added complication is that, as an agent traverses multiple hosts that are trusted to different degrees, its state can change in ways that adversely impact its functionality. In this paper, we discuss achievable security goals for mobile agents, and we propose an architecture to achieve these goals. The architecture models the trust relations between the principals of mobile agent systems. A unique aspect of the architecture is a "state appraisal" mechanism that protects users and hosts from attacks via state modifications and that provides users with flexible control over the authority of their agents.

1 Introduction

Currently, distributed systems employ models in which processes are statically attached to hosts and communicate by asynchronous messages or synchronous remote procedure calls. Mobile agent technology extends this model by including mobile processes, i.e., processes which can autonomously migrate to new hosts. Numerous benefits are expected; they include dynamic customization both at servers and at clients, as well as robust remote interaction over unreliable networks and intermittent connections [5, 11, 17].

Despite its many practical benefits, mobile agent technology results in significant new security threats from malicious agents and hosts. In fact, security issues are recognized as critical to the acceptability of distributed systems based on mobile agents. The primary added complication is that, as an agent traverses multiple machines that are trusted to different degrees, its state can change in ways that adversely impact its functionality. In this paper, we will discuss achievable security goals for mobile agents, and we will propose an architecture to achieve these goals. We use existing theory—the distributed authentication theory of Lampson et al. [10]—to clarify the architecture and to show that it meets its objectives.

---

* Work supported by the MITRE-Sponsored Research Program.

The process of deducing which principal made a request is called *authentication*. In a distributed system, authentication is complicated by the fact that a request may originate on a distant host and may traverse multiple machines and network channels that are secured in different ways and are not equally trusted [10]. The process of deciding whether or not to grant a request—once its principal has been authenticated—is called *authorization*. The authentication mechanism underlies the authorization mechanism in the sense that authorization can only perform its function based on the information provided by authentication, while conversely authentication requires no information from the authorization mechanism.

State Appraisal The unique aspect of our architecture is a "state appraisal" mechanism. State appraisal lies above the lower authentication layer, and provides input to an authorization mechanism like those of static distributed systems. When an agent arrives at a new site of execution, it must decide what privileges it will need at that site. A state appraisal function computes a set of privileges to request as a function of the state of the agent when it arrives at the new execution site. After state appraisal has determined which permissions to request, the authorization mechanism on the new execution site may then determine which of the requested permissions it is willing to grant.

The state appraisal mechanism serves several purposes:

1. It can protect a host from attacks, when these attacks alter the states of agents in dangerous but detectable ways;
2. It can protect an agent's author and sender (the user who dispatched this agent) from misuse of the agent in their name via dangerous but detectable state modification;
3. It can check whether an agent's state meets important state invariants;
4. It enables an agent's privilege at a new host to be dependent on the agent's current state, and therefore on the task to be carried at that host.

Not all state alteration can be detected, because agents travel to new hosts to acquire information that is not available elsewhere. Some deceptive alterations of the agent's state will be indistinguishable from the normal result of different (but possible) information on the remote host. However, alterations that would cause the agent to become harmful—either to sites it visits later or else to the user who dispatched it—can frequently be detected.

Our work contrasts with other work on mobile agent security [12, 13, 14, 16, 17] because it focuses on the state information that agents carry with them. We also explain the relationship between state appraisal, authentication, and authorization. We emphasize agents written by known software developers, which we think will be the predominant way of using software agents; most other work looks at security for agents written by unknown parties.

We avoid making assumptions about the environment offered by different sites of execution. In particular, we do not assume that the agents can count on protection from the operating system at those sites. We believe that many of the most useful applications for mobile agents will be in heterogeneous environments. Different sites will use different operating systems, none of them likely to provide a very high level of protection. Moreover, in these heterogeneous environments, some sites will be in hostile or at least competitive relations with each other. Thus, they cannot be expected to leave their operating systems unmodified, if modifying the systems—for instance to defeat security mechanisms—would further their competitive goals.

Mobile Agents and Languages A mobile agent is a program that can migrate from one networked computer to another while executing. This contrasts with the client/server model where non-executable messages traverse the network, but the executable code remains permanently on the computer on which it was installed. Mobile agents have numerous potential benefits. For instance, in a specialized search of a large free-text database, it may be more efficient to move the program to the database server rather than to move large amounts of data back to the client's host.

In recent years, several programming languages for mobile agents have been designed. These languages make different design choices as to which components of a program's state can migrate from machine to machine. In Java [11], only program code can migrate; no state is carried with the programs. In Obliq [1], first-class function values (closures) can migrate; closures consist of program code together with an environment that binds variables to values or memory locations [16]. In Kali Scheme [2], again, closures can migrate; however, since continuations [8, 6] are first-class values, Kali Scheme permits entire processes to migrate autonomously to new hosts. In Telescript [17], functions are not first-class values; however, Telescript provides special operations that permit processes to migrate autonomously.

In this paper, we adopt a fairly simple but general model of mobile agents. *Agent interpreters* run on individual networked computers and communicate among themselves using host-to-host communication services. An *agent* consists of code together with execution state. The state may include a program counter, registers, environment, recursion stack, and store; the agent executes by being interpreted by an agent interpreter.

Agents communicate among themselves by message passing. In addition, agents can invoke a special asynchronous "remote apply" operation that applies a closure to arguments on a specified remote interpreter. Remote procedure calls can be implemented with this primitive operation and message passing. Agent migration and cloning can also be implemented with this primitive operation, using first-class continuation values.

Example: Travel Agents, Mobile Agents to Plan Travel We turn now to an example mobile agent system. We believe that it is typical of many—though not of all—ways that mobile agents will be used. We will use the example to extract the most important principles that a security architecture for mobile agents should obey.

Consider a mobile agent that visits sites run by airlines, hotel chains, and rental car companies searching for a travel plan that meets a customer's requirements. We focus on four kinds of hosts: the personal communication systems of the end customers, the hosts run by travel agencies in the traditional sense of organizations that broker travel arrangements, and the hosts run by the competing airlines, hotel chains, and car rental firms. Let us refer to the airlines as Airline 1 and Airline 2, which we assume for the sake of this example do not share a common reservation system.

The mobile agent is programmed by the travel agency. A customer dispatches the agent to the Airline 1 server where the agent queries the flight database. With the results stored in its environment, the agent then migrates to the Airline 2 server where again it queries the flight database. From either of these hosts, it may visit a hotel host, where it may be eligible for a special deal depending on whether the customer will be traveling on an allied air carrier. The agent compares flight and fare information, decides on a travel plan, migrates to the appropriate airline and hotel hosts, and reserves the desired flights and rooms. Finally, the agent returns to the customer with the results.

The customer can expect that the individual airlines and hotels will provide true information on flight schedules and fares in an attempt to win her business, just as we assume nowadays that the reservation information the airlines provide over the telephone is accurate, although it is not always complete.

However, the airline servers are in a competitive relation with each other. The airline servers illustrate a crucial principle: *For many of the most natural and important applications of mobile agents, we cannot expect all the participants to trust one another.*

There are a number of attacks they may attempt. For instance, the second airline server may be able to corrupt the flight schedule information of the first airline, as stored in the environment of the agent. It could surreptitiously raise its competitor's fares, or it could advance the agent's program counter into the preferred branch of conditional code. Thus, the mobile agent cannot decide its flight plan on an airline host since the host has the ability to manipulate the decision. Instead, the agent would have to migrate to a neutral host such as the customer's host or a travel agency host, make its flight plan decision on that host, and then migrate to the selected airline to complete the transaction. This attack illustrates a principle: *An agent's critical decisions should be made on neutral hosts, which is to say hosts trusted by its sender.*

A second kind of attack is also possible: the first airline may hoodwink the second airline, for instance when the second airline has a cheaper fare available. The first airline's server surreptitiously increases the number of reservations to be requested, say from two seats to 100. The agent will then proceed to reserve 100 seats at the second airline's cheap fare. Later, legitimate customers will have to book their tickets on the first airline, as the second believes that its flight is full. This attack suggests a third principle: *a migrating agent can become malicious by virtue of its state being corrupted.*

Moreover, it may not be sufficient to seal certain state components cryptographically, such as the number of seats to be requested, which in our example was two. Rather, we would like to be able to ensure that a state invariant is preserved: in this case, that the sum of the number of seats already booked and those still to be requested should remain constantly the value two. Otherwise, the first airline may be able to send the same agent to the second airline repeatedly, booking two more unnecessary seats on each visit.

On the other hand, some organizations may trust each other, as for instance in the case where they are divisions of the same corporation. An agent arriving from a trusted partner may be subjected to less security examination (to reduce overhead), or it may be accorded special privileges. *Authentication and authorization may be handled specially between hosts with reciprocal trust.*

2 Security Goals

There are some basic constraints on what security goals are achievable. We assume that different parties will have different degrees of trust for each other, and in fact some parties may be in a competitive or even hostile relation to one another. As a consequence, we may infer that one party cannot be certain that another party is running an untampered interpreter. An agent that reaches that party may not be allowed to run correctly, or it may be discarded. The interpreter may forge messages purporting to be from the agent. Moreover, the interpreter may inspect the state of the agent to ferret out its secrets. For this reason, we assume that agents do not carry keys. In particular, we claim that agents *cannot* carry keys in a form that can be used on untrusted interpreters.

Existing approaches for distributed security [9] do allow us to achieve several basic goals. These include authenticating an agent's author and its sender, checking the integrity of its code, and offering it privacy during transmission, at least between interpreters willing to engage in symmetric encryption. We have discussed these points in more detail in [4].

However, at least three crucial security goals remain:

1. Certification that an interpreter has the authority to execute an agent on behalf of its sender;
2. Flexible selection of privileges, so that an agent arriving at an interpreter may be given the privileges necessary to carry out the task for which it has come to the interpreter; and
3. State appraisal, to ensure that an agent has not become malicious as a consequence of alterations to its state.

3 Authentication

Authentication is the process of deducing which principal has made a specific request. In a distributed system, authentication is complicated by the fact that a request may originate on a distant host and may traverse multiple machines and network channels that are secured in different ways and are not equally trusted. For this reason, Lampson and his colleagues [10] developed a logic of authentication that can be used to derive one or more principals who are responsible for a request.

Elements of a Theory of Authentication The theory—which is too rich to summarize here—involves three primary ingredients. The first is the notion of *principal*. Atomic principals include persons, machines, and roles; groups of principals may also be introduced as principals; and in addition principals may also be constructed from simpler principals by operators. The resulting compound principals have distinctive trust relations with their component principals. Second, principals make *statements*, which include assertions, requests, and performatives.[1] Third, principals may stand in the *"speaks for"* relation; one principal P_1 speaks for a second principal P_2 if, when P_1 **says** s, it follows that P_2 **says** s. This does not mean that P_1 is prevented from uttering phrases not already uttered by P_2; on the contrary, it means that if P_1 makes a statement, P_2 will be committed to it also. For instance, granting a power of attorney creates this sort of relation (usually for a clearly delimited class of statements) in current legal practice. When P_1 speaks for P_2, we write $P_1 \Rightarrow P_2$. One of the axioms of the theory allows one principal to pass the authority to speak for him to a second principal, simply by saying that it is so:

$$(P_1 \text{ says } P_2 \Rightarrow P_1) \supset P_2 \Rightarrow P_1$$

This is called the *hand-off* axiom; it says that a principal can hand his authority off to a second principal. It requires a high degree of trust.

Three operators will be needed for building compound principals, namely the **as, for**, and quoting operators. If P_1 and P_2 are principals, then P_1 **as** P_2 is a compound principal whose authority is more limited than that of P_1. P_2 is in effect a *role* that P_1 adopts. In our case, the programs (or rather, their names or digests) will be regarded as roles. Quoting, written $P \mid Q$ is defined straightforwardly: $(P \mid Q)$ **says** s abbreviates P **says** Q **says** s.

The **for** operator expresses *delegation*. P_1 **for** P_2 expresses that P_1 is acting on behalf of P_2. In this case P_2 must delegate some authority to P_1; however, P_1 may also draw on his own authority. For instance, to take a traditional example, if a database management system makes a request on behalf of some user, the request may be granted based on two ingredients, namely the user's identity supplemented by the knowledge that the database system is enforcing some constraints on the request. Because P_1 is combining his authority with

---

[1] A statement is a *performative* if the speaker performs an action by means of uttering it, at least in the right circumstances. The words "I do" in the marriage ceremony are a familiar example of a performative. Similarly, "I hereby authorize my attorneys, Dewey, Cheatham and Howe, jointly or severally, to execute bills of sale on my behalf." Semantically it is important that requests and performatives should have truth values, although it is not particularly important how those truth values are assigned.

P_2's, to authenticate a statement as coming from P_1 for P_2, we need evidence that P_1 has consented to this arrangement, as well as P_2.

Mobile agents require no additions to the theory presented in [10]; the theory as it exists is an adequate tool for characterizing the different sorts of trust relations that mobile agents may require.

Atomic Principals for Mobile Agents Five categories of basic principals are relevant:

- The *authors* (whether people or organizations) that write programs to execute as agents;
- The *programs* they create, which, together with supplemental information, are signed by the author;
- The *senders* (whether people or other entities) that send agents to act on their behalf. A sender may need a trusted device to sign and transmit agents;
- The *agents* themselves, consisting of a program together with data added by the sender on whose behalf it executes, signed by the sender;
- The *interpreters* that execute agents; they may transfer the agents among themselves, and may eventually return results to the sender.

Naturally, an implementation will also require one or more certification authorities, but their role is perfectly standard and we will not discuss them further.

The Natural History of an Agent There are three crucial types of events in the life history of an agent. They are the creation of the underlying program; the creation of the agent; and migration of the agent from one execution site to another. These events introduce compound principals built from the atomic principals just given.

Program Creation. The author of a program prepares source code and a state appraisal function **max** for the program. The function **max** will calculate the maximum safe permissions to be accorded an agent running the program, as a function of its current state.

In addition, an access control list (or other mechanism) may also be included for determining which users are permitted to send the resulting agent.

After compiling the source code for the program and its state appraisal function, the author C then compiles these pieces, constructs a message digest D for the result, and signs that with her private key. By doing so, she permits the program to make statements on her behalf, in her role as author of this program. That is, D, when attributing a statement to C, may speak for the compound principal C **as** D (formally, $D \,|\, C \Rightarrow C$ **as** D).[2]

---

[2] Since we regard D as a *name* of the program of which it is a digest, we regard actions performed by the program while executing as utterances of D.

Agent Creation. To prepare a program for sending, the sender attaches a second state appraisal function, called the request function; this will calculate the permissions the sender wants an agent running the program to have, as a function of its current state. We will call the sender's state appraisal function **req**. For some states Σ, $\mathbf{req}(\Sigma)$ may be a proper subset of $\mathbf{max}(\Sigma)$; for instance, the sender may not be certain how D will behave, and she may want to ensure she is not liable for some actions.

The sender may also include an interpreter access control list (or other mechanism) specifying interpreters that are allowed to run the resulting agent on the sender's behalf, either via delegation or hand-off.

The sender S attaches her name, and then she computes a message digest A for the following items: the program, its digest D, the function **req**, S's name, and a counter S increments for each agent she sends. She signs the message digest A with her private key.

This signature says that the resulting agent A may make statements for the compound principal A **for** S. This is a delegation, which requires some sort of acceptance by A. This acceptance amounts to permission for S to use A. The acceptance may then be attested by the access control list, mentioned above as a component of D, for determining the users authorized to send agents built from D. Alternatively, if C wants D to be usable by the general public, this acceptance may be vacuous. As a consequence of the delegation, A, when attributing a statement to S, may speak for the compound principal A **for** S (formally, $A\,|\,S \Rightarrow A$ **for** S).

In addition, A can speak for D: Statements made by an agent A are statements made by its program, and D is the digest of that program.

Before the sender dispatches A, she also attaches a list of parameters, which are in effect the initial state Σ_0 for the agent. The state is not included under any cryptographic seal, because it must change as the agent carries out its computation. However, S's request function may impose invariants on the state.

Agent Migration. When an agent is ready to migrate from one interpreter to the next, the current interpreter must construct a message containing the agent A, its current state Σ, the current interpreter I_1, the principal P_1 on behalf of whom I_1 is executing the agent, and a description of the principal P_2 on behalf of whom the next interpreter I_2 should execute the agent starting from Σ.

The authentication machinery can be construed as providing a proof that $I_2\,|\,P_2 \Rightarrow P_2$. Depending on whether I_2 is trusted by I_1 or by the agent A, four different values of P_2 are possible, expressing different trust relationships.

1. I_1 can hand the agent off to I_2; I_2 will then execute the agent on behalf of P_1. In this case, $I_1\,|\,P_1$ **says** $I_2\,|\,P_1 \Rightarrow P_1$. P_2 is P_1.
2. I_1 can delegate the agent to I_2. I_2 will combine its authority with that of P_1 while executing the agent. P_2 is I_2 **for** P_1.
3. The agent can directly hand itself off to I_2. I_2 will execute A on behalf of the agent. In this case, $A\,|\,S$ **says** $I_2\,|\,(A$ **for** $S) \Rightarrow (A$ **for** $S)$. This statement may be contained in an interpreter access control list the sender has attached to the agent. P_2 is A **for** S.

4. The agent can delegate itself to I_2. I_2 will then combine its authority with that of the agent while executing A. The delegation statement may be contained in an interpreter access control list the sender has attached to the agent. In this case, P_2 is I_2 for A for S.

In the first case, I_2 does not appear in the resulting compound principal. This requires I_1 to trust I_2 not to do anything I_1 would not be willing to do. In the third and fourth cases, because the agent itself is explicitly expressing trust in I_2, the resulting compound principal does not involve I_1. The agent trusts I_2 to appraise the state before execution. Assuming that the result of the appraisal is accepted, I_1 has discharged its responsibility.

In all four cases, if P_1 is of the form Q for $...(A$ for $S)$, where the initial chain of delegations Q for $...$ may be vacuous, then P_2 is also of the same form. Since agent creation—which serves as a base case—yields the principal A for S, by induction the relevant principal is always of the form shown.[3]

What happens when an interpreter I_2 receives a message requesting that it execute an agent? The message contains an agent $(A$ for $S)$, together with its current state Σ and the name of a principal P_2 on behalf of whom I_2 will execute it. I_2 must evaluate the certificates contained in the message to authenticate P_2. This may require it to fetch certificates from a directory service for principals it does not recognize. It will also check the author's signature on the program and the sender's signature on the agent. However, the mechanisms needed for this purpose are well-understood [10]; indeed, they provide a proof that $I_2 \mid P_2 \Rightarrow P_2$. We have now met the first of the security goals proposed in Section 2, namely certification that an interpreter has the authority to execute an agent, ultimately on behalf of its sender.

Trust Relationships for Travel Agents We now return to our travel agents example (Section 1) and describe how the various trust relationships of that example can be expressed in our security architecture.

In the example, a travel agency creates a travel reservation program and a state appraisal function while a customer adds a permit request function. The customer also provides certificates to hand off or delegate authority to interpreters. For instance, the customer's certificates may hand off authority to her own interpreter and to a neutral travel agency interpreter (since she trusts them), but her certificates may only delegate authority to Airline 1 and Airline 2 (since they have vested interests). The customer sends the agent to her interpreter, with an initial state containing her desired travel plans.

As its first task, the agent migrates to the Airline 1 host I_1. The agent contains a certificate that directly delegates to Airline 1 the authority to speak on its behalf. Airline 1 accepts this delegation and runs the agent as I_1 for A for S. In our architecture, this kind of trust relationship is an example of the *agent delegating its authority* to Airline 1 (case 4). This ensures that Airline 1 takes

---

[3] Indeed, we may regard agent creation as an instance of case 3, where the new interpreter I_2 is the sender's local host.

responsibility while speaking for the agent, for instance, while making airline reservations on the agent's behalf.

The agent now seeks to gather hotel reservation information. Airline 1 owns a hotel chain and has strong trust in its hotels such as Hotel 1. It sends the agent to the Hotel 1 host I_2 and gives Hotel 1 whatever authority it has over the agent. Hotel 1 runs the agent as I_1 **for** A **for** S, which is the principal that I_1 hands it. This kind of trust relationship is an example of Airline 1's *interpreter handing off its authority* to Hotel 1 (case 1). As a consequence of this trust, I_2 may grant the agent access to a database of preferred room rates.

Next, the agent migrates to Airline 1's preferred car rental agency Car Rental 1, whose interpreter is I_3. Since Airline 1 does not own Car Rental 1, it delegates its authority to Car Rental 1 which runs the agent as I_3 **for** I_1 **for** A **for** S. This causes Car Rental 1 to take responsibility while speaking on Airline 1's behalf. It also gives the agent combined authority from I_1 and I_3; for instance, the agent can obtain access to rental rates negotiated for travelers on Airline 1. Airline 1's interpreter *has delegated its authority* to Car Rental 1 (case 2).

The agent now migrates to the Airline 2 host I_4. The agent contains a certificate that directly delegates to Airline 2 the authority to speak on its behalf. Airline 2 accepts this delegation and runs the agent as I_4 **for** A **for** S, again case 4. Airline 1's interpreter I_1 has now discharged its responsibility; it is no longer an ingredient in the compound principal.

Once the agent has collected all the information it needs, it migrates to the customer's trusted travel agency (Travel Agency 1) host I_5 to compare information and decide on an itinerary. The agent contains a certificate that directly hands Travel Agency 1 the authority to speak on its behalf. Travel Agency 1 can thus run the agent as A **for** S. This permits Travel Agency 1 to make critical decisions for the agent, for instance, to make reservations or purchase a ticket. This kind of trust relationship is an example of the *agent handing off its authority* to Travel Agency 1 (case 3).

4 Authorization

The result of the *authentication* layer is a principal P_2 on behalf of whom I_2 has been asked to execute the agent. The purpose of the *authorization* layer is to determine what level of privilege to provide to the agent for its work. The authorization layer has two ingredients. First, the agent's state appraisal functions are executed; their result is to determine what privileges ("permits") the agent would like to *request* given its current state. Second, the interpreter has access control lists associated with these permits; the access control lists determine which of the requested permits it is willing to *grant*.

We will assume that the request is for a set α of permits; thus, a request is a statement of the form *please grant* α. In our approach, agents are programmed to make this request when they arrive at a site of execution; the permits are then treated as capabilities during execution: no further checking is required.

We distinguish one special permit **run**. By convention, an interpreter will run an agent only if it grants the permit **run** as a member of α.

The request is made by means of the two state appraisal functions. The author-supplied function **max** is applied to Σ returning a maximum safe set of permits. The sender-supplied appraisal function **req** specifies a desired set of permits; this may be a proper subset of the maximum judged safe by the author. However, it should not contain any other, unsafe permits. Thus, we consider P_2 to be making the conditional statement:

$$if\ \mathbf{req}(\Sigma) \subseteq \mathbf{max}(\Sigma)\ then\ please\ grant\ \mathbf{req}(\Sigma)\ else\ please\ grant\ \emptyset$$

I_2 evaluates $\mathbf{req}(\Sigma)$ and $\mathbf{max}(\Sigma)$. If either **req** or **max** detects dangerous tampering to Σ, then that function will request $\emptyset$. Likewise, if **req** makes an excessive request, then the conditional ensures that the result will be $\emptyset$. Since $\mathbf{run} \notin \emptyset$, the agent will then not be run by I_2. Otherwise, P_2 has requested some set α_0 of permits.

In the logic of authentication presented in [10], authorization—the *granting* of permits—is carried out using access control lists. Logically, an access control list is a set of formulas of the form $(Q \textbf{ says } s) \supset s$, where the statements s are requests for access to resources. If a principal P **says** s_0, then I_2 tries to match P and s_0 against the access control list. For any entry $(Q \textbf{ says } s) \supset s$, if $P \Rightarrow Q$ and $s_0 \supset s$, then I_2 may infer s, thus effectively granting the request. This matching may be made efficient if P, Q, and s take certain restricted syntactic forms.

Since we are concerned with requests for sets of permits, if $\alpha \subseteq \alpha_0$ then *please grant α_0* $\supset$ *please grant α*. Hence, a particular access control list entry may allow only a subset of the permits requested. The permits granted will be the union of those allowed by each individual access control list entry

$$(Q \textbf{ says } please\ grant\ \alpha) \supset please\ grant\ \alpha$$

that matches in the sense that $P_2 \Rightarrow Q$ and $\alpha \subseteq \alpha_0$.

Authorization for Travel Agents We again return to our example of mobile travel agents, in order to illustrate how state appraisal functions may be used to achieve their security goals. In particular, we will stress the goals 2 and 3 of Section 2, namely flexible selection of permits and the use of state appraisal functions to detect malicious alterations.

In our first example, we will illustrate how the flexible selection of privilege may benefit the servers, in this case the airlines. Let us suppose that agents requesting full-fare, unrestricted tickets are to be given priority over those requesting restricted tickets at discount fares. Since the author of the program knows best how these facts are stored in the agent's state, he knows how to perform this test. It may thus be incorporated into the state appraisal function **max**. Since the author is a disinterested, knowledgeable party, the interpreter can safely grant a requested privilege whenever it is within $\mathbf{max}(\Sigma)$. The priority treatment might consist of faster service, or access to a larger pool of seats.

The flexible selection of privilege may also benefit the sender. For instance, when the agent returns to the travel agency's trusted interpreter, it may attempt to book a ticket if sufficient information has already been retrieved. The sender may decide that she wants at least four airlines to be consulted. Thus, she writes—or selects—a permit request function **req** that, on reaching the travel agency's host, checks the number of candidate itineraries in the agent's state.If this is at least four, then she requests the **make-booking** permit. An exception-handling mechanism will send the agent out for more information if it tries to make a booking without this permit.

State appraisal may also be used to disarm a maliciously altered agent. Let us alter our example slightly so that the agent maintains—in its state—a linked list of records, each of which represents a desired flight. The code that generates this list ensures that it is finite (free of cycles); the code that manipulates the list preserves the invariant. Thus, there is never a need for the program to check that this list is finite. However, when an agent is received, it is prudent for the state appraisal function to check that the list has not been altered in transit. For if it were, then when the agent began to make its reservations, it would exhaust the available seats, causing legitimate travelers to choose a different carrier.

5 Conclusion

In this paper, we have briefly described a framework for authenticating and authorizing mobile agents, building on existing theory. Our approach models a variety of trust relations, and allows a mobile agent system to be used effectively even when some of the parties stand in a competitive relation to others. We have introduced the idea of packaging state appraisal functions with an agent. The state-appraisal functions provide a flexible way for an agent to request permits, when it arrives at a new interpreter, depending on its current state, and depending on the task that it needs to do there. The same mechanism allows the agent and interpreter to protect themselves against attacks in which the state of the agent is modified at an untrustworthy interpreter or in transit. We believe that this is the primary security challenge for mobile agents, beyond those implicit in other kinds of distributed systems.

References

1. L. Cardelli. A language with distributed scope. In *Proceedings of the 22nd ACM Symposium on Principles of Programming Languages*, pages 286–298, 1995. http://www.research.digital.com/SRC/Obliq/Obliq.html.

2. H. Cejtin, S. Jagannathan, and R. Kelsey. Higher-order distributed objects. *ACM Transactions on Programming Languages and Systems*, 17(5):704–739, September 1995. http://www.neci.nj.nec.com:80/PLS/Kali.html.

3. D. Chess, B. Grosof, C. Harrison, D. Levine, C. Parris, and G. Tsudik. Itinerant agents for mobile computing. IEEE *Personal Communications Magazine*, 2(5):34–49, October 1995. http://www.research.ibm.com/massive.

4. W. Farmer, J. Guttman, and V. Swarup. Security for mobile agents: Issues and requirements. In *National Information Systems Security Conference*. National Institute of Standards and Technology, October 1996.

5. C. G. Harrison, D. M. Chess, and A. Kershenbaum. Mobile agents: Are they a good idea? Technical report, IBM Research Report, IBM Research Division, T.J. Watson Research Center, Yorktown Heights, NY, March 1995. http://www.research.ibm.com/massive.

6. C. Haynes and D. Friedman. Embedding continuations in procedural objects. *ACM Transactions on Programming Languages and Systems*, 9:582–598, 1987.

7. IBM Corporation. Things that go bump in the net. Web page at http://www.research.ibm.com/massive, 1995.

8. IEEE Std 1178-1990. *IEEE Standard for the Scheme Programming Language*. Institute of Electrical and Electronic Engineers, Inc., New York, NY, 1991.

9. Charlie Kaufman, Radia Perlman, and Mike Speciner. *Network Security: Private Communication in a Public World*. PTR Prentice Hall, Englewood Cliffs, 1995.

10. B. Lampson, M. Abadi, M. Burrows, and E. Wobber. Authentication in distributed systems: Theory and practice. *ACM Transactions on Computer Systems*, 10:265–310, November 1992. http://DEC/SRC/research-reports/abstracts/src-rr-083.html.

11. Sun Microsystems. Java: Programming for the internet. Web page available at http://java.sun.com/.

12. Sun Microsystems. HotJava: The security story. Web page available at http://java.sun.com/doc/overviews.html, 1995.

13. J. Tardo and L. Valente. Mobile agent security and Telescript. In *IEEE CompCon*, 1996. http://www.cs.umbc.edu/agents/ security.html.

14. C. Thirunavukkarasu, T. Finin, and J. Mayfield. Secret agents — a security architecture for KQML. In *CIKM Workshop on Intelligent Information Agents*, Baltimore, December 1995.

15. T. D. Tock. An extensible framework for authentication and delegation. Master's thesis, University of Illinois at Urbana-Champaign, Urbana, IL, 1994. ftp://choices.cs.uiuc.edu/Papers/Theses/MS.Authentication.Delegation.ps.Z.

16. Leendert van Doorn, Martín Abadi, Mike Burrows, and Edward Wobber. Secure network objects. In *Proceedings, Symposium on Security and Privacy*, pages 211–221. IEEE Computer Society, 1996.

17. J. E. White. Telescript technology: Mobile agents. In *General Magic White Paper*, 1996. Will appear as a chapter of the book Software Agents, Jeffrey Bradshaw (ed.), AAAI Press/The MIT Press, Menlo Park, CA.

Server-Supported Signatures

N. Asokan[1,2], G. Tsudik[1,3], M. Waidner[1]

[1] IBM Zürich Research Laboratory, CH-8803 Rüschlikon, Switzerland
email: {aso,wmi}@zurich.ibm.com
[2] Department of Computer Science, University of Waterloo, Waterloo, Canada.
[3] Information Sciences Institute, University of Southern California, USA.
email: gts@isi.edu

Abstract. Non-repudiation is one of the most important security services. In this paper we present a novel non-repudiation technique, called Server-Supported Signatures, S³. It is based on *one-way hash functions* and *traditional digital signatures*. One of its highlights is that for ordinary users the use of asymmetric cryptography is limited to signature *verification*. S³ is efficient in terms of computational, communication and storage costs. It also offers a degree of security comparable to existing techniques based on asymmetric cryptography.

Keywords: digital signatures, non-repudiation, electronic commerce, network security, distributed systems, mobility.

1 Introduction

Computers and communication networks have become an integral part in the daily lives of many people. Systems to facilitate commercial and other transactions have been built on top of large open computer networks. Oftentimes these transactions must have some legal significance if they are to be useful in real life. Non-repudiation is one of the essential services that must be provided in order to attach legal significance to transactions and information transfer in general.

Existing techniques for non-repudiation are based primarily on either symmetric or asymmetric cryptography. Practically secure symmetric techniques are computationally more efficient but require unconditional trust in third parties. "Unconditional" means that if such a third party cheats, the victim cannot prove this to an arbitrator (e.g., a court). Practically secure asymmetric techniques (which we refer to as "traditional digital signatures") are computationally less efficient but can be constructed in a way that allows one to prove cheating by third parties. We call a third party whose cheating can be proven to an arbitrator **a verifiable third party**.

We present a novel non-repudiation technique, called **Server-Supported Signatures, S³**. It is based on *one-way hash functions* and *traditional digital signatures*. Like well-constructed asymmetric techniques, S³ uses only verifiable third parties. However, for ordinary users, S³ limits the use of asymmetric cryptographic techniques to signature *verification*. All signature *generations* are done

by third parties, called *signature servers*. For some signature schemes, e.g., RSA
with a public exponent of 3, verifying signatures is significantly more efficient
than generating them [Sch96].

This paper is organized as follows. We begin in the next section by briefly
reviewing the standardization activities in the area of non-repudiation. Section 2
provides some more motivation for alternative non-repudiation techniques. The
actual design of S³ is described in Sections 3 and 4. Some variations are addressed
in Section 5 and Section 6 discusses performance and storage costs. The paper
concludes in Section 7 with a brief review of related work.

2   Background and Motivation

The International Standardization Organization (ISO) is in the process of stan-
dardizing techniques to provide non-repudiation services in open networks. Current versions of the draft ISO standards [ISO95a, ISO95b, ISO95c] identify various classes of non-repudiation services. Two of these are of particular interest:

- **Non-repudiation of Origin (NRO)** guarantees that the originator of a
  message cannot later deny having originated that message.
- **Non-repudiation of Receipt (NRR)**[4] guarantees that the recipient of a
  message cannot deny having received that message.

Non-repudiation for a particular message is obtained by constructing a **non-
repudiation token**. The non-repudiation token must be such that it can be
verified by:

- the intended recipients of the token (e.g., in the case of NRO, the recipient
  of the message; in the case of NRR, the originator of the message), and
- in case of a dispute, by a mutually acceptable *arbitrator*.

The draft ISO standards divide non-repudiation techniques into two classes:

- *Asymmetric non-repudiation techniques* are based on digital signatures schemes,
  i.e., on public-key cryptography. The main (and likely the only) difficulty
  in using digital signature schemes is the computational cost involved. This
  is a particularly serious issue when "anemic" portable devices (like mobile
  phones) are involved.
  Non-repudiation is based on certification of the signer's public key by a *certification authority*. Trust in this certification authority can be minimized
  by an appropriate *registration procedure*, e.g., if the signer and the authority
  have to sign a paper contract listing the signer's and certification authority's public keys, responsibilities, and liabilities, maybe in front of a notary
  public. In the worst case the certification authority could cheat the user by

---

[4] The ISO documents call this "non-repudiation of delivery (NRD)" We use the term
"receipt" since we feel that the term "delivery" is more appropriate to describe the
function performed by the message transport system.

issuing a certificate with a public key chosen by a cheater. But the supposed signer could deny all signatures based on this forged certificate, by citing the contract signed during registration. Thus, trust is reduced to trust in the verifiability of the registration procedure.

- *Symmetric non-repudiation techniques* are based on symmetric message authentication codes (MACs) and trusted third parties that act as witnesses. Generating and verifying message authentication codes are typically lightweight operations, compared to digital signature operations.

  The signer has to trust the third party unconditionally, which means that the third party could cheat the user without giving the user any chance to deny forged messages. One could reduce this trust by using several third parties in parallel or by putting the third party in tamper resistant hardware. Both approaches increase bith cost and complexity while none of them solves the problem completely.

In the following we present a new, light-weight technique for non-repudiation services, *server-supported signatures*. It uses both traditional digital signatures(based on asymmetric cryptographic techniques) and one-way hash functions, in order to minimize the computational costs for ordinary users. Our main motivation arises from the typical mobile computing environments where the mobile entities have considerably less computing power than the static entities.

3 Server-Supported Signatures for Non-repudiation of Origin

3.1 Preliminaries: One-way Hash Functions

Intuitively, a one-way function $f()$ is a function such that given an input string x it is easy to compute $f(x)$, but given a randomly chosen y it is computationally infeasible to find an x' such that $f(x') = y$. A one-way hash function is a one-way function $h()$ that operates on arbitrary-length inputs to produce a fixed length value. x is called the *pre-image* of $h(x)$.

A large number of practically secure and efficient one-way hash functions have been invented, e.g., SHA or MD5 [Sch96].

One-way hash functions can be recursively applied to an input string. The notation $h^i(x)$ denotes the result of applying $h()$ i times recursively to an input x. That is,

$$h^i(x) = h(h(h(\ldots(i\ times)\ldots h(x)\ldots)))$$

Such recursive application results in a *hash-chain* that is generated from the original input string:

$$h^0(x) = x, h^1(x)\ldots h^n(x)$$

3.2 Model and Notation

We distinguish three types of entities in the system:

- *Users* – participants in the system who wish to avail themselves of the non-repudiation service while sending and receiving messages among themselves.
- *Signature Servers* – special entities responsible for actually generating the non-repudiation tokens on behalf of the users.
- *Certification Authorities* – special entities that are responsible for linking public keys with identities of users and servers.

Signature servers and certification authorities will be verifiable third parties, from the users' point of view.

All entities agree on a one-way hash-function $h()$ and a digital signature scheme. Entities should "personalize" the hash function by always including their unique name as an argument. Therefore, **every occurrence of $h(x)$ below really means $h(O, x)$, where O is the entity computing the one-way hash.**

The result of digitally signing a message x with signature key SK is denoted by $(x)SK$. The users' security depends on the one-way property of $h()$, i.e., the one-way property must hold even against the servers.[5]

In order to minimize the computational overhead for users, $h()$ must be efficiently computable, and digital signatures must be efficiently *verifiable*. Only signature servers and certification authorities must be able to *generate* signatures. MD5 as hash function and RSA with public exponent 3 as signature scheme would be reasonable choices.

Each user, O (O as in *Originator*) generates a secret key, K_O, randomly chosen from the range of $h()$. Based on K_O, user O computes the hash-chain $K_O^0, K_O^1, \ldots K_O^n$, where $K_O^0 = K_O$, $K_O^i = h^i(K_O) = h(K_O^{i-1})$. $PK_O = K_O^n$ constitutes O's *root public key*. Root public key K_O^n will enable O to authenticate n messages[6].

Each signature server, S, generates a pair of secret and public keys, (SK_S, PK_S), of the digital signature scheme. Each certification authority, CA, does the same. CA is responsible for verifiably binding a user O (server S) to her root public key PK_O (its public key PK_S). We assume that the registration procedure is constructed in a way such that CA becomes a verifiable third party.

---

[5] Hash functions such as SHA or MD5 are one-way for *all* parties, i.e., practically this is no problem. But note that usually so-called cryptographically strong hash-functions are invertible for the party that generated the hash-function.

[6] This is no real limitation: Before the old root public key is consumed completely a new root public key can be generated and authenticated using the old root public key.

> **Notation Summary**
> $h()$ - one-way hash function
> SK_X - secret key known only to entity X
> K_O^i - user O's $(n-i)$-th public key
> $(x)SK$ - digital signature on message x with secret key SK

3.3 Initialization

To participate in the system, a user O chooses a signature server S that shall be responsible for generating signatures on O's behalf, generates a random secret key K_O, and constructs the hash-chain. As will be described below, O can cause S to transfer the signature generation responsibility to another signature server S', if required (e.g., because O is a mobile user who wishes to always use the closest server available).

O submits the root public key $PK_O = K_O^n$ to a CA for certification. A certificate for O's root public key is of the form[7] $(O, n, PK_O, S)SK_{CA}$. The registration performed by O and CA must be verifiable, as discussed earlier. CA may make the certificate available to anyone via a directory service. O then deposits the certificate received from CA with S.

Each signature server S acquires a certificate on PK_S from a certification authority. Since these are ordinary certificates for digital signatures we do not need to describe them here.

For the sake of simplicity, we do not include the certificates in the following protocols. They might be attached to other messages, or retrieved using a directory service. We assume that the necessary certificates are always available to anyone who needs to verify a signature.

3.4 Generating NRO Tokens

The basic idea is to exploit the digital signature generation capability of a signature server to provide non-repudiation services to ordinary users. The basic protocol, providing non-repudiation of origin, is illustrated in Figure 1. We assume that a user O wants to send a message m along with an NRO token to some recipient R. The first protocol run uses $i = n$; i is decreased during each run.

1. O begins by sending (O, m, i) to its signature server S along with O's current public key K_O^i in the first protocol flow.[8]

---

[7] We ignore all information typically contained in a certificate but not relevant to the discussion at hand; e.g., organizational data such as serial numbers, expiration dates, etc.

[8] In case O does not want to reveal the message to S for privacy reasons, m can be replaced by a hash of m.

2. S verifies the received public key based on O's root public key (and O's certificate obtained from CA), i.e., checks that $h^{n-i}(K_O^i) = PK_O$. The signature server S has to ensure that only one NRO can be created for a given (O, i, K_O^i). If a message on behalf of O containing K_O^i has not yet been signed, S signs (O, m, i, K_O^i), records K_O^i as consumed, and sends the signature back to O in the second flow.

3. O verifies the received signature and records K_O^i as consumed, i.e., replaces i by $i - 1$. The NRO token for R consists now of

$$(O, m, i, K_O^i)SK_S, K_O^{i-1}$$

O produces this token, i.e., actually authenticates m, by revealing K_O^{i-1}. In Figure 1 we assumed that the NRO token is sent to R via S is the third flow. Alternatively, O can send the token to R directly.

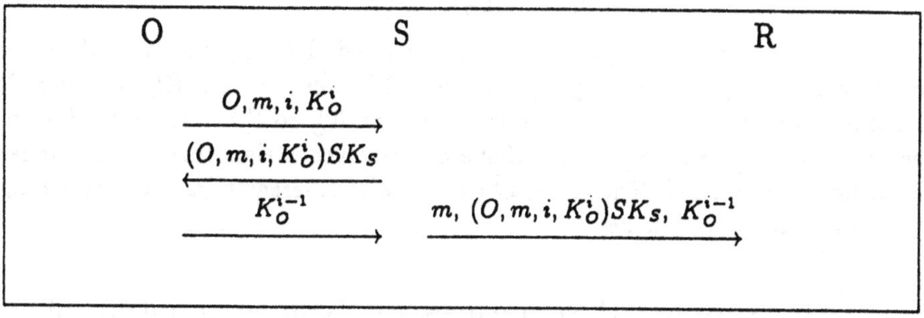

Fig. 1. Protocol providing non-repudiation of origin

K_O^i is referred as the **token public key** of the $(n - i + 1)$st non-repudiation token, $(O, m, i, K_O^i)SK_S, K_O^{i-1}$.

Note that O must consume the token public keys in sequence, i.e., must not skip any of them. In particular, O must not ask for a signature using K_O^{i-1} as token public key unless she has received S's signature under K_O^i. Otherwise, S could use that to create a fake non-repudiation token.

3.5 Dispute Resolution

In case of a dispute, R can submit the NRO to an arbitrator. The arbitrator will verify the following:

- the public keys are certified by CA,
- the signature in the token by the signature server is valid,
- the token public key is in fact a hash alleged pre-image in the token, and

- the root public key can be derived from the token public key by repeated hashing.

If these checks are successful, then the originator is allowed the opportunity to *repudiate* the token by

- proving that CA cheated:
  - If O has registered with CA, O can show a certificate on a different root public key.
  - Otherwise CA will be asked to prove that root public key was registered by O (i.e., showing the signed contract with O).
- proving that S cheated by showing a different token corresponding to the same token public key.

Note that in case CA is honest, to falsely claim that O has sent a message m', a cheating R has to produce an NRO token of the form:

$$(O, m', i, K_O^i)SK_S, K_O^{i-1}$$

If O has not revealed K_O^{i-1} yet, it is presumed that anyone else will find it computationally infeasible to generate this NRO token, even if K_O^i is known. If O has already revealed K_O^{i-1} she must have sent K_O^i to S before. According to the protocol, O reveals K_O^{i-1} only if she has received a signature from S under K_O^i which satisfied her. Therefore, O can show a different token corresponding to the same token public key.

4 Server-Supported Signatures for Non-repudiation of Origin and Receipt

Non-repudiation of receipt (NRR) can be easily added to the basic protocol. Before sending m to R, S can ask R for an NRO token for ("NRR", $h(m)$) which is then passed on to O. This is illustrated in Figure 2. The NRR token consists of:

$$(R, (\text{"NRR"}, h(m)), j, K_R^j)SK_S, K_R^{j-1}$$

Since this protocol is just two interleaved instances of the basic NRO protocol, it still guarantees that O and R can repudiate all forged NRO and NRR tokens, respectively.

Notice that the present protocol actually implements *fair-exchange* of m (NRO token) and its receipt (NRR token), based on S as trusted third party. If S behaves dishonestly, no fairness can be guaranteed, i.e., O might not receive the NRR token or R might not receive m or the NRO token.

Depending on the application R might request to receive m already in the second flow. This allows R to refuse generating the NRR token after he has actually received m, but avoids the problem that R has to trust that he will receive m *after* he has already acknowledged having received it.

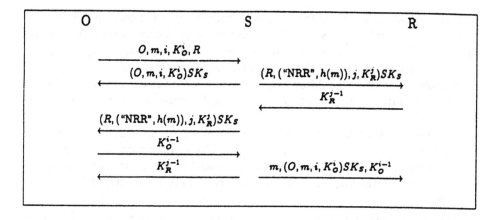

Fig. 2. Protocol providing non-repudiation of origin and receipt

5 Variations on the Theme

5.1 Reducing Storage Requirements

In order to deny forged non-repudiation tokens, O has to store *all* signatures received from S, which might be a bit unrealistic for a device that is not even able to compute signatures. One can easily avoid this storage problem by including an additional field in S's signature that serves as a commitment on all the previous signatures made by S for that hash-chain;i.e., an NRO token looks like

$$NRO^i := ((O, m, i, K_O^i, H^i)SK_S, K_O^{i-1})$$

Value H^i is recursively computed by $H^n := K_O^n$ and $H^{i-1} := f(H^i, NRO^i)$. $f()$ is a one-way hash function (it may be the same as $h()$).

O has to store the last value H^i and the last signature received from S only. S has to store all signatures, and has to provide them to O in case of a dispute. If S cannot provide a sequence of signatures that fits to the hash value contained in the last signature received by O, the arbitrator allows O to repudiate all signatures and assumes that S cheated.

This idea of chaining previous signatures was used by *Haber and Stornetta* [HS] for the construction of a time-stamping service, based on the observation that the sequence of messages in H^i cannot be changed afterwards. One could combine their protocols with ours, using S as time-stamping sever.

5.2 Increasing Robustness

As mentioned above, a signature server will sign exactly one message for a given user per public key (K_O^i) in the hash-chain. However, anyone can send a signature request in the form of the first flow, i.e., (O, m, i, K_O^i).

If the signature server does not subsequently receive the corresponding pre-image of the current public key (K_O^{i-1}), the current public key is rendered invalid regardless. This implies that an attacker can succeed in invalidating an entire chain of a user by generating fake signature requests in her name.

An obvious solution would be to require O and S to share a secret key to be used for computing (and verifying) message authentication code over the first protocol flow.

An alternative solution is to give users the ability to invalidate token public keys without having to create a new chain. The construction is only slightly more complicated than the basic protocol: instead of one chain, each user generates *two* chains (computed with two different hash functions): $K_O^n, \ldots, K_O^0$ and $\hat{K}_O^n, \ldots, \hat{K}_O^0$.

Each token public key is now a pair of hash values, say, $(K_O^i, \hat{K}_O^j)$. If O receives $(O, m, i, K_O^i, \hat{K}_O^j)SK_S$, she can either *accept* or *reject* that:

- O accepts by revealing K_O^{i-1}. The next token public key is $(K_O^{i-1}, \hat{K}_O^j)$.
- O rejects by revealing $\hat{K}_O^{j-1}$. The next token public key is $(K_O^i, \hat{K}_O^{j-1})$.

On receiving K_O^{i-1} or $\hat{K}_O^{j-1}$, server S creates

- the **non-repudiation token** $(O, m, i, K_O^i, \hat{K}_O^j, K_O^{i-1})SK_S$ or
- the **invalidation token** $(O, m, i, K_O^i, \hat{K}_O^j, \hat{K}_O^{j-1})SK_S$

respectively. The new token public key is $(K_O^{i-1}, \hat{K}_O^j)$ or $(K_O^i, \hat{K}_O^{j-1})$, respectively.

The additional signature by S is necessary since for one signature

$$(O, m, i, K_O^i, \hat{K}_O^j)SK_S$$

it can easily happen that both K_O^{i-1} and $\hat{K}_O^{j-1}$ become public, i.e., the combination of the first signature with one pre-image would not be unambiguous and recipient R could not depend on what he receives. Note that a cheating S could generate both tokens for the same token public key, but O could easily prove that S cheated by showing the token received.

5.3 Support for Roaming Users

In the basic protocol, the trust placed on the signature server is quite limited – it is trusted only to protect its secret key from intruders and to generate signatures in a secure manner. This limited trust enables a mobile user to make use of a signature server in foreign domains while roaming (or travelling). Normally the signature server in the user's home domain will be *in charge* of the user's hash-chain. Whenever the user requests to be transferred to a signature server in a different domain, an agreement could be signed by the two signature servers involving the transfer of the user's current public key.

In other words, instead of having a single root public key certificate (which includes the identity of the "home" signature server), a chain of public key certificates could be used. The chain consists of the root public key certificate signed by the home CA and one *hand-off certificate* every time the charge for the user's public key has changed hands:

$$(O, n, K_O^n, S)SK_{CA}$$

$$(O, n_l, K_O^{n_l}, S_l)SK_{S_{l-1}}, \ for \ 0 < n_l < n, l > 0$$

To effect a change in charge, the following procedure is carried out:

1. The user O sends a request for change of charge to both the current signature server S_{l-1} and the intended signature server S_l. Since this request must be non-repudiatable, this step is essentially a run of the basic protocol to generate a NRO token with a message that means "change of charge from S_{l-1} to S_l requested" for token public key $K_O^{n_l - 1}$.
2. When the NRO token is received and verified by S_{l-1}, it generates a corresponding hand-off certificate described in the previous paragraph and sends it to both O and S_l. It will no longer generate signatures on behalf of O for that hash-chain unless charge is explicitly transferred back to it at some point. In addition, it will store both the hand-off certificate and the corresponding NRO token.
3. When S_l has received both the NRO token and the hand-off certificate, it will be ready to generate signatures on behalf of O.

5.4 Key Revocation

As with any certificate-based system, there must be a way for any user O to revoke her hash-chain[9]. If the currently secret portion O's hash-chain (say K_O^i, for $i = p - 1, p - 2, \ldots 1$) has been compromised, O will detect the fact when she attempts to construct an NRO the next time for the token public key K_O^p: S will return an error indicating the current token public key $K_O^q (q < p)$ from S's point of view. O can attempt to limit the damage by doing one of the following:

1. invalidate all remaining token public keys $K_O^i (i = q, q-1, \ldots 1)$ by requesting NRO tokens for them, or
2. notifying S to invalidate the remaining hash-chain by sending it a non-repudiatable request to that affect and receiving a non-repudiatable statement from S stating that the hash-chain has been invalidated. This can be implemented similar to the invalidation tokens described in Section 5.2 – except in this case the token would invalidate the entire chain and not just a single key.

---

[9] Revocation by authorities is not an issue in this system since the user has to interact with the signature server for the generation of every new NR token anyway.

5.5 Similar Constructions

In a more general light, the signature server in S^3 can be viewed as a "translator" of signatures: *it translates one-time signatures based on hash-functions into traditional digital signatures.* The same approach can be used to combine other techniques in such a way that the result provides some features that are not available from the constituent techniques by themselves.

For example, one could select a traditional digital signature scheme (say D_1) where signing is easier than verification (e.g. DSS) and one (say D_2) where verification is easier than signing (e.g. RSA with a low public exponent) and construct a similar composite signature scheme. The signature key of an entity X in digital signature scheme D is denoted by SK_X^D. To sign a message m, an originator O would compute $(m)SK_O^{D_1}$ and pass it along with the message m to the signature server S. If the server can verify the signature, it will translate it to $(m, (m)SK_O^{D_1})SK_S^{D_2}$. In other words, the composite scheme allows digital signatures where both signing and verification are computationally inexpensive.

6 Analysis

Computation: Users need to be able to compute one-way hashes, and to verify digital signatures. Only the signature servers and CAs are required to generate signatures.

Storage: Using the improvement described in Section 5.1, users need to store only the last signature received from S, the pre-image of the current token public key and the sequence number, and the public keys needed to verify certificates.

Signature servers need to store all generated signatures in order to provide them to the users in case they request them. The stored signatures are necessary only in case of a dispute. Therefore, they can be periodically down-loaded to a secure archive.

Communication: The communication overhead of S^3 is comparable to that of standard symmetric non-repudiation techniques, since a third party, S, is involved in each generation of a non-repudiation token.

Using traditional digital signatures, the involvement of third parties can be restricted to exception handling, while the token generation is a two-party protocol. The price to be paid for this gain in efficiency is that revocation of signature keys becomes more complicated. Note that in S^3, revoking a key is trivial. O just has to invalidate the current chain.

Security: In the preceding sections, we demonstrated that as long as the registration procedure, digital signature scheme and one-way hash function are secure, both users and signature servers are secure with respect to their respective objectives. Furthermore, the security of originators depends on the strength of the one-way hash function and not on the security of the digital signature scheme.

7 Related Work

Although non-repudiation of origin and receipt are among the most important security requirements, only a few basic protocols exist. See [For94] for a summary of the standard constructions. We are not aware of any previous work that aims to minimize the computational costs (on the protocol level) for ordinary users while providing the same security as standard non-repudiation techniques based on asymmetric cryptography.

The efficiency problem as addressed by specific designs of signature schemes was mainly motivated by the limited computing power of smart cards and smart tokens. [Sch96] lists most known proposals. Typically they are based on pre-processing or on some asymmetry in the complexity of signature generation and verification (i.e., either sender or recipient must be able to perform complex operations, but not both.) Note that although server-supported signatures use a signature scheme that is asymmetric with respect to signature generation and verification, ordinary users are *never* required to generate signatures; thus, both sender and recipient are assumed to be computationally weak.

There had been other proposals to use one-way hash functions to construct signatures. Merkle's paper [Mer87] includes an overview of these efforts. The original proposals in this category were impractical: A proposal by Lamport/Diffie requires a "public key" (i.e. an object that must be bound to the signer beforehand) and two hash operations to sign *every* bit. Using an improvement attributed to Winternitz, with a single public key and (which is the nth hash image of the private key) and n hash operations, one can sign a single message of size $log_2 n$ bits. Merkle introduced the notion of using a tree structure [Mer87]; in one version of his proposals, with just a single public key, it is possible to sign an arbitrary number of messages. But, it still took either a large number of hash operations or a large amount of storage in order to sign more than a handful of messages corresponding to the same public key.

Motivated by completely different factors, *Pfitzmann et al.* [PPW91, Pfi] proposed a fail-stop signature protocol which uses the same ideas as S^3. There, the signature server is also the recipient of the signature, and the goal is to achieve unconditional security for the signer against the server (in the sense of fail-stop signatures). The protocol has a similar structure as the one in Section 1.[10] Because of the specific security requirements, all parties have to perform complex cryptographic operations, and signatures are not easily transferable.

---

[10] It uses a so-called bundling function $h()$ instead of the conceptionally simpler hash function used in S^3. A value $h(x)$ is used as O's current public key. To give a NRO token for message m to S, the signer O sends m to S, which answers by $(m, h(x))SK_S$. Finally O sends x to S, which terminates the protocol. The NRO token for S is $(m, h(x))SK_S, x$. The consumed public key $h(x)$ can be renewed by including a new public key $h(x')$ in m.

8 Acknowledgments

We are indebted to Michael Steiner for his perceptive feedback on previous versions of this paper. We would also like to thank Didier Samfat for making us interested in the original problem.

References

[For94] Warwick Ford. *Computer Communications Security – Principles, Standard Protocols and Techniques*. Prentice Hall, New Jersey, 1994.

[HS] Stuart Haber and W. Scott Stornetta. How to time-stamp a digital document. Journal of Cryptology 3/2 (1991) 99-111.

[ISO95a] ISO/IEC JTC1, Information Technology, SC 27. 2nd ISO/IEC CD 13888-1 Information Technology - Security Techniques - Non-repudiation - Part1: General Model. ISO/IEC JTC 1/SC 27 N 1105, May 1995.

[ISO95b] ISO/IEC JTC1, Information Technology, SC 27. 2nd ISO/IEC CD 13888-2 Information Technology - Security Techniques - Non-repudiation - Part2: Using symmetric encipherment algorithms. ISO/IEC JTC 1/SC 27 N 1106, July 1995.

[ISO95c] ISO/IEC JTC1, Information Technology, SC 27. ISO/IEC CD 13888-3 Information Technology - Security Techniques - Non-repudiation - Part3: Using asymmetric techniques. ISO/IEC JTC 1/SC 27 N 1107, September 1995.

[Mer87] Ralph C. Merkle. A digital signature based on a conventional encryption function. In Carl Pomerance, editor, *Advances in Cryptology – CRYPTO '87*, number 293 in Lecture Notes in Computer Science, pages 369–378, Santa Barbara, CA, USA, August 1987. Springer-Verlag, Berlin Germany.

[Pfi] Birgit Pfitzmann. Fail-stop signatures; principles and applications. Proc. Compsec '91, 8th world conference on computer security, audit and control, Elsevier, Oxford 1991, 125-134.

[PPW91] Andreas Pfitzmann, Birgit Pfitzmann, and Michael Waidner. Practical signatures where individuals are unconditionally secure. Unpublished manuscript, available from the authors (pfitzb@informatik.uni-hildesheim.de), 1991.

[Sch96] Bruce Schneier. *Applied Cryptography: Protocols, Algorithms, and Source Code in C*. John Wiley & Sons Inc., New York, second edition, 1996.

Limitations of the Approach of Solving a Network's Security Problems with a Firewall

Stefano Zatti, *European Space Agency, ESRIN, Frascati, Italy* (Chair)
Refik Molva, *Ecole EURECOM, Sophia Antipolis, France*
Angelo Tosi, *Price Waterhouse, Zurich, Switzerland*
Gene Tsudik, *Information Sciences Institute, Marina Del Rey, CA USA*
Helmut Kurth, *IABG Munich, Germany*

Abstract

The panel discussion will focus on current usage of firewalls, user expectations, and limitations of today's approach. It will then look into future evolution and possible enhancements of the solutions currently available on the market, that are desirable to strengthen the security of the installations to be protected.

The following topics are likely to be topics of discussion:

- Common uses and configurations of firewalls today
- Firewalls and Beyond
- Common use of firewalls in today's networks
- Limitations of firewalls in today's networks
- Requirements for enhancements to the firewall technology.
- Firewalls and emerging services: WWW, hot Java, Electronic Commerce
- Firewalls and high speed networking: End-to-end argument, ATM, etc.

Introduction

Firewalls are being touted as the ironclad solution for establishing outposts on the Internet and effectively controlling the flow of network traffic crossing administrative network boundaries.

While well-designed firewalls can be successfully deployed for the purpose of tunnelling (securing traffic flowing between a pair firewalls) and controlling in- and out-bound access, there remain some limitations. One of the most notable is the inability of authenticating the origin and contents of incoming traffic whenever this traffic does not originates behind a peer firewall. In other words, firewalls can be fooled by counterfeiting the callers' information.

As an example, consider a Telnet session originating within a private network. The outbound half of the session can be effectively secured and controlled. However, unless the external destination is also protected by a (trusted) peer firewall, the inbound half of the session is fair game for intruders.

It appears -- at least initially -- that the above-illustrated problem is unsolvable...

What's new about new technologies like ATM with respect to firewalls ?

Two points for discussion:

- The possibility to improve security: full fledged, application-level access control can be implemented by integrating security functions into the network control structures of new technologies, like the signalling protocols of ATM. The security functions thus obtained ca be cryptographically strong, contrary to today's packet filters.

- Inherent limitations and new exposures: because of the current trend in high speed network-ing, the protocols at the network level get leaner and security checks performed "on the fly" become incompatible with the network protocols and the speed requirements. The only pos-sible placement for authentication and access control functions is out of band as part of the network control system. Apart from this limitation, virtual networking functions brought by the new technologies like ATM create new exposures mostly because the physical separa-tions typical of classical network technologies do not exist in the virtual implementations using the new technologies. The best example of this problem is LAN-emulation over ATM, that completely lacks the physical separation of real LANs interconnected by a net-work-level router. Thus a firewall enforcing access control on the LAN protocols cannot prevent a terminal of a virtual LAN from establishing an unauthorized connection by using the lower level ATM protocols.

Users' view of firewall technologies

- What are the main characteristics of today's market of computer and network security? Fire-walls in the framework of a company's security strategy: why does a company need secu-rity? Which resources do need what kind of protection, and how can a company choose the most appropriate security level?
- Different users - employees as well as customers - need access to different resources: e.g. marketing people need to promote the company's products to customers; sales representa-tives need remote access to specific, often sensitive product information. How can network security satisfy all these needs.
- Technical and organizational problems experienced by companies in using firewalls (e.g. configuration management, user interface, human resources planning).
- Problems in using firewalls to secure an already existing network infrastructure.
- How can a company profit of emerging Internet services (Electronic Commerce, WWW advertising, etc.) while controlling its exposure to security risks? User requirements to future firewall technology.

Sleepy Network-Layer Authentication Service for IPSEC *

Shyhtsun F. Wu[1]

Computer Science Department, North Carolina State University, Raleigh, NC
27695-8206. wu@csc.ncsu.edu

Abstract. Network-layer authentication security services are typically pessimistic and static. A conservative IP security gateway checks/verifies the authentication information for every packet it forwards. This implies that, even there is no bad guy in the network, the authentication check is still performed for every packet. In this paper, we examine a sleepy approach, where the gateways normally do not authenticate or verify the packets unless security attacks are detected. We propose a security protocol, *SSGP (Sleepy Security Gateway Protocol)*, residing on top of the *IPSEC (Internet Security Protocol)*. One important feature of SSGP is the collaboration model between network and application layer security mechanisms.

1 Introduction

In the Internet, the *demilitarized zones (DMZ)* separated by firewalls or security gateways[CB94] are static. The system administrators decide the configuration options about the firewalls, which remain unchanged for months or years. For instance, packet filtering firewalls consistently check every incoming packets and reject unauthenticated packets. The checking is done even when there is NO security attack to the networking system.

Traditionally, these gateways are provided only in the transport or application layer. Implementing this type of filtering mechanisms in the *network/IP* layer is beneficial but causes the potential performance problem as mentioned in section 3 of RFC1636 [BCCH94] as well as section 5.3 of RFC1825 [Atk95]. For example, in *swIPe* [IB93], if the security check is done in purely software, then it is measured that we need to pay 100 microseconds per IP packet plus 1 microsecond per byte for MD5 and 10 microseconds per byte for DES. One obvious way to improve the performance is to use some hardware solutions (*e.g.*

---

* This research is supported by Center for Advanced Computing and Communication.

[Ebe92]). However, as pointed out in [Lin94], since the network layer itself generally is implemented in software, it is hard to make effective use of cryptographic hardware.

Generating and verifying the MAC (message authentication code) for every IP packet consume the network resources. The performance of the most commonly used MAC scheme, MD5, can be found in [Tou95]. On the other hand, more and more Internet applications have their own authentication process. For example, Kerberos [NT94], SNMPv2 [GM93], MobileIP's Registration Protocol [Per96], and the next release of Java [Mic, DFW96, WDH+96] have or will have built-in application layer authentication mechanisms. This means that the same IP payload will pass through the MAC process twice, one in the network layer and another in the application layer. The problem is that whether we could do something smart to reduce the security overheads.

In this paper, *SSGP (Sleepy Security Gateway Protocol)* is presented to efficiently offer network-layer authentication services for IPSEC. The key element of SSGP is the *Sleepy Security Gateway (SSG)* which might be in either one of the following two different modes: *sleepy* and *wakeup*. In the following sections, through two different examples, we will show how SSGP works.

2 A Simple Example of SSGP

2.1 Problem

In Figure 1, a system administrator establishes a connection with the management agent across a segment of public Internet. According to the IPSEC architecture, we have two security gateways, SSG_A and SSG_B, and establish a secure channel over the insecure public internet. This scheme is sufficient for outside intruders but not good enough for insider. Therefore, we need an application-layer security mechanism or an intrusion detection module to protect the application against the insider's attacks. Please note that if we only have inside intruders, then the security checks being performed by SSG_A and SSG_B are wasted.

2.2 Answer

Assume that we do have an application-layer mechanism (e.g., SNMPv2) to authenticate the application PDU (e.g., SNMP PDU). Then, even no IP layer security mechanism exists, the application is safe in the sense that it will not accept any unauthenticated packets. This is true for attacks from either the

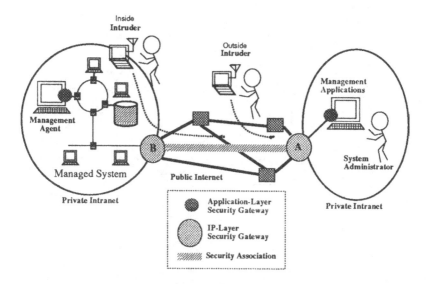

Fig. 1. Application and IP Security

insider or the outsider. However, the application might suffer from heavier incoming traffic load because all the attack packets can now be delivered to the host directly. And, the application needs to spend time to filter out those bad PDUs. For example, without network-layer protection, in [Zor94, Wu95], it is identified that the performance of the SNMPv2 agent drops significantly under denial-of-service attacks.

The application-layer security module detects bad PDUs. For example, SNMPv2 security module dropped packets with wrong key-MD5 authentication and replayed packets. This detection information should be forwarded to the security management module. This management module wakes up sleepy security gateways (SSGs) protecting this application. Based on the *security association* relations defined in [Atk95], these waked-up SSGs might wake up more SSGs. As shown in Figure 2, SSG_A has been waked up by the security management module who received a report from an application. Because a security association exists between SSG_A and SSG_B, SSG_A wakes up SSG_B.

At this point, all the packets from the agent to the administrator are authenticated in the public Internet. The original IP packet from the SNMP agent (*Agent*) to the SNMP management application (*M App*) looks like:

$$IP(Agent, MApp) = \boxed{Prot_{UDP}, IP_{src}^{Agent}, IP_{dst}^{MApp} : \boxed{IPpayload}}.$$

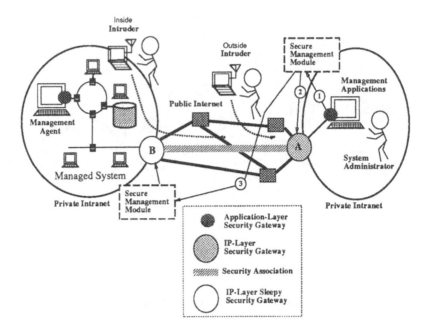

Fig. 2. SSGP: Simple Example

The SSG authenticated packet format, $IP_{encap}(SSG_B, SSG_A)$, is:

$$\boxed{Prot_{SSGP}, IP_{src}^{SSG_B}, IP_{dst}^{SSG_A} : \boxed{\boxed{Auth_{SSG_B}^{SSG_A}}\ \boxed{IP(Agent, MApp)}}},$$

where the $Auth_{SSG_B}^{SSG_A}$ is

$$\boxed{ID_{SSG_B}, ID_{SSG_A}, Seq\sharp},$$

plus:

$$MD5(K_{AB}, ID_{SSG_B}, ID_{SSG_A}, Seq\sharp, \boxed{IP(Agent, MApp)}, K_{AB}).$$

When this encapsulated IP packet is received by SSG_A, it will be decapsulated by SSG_A and delivered to $MApp$ with the following format:

$$IP_{decap}(Agent, MApp) = \boxed{IP(Agent, MApp)}\ \boxed{Auth_{SSG_B}^{SSG_A}}.$$

We append the authentication certificate, $Auth_{SSG_B}^{SSG_A}$, at the end of the packet. This information is useful for deciding the attack sources as we will explain later. The reason for appending this certificate at the end of a regular IP packet is to ensure the compatibility between SSGP packets and normal IP packets.

If we only have outside intruders, then, in theory, no more bad packets will get to the protected host $MApp$. If $MApp$ still receives bad packets and SSG_A did NOT find any unauthenticated packets, then we conclude we only have "inside intruders." Otherwise, we are under attacks of both insiders and outsiders simultaneously.

We learn three things from the above results:

1. If no attack exists, then we do not pay the network layer authentication overhead. We always need to pay the application security overhead though.
2. Correlating intrusion information from two different layers, *i.e.*, network and application layers, we will be able to tell the location of the attack sources. This location information is valuable for security management.
3. If we know that the attack sources are purely from insiders, then we know that the network layer authentication does not help at all. In this case, we should put the waked-up SSGs back to sleep again.

3 Another Example of SSGP

3.1 Problem

In Figure 3, we have four SSGs and we assume that the public network is partitioned into four different zones by these SSGs. We assume that there are security associations ($\Leftrightarrow$) between (SSG_A, SSG_B) and (SSG_C, SSG_D). I.e., $SSG_A \Leftrightarrow SSG_C$, $SSG_A \Leftrightarrow SSG_D$, $SSG_B \Leftrightarrow SSG_C$, $SSG_B \Leftrightarrow SSG_D$. However, there is no such relation between SSG_A and SSG_B i.e., $(SSG_A \not\Leftrightarrow SSG_B)$. I.e., the IPSEC traffic from SSG_B to SSG_A must flow through either SSG_C or SSG_D. Previously, we have shown how we can use SSGP to decide whether the attack is from inside or outside. In this example, we would like to decide which zone the attack source resides.

3.2 Answer

At the beginning, all SSGs (A,B, C and D) are in sleepy mode. When the application detects an attack, it will wake up SSG_A first. Then, SSG_A will wake up both SSG_C and SSG_D. The packets authenticated by SSG_C and SSG_D include an authentication path information. Thus, when the application detects an attack, by looking at the authentication certificate appended after the IP packet, we can tell whether this attack packet is from SSG_C or SSG_D. In other words, if

$$IP_{decap}(Agent, MApp) = \boxed{IP(Agent, MApp)} \ \boxed{Auth^{SSG_A}_{SSG_C}},$$

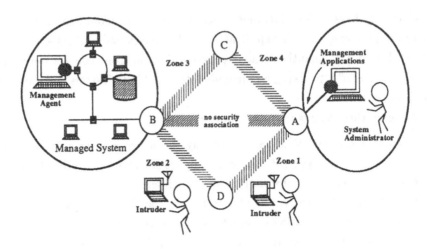

Fig. 3. SSGP: Another Example

then, we know this packet is from SSG_C.

If from now on the application does not observe any attack, while SSG_A detects some unauthenticated IP packets, then we know that the attack source must be either Zone 1 or 4. It depends on the network topology and configuration, and sometimes it may not be possible to further distinguish Zone 1 and 4. In this case, SSG_B will sleep all the time.

Similarly, if the application is still under attack and SSG_A does not detect bad packets, then the attack source must be in either Zone 2, Zone 3 or from an insider. At this point, the attacking packet should be presented to the security management module, and the module can tell whether it is from SSG_C or SSG_D by looking at the appended authentication certificate. If this attack packet is indeed from SSG_C, then SSG_C will wake up SSG_B. Now, an IP packet will pass through two separate IPSEC channels: $SSG_B \Leftrightarrow SSG_C$ and then $SSG_C \Leftrightarrow SSG_A$. The packet from SSG_B to SSG_C is

$$\boxed{Prot_{SSGP}, IP_{src}^{SSG_B}, IP_{dst}^{SSG_C} : \boxed{\boxed{Auth_{SSG_B}^{SSG_C}}\ \boxed{IP(Agent, MApp)}}},$$

where the $Auth_{SSG_B}^{SSG_C}$ is

$$\boxed{ID_{SSG_B}, ID_{SSG_C}, Seq\#},$$

plus

$$MD5(K_{BC}, ID_{SSG_B}, ID_{SSG_C}, Seq\#, \boxed{IP(Agent, MApp)}, K_{BC}).$$

At SSG_C,

$$IP_{decap}^{SSG_C}(Agent, MApp) = \boxed{IP(Agent, MApp) \;\Big|\; Auth_{SSG_B}^{SSG_C}}.$$

Then SSG_C will encapsulate the packet again using SSGP and send it to SSG_A. So, $IP_{encap}(SSG_C, SSG_A)$ looks like:

$$\boxed{Prot_{SSGP}, IP_{src}^{SSG_C}, IP_{dst}^{SSG_A} \; : \; \boxed{\boxed{Auth_{SSG_C}^{SSG_A}} \;\Big\|\; \boxed{IP_{decap}^{SSG_C}(Agent, MApp)}}},$$

where the $Auth_{SSG_C}^{SSG_A}$ is

$$\boxed{ID_{SSG_C}, ID_{SSG_A}, Seq\sharp},$$

plus,

$$MD5(K_{AC}, ID_{SSG_C}, ID_{SSG_A}, Seq\sharp, \boxed{IP_{decap}^{SSG_C}(Agent, MApp)}, K_{AC}).$$

Finally, at SSG_A, the packet being delivered to $MApp$ is:

$$\begin{aligned}
IP_{decap}^{SSG_A}(Agent, MApp) &= \boxed{IP_{decap}^{SSG_C}(Agent, MApp) \;\Big|\; Auth_{SSG_C}^{SSG_A}} \\
&= \boxed{IP(Agent, MApp) \;\Big|\; Auth_{SSG_B}^{SSG_C} \;\Big|\; Auth_{SSG_C}^{SSG_A}}.
\end{aligned}$$

Please note that this packet will then have two authentication certificates appended. At this point, it depends on whether we will observe another attack to decide the attack source location.

4 Attack Detection in the Application Layer

SSGP is a lazy security protocol. When no application or intrusion detection system complains about attacks, the $SSGs$ will not perform any authentication check. Thus, when no attack presents, the network is equivalent to an unsecure IP network. At this stage, even *untrusted hosts* can enjoy the network services.

We use SNMPv2 as an example to describe our idea about application-layer attack detection. In Figure 4, the security gateway in the SNMPv2 agent is in the application layer. An SNMPv2 PDU might be rejected for two reasons: authentication failure or freshness constraint.

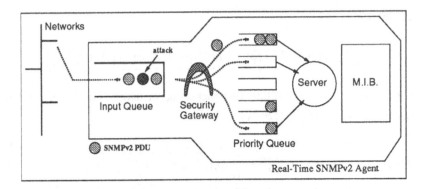

Fig. 4. Real-Time SNMPv2 Agent

4.1 Authentication Failure

If an PDU has an incorrect MD5 signature, this PDU may be an attack, an error in MD5 key configuration, or even a software bug. In any case, we should treat it as an attack and notify the security management module. If this is an error or bug, the SSGP protocol will treat it as an insider attack and, therefore, all *SSG*s should go back to sleep. Then, some network management modules or system administrators should be notified about this problem.

In a wireless network, since the bit error rate is higher, sometimes the link layer checksum mechanism might not correct/detect all the errors in the message. This could also cause incorrect MD5 signatures. Therefore, when accessing SNMP agents across wireless links (*e.g.*, CDPD [CDP95]), we can not conclude immediately the existence of attacks by justing detecting one single bad PDU. It depends on the link error rate to decide how many bad PDUs are enough to notify the management module.

4.2 Freshness Constraint

In SNMPv2, a received PDU might violate the freshness constraint. It could be a replay attack, a duplicated IP packet, or a large network delay. One heuristic is to set a second deadline for the PDU. If the PDU violates the first deadline, it is silently dropped. If it also violates the second deadline, we consider it an attack.

4.3 Attack Detection by Intrusion Detection Systems

Many existing applications do not have any built-in security mechanisms. Therefore, we need to build an intrusion detection system (IDS) [Den87, SRS91] to protect them. For example, in NCSU, we are using SNMPv1 (which has no security by itself) on top of Kerberos. Currently, we are building an IDS for SNMPv1 by monitoring the SNMPv1 traffic in our network.

4.4 Summary

No golden rules exist for the application layer attack detection. We must define the detection policies case by case. For example, to build a detection module for SNMP[WMBL94, WMB93] or Kerberos[NT94, BM90], we need to understand the application layer protocols themselves very well. Furthermore, we need to know what environment we run this application, *e.g.*, ATM or wireless.

5 Security Management Modules (SMM)

Security Management Module (SMM) is a key component in a SSGP system. SMM needs to communicate with both network and application layer security mechanisms. In our current prototype implementation, the SMM will interact with SNMP agents, while the agents collects intrusion information from network and application layers. In this section, the architecture of SMM is presented.

5.1 Intrusion Detection MIB

An *Intrusion Detection MIB (IDMIB)* is an abstraction of detected intrusion with standard management information interfaces (*e.g.*, SNMP or CMIP). An IDMIB specification document should describe what types of information are available in the MIB. For instance, an *intrusion event table (IET)* in the IDMIB collects all the locally detected intrusion events. This table (IET) offers valuable management information for local or even remote SMMs. All information requests from SMMs must be handled by management protocol agents (*e.g.*, SNMP agent).

5.2 Attack Detection

In SSGP, network applications themselves and/or intrusion detection systems are capable of detecting intrusion events. Detected events will be stored in the IET. An IET entry (*i.e.*, a row in the IET) consists of attributes (*i.e.*, columns in the IET) related to a detected intrusion event. These attributes may include the attack PDU with its original IP header, the attack type, and a timestamp.

When the networking system is under serious attacks, IET is updated frequently. And, the information kept in the IET is called *rapidly changing data* [Wu95]. In this case, it is important to maintain the information flows between the IDMIB agents and the SMMs. Sometimes, it is more efficient to have agents notify SMMs about newly detected intrusion events. However, there are also cases where it is better to let the SMMs periodly poll the information out of the IDMIB. In practice, a security management system will perform both polling and event notification.

5.3   Attack Isolation

A local SMM with a local IDMIB sometimes can not handle certain global attacks. For instance, in Figure 2, the SMM behind SSG_A observes attacks, but by itself it can not handle the problem properly. Therefore, SMMs must communicate with each other, exchange intrusion management information, and then a set of collaborating SMMs can decide the correct sources of attacks.

6   Security Consideration

We consider the following security concerns for SSGP:

Security-Sensitive Applications: There are certain important applications that could have very weak security by itself and also it is very hard to build an IDS to protect them. These applications should never be protected by a sleepy security gateway. In other words, the network administrator should configure the SSG such that it will never go to sleep. It is also important to identify what applications are suitable for the SSGP protection and what are not.

Evil Application Detection: If a protected application is evil, then it could complain about attacks while the attacks do not exist. These will wake up SSG gateways unnecessarily. The problem of detecting such evil/faulty applications is another IDS/security management problem. However, in the worst case, the SSGP will just converge to the static IPSEC architecture.

Compromised SSG Gateways: Compromised SSG gateways can wake up other SSG gateways viciously. In fact, without SSGP, if a security gateway in plain IPSEC is compromised, then many serious attacks can happen. To detect this type of problems is extremely important and generally an open problem.

SNMP Security: We use SNMPv2 in our experiments because of its availability today. We expect that a securer version of SNMP will be standardized in the near future.

7 Related Works

Network layer security for IP has been studied in [Bel96, Orm96, CGHK95, WB96, IB93]. Most of these works focus on design and implementation of a network security system similar to IPSEC [Atk95]. The SSGP work presented here went one step further by examining how IPSEC can be used to provide secure and high performance network services.

Security management and intrusion detection system have also been studied extensively (*e.g.,* [Den87, SRS91]). Both logical and statistical approaches have been proposed to handle different types of intrusion. SSGP offers an attractive architecture to integrate IPSEC and the results produced by the IDS community.

8 Conclusion

The IPSEC architecture [Atk95] specified only the security building blocks that we could use for Internet security. It has pointed out certain performance overheads for employing the standardized protocols. However, where and how to put these security building blocks in today's internet is a big open problem. It is very clear that careless placement of these blocks will not secure the network but reduce the available bandwidth. Therefore, in this paper, we propose SSGP as a solution to support secure and high performance authentication services on top of IPSEC. We feel that SSGP is an interesting option for the network administration to protect applications with application-layer security mechanisms.

SSGP defines an architecture about how application and network layer security mechanisms could collaborate under the framework of IPSEC. The collaboration between the security management modules and the SSGP/IPSEC offers the following advantages:

efficiency: SSGP saves unnecessary security checks. The SSG gateways will sleep when either there is no attack or they can not help because it is an insider attack.

isolation: SSGP isolates an outsider attack in its zone by waking up all the SSG gateways around that particular zone.

identification: SSGP identifies the possibility of insider attacks by comparing the security information from both network and application layers.

Currently, we are implementing a prototype version of SSGP/IPSEC and hopefully through this experimental system building process, we will learn more about the strength and weakness of SSGP. Our prototyping experiment is being built on top of Linux PCs with EtherNet and AT&T WaveLan cards. We need to modify the networking module code for participating routers/gateways. We also need to modify the applications so that it will observe/report attacks. Finally, we are using CMU's SNMPv2 package to implement the security management module.

In both SSGP and IPSEC, the insider attack will not be detected until it hits the target host's detection module (*e.g.*, MApp). It will be much nicer, while tracking the insider attacks, if we could perform the application layer detection much earlier. One idea that we are working on is to implement the application detection module as a Java applet. Then, in theory, we could send this applet to the SSG gateway and run it over there. For example, if the attack is from SSG_B in our previous examples, then we could ask SSG_B to load this applet and eliminate the attacks right at that point. The current release of Java does not allow this to happen because of the security concerns of Java itself. We are currently implementing LAVA [WDH+96], a securer version of Java, for this purpose.

Acknowledgments

Matt Blaze encouraged me to look into the problem of performance versus security. Some of the ideas here came out of my Ph.D. thesis which was supervised and shaped by Professor Gail E. Kaiser. Many members in the Secure and Highly Available Networking Group (SHANG) at NCSU have contributed to this work one way or the other. Especially, I want to thank XinYuan Wang, Brian Vetter, Hicong Fu, Tim Sluss and Ilia Baldine.

References

[Atk95]   R. Atkinson. Security Architecture for the Internet Protocol. RFC 1825, August 1995.

[BCCH94] R. Braden, D. Clark, S. Crocker, and C. Huitema. Report of TAB Workshop on Security in the Internet Architecture. RFC 1636, June 1994. Network Working Group.

[Bel96]   Steven M. Bellovin. Problem Areas for the IP Security Protocols. Draft, March 1996.

[BM90]   S.M. Bellovin and M. Merritt. Limitations of the Kerberos Authentication System. *Computer Communication Review*, 20(5):119–132, October 1990.

[CB94]   William R. Cheswick and Steven M. Bellovin. *Firewalls and Internet Security*. Addison Wesley, 1994.

[CDP95]   Cellular Digital Packet Data System Specification. CDPD Forum, Release 1.1, January 1995.

[CGHK95]   Pau-Chen Cheng, Juan A. Garay, Amir Herzberg, and Hugo Krawczyk. Design and Implementation of Modular Key Management Protocol and IP Secure Tunnel on AIX. In *1995 IEEE Symposium on Research in Security and Privacy*, May 1995.

[Den87]   Dorothy Denning. An Intrusion-Detection Model. *IEEE Transactions on Software Engineering*, SE-13(2):222–232, February 1987.

[DFW96]   D. Dean, E.W. Felten, and D.S. Wallach. Java Security: From HotJava to Netscape and Beyond. In *1996 IEEE Symposium on Security and Privacy*, pages 190–200, May 1996.

[Ebe92]   Hans Eberle. A High-Speed DES Implementation for Network Applications. Technical Report 90, DEC SRC, Palo Alto, CA, September 1992.

[GM93]   J. Galvin and K. McCloghrie. Security Protocols for version 2 of the Simple Network Management Protocol (SNMPv2). RFC 1446, May 1993. Network Working Group.

[IB93]   John Ioannidis and Matt Blaze. The Architecture and Implementation of Network-Layer Security Under Unix. In *4th Usenix Security Symposium*, October 1993.

[Lin94]   Mark H. Linehan. Comparison of Network-Level Security Protocols. Technical Report White Paper, IBM Research Division, June 1994.

[Mic]   Sun Microsystems. HotJava(tm): The Security Story. Java home page.

[NT94]   B. Clifford Neuman and Theodore Ts'o. Kerberos: An Authentication Service for Computer Networks. *IEEE Communications Magazine*, pages 33–38, September 1994.

[Orm96]   Hilarie Orman. Evolving an Implementation of a Network Level Security. Technical Report TR-95-15, CS Department, University of Arizona, Tucson, AZ, January 1996.

[Per96]   Charles Perkins. IP Mobility Support, draft 15. Internet Draft, IETF, February 1996. Mobile IP Working Group.

[SRS91]   et. al. Steven R. Snapp. DIDS (Distributed Intrusion Detection System) - Motivation, Architecture, and an Early Prototype. In *14th National Computer Security Conference*, pages 167–176, October 1991.

[Tou95]   Joseph Touch. Performance Analysis of MD5. In *SIGCOMM: Communications Architectures, Protocols and Applications*, pages 77–86, Cambridge, MA, September 1995.

[WB96]   David A. Wagner and Steven M. Bellovin. A Bumper in the Stack Encryptor for MS-DOS Systems. In *IEEE Symposium on Network and Distributed Systems Security*, 1996.

[WDH+96] S. F. Wu, M.S. Davis, J. Hansoty, J. Yuill, J. Webster, and X. Hu. LAVA: Secure Delegation for Mobile Applets. Technical Report TR-96-05, Computer Science Department, North Carolina State University, June 1996. submitted.

[WMB93]   Shyhtsun F. Wu, Subrata Mazumdar, and Stephen Brady. EMOSY: An SNMP Protocol Object Generator for the PIMIB. In *IEEE First International Workshop on System Management*, Los Angeles, CA, April 1993.

[WMBL94] Shyhtsun F. Wu, Subrata Mazumdar, Stephen Brady, and David Levine. On Implementing a Protocol Independent MIB. In *Network Management and Control, volume 2*, pages 309–329. Plenum Press, New York, 1994.

[Wu95]   Shyhtsun F. Wu. ϵ-*Consistent Real-Time Monitoring for Rapidly Changing Data*. PhD thesis, Columbia University, Computer Science Department, New York, NY, July 1995.

[Zor94]   Vasilios Zorkadis. Security versus Performance Requirements in Data Communication Systems. In *Computer Security - ESORICS 94*, pages 19–30, Brighton, UK, November 1994.

Certified Electronic Mail

Jianying Zhou and Dieter Gollmann

Department of Computer Science
Royal Holloway, University of London
Egham, Surrey TW20 0EX
United Kingdom
email: {zhou, dieter}@dcs.rhbnc.ac.uk

Abstract. This paper examines certified mail delivery in postal systems and derives the essential requirements that may be met by a service called certified electronic mail. Protocols are presented to demonstrate how various flavours of certified electronic mail services may be implemented.

Keywords: certified electronic mail, communications security, protocol design

1 Introduction

In many areas, 'pen-and-paper' procedures are being replaced by electronic mechanisms which can improve efficiency and provide better service. However, this transfer is not always easy. Much of the tradition, culture, and law that has been developed to provide protection in social contexts cannot readily be adapted to electronic procedures. On the other hand, cryptographic mechanisms can provide a new range of protection services in the electronic world. Indeed, Diffie has argued that communication security is "the transplantation of fundamental social mechanisms from the world of face to face meetings and pen and ink communication into a world of electronic mail, video, conference, electronic funds transfers, electronic data interchange, and, in the not too distant future, digital money and electronic voting" [6].

Electronic mail has today become an important application of computer networks. There are two main non-proprietary electronic mail (email) systems in widespread use, namely the Internet email system, specified in various RFCs, e.g. [1, 4, 10], and X.400, specified in the CCITT X.400 series recommendations [2]. Once email is used as a standard means of communications, it is natural to ask for the electronic equivalent of more specialised services offered by postal agencies. One such service, providing added protection for mail items, is certified mail. In this paper, we examine the requirements certified electronic mail should meet and the features that may distinguish certified electronic mail from other related services. This discussion not only leads to the specification of certified electronic mail protocols, it also highlights general issues in the definition and design of communications security services.

The paper is organized as follows. The next section gives a model of certified mail delivery in postal systems. In Section 3, we discuss a fictitious application of electronic mail and state the essential requirements that should be met by certified electronic mail. The relation between a certified mail service and other security services is also analysed in this section. We propose three versions of a certified electronic mail protocol (CEM) in Section 4, demonstrating a trade-off between the security properties achieved and the cryptographic infrastructure required.

2   Certified Mail

By choosing the name certified electronic mail (CEM) for a communications security service, we invoke the images of a familiar postal service. It is then only fair to ask that the objectives of CEM should not diverge too much from those of its precursor. We therefore start with a look at three kinds of certified mail services provided by the Royal Mail in the United Kingdom.

Recorded Mail This is a traceable delivery service, suitable for sending important documents. It has the following properties:

- provides a certificate of posting as proof that a letter or packet has been posted,
- signature collected on delivery,
- a *Local Call* telephone enquiry centre for confirmation of delivery,
- available with First or Second class post.

Special Delivery This is a guaranteed next day delivery service, suitable for sending urgent documents. It has the following properties:

- guarantees next day delivery by 12.30pm to most UK destinations,
- a *Local Call* telephone enquiry centre for up-to-date status and confirmation of delivery,
- signature collected on delivery.

Registered Mail This is a guaranteed next day delivery service with compensation, suitable for sending urgent documents, money, and valuable items. It has the following properties:

- guarantees next day delivery by 12.30pm to most UK destinations,
- compensation for loss or damage up to a maximum of £500,
- a *Local Call* telephone enquiry centre for up-to-date status and confirmation of delivery,
- signature collected on delivery.

In the above services, if nobody is available to receive the item, a card is left to advise the recipient that a mail item can be collected from the nearest Royal Mail delivery office. If the item is not collected within 3 weeks (1 week for Recorded mail items), it will be returned to the sender. The sender can track the progress of delivery by making a phone call to the enquiry centre or by paying an extra fee for automatic information.

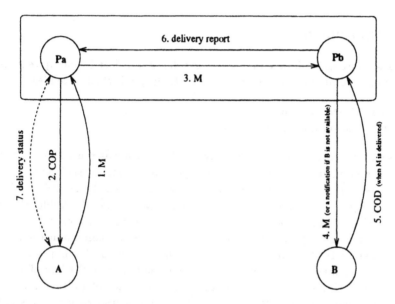

Fig. 1. Schematic Description of Certified Mail

A schematic description of certified mail is given in Figure 1. The sender A submits its mail M at a local post office P_a. P_a gives a certificate of posting (COP) to A, then sends A's mail to the recipient B's local post office P_b. P_b delivers A's mail to B and collects B's signature on a certificate of delivery (COD), or leaves a message asking B to collect its mail. Delivery is a face to face transaction between P_b and B, therefore the exchange of the mail and the COD with B's signature is guaranteed. A delivery report could be sent back from P_b to P_a by request. If necessary, A may make an enquiry to P_a about the delivery status of its mail which could be in delivery, awaiting collection, delivered with COD, non-deliverable, or lost.

The security properties guaranteed by certified mail are limited. Integrity and confidentiality of a mail item are only protected by placing the mail item in an envelope. Certified mail itself will not detect manipulation of a mail item. Usually, the sender and recipient have to combine to establish such an incidence.

Certified mail establishes a contractual relationship between the sender and the postal agent. A certificate of posting proves that the postal agent undertook to deliver a particular mail item. However, the content of the mail item is not verified in any way by the postal agent, so the sender cannot use *COP* as a proof of submission. The certificate of delivery proves that a particular mail item was delivered to the recipient. Again, *COD* cannot be interpreted as evidence sufficient to establish non-repudiation of receipt of the contents of the mail item.

3   Requirements

In postal systems, ordinary mail items get delayed or lost for many reasons. For important mail items, we thus may use certified mail which provides

- report of delivery, and
- compensation for lost mail items.

Mail sent over computer networks may also be lost or mis-routed due to network faults or system crashes. In current electronic mail systems, such as the Internet mail system, if a mail item fails to be delivered, it will be returned. If a mail item is delayed, the sender will receive a warning message. In X.400, the sender can specifically ask to be notified about the successful delivery of a mail item. This option is usually switched off because of the extra communication burden. Compensation for lost mail is not part of these services. As mail systems can, and will, copy mail items, compensation would not refer to the loss of a physical item but to a situation where the mail service lost track of an item and failed to advise the sender in time. We can formulate the essential requirements of CEM as:

> *Report of delivery and compensation for lost mail* — The sender collects evidence that the delivery agent undertook to deliver the mail item and that the mail item was delivered to the intended recipient. The delivery agent can also discharge its duty to the sender by giving a notification before an agreed deadline that the mail could not be delivered.

3.1   A Fictitious Application of CEM

A fictitious application may help to demonstrate the purpose of a certified electronic mail (CEM) service. A software house *A* sells its products over the Internet. A potential buyer *B* enquires about one of *A*'s products. *A* ships an inspection copy. What could happen next?

- The inspection copy arrives intact, *B* installs it, tests it, is satisfied, and places an order with *A*.
- The delivery agent employed by *A* returns the mail as undeliverable. If *A* suspects a problem with the delivery agent, it resends its inspection copy via a more competent service provider.

- The inspection copy never arrives. B turns to a different supplier and A has lost a business opportunity.
- The inspection copy arrives in a corrupted state. (Maybe, one of A's competitors has replaced it with a particularly lousy piece of code.) Again, B may be unhappy and turn to a different supplier.

Evidently, A should protect itself against

- loss of the mail item containing its software, and
- corruption of that mail item.

Certified mail addresses the first threat. If a mail item has been lost by the delivery agent, i.e. if A has not been informed about the status of delivery before a given deadline, A can claim compensation.

3.2 Relation to Other Security Services

Let us now consider integrity protection. Of course, this service could be tied in with CEM. However, it is definitely not necessary to do so. In our fictitious application, the sender A could attach its signature to the software shipped. B then can detect changes to the software and verify that it came from A. The delivery agent has no role to play in this verification. Even more, a delivery agent that works incorrectly will not corrupt the integrity service. (Messages may be corrupted, but corrupted messages will not be accepted as genuine.)

Equally, confidentiality protection need not be an aspect of certified mail. In the electronic world, it could be provided by a separate service, like PEM (Privacy Enhanced Mail) [7] or MOSS (MIME Object Security Services) [5].

We can also distinguish a certified mail service from a service for non-repudiation of origin and receipt. Non-repudiation of origin and receipt prevent entities from denying that they have sent or received certain messages [12]. This is a relation between the originator and the recipient, referring to the content of a message. Trusted third parties only help in establishing non-repudiation evidence and settling disputes. In contrast, a certified mail service is offered by the postal agent to the mail sender to guarantee the delivery of a mail to its destination. This is a relation between the mail sender and the delivery agent, without any reference to the content of the message. The mail recipient only helps the delivery agent to prove to the mail sender that the mail was delivered.

In electronic commerce, we may want a payment on delivery service. NetBill [3] defines *certified delivery* as an atomic method to guarantee payment when electronic goods are delivered. A trusted third party, the NetBill server, is involved in this protocol. Both merchant and client have a contractual relationship with the NetBill server and the protocol combines a non-repudiation service with a delivery service so that the client can obtain an item only when merchant and client are committed to that transaction.

4 Certified Electronic Mail

When designing a certified electronic mail protocol, a few important differences between postal delivery and electronic mail have to be noted. In postal systems, mail items exist physically and value is attached to the mail item itself. Postmen deliver the mail to the recipient in a face to face meeting. In computer networks, mail items can exist in several copies and senders are less concerned about the loss of such a copy than about timely delivery. Furthermore, when an electronic mail message is delivered, the recipient may be reluctant to acknowledge the message after having read its content. If this is deemed to be a problem, direct delivery has to be replaced by some other process to establish a certified electronic mail service.

The security elements built into X.400 [2] enable the provision of a number of different security services. The elements which may be of relevance for a certified electronic mail service are *proof of submission, non-repudiation of submission, proof of delivery*, and *non-repudiation of delivery*. Proof of delivery, or its stronger version non-repudiation of delivery, allows the originator of a message to obtain from the recipient a proof that the message has been delivered unaltered. This is more than originally required from certified mail. We will consider a weaker service that provides delivery reports referring to message labels rather than to the message contents.

In store and forward systems like X.400, messages are delivered by the message transfer system first to a message store (MS) and may later be retrieved by a user agent (UA). We thus can distinguish between services that report on delivery to a message store and those that require evidence from the user agent. A certified electronic mail service may use both options. As pointed out in [8, 9], proof of delivery to an MS is not possible if the message content is encrypted (unless the MS is given the UA's private key) because the message receipt has to be generated at the point in time when the message is delivered to the MS and is required to include a signature of the cleartext message content, which is only available to an entity possessing the recipient's private key. Our certified mail protocol avoids this problem as it only refers to message labels.

4.1 Notation

In our electronic model of certified mail (see Figure 2), A and B are mailbox programs rather than human users. $P_1, \ldots, P_n$ are a set of network mail servers acting as delivery agents to relay messages between A and B. The notation in the protocol description is as follows.

- X, Y: concatenation of two messages X and Y.
- $[X]$: message X is optional.
- $H(X)$: a one-way hash function of message X.
- $sK(X)$: digital signature of message X with the private key K.

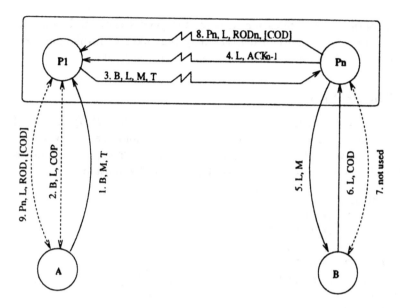

Fig. 2. Protocol CEM

- S_A: the private signature key of principal A.
- $A \rightarrow B : X$: principal A sends message X to principal B.
- $A \leftrightarrow B : X$: principal A pulls message X from principal B.
- M: mail item sent from A to B.
- L: a unique label chosen by P_1 to identify mail item M.
- T: deadline by which a delivery report or a non-deliverable notification should be available, chosen by A and agreed by P_1.
- $COP = sS_{P_1}(B, L, M, T)$: Certificate of Posting for M. In addition to the service offered by ordinary mail where COP and M do not have a direct link, the message is included in the signature. Thus, the mail sender can check whether the delivery agent acknowledged the submitted mail. It also includes a deadline for providing delivery status.
- $ACK_i = sS_{P_{i+1}}(P_i, B, L)$: Acknowledgement of the labeled mail item from P_i, $i = 1, \ldots, n-1$.
- $COD = sS_B(P_n, L, M)$: Certificate of Delivery of the labeled mail item.
- $ROD_j = sS_{P_j}(P_n, L)$: Report of Delivery of the labeled mail item. We use ROD for the Report of Delivery generated by P_1.

4.2 Cryptographic Infrastructure

Our protocol employs digital signatures to generate certificates like COP, COD, and ROD. We assume that all users and mail servers have the ability to digitally sign messages. The mail servers have to be able to verify signatures of neighbouring mail servers and of the users they deliver mail to. Users only need to be able to verify signatures of the mail servers they submit mail to but do not necessarily have verification keys for the parties they send mail to. A user wanting to query a report of delivery may thus have to invoke another service to check the certificate of delivery signed by the recipient.

4.3 The Protocol

Protocol CEM has four phases. Steps 2 and 9 are *"ftp get"* operations [11]. We assume that network failures are not permanent and that every message will *eventually* arrive at the intended recipient. If A and B are in the domain of the same mail server, i.e. $n = 1$, Steps 3, 4 and 8 will be omitted.

(1) Submission:
    1. $A \rightarrow P_1 : B, M, T$
    2. $A \leftrightarrow P_1 : B, L, COP$
(2) Relay: $i = 1, \ldots, n - 1$
    3. $P_i \rightarrow P_{i+1} : B, L, M, T$
    4. $P_{i+1} \rightarrow P_i : L, ACK_i$
(3) Delivery:
    5. $P_n \rightarrow B : L, M$
    6. $B \rightarrow P_n : L, COD$
    7. not used
(4) Confirmation:
    8. $P_n \rightarrow P_1 : P_n, L, ROD_n, [COD]$
    9. $A \leftrightarrow P_1 : P_n, L, ROD, [COD]$

This protocol can be elaborated depending on the application, e.g. by setting a deadline to limit the time mail items and delivery reports are available to the public so that the delivery agents do not need to store all mail items and delivery reports forever. We now describe the steps of protocol CEM in more detail.

1. $A \rightarrow P_1$: A sends the mail item, the name of the recipient and the delivery deadline to P_1. A could resend this message until it has retrieved the certificate of posting from P_1.
2. $A \leftrightarrow P_1$: If P_1 agrees with the delivery deadline, P_1 issues the certificate of posting with a unique label L and puts it in a publicly readable directory. A can fetch COP to check whether P_1 received the mail unchanged. If the check fails, A can resend the mail.
3. $P_i \rightarrow P_{i+1}$: P_i relays the mail item, the unique label, the name of the recipient and the delivery deadline to P_{i+1}. P_i could resend this message until it has received an acknowledgement from P_{i+1}.
4. $P_{i+1} \rightarrow P_i$: P_{i+1} acknowledges the labeled mail item received from P_i. If P_i does not receive this acknowledgement within its timeout period, it will inform A that the mail could not be delivered.
5. $P_n \rightarrow B$: P_n sends the mail item M and the label L to B.
6. $B \rightarrow P_n$: B returns the signed certificate of delivery COD to P_n. If P_n does not receive COD within its timeout period, it will inform A that the mail could not be delivered.

8. $P_n \to P_1$: A report of delivery, and optionally COD are relayed back from P_n to P_1. Then P_1 will store its ROD, and optionally COD, in a publicly readable directory. If P_1 does not receive the report of delivery before the deadline T, it will inform A that the mail could not be delivered.

9. $A \leftrightarrow P_1$: A fetches ROD, and optionally COD from P_1. The delivery agent is responsible for maintaining consistency among COP, ROD and COD.

In this protocol, the delivery agent either notifies A that the mail item could not be delivered or indicates delivery by presenting a report of delivery. The certificate of delivery signed by B can be included as supporting evidence. The delivery agent can do so only if the mail had actually been delivered but A would need B's verification key to check the link between ROD and COD. Such a check would also detect delivery of a corrupted mail item. The recipient has no way of verifying where the message came from or whether it was modified during transport.

As the recipient sees the message before signing the certificate of delivery, the protocol suffers from the *selective receipt* problem, a problem that also exists in X.400 security services like proof of delivery and non-repudiation of delivery. In our fictitious application, the following course of events is possible. The buyer B likes the software but does not want to pay for it. So, B does not acknowledge receipt. After a timeout period, the delivery agent informs A that its mail could not be delivered. B hopes that A will not check B's premises later on.

4.4 CEM-nsr: No Selective Receipt

The following CEM version prevents selective receipt by changing the certificate of delivery to $COD = sS_B(P_n, L)$, and the delivery phase to:

5. $P_n \to B : L$
6. $B \to P_n : L, COD$
7. $B \leftrightarrow P_n : L, M$

In this version, P_n informs B that a mail item labeled L is awaiting collection. We assume that the delivery agent places mail item M in a publicly readable directory after receiving COD from B. Now, B can retrieve the mail item. If the mail item is put into the directory before, there is no protection against selective receipt. If the mail item is not placed in the directory at all, then B does not get the mail item. When B is unable to retrieve the message, it will take steps beyond the protocol to alert the user community about its communications problems with that particular delivery agent.

The recipient still cannot verify the integrity of the mail fetched from the delivery agent. The mail sender obtains evidence that the recipient acknowledged a notification for a mail item with the correct label but has no evidence that the recipient did indeed receive the correct mail.

4.5   CEM-ip: No Selective Receipt with Integrity Protection

When the sender A wants B to acknowledge that the correct item was received, A could use a service providing non-repudiation of receipt. Such a service requires further security infrastructure to be in place, and may thus be quite expensive. Hence, A could settle for less and only ask for evidence that the correct mail item was ready for collection by B. There is still no guarantee that B will collect this message. Given that CEM is an arrangement between A and the delivery agent, this requirement is reasonable. The delivery agent has no authority over B and may be reluctant to pay compensation if B is at fault. Again, integrity protection inserted by A may alert B when it has retrieved a wrong message.

To provide the mail sender with sufficient information for integrity verification while avoiding the selective receipt problem, we change the certificate of delivery to $COD = sS_B(P_n, L, H(L, M))$.

5. $P_n \rightarrow B : L, H(L, M)$
6. $B \rightarrow P_n : L, COD$
7. $B \leftrightarrow P_n : L, M$

In Step 5, the delivery agent sends $H(L, M)$ with the unique label L. The recipient can use $H(L, M)$ to verify the mail fetched at Step 7. Alternatively, P_n could send M encrypted under a key K in Step 5, release the key in Step 7, and include the key in its report of delivery. However, we prefer the version using a cryptographic hash function because of its lower computational overheads.

When the delivery agent supplies a wrong message M' with hash value $H(L, M')$, B will accept M' as genuine. However, a check of COD will detect that B was notified about a wrong message and the sender can take steps beyond the protocol to rectify the situation. When the delivery agent supplies M' with $H(L, M)$, B will note the discrepancy and retry to fetch M. If this fails persistently, or if the message cannot be retrieved at all, B will take steps beyond the protocol to alert the user community about its communications problems with that particular delivery agent.

When a bogus delivery agent has sent $L, H(L, M')$ to B and B responds with $COD = sS_B(P_n, L, H(L, M'))$, P_n will note the discrepancy and A will not be notified about the success of delivery. However, B will not detect that it retrieves the wrong message M'. When B replies to the notifications $L, H(L, M)$ from P_n and $L, H(L, M')$ from a bogus delivery agent, B cannot determine which notification was genuine. As far as P_n and A are concerned, the message M was delivered but B may wrongly retrieve M'.

It is not difficult for B to protect itself against such a situation. Whenever B is notified about a mail with label L, B will reject any further notifications with the same label until it has retrieved the corresponding mail item. Of course, genuine delivery agents may be concerned about bogus competitors and offer integrity protection mechanisms of their own. For example, P_n could sign the notification to B. However, this implies that B is able to verify signatures and is in possession of a certified verification key for P_n. As a matter of fact, B will require those keys for all agents that may deliver certified mail to B.

4.6 Compensation

The delivery agent agrees to compensate A if A has a COP with label L and the delivery agent fails to supply a ROD and COD with label L for the correct message, if applicable, signed by the intended receiver within an agreed period of time. Timestamping of ROD is outside the scope of this protocol. Instead of ROD and COD, the delivery agent can also supply a notification that the mail could not be delivered. Of course, the delivery agent can always create such a notification before the deadline. In our fictitious application, A then at least knows about the delivery problem and can use another delivery agent.

The delivery agent ought to be reluctant to *guarantee* to deliver A's mail. It would have to rely on A to specify B's address correctly and on B to be ready to receive mail. Such a guarantee only makes sense if B is controlled by the delivery agent to the extent that the delivery agent can check the correctness of B's address and guarantee that B will be ready. Typically, such a situation arises when B is a message store under the delivery agent's control.

5 Conclusion

There are three aspects to this paper. First and foremost, it uses certified electronic mail in an attempt to show how to properly identify requirements for a secure communication service. It is often quite tempting to add any reasonable protection requirements to the list of intended features. There is no doubt that such an all encompassing service may be useful, but it will quite likely also be rather expensive. Every new encryption, every new signature demands appropriate management of the new keys introduced to the system. The more cryptographic functions we use, the more elaborate our security infrastructure will be. Given that the customers will have to pay for this infrastructure, we should place our services where it is most cost effective. This observation may be obvious, but it is worth repeating.

Secondly, we have defined CEM to protect only against loss and delayed delivery of mail items. We decided to treat integrity protection and non-repudiation of receipt as different services, which may be offered in conjunction with CEM, but are not an integral part of CEM. If we only ask for a report of delivery, then present electronic mail systems already include CEM as an option.

Finally, we have given protocols to demonstrate how various flavours of CEM may be implemented. We observe a trade-off between the guarantees the sender can obtain and the assumptions it wants to make about the behaviour of the recipient and of the delivery agent. Protocol CEM does not make any assumptions about the delivery agent, but the recipient may decide not to acknowledge a message it has received. Protocols CEM-nsr and CEM-ip avoid the selective receipt problem but rely on the delivery agent to make messages available once the recipient has acknowledged the corresponding notification.

Acknowledgements

We have benefited from discussions with colleagues in the Information Security Group. Comments from Chris Mitchell and Wenbo Mao on the draft of this paper are appreciated. We are also grateful to the anonymous referees for their important suggestions for improvements to this paper. The first author would like to thank the British Government and the K C Wong Education Foundation for their support through an ORS Award and a K C Wong Scholarship.

References

1. N. Borenstein and N. Freed. *Multipurpose Internet mail extensions (MIME)*. RFC 1521, September 1993.
2. CCITT. *Recommendation X.400: Message handling system and service overview*. November 1988.
3. B. Cox, J. D. Tygar and M. Sirbu. *NetBill security and transaction protocol*. Proceedings of the First USENIX Workshop on Electronic Commerce, July 1995.
4. D. Crocker. *Standard for the format of ARPA Internet text messages*. RFC 822, August 1982.
5. S. Crocker, N. Freed, J. Galvin and S. Murphy. *MIME object security services*. RFC 1848, October 1995.
6. W. Diffie. *The impact of a secret cryptographic standard on encryption, privacy, law enforcement and technology*. Hearings before the Subcommittee on Telecommunications and Finance of the Committee on Energy and Commerce, House of Representatives, One Hundred Third Congress, First Session, Serial No. 103-53, pages 111-116, April 29 and June 9, 1993.
7. S. T. Kent. *Internet privacy enhanced mail*. Communications of the ACM, 36(8):48-60, August 1993.
8. C. J. Mitchell, M. Walker and D. Rush. *CCITT/ISO standards for secure message handling*. IEEE Journal on Selected Areas in Communications, 7(4):517-524, May 1989.
9. C. J. Mitchell, D. Rush and M. Walker. *A secure message architecture implementing the X.400-1988 security features*. The Computer Journal, 33(4):290-295, 1990.
10. J. B. Postel. *Simple mail transfer protocol*. RFC 821, August 1982.
11. J. B. Postel and J. K. Reynolds. *File transfer protocol*. RFC 959, October 1985.
12. J. Zhou and D. Gollmann. *A fair non-repudiation protocol*. Proceedings of the 1996 IEEE Symposium on Security and Privacy, pages 55-61, Oakland, CA, May 1996.

Distributed Proctoring

Bruce Schneier *   John Kelsey **   Jay Walker ***

Abstract. We develop a protocol for "distributed proctoring" which allows a network of graders to grade individual problems solved by a network of test takers. The mutual anonymity of the test takers and graders is ensured using anonymous MIXs, but an audit trail is provided in the event of a grading dispute. We discuss other applications for this protocol, more generally defined as "digital piecework."

1 Introduction

We would like to take some submission from a user (e.g. a contest entry, a solution to a problem in an exam, or a paper submitted to a refereed electronic journal) and pass it anonymously to be judged by one or more graders. We want the graders to be able to send an authenticated result back, and we need to be able to pay them for their work. Eventually, we will make some decision on the basis of this result: an exam is given a grade, a paper accepted or rejected, a winner declared in a contest. We call this general problem "Distributed Proctoring."

There are many applications for this kind of protocol, and it can be more generally thought of as "Digital Piecework." Alice has a problem requiring human judgment (grading test answers, in the example above) which can possibly be divided into several pieces (each test question can be graded individually). There is a network of experts (graders) who are available to solve problems (they log onto the system at will, and are sent test answers to grade as they become available). The experts solve the problems (grade the questions) and transmit their solutions back to Alice. This system could be anonymous or not. Alice needs to be able to verify the experts' credentials (they must post certified copies of their credentials) and possibly their identity, and some means of paying them for their work.

There could be an entire network devoted to digital piecework. Experts in a variety of fields could post their credentials, and people needing expertise could post their requests. An "experts wanted" list might look like:

- I want an academic paper on quantum mechanics reviewed anonymously by three qualified academics not located in the U.S. The reviews are due on a particular date.

* Counterpane Systems, 101 East Minnehaha Parkway, Minneapolis, MN 55419 schneier@counterpane.com
** Counterpane Systems, 101 East Minnehaha Parkway, Minneapolis, MN 55419 kelsey@counterpane.com
*** Walker Digital, Inc., 4 High Ridge Park, Stamford, CT 06905

- I am a businessman in the steel salvage business with a question as to how to handle a personnel problem. I would like my question answered by a personnel professional at a Fortune 1000 company who is not in the steel business and who has dealt with the same or similar problem at least five times in their own company. I am willing to pay $100 for answers or at least 250 words. Anonymity is acceptable, but I will pay an extra $100 if the person is identified to me and I am allowed to call him.
- I am an attorney who is seeking other businesses who have had a problem with the XYZ company's plastic products. I will pay $50 for each documented example of problems, up to 100 problems.
- I am looking to decode a hieroglyphic unearthed on a site in Israel. I will pay $50 for each solution of at least ten words, and $500 for the complete solution. Answers will be accepted from 4 candidates who send me their credentials.
- I am seeking to hire a qualified structural engineer for a two-week assignment performing a weight-load analysis for various wooden bridges.
- I am arguing with an insurance company, and need three independent medical opinions no later than the following Friday. I seek only the opinions of doctors who are board-certified inner ear specialists and who have been practicing for five or more years. Each opinion must be at least 200 words in length. If the opinion is anonymous or unofficial, I'll pay $100. If the opinion is the physician's official opinion, I'll pay $250.
- I am looking to find Alice Smith, last known address 100 York Street, Anytown, USA. I will pay $500 to the first person who provides me with a verified place of employment for this person.
- To all people who have eaten at my restaurant, I will pay $5 for a 100 word description of how to improve my service or menu: limit, 50 people.

For the rest of this paper, we will restrict our discussion to the distributed proctoring problem. Many security issues arise in this kind of protocol. Among them:

a. How do we know that the test's rules are being followed?
b. How do we know that the grader is grading tests impartially and correctly?
c. How do we ensure anonymity of the test takers and graders?
d. How do we prevent collusion between some test takers and some graders?
e. How do we prevent outside interference with the process?

1.1 Notation and Conventions

a. $PKE_{PK_U}(X)$ represents the public-key encryption of X under public key PK_U.
b. $SIGN_{SK_U}(X)$ represents the digital signature of X under private key SK_U.
c. $E_{K_0}(X)$ represents the symmetric encryption of X under key K_0.
d. PK_U represents the public key of user U.

e. SK_U represents the private key of user U.

f. ID_U represents the identification number or code of user U.

g. X, Y represents the concatenation of X with Y.

2 Techniques

2.1 Anonymity and MIXs

An "anonymous MIX" is an intermediary communications node which attempts to make it very difficult for anyone to trace the path of a message which passes through the MIX. The idea behind MIXs is discussed in [Cha81], and is used in election schemes [Cha81, PIK94] and anonymous remailers on the Internet [Sch95, TG96]. In our protocol, we use anonymous MIXs to prevent an eavesdropper who has access complete access to the network's traffic from being able to compromise the system.

When Alice sends Bob a message through an anonymous MIX, the following (roughly) takes place:

1. Alice wishes to send message P to Bob anonymously. She first forms

    K_0 = a random session key.

    Z_0 = an all-zero string of some random length.

    $X_0 = PKE_{PK_M}(K_0)$, where PK_M is the MIX's public key.

    $M_0 = X_0, E_{K_0}(ID_B, Z_0, P)$, where ID_B represents Bob's identity.

    She then sends M_0 to the MIX. Note that Alice may also have encrypted and digitally signed the message she's sending to Bob. This has no bearing at all on how the MIX processes it.

2. The MIX receives M_0. It decrypts this into ID_B, P. It looks up Bob's public key from ID_B, and then forms

    K_1 = a random session key.

    Z_1 = an all-zero string of some random length.

    $X_1 = PKE_{PK_B}(K_1)$, where PK_B is Bob's public key.

    $M_1 = X_1, E_{K_1}(Z_1, P)$.

    It waits some random amount of time before sending M_1 to Bob. During this time, it is processing many other messages, both sending and receiving them.

3. Bob receives M_1. He decrypts it and recovers P.

In order to anonymize messages that pass through a MIX, we must have a fairly large volume of messages coming in and out and a random delay involved in forwarding those messages. Otherwise, it is possible for an opponent to watch and time messages going into and coming out of the MIX, and use this information to determine the source and destination of each message. The whole point of the strings of random-length all-zero string (it can be a random-length string of any random bits, but there needs to be some way to determine where Z_i ends and P

begins) is to disguise the size of the messages; an eavesdropper who watches the messages coming in and out of the MIX cannot link them by their size. Messages may also be broken into many pieces to avoid this problem. Similarly, messages must be encrypted to the MIX, so that the messages can be decrypted and then re-encrypted with a different key.

2.2 Steganography, Marking, and Collusion

There exist techniques for embedding a hidden message in almost any free-format data. This can be used to allow Alice to mark her submission in some invisible way, so that if Bob is colluding with her, he can identify her submission. Given that submissions generally need to be free-format, there is not a general cryptographic solution for this problem.

The study of how to embed invisible marks and messages in other messages is called steganography. Many such techniques of varying quality are well-publicized. However, one general rule is that it is very hard to eliminate any chance of such hidden information without radically altering the "covertext" data. However, proper design of the tests may help make it hard to insert covert signals into the submission in practice. Mainly, however, we rely on the difficulty of making contact with the graders and bribing or threatening very many of them into co-operating, to make this attack less threatening.

3 The Protocol

In this protocol, the players are:

- Alice — the user submitting something to be judged.
- Bob — the person judging Alice's submission.
- Carol — the person coordinating the whole thing. She is completely trusted by all parties.
- Dave — a person who may want to have Alice prove the results to him.

We use public-key cryptography for encryption and digital signatures. The exact algorithms are unimportant at the protocol level; an overview of the techniques involved is [Sch96]. All public keys are signed by some certification authority. Certificates can be sent with messages, and different keys can be used for encryption and digitial signatures. Carol knows everyone's public key, and everyone knows hers. The anonymous MIXs either know everyone's public keys, or their public keys are sent along with their identities. Everyone is assumed to know the MIXs' public keys.

3.1 The Basic Protocol

1. Alice creates some submission, S. This may be in response to a question from an exam booklet, or a contest, or a post submitted to a moderated newsgroup, or whatever. She then forms

K_0 = a random session key. This should not be confused with the key Alice uses to send the message to the anonymous MIX.

R_0 = a random challenge either generated by Alice or given to her by someone else, depending on application. In some cases, R_0 is used to seed the test machine.

$X_0 = PKE_{PK_C}(K_0)$, where PK_C is Carol's public key.

$X_1 = SIGN_{SK_A}(ID_A, R_0, S)$, where SK_A is Alice's private key and ID_A represents Alice's identity.

$M_0 = X_0, E_{K_0}(ID_A, R_0, S, X_1)$.

She sends M_0 to Carol via an anonymous MIX.

2. Carol receives M_0. She decrypts it, and verifies the signature. She also verifies that she's never seen this submission before. She randomly selects a Bob out of all the graders available. She then forms

K_1 = a random session key.

N = a random submission identifier.

T_1 = a timestamp.

$X_2 = PKE_{PK_B}(K_1)$, where PK_B is Bob's public key.

$X_3 = SIGN_{SK_C}(ID_C, N, T_1, I, S)$, where SK_C is Carol's private key and ID_C represents Carol's identity, and where I are the grading instructions.

$X_4 = E_{K_1}(ID_C, N, T_1, I, S, X_3)$

$M_1 = X_2, X_4$.

She sends M_1 to Bob via anonymous MIX. She stores N, ID_A, R_0, S, and T_1.

3. Bob receives M_1. He decrypts it, and verifies the signature and timestamp. He then grades the submission, S, according the the instructions, I. When this is finished, he has formed a grade, G. He then forms

K_2 = a random session key.

$X_5 = PKE_{PK_C}(K_2)$.

$X_6 = SIGN_{SK_B}(ID_B, N, G)$, where SK_B is Bob's private key and ID_C represents Bob's identity.

$X_7 = E_{K_2}(ID_B, N, G, X_6)$

$M_2 = X_5, X_7$.

He sends M_2 to Carol via anonymous MIX.

4. Carol receives M_2. She decrypts it and verifies the signature. She searches for the matching N among her currently active submissions. If she doesn't find it, an error has occurred, and someone will need to follow up, but the protocol ends. If she does find it, however, she notes that Bob has returned the submission (so he can be paid for it). She then looks up Alice's challenge, address, and timestamp, and forms

K_3 = a random session key.

T_2 = a new timestamp.

$X_8 = PKE_{PK_A}(K_3)$, where PK_A is Alice's public key.

$X_9 = SIGN_{SK_C}(ID_A, R_0, T_2, S, G)$.

$M_3 = X_8, E_{K_3}(ID_A, R_0, T_2, S, G, X_9)$.

Carol sends M_3 to Alice via anonymous MIX.

5. Alice receives M_3, and verifies the signature. She now has an authenticated grade on this submission, along with a timestamp to show when she submitted it.

In step (1), Alice encrypts the submission under the public key of Carol, the co-ordinator of the proctoring system. This gives Alice some confidentiality (important for some kinds of tests), makes it harder for others to copy Alice's submission, and also prevents an eavesdropper from seeing Alice's specific submission, and thus being able to easily trace it.

Alice also signs the submission under her own private key. This prevents someone from changing Alice's submission, either to help or hurt her score, without knowledge of her private key. If we are concerned that Alice may give or lose her private key to someone else interested in changing her submission, then we can also have the test-taking machine digitally sign the submission with a key that's kept in tamper-resistant storage somewhere.

Alice incorporates a random challenge into her submission. This allows another party, Dave, to verify that she's actually getting these results, without having to look over her shoulder and verify her score.

In step (2), Carol generates and uses N, an anonymous identification code for this submission. This allows her to efficiently cross-reference between submissions already sent out to graders, and those waiting for a return from the graders. Carol needs to verify that she has never seen the submission before, in order to prevent Alice from submitting multiple S values and keeping the one with the best grade. In some applications she can check R_0; in other applications she needs to keep a database of which exam questions Alice has already answered.

Carol's timestamp prevents simple replay attacks. Her public-key and symmetric encryption prevents loss of confidentiality of submissions, and also to complicate attempts to figure out which submission went to which grader. Finally, her digital signature ensures that graders don't grade bogus submissions, and that nobody can change any of these submissions without being noticed.

In step (4), Carol signs the message; this authenticates the grade for Alice and Dave, as well as ensuring that no malicious or accidental changes to the grade have occurred. Carol encrypts the message, ensuring Alice's confidentiality. And Carol includes both a timestamp (from when the submission was received) and R_0. This allows Alice and Dave to be certain that this isn't simply a replay of someone else's successful test result. It also contains S, so that Alice can immediately notice any changes that have occurred in S.

At this point Alice must also verify that she expected X_7 from Bob. Otherwise, if N were easy to guess, Alice could send the grade that she wanted to Carol before Bob did. Or another grader could send a grade to Carol for a pending submission and receive pay, even if that grader was not assigned to the submission.

3.2 Enhancements and Variations

Showing Results to Someone Else If Alice is making a submission whose result she must show Dave, then she gets R_0 from Dave. In this way, she is able to prove that there is no replay going on.

Preventing Signaling by Dave If Alice is concerned that Dave might pass use R_0 as a subliminal channel [Sim85, Sim94] to pass information to Carol, they can mutually agree on R_0. The simplest way is probably as follows:

1. Alice generates random R_1, and sends Dave $hash(R_1)$.
2. Dave sends Alice R_2.
3. Alice generates $R_0 = R_1 \oplus R_2$.
4. Alice makes her submission, and receives her answer back.
5. Alice sends Dave R_1 and the response she received from Carol.

Auditing the Performance of the Graders Sometimes, it may be important to judge the graders' competence and impartiality. In this case, the same questions or submissions can be sent to both a trusted grader and an untrusted one. Then, the answers can be compared. Alternatively, each submission might have some chance of being sent out to more than one grader. Significant disagreements would cause Carol to review both grades, and possibly to determine that one grader was being partial or incompetent.

3.3 What Can Go Wrong?

- The anonymous MIXs may fail, making it possible for a network eavesdropper to determine which graders graded which submissions. This opens up possibilities for all kinds of potential problems, especially involving bribery or blackmail of the graders. If Carol adds random delays in steps (2) and (4), she can act as an anonymous MIX herself, though it would still be preferable to use a larger set of anonymous MIXs as well. Additionally, she may wish to agree ahead of time with some of the graders and test-takers, or with others, to send and receive "null messages," which look like real messages until decrypted. This could happen either because the MIX machines are subverted, or because they don't have enough traffic, don't have random enough delays, etc.
- If the public key or symmetric encryption algorithms are broken or badly implemented, then the anonymity of the graders and users can be compromised.
- If the digital signature or hashing algorithms are broken or badly implemented, then it will be possible to carry out active attacks in which Alice's submission is replaced with a better (or worse) submission.

- Some test-takers may conspire with some graders to get unfairly high grades. In most cases, this can be done using some steganographic techniques to embed an identification string into the submission, and possibly even into the grade. The only general solution to this seems to be to make sure that the graders are audited occasionally, and to ensure that most graders are honest.
- Graders may be incompetent or dishonest, and not do a thorough job grading.
- Depending on the way graders are rewarded for their work, it may be possible to acquire a list of all the graders. This would make blackmail or bribery far simpler. Where possible, anonymous payment methods should be used.

4 Applications

There are many possible applications based on these ideas. Three are discussed briefly in this section.

4.1 Distributed Proctoring of Exams

Distributed proctoring of exams simply allows a user to take an exam under some simple scrutiny to prevent cheating, and then allows that exam to be graded by people who have never met the user and probably never will.

The protocol discussed in subsection 3.1 is directly used for this application. Alice's instructor, Dave, gives her random challenge R_0. She responds, after taking the exam, with the response returned to her by Carol. Carol, of course, keeps a database to ensure that Alice only responds with one answer to each exam question.

One potential problem is that the graders may not be very consistent. Many people who grade exams or programs try to grade them all in one sitting to avoid treating one group of students differently than another. It may make sense to require the same grader to grade many exams, or the same problems from many submissions. Alternatively, it may make sense to have several graders judge each exam, and average out their scores, or even normalize test scores based on averages per grader.

4.2 Judging a Contest

Contests go on all the time. Some ask participants to sketch a suggested new company logo, or come up with a new slogan. Others might ask the participants to estimate some number (like the number of jelly beans that fit in a large room), or solve some puzzle (such as a very large and complex crossword puzzle.) Distributed proctoring in this case is used to impartially judge contest submissions.

Contest submissions are different from exams in that they are probably graded by several people in sequence, as the graders weed out all but the best submissions. The only major change in this application's use of the protocol in section 3.1 is that steps (2) through (4) may take place many times for the same submission. Each time, Alice is notified of how her submission has fared. Eventually, if Alice is the winner, she is sent her final notification. For judging a contest, Carol may send each submission to several judges at once, and then take the average of their grades as the true score. There may then be a final judgement between the most promising three or four submissions.

Along with the things discussed in section 3.3, there are other potential problems here:

- These contests may have monetary prizes. This raises a whole set of possible problems regarding payment protocols and such. Also, many attacks become worth considering when there is a large potential payoff for succeeding.
- Contests with a single corrct or best answer, or a straightforward judging criteria, would never need a set of human graders. However, the more subjective the grades are, the harder it is to determine whether a given grader is giving some submissions better treatment than others. This implies that judgements should probably be done using many different graders, and averaging their scores somehow.

4.3   Refereeing a Journal or Newsgroup Submission

Moderated Usenet newsgroups and internet mailing lists have existed for a while now, and refereed technical journals for much longer. The technical journal of the future will probably look like a marriage of the two. A distributed proctoring system is useful in getting a submission directly to one or more referees. Depending on the application, there may be several levels of refereeing between initial submission and final acceptance.

For most moderated newsgroups, the intent of moderation is simply to filter out irrelevant or inappropriate submissions. The moderators seldom (if ever) filter the submissions for quality and originality of technical work. The problem in moderating a newsgroup is dealing with volume.

Distributed proctoring works here because a large number of graders can each take part in moderating the newsgroup. Most newsgroup articles can be filtered for relevance and appropriate topic pretty quickly. If there is some method by which people pay to receive or use the newsgroup, then each moderator can be paid according to how many articles he grades. (The quality of his judgement will also come into play, probably in determining whether or not he will continue to be a moderator for the group.) The protocol described in section 3.1 is followed, except that in step (d), Carol posts Alice's submission to the newsgroup. In some cases, she also includes the grade. Note that the grade may be more about the post's topic (keywords, for example) than about its quality.

Technical journals are quite different. Most have a much more narrow audience, and they generally filter for technical quality of the submissions. Grading will take longer for a technical journal, and there will probably be several graders involved. Also, for a technical journal, it is quite reasonable for the graders to reject the submission for now, but make some suggestions for ways to make the submission acceptable at a later time.

Distributed proctoring works well here because the grading process needs to be anonymous, and because while there needs to be a thorough review of submissions, turn-around time is also important. For this application, the protocol in section 3.1 is modified in step (2): the submission is probably sent out to several graders. The final grade is based on all the grades collected: possibly a majority vote of accept or reject. However, all comments are passed back to Alice in step (4). It would not be unusual for Alice to alter the submission based on those recommendations before resubmitting it for final approval. Final approval means that in step (4) of the protocol, Carol forwards the submission to the journal's printing or remailing system, as well as to Alice.

Along with the things discussed in section 3.3, there are other potential problems here:

- Moderators or referees may not do a thorough enough job grading the submissions. For example, a dishonest newsgroup moderator might only read the first paragraph of a submission before deciding to accept or reject it. The auditing techniques discussed above should minimize this problem. Also, there will probably be a record kept of each grader's acceptances and rejections. There may even be a way to allow the subscribers to rate the submissions' quality, and thus effectively grade the graders.

5   Conclusions

There exists a need to efficiently match people with expertise with people requiring that expertize; exam proctoring is only one example of this. We have shown how to use anonymous MIXs to support this commerce in expertise. Potential applications include buying expert opinions, hiring of temporary, part-time, and permanent employees, and marketing research. The more diverse the applications that use the MIX protocol, the more security inherent in the system.

6   Acknowledgments

The authors would like to thank Steve Bellovin, Chris Hall, James Jorasch, and David Wagner for their helpful comments and suggestions. The digital piecework protocols are patent pending in the United States and other countries.

References

[Cha81]   D. Chaum, "Untraceable electronic mail, return addresses, and digital pseudonyms," *Communications of the ACM*, v. 24, n. 2, Feb 1981, pp. 84-88.

[PIK94]   C. Park, K. Itoh, and K. Kurosawa, "Efficient Anonymous Channel and All/Nothing Election Scheme," *Advances in Cryptology — EUROCRYPT '93 Proceedings*, Springer-Verlag, 1994, pp. 248-259.

[Sch95]   B. Schneier, *E-Mail Security*, John Wiley & Sons, 1995.

[Sch96]   B. Schneier, *Applied Cryptography, 2nd Edition*, John Wiley & Sons, 1996.

[Sim85]   G. Simmons, "The Subliminal Channel and Digital Signatures," *Advances in Cryptography — EUROCRYPT '84 Proceedings*, Springer-Verlag, 1985, pp. 51-57.

[Sim94]   G. Simmons, "Subliminal Channels: Past and Present," *European Transactions on Telecommunications*, v. 5, n. 4, 1994, pp. 459-473.

[TG96]   G. Tsudik and C. Gulcu, "Mixing E-mail with BABEL," *ISOC Symposium on Network and Distributed System Security '96*, to apprear.

Merging Heterogeneous Security Orderings

P.A. Bonatti[1], M.L. Sapino[1] and V.S. Subrahmanian[2*]

[1] Università di Torino
{bonatti,mlsapino}@di.unito.it
[2] University of Maryland
vs@cs.umd.edu

Abstract. The problem of integrating multiple heterogeneous legacy databases is an important problem. Many papers [7, 9, 3] to date on this topic have assumed that all the databases comprising a mediated/federated system share the same security ordering. This assumption is often not true as the databases may have been developed independently by different agencies at different points in time. In this paper, we present techniques by which we may merge multiple security orderings into a single unified ordering that preserves the security relationships between orderings. We present a logic programming based approach, as well as a graph theoretical approach to this problem.

Keywords: Theoretical Foundations of Security, Heterogeneous Mediated/Federated Systems.

1 Introduction

Complex applications in today's rapidly changing world require the ability to access a wide variety of distributed, heterogeneous data sources. In order to assist the *author* of such complex applications, Wiederhold [14, 15] has proposed the important concept of a *mediator* as a paradigm for integrating heterogeneous data and software. Major efforts towards the construction of mediators are currently underway at many universities and companies [12, 1, 4, 10].

One of the fundamental problems faced by each and every one of these efforts is the problem of *security*. Besides the standard problems related to security in databases and information systems, one has to tackle specific problems raised by the heterogeneous nature of data sources. In particular, it is not reasonable to assume that all packages participating in a mediated system and the mediator itself use the same security orderings.

* Partially supported by the Army Research Office under grant DAAH-04-95-10174, by the Air Force Office of Scientific Research under grant F49620-93-1-0065, by ARPA/Rome Labs contract Nr. F30602-93-C-0241 (Order Nr. A716), by NSF Young Investigator award IRI-93-57756, by NSF award IRI-93-14905, and by the Army Research Laboratory under Cooperative Agreement DAAL01-96-2-0002 Federated Laboratory ATIRP Consortium.

For example, a Supply Mediator might use an **inventory** relation, created by an Army Logistics agency, and a GIS database, developed by a defense contractor, and it may very well be the case that these two groups used different security orderings in their design. A mediator must be able to *automatically combine the security orderings used by the different packages in a semantically meaningful and security-preserving way.* Such a combination will result in a new security level ordering that can be used by the mediator. In this paper, we will present methods by which different security orderings used by individual packages may be neatly *combined* into a new security ordering that captures the essential properties of the constituent orderings. Furthermore, we will show that this combination may be elegantly implemented using well known logic programming techniques and graph algorithms, and is solvable in polynomial time.

In the next section, we introduce the basic principles of our approach to the combination of heterogeneous security orderings. In Sec. 3, we introduce an axiomatization of the combinability problem based on a logic program P, and show how a global security ordering can be computed by querying P. In Sec. 4 we introduce an alternative approach, based on a graph representation of the problem, which leads to more efficient algorithms. We conclude with a section on related work.

2 Combining Heterogeneous Security Orderings

A *security ordering* is a partial order $(S, \leq)$, where S is a set of security levels and $\leq$ is a partial order over S. Intuitively, in an individual data source, each user is assigned a security level that determines the user's capabilities; higher security levels correspond to higher clearance. Informally speaking, we would like to construct a security ordering $(S, \leq)$ that takes into account and semantically merges the security orderings $(S_1, \leq_1), \ldots, (S_z, \leq_z)$ that are used by the different packages participating in a mediated system. Users may then be assigned security levels from the merged ordering $(S, \leq)$.

Example 1. Figure 1 shows two different security orderings used by two relational DBs, **db1** and **db2**. The first database uses the ordering **u** (unclassified), **s** (secret), **ts** (top-secret), **ts-sci1**, and **ts-sci2**, where **ts-sci** stands for top-secret special compartmented information. The classification levels of **db2** may be read similarly. For now, the reader can ignore the dotted line in Figure 1. There are several things to note, however. As **db1** and **db2** may have been created independently, it is entirely possible that these orderings refer to different things. For example, it may well be the case that the classification level **ts** in $(S_1, \leq_1)$ is equal to the classification level **s** in $(S_2, \leq_2)$. Later (Example 2) we will show how this may be captured within our framework. □

The aim of this section is to find a way of *combining* a given set of security orderings $(S_1, \leq_1), \ldots, (S_z, \leq_z)$. In our framework, we will merge the given security orderings into a new ordering in such a way that certain constraints are preserved. These constraints express relationships between security levels in

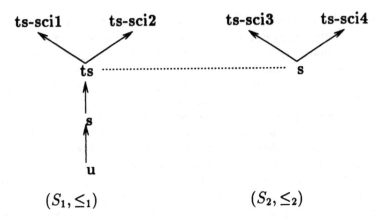

Fig. 1. Two different Security Orderings

different security orderings, thus providing us with information on how these different security orderings are linked. In order to avoid confusion, we will write $x : i$ to denote the security level x of the ordering $(S_i, \leq_i)$.

Definition 1. An *interoperation security constraint set* is a set of statements of the form $x : i \preceq y : j$ or $x : i \npreceq y : j$ where $x \in S_i$ and $y \in S_j$ and $i \neq j$. Sometimes, when an interoperation security constraint set contains both the constraints $x : i \preceq y : j$ and $y : j \preceq x : i$, we will replace them by the single constraint $x : i = y : j$. Similarly, when both $x : i \preceq y : j$ and $y : j \npreceq x : i$ belong to an interoperation security constraint set, we will sometimes replace them with $x : i \prec y : j$.

Example 2. Returning to the security orderings of Figure 1 (cf. also Example 1), it may very well be the case that ts of ordering $(S_1, \leq_1)$ and s of ordering $(S_2, \leq_2)$ are identical, and so are **ts-sci1** and **ts-sci4**. In this case, we have *two* members in our interoperation security constraint set; these are:

$$\text{ts} : 1 = \text{s} : 2; \quad \text{ts-sci1:1} = \text{ts-sci4:2}.$$

□

Given the security orderings $(S_1, \leq_1) \ldots (S_z, \leq_z)$, and a set of interoperation security constraints ISC, we have to find a new, global security ordering $(S, \preceq)$ and a family of functions $\psi_i : S_i \to S$ $(1 \leq i \leq z)$, translating the given security levels into the new ones,[3] such that:

(C1) the original orderings are preserved, i.e., for all x, y in any given S_i,

$$\psi_i(x) \preceq \psi_i(y) \leftrightarrow x \leq_i y;$$

---

[3] In other words, $\psi_i(x)$ is the new security level, corresponding to the given security level x of S_i.

(C2) the interoperation constraints are satisfied, that is,

$$(x : i \preceq y : j) \in \mathsf{ISC} \rightarrow \psi_i(x) \preceq \psi_j(y),$$
$$(x : i \npreceq y : j) \in \mathsf{ISC} \rightarrow \psi_i(x) \npreceq \psi_j(y).$$

Definition 2. A set of security orderings $\mathcal{H} = \{(S_1, \leq_1), \ldots, (S_z, \leq_z)\}$ is said to be *combinable* w.r.t. a set of interoperation security constraints, ISC, iff there exist a partially ordered set $(S, \preceq)$ and a family of *translation functions* ψ_i : $S_i \rightarrow S$ $(1 \leq i \leq z)$, such that conditions (C1) and (C2) hold. In this case, we say that $(S, \preceq), \psi_1, \ldots, \psi_z$ constitute a *witness* to the combinability of $\mathcal{H}$.

Example 3. Let us return to the security ordering of Figure 1 and the interoperation security constraints of Example 2. The partial ordering shown in Figure 2 constitutes a witness to the combinability of such orderings, together with the following translation functions: $\psi_1 : S_1 \rightarrow S$ is the identity function, while $\psi_2 : S_2 \rightarrow S$ is the map:

$$\mathsf{s} \mapsto \mathsf{ts}; \quad \mathsf{ts\text{-}sci3} \mapsto \mathsf{ts\text{-}sci3}; \quad \mathsf{ts\text{-}sci4} \mapsto \mathsf{ts\text{-}sci1}.$$

$\square$

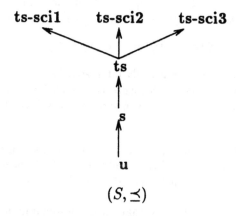

Fig. 2. A security ordering that merges $(S_1, \leq_1)$ and $(S_2, \leq_2)$

Example 4. Let us return to the security orderings of Figure 1 and consider the situation when the interoperability constraint set contains the statements:

$$\mathsf{s} : 1 = \mathsf{ts\text{-}sci3} : 2, \quad \mathsf{ts} : 1 = \mathsf{s} : 2.$$

These orderings are not combinable with respect to the above interoperation constraints. In fact, $\mathsf{ts{:}1} = \mathsf{s{:}2} \preceq \mathsf{t\text{-}sci3{:}2} = \mathsf{s{:}1}$. This violates the principle of preservation of the given orderings, (C1), because $\mathsf{ts{:}1}$ is not smaller than $\mathsf{s{:}1}$ in the given ordering. $\square$

Remark. Condition (C1) implies that each ψ_i must be *order-preserving* and *injective* (cf. [2]), that is, $x \leq_i y \to \psi_i(x) \preceq \psi_i(y)$, and $x \neq y \to \psi_i(x) \neq \psi_i(y)$. These conditions, however, are not equivalent to (C1) (essentially, the "only if" part of (C1) is not entailed, because every partial order can be linearized). We omit the details here, because they are not relevant in this context.

Given $(S_1, \leq_1), \ldots, (S_z, \leq_z)$ and ISC, there are several natural problems to solve. First, we have to check combinability. Then, if possible, a "conservative" witness should be computed; by "conservative", we mean that security levels belonging to different orderings should not be equated or made to satisfy an inequality in the merged ordering unless doing so is absolutely necessary to satisfy the combinability conditions (C1) and (C2). If the given orderings are not combinable w.r.t. ISC, then we need to find a minimal relaxation of the constraints that allows for combinability. In the following sections, we will show how we can solve these problems by exploiting logic programming techniques and standard algorithms on graphs.

But first, we show that conservative witnesses are essentially unique; therefore, it does not really matter which witness we choose, as far as it enjoys conservativity. For this purpose, we formalize the notion of conservativity.

Definition 3. A witness $(S^*, \preceq^*), \psi_1^*, \ldots, \psi_z^*$ of the combinability of $\mathcal{H}$ w.r.t. ISC is *maximally conservative* iff, for all other such witnesses $(S, \preceq), \psi_1, \ldots, \psi_z$,

$$\psi_i^*(x) \preceq^* \psi_j^*(y) \to \psi_i(x) \preceq \psi_j(y).$$

Besides conservativity, we are naturally interested in witnesses that do not contain "useless" security levels, in the sense that each level in the witness corresponds to some level in one of the given security orderings. These witnesses are called *parsimonious*.

Definition 4. Let $\mathcal{H} = \{ (S_1, \leq_1), \ldots, (S_z, \leq_z) \}$ be a set of security orderings. A witness $(S^*, \preceq^*), \psi_1^*, \ldots, \psi_z^*$ of the combinability of $\mathcal{H}$ is *parsimonious* iff for all $x^* \in S^*$, there exists $x : i$ such that $x^* = \psi_i^*(x)$.

In the next section, we will show that each combinable $\mathcal{H}$ has a maximally conservative and parsimonious witness (cf. Theorem 9 and Corollary 10). Here we prove that all such witnesses are isomorphic to each other, and hence, roughly speaking, they are essentially the same object.

Theorem 5. *Let* $(S^*, \preceq^*), \psi_1^*, \ldots, \psi_z^*$ *and* $(S', \preceq'), \psi_1', \ldots, \psi_z'$ *be witnesses of the combinability of* $\mathcal{H}$ *w.r.t.* ISC. *If they are parsimonious and maximally conservative, then they are isomorphic. Moreover, there is an isomorphism* $f : S^* \to S'$ *such that* $f \circ \psi_i^* = \psi_i'$, *that is, the diagram in Fig. 3 commutes.*

Proof. To show that the two witnesses are isomorphic, we have to prove that (i) there is a bijection $f : S^* \to S'$, and (ii) f preserves the orderings, that is, $x^* \preceq^* y^*$ iff $f(x^*) \preceq' f(y^*)$.

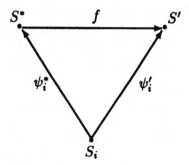

Fig. 3. This diagram commutes, for all $i = 1, \ldots, z$

(i) The function f is constructed as follows. For each element $x^* \in S^*$, consider the set $X = \{ x : i \mid \psi_i^*(x) = x^* \}$ (X is not empty because $(S^*, \preceq^*)$, $\psi_1^*, \ldots, \psi_z^*$ is parsimonious), and define $f(x^*) = \psi_i'(x)$, for an arbitrary $x : i \in X$.

To see that f is well defined, we have to show that the choice of $x : i$ does not influence the value of f. For this purpose, it suffices to prove

(i') for all $x : i$, $y : j$ in X, $\psi_i'(x) = \psi_j'(y)$.

Note that, for all pairs of elements $x : i$, $y : j$ in X, $\psi_i^*(x) = x^* = \psi_j^*(y)$ holds; furthermore, $\psi_i^*(x) = \psi_j^*(y)$ iff $\psi_i^*(x) \preceq^* \psi_j^*(y)$ and $\psi_j^*(y) \preceq^* \psi_i^*(x)$, iff $\psi_i'(x) \preceq' \psi_j'(y)$ and $\psi_j'(y) \preceq' \psi_i'(x)$ (since the two witnesses are maximally conservative), iff $\psi_i'(x) = \psi_j'(y)$. This completes the proof that f is well defined.

Next we prove that f is a bijection. To see that f is surjective, note that for all $x' \in S'$, there exists $x : i$ such that $\psi_i'(x) = x'$ (because $(S', \preceq')$, $\psi_1', \ldots, \psi_z'$ is parsimonious); then, by definition of f, $f(\psi_i^*(x)) = x'$. To see that f is injective, assume that $f(x^*) = f(y^*)$; we have to show $x^* = y^*$. By definition of f, there exist $x : i$ and $y : j$ such that

$$\psi_i^*(x) = x^* \tag{1}$$
$$f(x^*) = \psi_i'(x) \tag{2}$$
$$\psi_j^*(y) = y^* \tag{3}$$
$$f(y^*) = \psi_j'(y) \tag{4}$$

From $f(x^*) = f(y^*)$, (2) and (4), it follows that $\psi_i'(x) = \psi_j'(y)$; this implies $\psi_i^*(x) = \psi_j^*(y)$, because the two witnesses are maximally conservative (see the proof of (i') above). From this fact, (1) and (3), derive $x^* = y^*$. This completes the proof that f is injective, and the proof that f is a bijection.

(ii) Consider two elements $x : i$, and $y : j$ such that $\psi_i^*(x) = x^*$ and $\psi_j^*(y) = y^*$ (they exist because $(S^*, \preceq^*), \psi_1^*, \ldots, \psi_z^*$ is parsimonious). Clearly, $x^* \preceq^* y^*$ iff $\psi_i^*(x) \preceq^* \psi_j^*(y)$, iff $\psi_i'(x) \preceq' \psi_j'(y)$ (maximal conservativity of the two witnesses) iff $f(x^*) \preceq' f(y^*)$ (because $f(x^*) = \psi_i'(x)$ and $f(y^*) = \psi_j'(y)$, by definition of f).

Finally, note that f satisfies $f \circ \psi_i^* = \psi_i'$ by definition. □

Remark. If a witness $\mathcal{W}$ is maximally conservative but not parsimonious, then it contains a parsimonious, maximally conservative witness, which coincides with the restriction of $\mathcal{W}$ to the range of the translation functions. The proof is easy and is omitted here.

3 Logic Programming Approach

In this section we prove that the combinability problem can be solved in polynomial time by exploiting a suitable logic program. In the rest of the paper, without loss of generality, we will assume that each ordering $(S_i, \leq_i)$ is represented as a finite Hasse diagram (as shown in Figure 1).

The combinability problem can be represented in a natural way through a logic program P, that encodes (a) the given security orderings, (b) the standard properties that must be satisfied by the ordering $\preceq$ of the witness, and (c) the interoperation constraints ISC.

Definition 6. The Herbrand Universe U_P (i.e. the set of ground terms) of the program P consists of all the terms $x : i$ where $x \in S_i$, $(1 \leq i \leq z)$. The rules of P comprise:

1. the axiomatization of the reflexive, antisymmetric and transitive properties:
   $$X \leq X$$
   $$X \approx Y \leftarrow X \leq Y, Y \leq X$$
   $$X \leq Y \leftarrow X \leq Z, Z \leq Y$$
   Note that above, $\leq$ and $\approx$ are binary predicate symbols.
2. the facts
   $$x : i \leq y : i$$
   such that (x,y) is a link in the Hasse diagram of S_i (principle of autonomy);
3. the facts
   $$x : i \leq y : j.$$
   such that $(x : i \preceq y : j)$ is a constraint of ISC;
4. the rules
   $$non\_combinable \leftarrow x : i \leq y : i$$
   whenever x is not smaller than y in S_i (principle of security);
5. the rules
   $$non\_combinable \leftarrow x : i \leq y : j$$
   such that $(x : i \npreceq y : j)$ is a constraint of ISC.

Remark. The relation $\approx$ in P is an *equivalence relation.*

Remark. For all given security orderings $(S_i, \leq_i)$,

$$x \leq_i y \text{ implies } P \models x : i \leq y : i.$$

Example 5. Suppose we return to the two partial orderings of Fig. 1. The logic program P associated with the problem of combining these two security orderings is given in Fig. 4. Note that rule (a) is redundant, because if $\mathbf{ts} : \mathbf{1} \leq \mathbf{u} : \mathbf{1}$ then,

$$
\begin{aligned}
X &\leq X \leftarrow \\
X &\leq X \leftarrow X \leq Z, Z \leq Y \\
X &\approx X \leftarrow X \leq Y, Y \leq X \\
\mathbf{u} : 1 &\leq \mathbf{s} : 1 \leftarrow \\
\mathbf{s} : 1 &\leq \mathbf{ts} : 1 \leftarrow \\
\mathbf{ts} : 1 &\leq \mathbf{ts\_sci1} : 1 \leftarrow \\
\mathbf{ts} : 1 &\leq \mathbf{ts\_sci2} : 1 \leftarrow \\
\mathbf{s} : 2 &\leq \mathbf{ts\_sci3} : 2 \leftarrow \\
\mathbf{s} : 2 &\leq \mathbf{ts\_sci4} : 2 \leftarrow \\
\mathbf{ts} : 1 &\leq \mathbf{s} : 2 \leftarrow \\
\mathbf{s} : 2 &\leq \mathbf{ts} : 1 \leftarrow \\
\mathbf{ts\_sci1} : 1 &\leq \mathbf{ts\_sci4} : 2 \leftarrow \\
\mathbf{ts\_sci4} : 2 &\leq \mathbf{ts\_sci1} : 1 \leftarrow
\end{aligned}
$$

$$
\begin{aligned}
&non\_combinable \leftarrow \mathbf{s} : 1 \leq \mathbf{u} : 1 \\
&non\_combinable \leftarrow \mathbf{ts} : 1 \leq \mathbf{u} : 1 && (a) \\
&non\_combinable \leftarrow \mathbf{ts} : 1 \leq \mathbf{s} : 1 && (b) \\
&non\_combinable \leftarrow \mathbf{ts\_sci1} : 1 \leq \mathbf{u} : 1 && (*) \\
&non\_combinable \leftarrow \mathbf{ts\_sci1} : 1 \leq \mathbf{s} : 1 && (*) \\
&non\_combinable \leftarrow \mathbf{ts\_sci1} : 1 \leq \mathbf{ts} : 1 \\
&non\_combinable \leftarrow \mathbf{ts\_sci1} : 1 \leq \mathbf{ts\_sci2} : 1 \\
&non\_combinable \leftarrow \mathbf{ts\_sci2} : 1 \leq \mathbf{u} : 1 && (*) \\
&non\_combinable \leftarrow \mathbf{ts\_sci2} : 1 \leq \mathbf{s} : 1 && (*) \\
&non\_combinable \leftarrow \mathbf{ts\_sci2} : 1 \leq \mathbf{ts} : 1 \\
&non\_combinable \leftarrow \mathbf{ts\_sci2} : 1 \leq \mathbf{ts\_sci1} : 1 \\
&non\_combinable \leftarrow \mathbf{ts\_sci3} : 2 \leq \mathbf{s} : 2 \\
&non\_combinable \leftarrow \mathbf{ts\_sci4} : 2 \leq \mathbf{s} : 2 \\
&non\_combinable \leftarrow \mathbf{ts\_sci3} : 2 \leq \mathbf{ts\_sci4} : 2 \\
&non\_combinable \leftarrow \mathbf{ts\_sci4} : 2 \leq \mathbf{ts\_sci3} : 2
\end{aligned}
$$

Fig. 4. The program P for the orderings in Fig. 1

by transitivity, $\mathbf{ts} : \mathbf{1} \leq \mathbf{s} : \mathbf{1}$, and hence *non_combinable* can be derived through (b). Similarly, the rules marked with $(*)$ can be eliminated. In general, among the lower bounds of a security level, only the maximal ones need to be considered.

The following lemma shows that the above logic program is a sound formalization of the combinability problem, in the sense that the relations which are entailed by P must hold in every possible witness[4].

Lemma 7. *For all witnesses* $(S, \preceq), \psi_1, \ldots, \psi_z$ *of the combinability of* $\mathcal{H}$,

$$P \models x : i \leq y : j \text{ implies } \psi_i(x) \preceq \psi_j(y).$$

Proof. If $x : i = y : j$, then the property holds trivially. Otherwise, if $P \models x : i \leq y : j$, then $(x : i \leq y : j) \in T_P^\omega$, since P is a Horn program, and therefore there exists n such that $(x : i \leq y : j) \in T_P^n - T_P^{n-1}$.

By induction on n: if $x : i \leq y : j \in T_P^1$, then $x : i \leq y : j \in P$, which means that either $(x : i \preceq y : j) \in \mathsf{ISC}$, and then $\psi_i(x) \preceq \psi_j(y)$ by definition of witness, or $i = j$, and $x \leq_i y$, and then $\psi_i(x) \preceq \psi_i(y)$, by definition of witness . Assume that the lemma holds for all the facts $z : l \leq t : k \in T_P^n$, and consider $(x : i \leq y : j) \in T_P^{n+1}$. Since $(x : i \leq y : j) \in T_P^{n+1}$, there must be a ground instance $x : i \leq y : j \leftarrow x : i \leq z : l, z : l \leq y : j$ of a clause in P such that both $x : i \leq z : l$ and $z : l \leq y : j$ belong to T_P^n. Therefore, both $x : i \leq z : l$ and $z : l \leq y : j$ satisfy the inductive hypothesis: $\psi_i(x) \preceq \psi_l(z)$ and $\psi_l(z) \preceq \psi_j(y)$ From the transitivity of $\preceq$, $\psi_i(x) \preceq \psi_j(y)$. $\square$

Intuitively, if the given orderings are combinable, we can build a witness by querying the program P. The new security levels are obtained by collapsing all the pairs $x : i$ and $y : j$ such that P entails $x : i \approx y : j$. Technically speaking, this is obtained by taking the quotient $(U_P / \approx)$ as the witness domain. Similarly, the ordering is obtained by querying P, as specified below.

Definition 8. The *P-canonical security ordering* associated with $\mathcal{H}$ is $(S^*, \preceq^*)$, where

- S^* is the quotient set $(U_P / \approx)$;
- $X \preceq^* Y$ holds iff $P \models x : i \leq y : j$, for some $x : i \in X$ and $y : j \in Y$.

The translation functions are defined as $\psi_i^*(x) = [x : i]$, where $[x : i]$ denotes the equivalence class of $x : i$.

Theorem 9. $\mathcal{H}$ *is combinable iff* P *does not entail non_combinable*.

Proof. First we prove the "only if" part. Let $(S, \preceq), \psi_1, \ldots, \psi_z$ be a witness of the combinability of $\mathcal{H}$. Assume that $P \models non\_combinable$. This means that there exists n such that $non\_combinable \in T_P^n - T_P^{n-1}$. Therefore, either $x : i \leq$

---

[4] The proof of this lemma, as well as proofs of some others, require the use of an operator called T_P well known in logic programming [11] that may be associated with a logic program P. Due to space restrictions, we briefly state the definition here. T_P takes as input, a set I of ground atoms. $T_P(I)$ is the set $\{A \mid A \leftarrow B_1, \ldots, B_n \text{ is a ground instance of a rule in } P \text{ and } \{B_1, \ldots, B_n\} \subseteq I\}$. T_P may be iteratively applied as follows. $T_P^0 = \emptyset; T_P^{i+1} = T_P(T_P^i)$. $T_P^\omega = \bigcup_{i \geq 0} T_P^i$. It is well known [11] that T_P^ω is identical to the set of all ground atoms that are logically entailed by P.

$y : i \in T_P^{n-1}$, and $x \not\leq_i y$, or $x : i \leq y : j \in T_P^{n-1}$, and $(x : i \not\preceq y : i) \in$ ISC. In the first case $P \models x : i \leq y : i$, therefore, by Lemma 7, $\psi_i(x) \preceq \psi_i(y)$ and, by definition of witness $x \leq_i y$; a contradiction. Consider now the second case. $P \models x : i \leq y : j$, and therefore, by Lemma 7, $\psi_i(x) \preceq \psi_j(y)$. This contradicts the hypothesis $(x : i \not\preceq y : j) \in$ ISC, since, by definition of witness, it would imply $\psi_i(x) \not\preceq \psi_j(y)$. This means that also the second case is impossible, and therefore it cannot be the case that $P \models non\_combinable$.

We are left to prove that if $P \not\models non\_combinable$, then $\mathcal{H}$ is combinable. For this purpose, we show that the canonical security ordering $(S^*, \preceq^*)$, and the canonical translations $\psi_1^*, \ldots, \psi_z^*$, constitute a witness of its combinability.

Condition (C1) is satisfied. Indeed, assume $\psi_i^*(x) \preceq^* \psi_i^*(y)$, i.e., $[x : i] \preceq [y : i]$. Then, by definition, $P \models x : i \leq y : i$, and therefore it must be $x \leq_i y$ (otherwise, P would entail $non\_combinable$). On the other hand, if $x \leq_i y$, then $P \models x : i \leq y : i$ (Remark 3), and then, by definition, $[x : i] \preceq^* [y : i]$, i.e., $\psi_i^*(x) \preceq \psi_i^*(y)$.

Condition (C2) is satisfied. Indeed, if $(x : i \preceq y : j) \in$ ISC, then the fact $x : i \leq y : j$ belongs to the program P. By definition, $P \models x : i \leq y : j$ implies $[x : i] \preceq [y : j]$, i.e., $\psi_i^*(x) \preceq \psi_j^*(y)$.

On the other hand, if $(x : i \not\preceq y : j) \in$ ISC, then $P \not\models x : i \leq y : j$, otherwise P would entail $non\_combinable$. From $P \not\models x : i \leq y : j$ it follows, by definition, $[x : i] \not\preceq [y : j]$, and then $\psi_i^*(x) \not\preceq^* \psi_j^*(y)$. □

As a corollary of Theorem 9 and Lemma 7, we derive that the canonical security ordering and the canonical translations integrate the given security orderings $(S_i, \leq_i)$ by introducing the least possible number of dependencies, thereby achieving a maximally conservative composition.

Corollary 10. *If $\mathcal{H}$ is combinable then $(S^*, \preceq^*), \psi_1^*, \ldots, \psi_z^*$ is a maximally conservative and parsimonious witness.*

Since deduction from Horn clauses can be done in polynomial time [5], also the combinability check and the construction of a witness can be performed in polynomial time.

Theorem 11. *Let $n = \sum_{i=1}^{z} |S_i|$. Checking combinability and building the canonical ordering with the LP method can be done in time and space $O(n^3)$, that is, the size of the ground instantiation of the program.*

Proof. To check that $\mathcal{H}$ is combinable, it suffices to

- build the ground instance of the program P associated with $\mathcal{H}$, say P_{ground}. This can be done in time and space $O(n^3)$, since the axiomatization of the transitive property is the only rule in P in which three variables occur (the other rules contain at most two variables);
- compute the least model of P_{ground}. P_{ground} is a ground Horn program, and its least Herbrand model can be found in time and space linear in the size of P_{ground} [5], that is, $O(n^3)$;

– verify that *non_combinable* does not belong to the least model of P_{ground}. The size of the least model is linear in the size of the Herbrand Universe of P, that is, $O(n)$; checking if *non_combinable* belongs to such a model can be done in $O(n)$.

The total cost is therefore $O(n^3)$. □

The canonical ordering can be computed by a naive algorithm in time $O(n^4)$, by repeatedly scanning the least model of P (whose size is $O(n^2)$, and which can be computed in time $O(n^3)$, cf. the proof of the above theorem). The naive algorithm can be improved, but the cost is unlikely to drop below $O(n^3)$, as far as general query methods for function-free logic programs are used. In fact, the best general query methods have worst case complexity linear in the size of the ground instantiation of the program, that is $O(n^3)$ for P. We omit the details here, because these complexity bounds can be improved by adopting a different, more efficient technique, based on standard graph algorithms.

4 Composing Security Orderings Through Graph Algorithms

In this section we reformulate the notion of canonical security ordering in terms of the graph defined below. The final goal is obtaining more efficient algorithms for solving the various problems related to combinability.

Definition 12. The *graph associated with* $\mathcal{H} = \{(S_1, \leq_1), \ldots, (S_z, \leq_z)\}$ and ISC is $G = (V, E)$, where V (the set of vertices) is the set of all $x : i$ such that $x \in S_i$ ($1 \leq i \leq z$), and where E (the set of edges) is the set of all ordered pairs $(x : i, y : j)$ such that either

(1) $i = j$ and there is an edge from x to y in the Hasse diagram of S_i, or
(2) $i \neq j$ and $(x : i \preceq y : j) \in$ ISC.

The basic idea is that if two security levels belong to a cycle in G, then the two levels must be identified to satisfy (C1) and (C2). The rest of the section expands on this idea.

Definition 13. The *G-canonical security ordering* associated to $\mathcal{H}$ is $(S^+, \preceq^+)$, where S^+ is the set of strongly connected components[5] of the graph G associated to $\mathcal{H}$, and $x \preceq^+ y$ holds iff $x = y$ or there is a directed path in G from a member of x to a member of y. The *canonical translations* ψ_i^+ are defined by

$$\psi_i^+(x) = [x : i],$$

where $[x : i]$ denotes the strongly connected component containing $x : i$.

---

[5] Here, with a slight abuse of notation, we identify the strongly connected components of a directed graph with the maximal sets C of vertices such that each member of C can be reached from any other member of C through a directed path.

The following is a soundness lemma, stating that the dependencies that hold in the canonical security ordering must hold also in every witness.

Lemma 14. *Let $(S^+, \preceq^+)$ be the canonical security ordering of $\mathcal{H}$. Then, for all witnesses $(S, \preceq), \psi_1, \ldots, \psi_z$ of the combinability of $\mathcal{H}$,*

$$[x:i] \preceq^+ [y:j] \rightarrow \psi_i(x) \preceq \psi_j(y).$$

Proof. Assume that $[x : i] \preceq^+ [y : j]$. By definition, it follows that either $x : i = y : j$ or there must be a path from $x : i$ to $y : j$ in G. The first case is trivial, so we focus on the latter. Let the path be

$$x : i = x_1 : i_1, \; x_2 : i_2, \; \ldots, \; x_n : i_n = y : j.$$

By definition of the edges of G, we have that for all $k = 1, \ldots, n-1$ one of the following conditions holds:

(1) $i_k = i_{k+1}$ and $x_k \leq_{i_k} x_{k+1}$. In this case, by (C1), we have $\psi_{i_k}(x_k) \preceq \psi_{i_k}(x_{k+1}) = \psi_{i_{k+1}}(x_{k+1})$.

(2) $i_k \neq i_{k+1}$ and $(x_k : i_k \preceq x_{k+1} : i_{k+1}) \in \mathsf{ISC}$. Also in this case, we have $\psi_{i_k}(x_k) \preceq \psi_{i_{k+1}}(x_{k+1})$, by (C2).

It follows that $\psi_i(x) = \psi_{i_1}(x_1) \preceq \ldots \preceq \psi_{i_n}(x_n) = \psi_j(y)$, so, by transitivity, $\psi_i(x) \preceq \psi_j(y)$. $\quad\square$

This result, however, does not imply that the canonical ordering and the canonical translations constitute a witness, nor that $\mathcal{H}$ is combinable. For this purpose we prove the next theorems.

Theorem 15. $\mathcal{H}$ *is combinable iff the corresponding canonical ordering $(S^+, \preceq^+)$ and the canonical translations $\psi_1^+, \ldots, \psi_z^+$, constitute a witness to the combinability of $\mathcal{H}$.*

Proof. The "if" part is trivial. To prove the "only if" part, assume that $\mathcal{H}$ is combinable, and let $(S, \preceq), \psi_1, \ldots, \psi_z$ be a witness to the combinability of $\mathcal{H}$. We have to show that $(S^+, \preceq^+)$ and the canonical translations constitute a witness, i.e., that they satisfy the conditions (C1) and (C2). To prove the "if" part of (C1), assume $x \leq_i y$; then there is a path from x to y in the Hasse diagram of the security ordering S_i; by definition of G, there is a corresponding path from $x : i$ to $y : i$ in G; by definition of canonical ordering, it follows that $[x : i] \preceq^+ [y : i]$; then, by definition of ψ_i^+, $\psi_i^+(x) \preceq^+ \psi_i^+(y)$. This proves the "if" part of (C1). To prove the "only if part", assume that $\psi_i^+(x) \preceq^+ \psi_i^+(y)$; then, by definition of ψ_i^+, $[x : i] \preceq^+ [y : i]$; by Lemma 14, it follows that $\psi_i(x) \preceq \psi_i(y)$, and hence, by (C1), $x \leq_i y$. This completes the proof that (C1) holds.

We are left to prove that also (C2) is satisfied. For each constraint $(x : i \preceq y : j) \in \mathsf{ISC}$, G contains an edge from $x : i$ to $y : j$; therefore $[x : i] \preceq^+ [y : j]$, and hence $\psi_i^+(x) \preceq^+ \psi_j^+(y)$. This proves that all positive constraints are satisfied. Now assume that some negative constraint $(x : i \npreceq y : j) \in \mathsf{ISC}$ is not satisfied by the canonical ordering, that is, $\psi_i^+(x) \preceq^+ \psi_j^+(y)$. This is equivalent to $[x : i] \preceq^+ [y : j]$; by Lemma 14, it follows that $\psi_i(x) \preceq \psi_j(y)$. But then, the witness $(S, \preceq), \psi_1, \ldots, \psi_n$ would violate (C2), which is absurd. $\quad\square$

As a corollary of the above results, we derive that the new notion of canonical security ordering constitutes a maximally conservative witness.

Corollary 16. *If $\mathcal{H}$ is combinable then $(S^+, \preceq^+), \psi_1^+, \ldots, \psi_z^+$ is a maximally conservative and parsimonious witness.*

Therefore, by Theorem 5, the G-canonical witness is isomorphic to the P-canonical witness, i.e. the two approaches are equivalent, from a semantic point of view. On the contrary, there are some differences in efficiency. All the basic problems related to combinability outlined in the previous sections can be solved in polynomial time, with some improvements w.r.t. the logic programming approach.

Theorem 17. *Let n be the number of vertices of G, that is, $n = \sum_{i=1}^{z} |S_i|$.*

(i) *Deciding combinability can be done in time $O(n^2 \log n)$.*
(ii) *The canonical ordering $(S^+, \preceq^+)$ can be computed in time $O(n^2)$.*
(iii) *A maximal satisfiable subset of ISC can be computed in time $O(n^4 \log n)$.*

Proof. (*i*) To check that $\mathcal{H}$ is combinable, it suffices to verify that the canonical ordering and the canonical translations constitute a witness. This can be done through the following steps:

(a) Construct the associated graph G (time: $O(|G|)$).
(b) Compute the strongly connected components of G (time: $O(|G|)$, cf. [13]).
(c) Verify condition (C1). This can be done by constructing the set $L_i^+ = \{(x,y) \mid [x : i] \preceq^+ [y : i]\}$ and checking that it coincides with the set $L_i = \{(x,y) \mid x \leq_i y\}$ ($1 \leq i \leq z$). This can be done as follows:
   (c1) Construct L_i^+ and L_i as lists (time: $O(n^2)$).
   (c2) Sort L_i^+ and L_i under lexicographic order (time: $O(n^2 \log n^2)$).
   (c3) Verify that $L_i^+ = L_i$ (time: $O(n^2)$).
   Since the cost of (c2) dominates the cost of (c1) and (c3), the total cost of step (c) is $O(n^2 \log n^2)$.
(d) Verify condition (C2). Clearly, the positive constraints of ISC are satisfied by construction (cf. proof of Theorem 15), so we only have to check the negative constraints. This can be done by
   (d1) constructing the set $N = \{(x : i, y : j) \mid (x : i \npreceq y : j) \in \text{ISC}\}$ and the set $L^+ = \{(x : i, y : j) \mid [x : i] \preceq^+ [y : j]\}$ ($1 \leq i \leq z$); (time: $O(n^2)$);
   (d2) verifying that the intersection of L^+ and N is empty; this can be done in time $O(n^2 \log n^2)$ by sorting L^+ and N and then visiting them one time in parallel, in ascending order.

The total cost of step (d) is $O(n^2 \log n^2)$. Now, since the size of $|G|$ grows as n^2, in the worst case, we have that the cost of (a) and (b) is dominated by the cost of (c) and (d); therefore, the overall complexity of this algorithm is $O(n^2 \log n^2)$. Moreover, $n^2 \log n^2 = 2n^2 \log n$, and hence the asymptotic time complexity is $O(n^2 \log n)$.

(*ii*) Note that the canonical ordering can be constructed by performing steps (a) and (b), and by computing the set L^+ (cf. step (d1)) which yields the relation

$\preceq^+$. It follows immediately that the canonical ordering can be constructed in time $O(n^2)$.

(iii) Let $\chi_1, \ldots, \chi_k$ be any enumeration of ISC. For $i = 1, \ldots, k$ define

$$\mathsf{ISC}_0 = \emptyset,$$

$$\mathsf{ISC}_i = \begin{cases} \mathsf{ISC}_i & \text{if } \mathcal{H} \text{ is not combinable w.r.t. } \mathsf{ISC}_i \cup \{\chi_i\} \\ \mathsf{ISC}_i \cup \{\chi_i\} & \text{otherwise.} \end{cases}$$

Clearly, $\mathcal{H}$ is combinable w.r.t. ISC_0 (the given orderings remain unrelated), therefore, by construction, ISC_k is a maximal satisfiable subset of ISC. By (i), each iteration can be computed in time $O(n^2 \log n)$; moreover, $k \le n^2$, therefore ISC_k can be computed in time $O(n^4 \log n)$. $\qquad\qquad\square$

Remark. Point (iii) considers the worst case in which the size of ISC grows as n^2. However, in real applications, it seems reasonable to assume that the set of constraints is sparse. Clearly, if we assume that the cardinality of ISC is proportional to n, then the algorithm for computing a maximal satisfiable subset of ISC runs in time $O(n^3 \log n)$.

5 Related Work

Gong and Qian [6] studied the complexity of secure interoperation in a framework that is similar to ours in several respects. Their principles of autonomy and security are equivalent to our combinability condition (C1). The major difference between the two approaches lies in the treatment of negative constraints (*restricted access* relation in [6]). In the extended version of their paper, Gong and Qian note that a negative constraint can be violated by the transitive closure of the permitted accesses (permitted by the individual secure systems, or by the positive constraints, which they call *permitted access relation*). On the contrary, in our approach, negative constraints are satisfied by the transitive closure as well. Our combinability checking algorithm (which runs in time $O(n^2 \log n)$), is slightly more efficient than their security evaluation algorithm, whose complexity is $O(n^3)$. By using our methods for comparing sets of edges (cf. steps (c) and (d) in the proof of Theorem 17), the complexity of their algorithm can be reduced to $O(n^2 \log n)$, as well. When the interoperation constraints are not satisfiable, Gong and Qian consider appealing forms of constraint relaxation (e.g. which maximize the cardinality of the satisfiable subset) which we do not consider here; they show intractability results and characterize tractable subclasses for these problems.

Jones and Winslett [8] consider *role based* secure interoperation (as opposed to the clearance level approach) in object-oriented databases. In that framework, roles with identical attributes are identified; on the contrary, in the approaches based on security levels, different levels should be identified only if the interoperation constraints force them to coincide. In [8] no negative constraints are considered.

Acknowledgements. We thank Xiaolei Qian for her comments concerning the relationship between our algorithm and that of Gong and Qian.

References

1. Y. Arens, C.Y.Chee, C.N. Hsu and C. Knoblock. Retrieving and Integrating Data from Multiple Information Sources, *Intl. J. of Intelligent Cooperative Info. Systems*, 2, 2, pp. 127–158, 1994.
2. G. Birkhoff. *Lattice Theory*, American Math. Society, Providence, 1967.
3. K.S. Candan, S. Jajodia and V.S. Subrahmanian. Secure Mediated Databases, to appear in:*Proc. 1996 IEEE Conf. on Data Engineering.*
4. S. Chawathe, H. Garcia-Molina, J. Hammer, K. Ireland, Y. Papakonstantinou, J. Ullman and J. Widom. (1994) *The TSIMMIS Project: Integration of Heterogeneous Information Sources*, Proc. IPSJ Conf., Tokyo, Japan, Oct. 1994.
5. W.F. Dowling, J.H. Gallier. Linear-time algorithms for testing satisfiability of propositional Horn formulae. *Journal of Logic Programming*, 3:267-284, (1984).
6. L. Gong and X. Qian. (1996) Computational Issues in Secure Interoperation, *IEEE Trans. on Software Engineering*, 22, 1, pp. 43–52.
7. N. B. Idris, W. A. Gray and R. F. Churchhouse, Providing Dynamic Security Control in a Federated Database, *Proc. 1994 Intl. Conf. on Very Large Databases*, pp. 13–23.
8. V.E. Jones and M. Winslett. (1993) Secure Database Interoperation via Role Translation, in "Security for Object Oriented Systems (eds. B. Thuraisingham, R. Sandhu amd T.C. Ting), Springer Verlag.
9. D. Jonscher and K. R. Diittrich, An approach for building secure database federations, *Proc. 20th VLDB Conf.*, 1994.
10. Laks V.S. Lakshmanan, F. Sadri and I.N. Subramanian, On the logical foundations of schema integration and evolution in Heterogeneous Database Systems, *Proc. DOOD-93*, Phoenix, Arizona, 1993.
11. J.W. Lloyd. (1987) *Foundations of Logic Programming*, Springer.
12. V.S. Subrahmanian, et al. (1995) *HERMES: A Heterogeneous Reasoning and Mediator System*, submitted for publication.
13. R. Tarjan. Depth-first search and linear graph algorithms. *SIAM J. of Computing*, 1(2):146-160 (1972)
14. G. Wiederhold, Mediators in the Architecture of Future Information Systems, *IEEE Computer*, pp. 38–49, March 1992.
15. G. Wiederhold, Intelligent Integration of Information, *Proceedings of the ACM Conference on Management of Data*, pp. 434–437, 1993.

CSP and Anonymity

Steve Schneider and Abraham Sidiropoulos

Department of Computer Science
Royal Holloway, University of London
Egham, Surrey TW20 0EX

email: {steve,abraham}@dcs.rhbnc.ac.uk

Abstract. Security protocols are designed to meet particular security properties. In order to analyse such protocols formally, it is necessary to provide a formal definition of the property that they are intended to provide. This paper is concerned with the property of anonymity. It proposes a definition of anonymity within the CSP notation, discusses the approach taken by CSP to anonymity with respect to different viewpoints, and illustrates this approach on some toy examples, and then applies it to a machine-assisted analysis of the dining cryptographers example and some variants.

1 Introduction

The notion of anonymity is used in a wide variety of situations, from anonymous donations to anonymous transactions. Computer systems may be used to support anonymity, but the users have to be confident that their anonymity requirements are actually provided by the system.

This paper aims to provide the foundations of a process algebraic approach to analysing systems with regard to anonymity properties. Such an approach focuses on the interactions between system components and is appropriate for the analysis and verification of protocols designed to achieve these properties. This is in contrast to mathematical characterisations such as that of [Wai90], where attention is focused on the information contained in outputs of communication rounds. This paper fits within the general framework described in [PfW94], where the authors identify the need to discuss properties in terms of the sequences of interactions (traces) possible at the interface between the system and the users. It fits in with the aims of [Sch96] to define a number of security properties within CSP, providing a uniform framework for describing and analysing protocols and their properties.

The principal intention of this paper is to describe the use of CSP to define anonymity properties and to analyse anonymity protocols. CSP is an appropriate formal method for describing and analysing communications protocols because it is designed to describe systems in terms of components which interact by means of message passing. To this end it is important firstly to understand the concept of anonymity by examining the way it is generally used. Once a formal definition has been provided, it is explored and refined by applying it to known situations and confirming that the diagnosis provided by the definition corresponds to what is expected. It can then be used in the analysis of situations which are not already well understood, in order to see how it provides feedback and clarifies understanding.

This paper is structured as follows: Section 2 investigates the nature of anonymity; Section 3 introduces the relevant CSP notation and theory; Section 4 formulates a CSP definition of anonymity which aims to capture the concept, and illustrates the definition by applying it to a variety of simple situations. Notions of abstraction, crucial for the consideration of anonymity with respect to different viewpoints, are also discussed; Section 5 explores and illustrates these definitions on the well-understood Dining Cryptographers anonymity protocol, and discusses how the FDR model-checking tool [FSEL94] provides feedback during protocol analysis.

2 Anonymity notions

If we are to analyse anonymity as a security property it is crucial to define it in a precise way. There are many real life activities which may be done anonymously: examples include donating money, publishing poems, sending mail, voting, informing the police, and posting to bulletin boards. A formal definition should be applicable to this wide variety of situations.

A natural question that arises is whether anonymity is a property of events and messages or a property of agents. The scenarios described above suggest that the anonymity involved in a particular message or event is a property of the agents associated with that event or message. For example, in a specific voting situation where members of a party voted to elect a new leader we might have as a requirement that the voter associated with any particular vote should be anonymous. In another example, if someone informed the police, the informer would like to hide his identity. It is also the case that the police would like in some cases to hide the nature of the information itself. It seems that the hidden information itself (in contrast to the identity of the informant) would be better considered as confidential rather than anonymous. In this case, we use *confidentiality* to refer to messages whose content is to be kept secret, and *anonymity* to refer to messages whose originator or recipient is to be kept secret.

We can identify various aspects of anonymity:

1. It can be provided to agents as in the discussion above, where an agent wishes to hide his identity. In an anonymous mail, poem, donation, or informing police one wants to be anonymous.

2. Viewing the world from particular viewpoints, one may have anonymity with respect to some information but not with respect to other (more privileged) information. For example, with regard to an anonymous donation, the organisation receiving the donation may know the identity of the donor even if the general public does not. Hence the anonymity of the donor will be with respect to the absence of particular privileged information. Furthermore, the

anonymity is with respect to the relationship between the donor and the donation. The identity of the donor may be known in other contexts, but it is the fact that the connection between the donor and the donation is hidden which provides anonymity.

An issue that arises from this concerns who has control over withholding the particular privileged information that is required to provide anonymity. Chaum is concerned with this distinction, and has proposed protocols in which the agent himself is in possession of that information. He has written a number of papers [Cha85, Cha88] on the subject in which two main kinds of transaction are identified: payments, and credentials transactions. In Chaum's electronic cash scheme for example, the author promises anonymity of the digital coins user so that the bank cannot associate a payment with the payer without their consent. The argument of Chaum is that his system permits fraud detection and transaction tracing with the consent of the individual. His system also addresses other problems such as double spending of the same coin.

We can use credentials as another example of demonstrating anonymity. Credentials are usually needed to prove one's credibility and identity. With untraceable credentials using pseudonyms one's credibility is proven without divulging the identity. When one can have only one pseudonym per organisation the problem of double identity is also addressed. Additionally, if one uses different pseudonyms for different organisations nobody can trace him and with a suitable implementation the organisations can be convinced they are dealing with the correct individual. This saves the individual the trouble of giving potentially sensitive information in order to prove its identity. Both examples are published in [Cha85].

This paper is concerned with providing a formal definition which may be applied to this wide variety of situations. Although there are a variety of anonymity protocols, often the property which the protocol aims to guarantee is not explicitly defined. Formal definition provides the starting point for formal analysis. Anonymity protocols can then be described in CSP, and the resulting system can be analysed to show that the anonymity property is present.

3 CSP notation

CSP is an abstract language designed specifically for the description of communication patterns of concurrent system components that interact through message passing. It is underpinned by a theory which supports analysis of systems described in CSP. It is therefore well suited to the description and analysis of network protocols: protocols can be described within CSP, as can the relevant aspects of the network. Their interactions can be investigated, and certain aspects of their behaviour can be verified through use of the calculus. This section introduces the notation and ideas used in this paper. In particular, only the trace model for CSP is used here. For a fuller introduction to the language the reader is referred to [Hoa85].

Events Systems are modelled in terms of the events that they can perform. The set of all possible events (fixed at the beginning of the analysis) is denoted Σ. Events may be atomic in structure or may consist of a number of distinct components. For example, an event $put.5$ consists of two parts: a channel name put, and a data value 5. An example of events used in this paper are those of the form $look.i.j.v$ consisting of a channel $look$, the first participant i, the second participant j, and the value v being communicated. This may be thought of either as a channel $look$ which passes messages consisting of three components, or as a collection of channels $look.i.j$ which each pass a single component message. The CSP model treats these identically, though in this paper we will prefer to think in terms of the second possibility. If M and N are sets of messages, then $M.N$ will be the set of messages $\{m.n \mid m \in M \wedge n \in N\}$. If m is a single message then we elide the set brackets and define $m.N$ to be $\{m\}.N$. Thus for example the set of events $i.N.m = \{i.n.m \mid n \in N\}$. A channel c is said to be of type M if for any message $c.m \in \Sigma$ it is the case that $m \in M$; and for any $m \in M$ it is the case that $c.m \in \Sigma$.

Processes Processes are the components of systems. They are the entities that are described using CSP, and they are described in terms of the possible events that they may engage in. The process $STOP$ is the process that can engage in no events at all. If P is a process then the process $a \to P$ is able initially to perform only a, following which it will behave in the way described by P. The process $P \,\square\, Q$ (pronounced 'P choice Q') can behave either as P or as Q: its possible communications are those of P and those of Q. An indexed form of choice $\square_{i \in I} P_i$ is able to behave as any of its arguments P_i.

Processes may also be composed in parallel. If A is a set of events then the process $P \,\|[\,A\,]\|\, Q$ behaves as P and Q acting concurrently, with the requirement that they have to synchronise on any event in the synchronisation set A: in other words, any event in the set A can be performed only when both P and Q are simultaneously able to perform it, and they both participate in its occurrence. Events not in A may be performed by either process independently of the other. A special form of parallel operator in which the two components do not synchronise on any events is $P \,|||\, Q$ which is equivalent to $P \,\|[\,\{\}\,]\|\, Q$.

Events occurring in process descriptions may be renamed by use of an event renaming function $f : \Sigma \to \Sigma$. The process $f(P)$ performs the event $f(a)$ whenever P would perform a. The process $f^{-1}(P)$ can perform any event from the set $f^{-1}(a)$ whenever P can perform a.

Processes may be recursively defined by means of equational definitions. Process names must appear on the left hand side of such definitions, and CSP expressions which may include those names appear on the right hand side. For example, the definition

$$LIGHT = on \to off \to LIGHT$$

defines a process $LIGHT$ whose only possible behaviour is to perform on and off alternately.

Traces For the purposes of this paper we restrict attention to the trace semantics for CSP. This semantics associates a process P with the set of (finite) sequences of events $(traces(P))$ that it may possibly perform. Examples of traces include $\langle\rangle$ (the empty trace, which is possible for any process) and $\langle on, off, on \rangle$ which is a possible trace of $LIGHT$.

Analysing processes A process P is refined by a process Q (written $P \sqsubseteq Q$) if $traces(Q) \subseteq traces(P)$. This means that if P meets a specification then Q will also meet it. It also allows CSP processes to act as specifications: Q meets the specification P if it a refinement of it.

Model-checking techniques allow the refinement relation $P \sqsubseteq Q$ to be checked mechanically (for finite-state processes). There are a number of tools that have been designed to support model-checking. We will use the tool FDR which has been designed specifically for analysis of CSP processes. It takes two processes P and Q as input, and either confirms that Q is a refinement of P, or provides a witness trace tr which is a trace of Q but not of P (which is concrete evidence that $traces(Q) \not\subseteq traces(P)$). The trace tr is useful in debugging Q, since it contains information as to a behaviour of Q that is disallowed by the specification P.

Since two processes are equal if each refines the other, equality of processes can be checked by checking $P \sqsubseteq Q$ and $Q \sqsubseteq P$. The definition of anonymity presented below will require that a process P is equal to another process Q dependent on P. The tool FDR will allow automatic checking for this equality.

4 Formalisation

The point of formalisation is to allow a better analysis of the real-world situation. It is therefore necessary to translate the various aspects involved in anonymity into the formal method. In particular, the CSP approach should be able to model identities of agents, the various ideas of viewpoints of agents on the system, and the idea of sensitive information. Furthermore, the results of the analysis should provide feedback at the real-world level, in the sense that it should provide information concerning why anonymity does not hold in particular cases.

Anonymity is concerned with protecting the identity of agents with respect to particular events or messages. The messages themselves need not be protected. Hence it is natural to consider events in the system under analysis as consisting of two components: the identity of the agent performing that event, and the content itself. For anonymity, we consider events of the form $i.x$, where i is the identity of the agent, and x is the content of the event.

The point of anonymity is that a message that could have originated from one agent could equally have originated from any other (perhaps any other from some set of users). Hence we wish our definition to capture the notion that any message of the form $i.x$ could equally well have been of the form $j.x$. If the set $USERS$ consists of the set of all users whose identities should be masked by the system in providing anonymity, then the set of messages we wish to confuse for a given piece of information x is given by the set A:

$$A = \{i.x \mid i \in USERS\}$$

Rather than talk directly about the identity of users, we can capture anonymity by requiring that whenever any event from the set A occurs, it could equally well have been any other event. In terms of agent identity and content, this means that if an observer has access only to the content of the message then it is not possible to deduce the identity of the agent associated with it.

This may be encapsulated in an equation for the system P

Definition 1 A process P is *strongly anonymous* on an alphabet A if:

$$f_A^{-1}(f_A(P)) = P$$

where equality is with respect to traces, and

$$f_A(x) = \alpha \text{ if } x \in A$$
$$f_A(x) = x \text{ if } x \notin A$$

where $\alpha \notin \Sigma$

This definition states that if every occurrence of every event from A were renamed to some new dummy event α (thus considering all events from A to be equivalent) which is the situation in the process $f_A(P)$, then whenever an α is possible in this renamed process, any possible event from A should have been possible in the original process. The process $f_A^{-1}(Q)$ makes every event from A available whenever α is available in Q, so $f_A^{-1}(f_A(P))$ makes all events from A available whenever any such event is possible. The equation states that this process is identical to the original process P, which means that the process P makes all events in A available whenever any of them is.

Consequences of the definition A number of aspects of anonymity follow immediately from the definition:

1. If P is anonymous on both A and A', and $A \cap A' \neq \emptyset$ then P is anonymous on $A \cup A'$
2. If P is anonymous on A and $A' \subseteq A$ then P is anonymous on A'
3. Anonymity is not preserved by CSP refinement with respect to nondeterminism.

From these properties it can be seen that if P provides anonymity for A then it need not follow that some event from A *must* have occurred whenever any of them could have occurred. For example, if P provides anonymity for the set $\{0.gives, 1.gives\}$ and in some situation it was possible that $0.gives$ occurred, it need not be the case that either $0.gives$ or $1.gives$ must have occurred; it is also possible that some other event (such as $2.gives$) could have occurred, or even no such event at all. Anonymity on a set simply means that events from that set should be indistinguishable in the sense that if one could have occurred then so could any—it does not mean that this should be a maximal set.

Illustration of the definition As an example, consider a charity which accepts donations. In fact there are only two possible donors, and only one of them will provide a donation. If donor 0 offers to give, then he always gives £ 5; if donor 1 offers to give, then she always gives £ 10[1]. The charity always announces its thanks publicly (in the form 'we have received a donation'). This setup is described by the process $EX\,0$.

$$EX\,0 = 0.gives \rightarrow £5 \rightarrow thanks \rightarrow STOP$$
$$\square\ 1.gives \rightarrow £10 \rightarrow thanks \rightarrow STOP$$

The donors require anonymity concerning who decides to *give*. In other words, anonymity is required for the set $A = \{0.gives, 1.gives\}$.

To see whether this setup provides anonymity, we have to consider whether $f_A^{-1}(f^A(EX\,0)) = EX\,0$. In fact

$$f_A^{-1}(f_A(EX\,0)) = 0.gives \rightarrow £5 \rightarrow thanks \rightarrow STOP$$
$$\square\ 0.gives \rightarrow £10 \rightarrow thanks \rightarrow STOP$$
$$\square\ 1.gives \rightarrow £5 \rightarrow thanks \rightarrow STOP$$
$$\square\ 1.gives \rightarrow £10 \rightarrow thanks \rightarrow STOP$$

which has different traces to $EX\,0$. One of the traces it has is $\langle 0.gives, £10\rangle$ which is not possible for $EX\,0$. This indicates that the occurrence of the event £10 allows a distinction to be made between different events in A, and so the system does not provide anonymity. This situation corresponds to the scenario where the donors disguise themselves (so as not to be identified) but all other events are public.

Observation

The definition given above requires that any event from A should be made available whenever any of them is. From the point of view of a possible observer, this is intended to ensure that whenever the observer can *deduce* that one of the events was performed, then no knowledge is obtained about which event it was. The observer is able to make such deductions from the information which is available in the form of seeing events which the system has performed.

Anonymity is often with respect to particular observers or particular viewpoints. In other words, anonymity is provided in cases where an observer has access only to certain kinds of information, and might not be provided in cases where more information is available. For example, a donation to a charity would be anonymous if the only information available is details of the amounts of money passing through particular accounts, but might not be anonymous if all details of particular transactions are available.

---

[1] Names of donors have been removed to protect their identities

In general, an observer does not have complete access to all of the events occurring in a system, but has only limited or no direct access to some events. The events that an observer has access to could be captured as another set B.

It is an immediate requirement for anonymity that $A \cap B = \varnothing$. If an observer has direct access to the very events that we wish to mask, then it will always be possible to tell some events in A (in particular, those also in B) from some others.

The events that are not in A or B are those events that the observer does not have direct access to. From the point of view of modelling the system in order to analyse for anonymity, the other events should be *abstracted*, since the system to be analysed for anonymity should encapsulate the information available to the observer. There are a number of forms of abstraction, corresponding to various ways in which events can be hidden from the observer. CSP contains a number of abstraction mechanisms.

For example, in the process $EX0$ above an observer might have access only to event *thanks*. In this case $B = \{thanks\}$ and the other events, £5 and £10, should be abstracted away before analysis begins.

If C is the set of events that are to be abstracted from P, then the system to be analysed is $ABS_C(P)$, where ABS_C is one of the abstraction mechanisms to be discussed below. In each case the requirement will be to check

$$f_A(f_A^{-1}(ABS_C(P))) = ABS_C(P)$$

Hiding The most straightforward form of abstraction is *hiding*. In the process $P \setminus C$ (pronounced 'P hide C') all events in the set C that P is able to perform now become internal events, and their performance will no longer be visible to Ps environment.

If a set of events is hidden then they are entirely internal to the process, and observers obtain no direct information about their occurrence. It may of course be possible to deduce such information from the occurrence of visible events.

This form of abstraction would be used in cases where the observer is completely unable to observe the occurrence of events outside B.

In the case of $EX0$ this means that the occurrence of the cash transaction is completely invisible to an observer.

This form of abstraction yields the following analysis

$$EX0 \setminus C = 0.gives \to thanks \to STOP$$
$$1.gives \to thanks \to STOP$$

It is the case that $EX0 \setminus C$ satisfies the anonymity equation, that

$$f_A^{-1}(f_A(EX0 \setminus C)) = EX0 \setminus C$$

and so the system does provide anonymity on A when £5 and £10 are invisible to the observer. This is exactly what we would expect—all the observer can now see is the occurrence of event *thanks*, and this provides no information about which of the two possible initial events was actually performed.

Another example is provided by $EX1$, where donor 1 gives two donations.

$$EX1 = 0.gives \to £5 \to thanks \to STOP$$
$$\square \ 1.gives \to £10 \to £10 \to thanks \to STOP$$

This also provides anonymity when the set C is hidden. Although the second choice will lead to more activity, this will be completely hidden from the observer. In fact, $EX1 \setminus C = EX0 \setminus C$, from which it follows immediately that $EX1 \setminus C$ satisfies the anonymity definition.

Renaming It is also possible that an observer might know that some event is occurring, but unable to detect which. For example, a donation might be posted in an envelope. It may be clear to an observer that a donation is occurring, but its nature remains unknown. This situation can be modelled using the same renaming operation that was used in the definition of anonymity. The process describing the information available to the observer is given as $f_C(P)$, where C is the set of events to be abstracted.

In the case of $EX0$ this form of abstraction yields the following

$$f_C(EX0) = 0.gives \to envelope \to thanks \to STOP$$
$$1.gives \to envelope \to thanks \to STOP$$

It is the case that $f_A^{-1}(f_A(f_C(EX0))) = f_C(EX0)$, and so the system does provide anonymity on A when all that is known about £5 and £10 is when one of them occurs (but not which one). Again, this is exactly what we would expect—all the observer can now see is the occurrence of an *envelope* followed by event *thanks*, and this provides no information about which of the two possible initial events was actually performed.

In the case of $EX1$ an observer does have some indication of the abstracted activity, but no direct information concerning its precise nature. We obtain

$$f_C(EX1) = 0.gives \to envelope \to thanks \to STOP$$
$$1.gives \to envelope \to envelope \to thanks \to STOP$$

This process does not meet the anonymity definition, since the sequence of events $\langle 0.gives, envelope, envelope \rangle$ is not a trace of this process, but it is a trace of the renamed process $f_A^{-1}(f_A(f_C(EX1)))$. This illustrates the fact that it is possible for anonymity to fail even without any direct information to the observer, if the abstraction mechanism is not strong enough. If the event *thanks* were also abstracted in $EX1$ so the observer does not even have access to any information directly, the process would still fail to provide anonymity, since the observer can detect the level of abstracted activity.

Masking Another third of abstraction, first presented in [Ros94], corresponds to events being *masked* by the occurrence of other events which act as noise. In the charity example we consider the possibility that there are other donations flowing in, so in the case of any particular donation it is unclear whether it is from one of the donors we are interested in or whether it is from somewhere else. Events are observed but it is unclear whether they are events from the process of interest, or whether they are other events.

This form of abstraction is described by running the process P in parallel with $RUN(C)$, the process which can always perform any events from the set C. The resulting description $P \;|||\; RUN(C)$ is always able to perform an event from C, so an observer cannot know whether any particular occurrence of such an event was due to P or due to $RUN(C)$. $RUN(\{£5, £10\})$ models the situation of donations occurring from sources other than those we are considering. The fact that *thanks* is not also in the set indicates that *thanks* can occur only in response to the donors of interest. If *thanks* could also occur elsewhere, then that would also be contained in the set.

In this situation, the observer is in a position to know that P has *not* performed any events from C in the case where none have been performed. In any case, an observer will have an upper bound on the number of events from C that P has performed at any point—the total number of events from C that have been observed.

In the case of $EX0$, the situation is that donations come in from a variety of sources, and their values are known to an observer. The *thanks* event is not masked.

Analysis of $EX0$ in this situation reveals that anonymity is not provided in this case. The process $f_A^{-1}(f_A(EX0 \;|||\; RUN(C)))$ contains the seqnece of events $\langle 0.gives, £10, thanks \rangle$ as a possible trace, though it is not possible for the process $EX0 \;|||\; RUN(C)$. The reason anonymity breaks down is that although £5 and £10 events are masked, it is still possible for an observer to deduce that no such events have occurred, if none are performed by the masking process or by the process under consideration. Hence once a *thanks* event has occurred, if a £10 has occurred but no £5 events then it will be clear to the observer that $0.gives$ cannot have occurred. In such a situation, $0.gives$ is distinguishable from $1.gives$.

The same phenomenon also appears in $EX1$.

Combining masking and renaming These forms of abstraction combine naturally, and it is often appropriate to use a combination in a system where observers have different kinds of access to events. The system $P \setminus C \;|||\; RUN(D)$ for example describes the situation where no events from C can be observed, and events from D are masked.

A particularly natural combination is that of masking with renaming: the identity of particular events is not known, and their occurrence may be observed but may also be masked. In the charity case, this corresponds to donations being provided in envelopes, from the donors of interest and also from other donors. The situation is described by $f_C(P) \;|||\; RUN(\{envelope\})$ (where f_C maps events to *envelope*). The only information an observer has concerning the abstracted events is an upper bound on the number of such events—a total number of envelopes will have been seen, and so the process in question can have performed no more than this.

This form of abstraction yields anonymity for $EX\,0$:

$$f_C(EX\,0) \;|||\; RUN(\{envelope\}) = f_A^{-1}(f_A(f_C(EX\,0) \;|||\; RUN(\{envelope\})))$$

However, it does not yield anonymity for $EX\,1$. The process after the renaming, which is

$$f_A^{-1}(f_A(f_C(EX\,1) \;|||\; RUN(\{envelope\})))$$

has a trace $\langle 1.gives, envelope, thanks \rangle$ which is not possible for the left-hand process $f_C(EX\,0) \;|||\; RUN(\{envelope\})$. This indicates that if a single envelope is observed, and then *thanks* is observed, then the only possible donor is 0. An observer has an upper bound on the number of donations provided by the process under consideration (i.e. $EX\,1$) which is the number of *envelope* events that appear in the trace: one in this case. Since *thanks* will not occur for donor 1 after only one *envelope* we have a situation where an observer can distinguish one donor from the other.

In the case described by $EX\,2$, where donor 1 can receive thanks after a single donation, then anonymity is indeed provided under this form of abstraction, where masking and renaming are combined. The situation where donor 1 gives two donations is masked by donations coming in from other sources.

$$EX\,2 = 0.gives \rightarrow £5 \rightarrow thanks \rightarrow STOP$$
$$\Box\ 1.gives \rightarrow £10 \rightarrow £10 \rightarrow thanks \rightarrow STOP \Box\ £20 \rightarrow thanks \rightarrow STOP$$

Note that anonymity is not provided by $EX\,2$ if the form of abstraction is either simply masking or simply renaming.

5 The Dining Cryptographers

This protocol is taken from [Cha88]. The introductory example of the paper describes a situation in which three cryptographers share a meal. At the end of the meal, each of them is secretly informed by the NSA whether or not she is paying. Either at most one is paying, or else the NSA is itself picking up the bill.

The cryptographers would like to know whether it is one of them who is paying, or whether it is the NSA that is paying; but they also wish to retain anonymity concerning the identity of the payer if it one of them.

They each toss a coin, which is made visible to themself and their right-hand neighbour. Each cryptographer then examines the two coins that they can see. There are two possible announcements that can be made by each cryptographer: that the coins agree, or that they disagree. If a cryptographer is not paying then she will say that they agree if the results on the coins are the same, and that they disagree if the results differ; a paying cryptographer will say the opposite.

If the number of 'disagree' announcements is even, then the NSA is paying. If the number is odd, then one of the cryptographers is paying. The two cryptographers not paying will not be able to identify the payer from the information they have available.

Analysis

This protocol (and variants) will be coded up in CSP and analysed as follows:

1. The protocol will be analysed for functional correctness: that it can be decided from the cryptographers' announcements whether or not the NSA is paying.
2. It will be analysed from the point of view of anonymity of the payer with respect to an eavesdropper at another table
3. Anonymity of the payer with respect to the other cryptographers will be tested
4. The situation of one of the coins being double-headed will be analysed
5. The situation of four dining cryptographers will be analysed for anonymity of the payer where two of the other cryptographers pool their information

Modelling the protocol

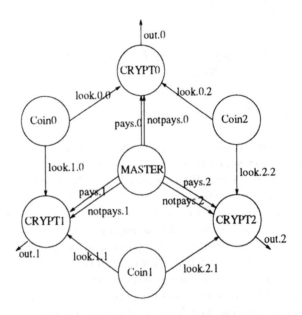

Figure 1: Components of the protocol

The protocol is modelled in CSP as the parallel combination of cryptographers and coins, and a master process dictating who pays, as illustrated in Figure 1. The events of the form $pays.i$ and $notpays.i$ are the instructions from the NSA concerning payment. Events of the form $look.i.j.x$ model cryptographer 1 reading value x from coin j. The channels $out.i$ are used for the cryptographers to make their declaration.

The $MASTER$ process nondeterministically chooses either to pay, or one of the cryptographers to pay.

$$MASTER = (\sqcap_{i:CRYPTNAMES}\ pays.i \to notpays.((i+1)\ \textbf{mod}\ 3)$$
$$\to notpays.((i+2)\ \textbf{mod}\ 3) \to STOP)$$
$$\sqcap\ notpays.0 \to notpays.1 \to notpays.2 \to STOP$$

Each cryptographer process follows the protocol. This is described in CSP as follows:

$$CRYPT(i) = notpays.i \to look.i.i?x \to look.i.((i+1)\ \textbf{mod}\ 3)?y \to$$
$$(\textbf{if}\ (x = y)\ \textbf{then}\ (out.i.agree \to STOP)$$
$$\textbf{else}\ (out.i.disagree \to STOP))$$
$$\square\ (pays.i \to look.i.i?x \to look.i.((i+1)\ \textbf{mod}\ 3)?y \to$$
$$(\textbf{if}\ (x = y)\ \textbf{then}\ out.i.disagree \to STOP$$
$$\textbf{else}\ out.i.agree \to STOP))$$

Each coin is modelled as a choice between reading heads and reading tails:

$$COIN(i) = HEADS(i) \sqcap TAILS(i)$$
$$HEADS(i) = look.i.i!heads \to HEADS(i)$$
$$\square\ look.((i-1)\ \textbf{mod}\ 3).i!heads \to HEADS(i)$$
$$TAILS(i) = look.i.i!tails \to TAILS(i)$$
$$\square\ look.((i-1)\ \textbf{mod}\ 3).i!tails \to TAILS(i)$$

The master either sends a pay message to one of the cryptographers or a don't pay message to all of them.

The system is constructed from the cryptographers and coins, which are two collections of independent processes.

$$CRYPTS = CRYPT(0)\ |||\ CRYPT(1)\ |||\ CRYPT(2)$$
$$COINS = COIN(0)\ |||\ COIN(1)\ |||\ COIN(2)$$

They must synchronise on the events representing the examination of coins and the $MASTER$ decides who is paying.

$$MEAL = ((CRYPTS\ |[\ look\ ]|\ COINS)\ |[\ pays, notpays\ ]|\ MASTER) \setminus notpays$$

It is also possible to provide a parametric description of the system for an arbitrary number n of cryptographers; but automatic verification will be possible only once a particular n is chosen.

Functional correctness The protocol is functionally correct if it is possible to distinguish the possibilities of a cryptographer paying from the NSA paying. The description of the protocol itself indicates how this is to be achieved: by means of counting the 'disagree' declarations and checking whether there were an odd or an even number of them.

Although this is very simple to express, if it is to be checked using FDR then it is necessary to construct an explicit CSP 'test-harness' to count the number of 'disagree' events and then output the result. This will be the process $COUNTS(0,0)$ below.

The specification then captures the idea that either one of the cryptographers pays, in which case an answer 'crypt' should result, or none of them pays and the answer 'nsa' should result:

$$SPEC = (\sqcap_{i:CRYPTNAMES}(pays.i \rightarrow crypt \rightarrow STOP))$$
$$\sqcap (nsa \rightarrow STOP)$$

The specification is that if one of the cryptographers is asked to pay, then the protocol yields 'crypt'; otherwise it yields 'nsa'.

The process of telling the difference is captured by $COUNTS(0,0)$ where $COUNTS(i,j)$ is defined as follows:

$$
\begin{aligned}
COUNTS(i,j) = (&\textbf{if } (i = 3) \\
&\textbf{then } (\textbf{if } (j = 0) \\
&\qquad \textbf{then } (crypt \rightarrow STOP) \\
&\qquad \textbf{else } (nsa \rightarrow STOP)) \\
&\textbf{else } out.i?x \rightarrow (\textbf{if } (x = disagree) \\
&\qquad\qquad\qquad\quad \textbf{then } COUNTS(i+1,j) \\
&\qquad\qquad\qquad\quad \textbf{else } COUNTS(i+1,((j+1) \bmod 2))))
\end{aligned}
$$

The meal together with the protocol captured by $COUNTS(0,0)$ is then captured as follows:

$$SYSTEM = (MEAL \,|[\,out\,]|\, COUNTS(0,0)) \setminus \{look, out\}$$

All of these descriptions are easily coded up within the CSP syntax required for FDR, which confirms that

$$SPEC \sqsubseteq SYSTEM$$

or in other words, that the system really does meet the specification: the protocol is correct.

Anonymity with respect to an outsider Anonymity is required for the system described by *MEAL*.

An observer sitting at the next table sees only the calls made by the cryptographers: such an observer has access only to the set *out*, as illustrated in Figure 2

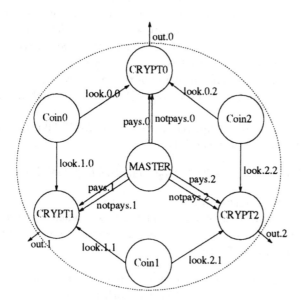

Figure 2 : The abstracted cryptographers

We may test for anonymity between all the cryptographers, by checking for anonymity on the set *pays*. The set of abstracted events in this case is all the internal events except *pays*, i.e. the set *look*.

We will use the abstraction $f_p(pays.i) = \alpha$ to identify all the *pays* events.

If the observer cannot even tell when a cryptographer is looking at a coin, then hiding abstraction is most appropriate. The check required for anonymity is therefore:

$$MEAL \setminus look \sqsubseteq f_p^{-1}(f_p(MEAL \setminus look))$$

On the other hand, if the observer can see when a cryptographer is looking at a coin, then renaming abstraction is appropriate: the observer can tell that some event is occurring, but does not know its precise nature. We may use the renaming function $f_l(look.i.j.x) = look.i.j$. The observer can tell which cryptographer is looking at which coin, but cannot tell what is seen.

The check required in this case is

$$f_l(MEAL) \sqsubseteq f_p^{-1}(f_p(f_l(MEAL)))$$

In both cases, FDR confirms that the relationship holds: that the protocol does provide anonymity.

Anonymity against other cryptographers The protocol is intended not only to provide anonymity against outsiders, but also against the other cryptographers. In this situation we require that any particular cryptographer cannot distinguish between the other two $pay.i$ events on the strength of the available information. Now there is much more information with which to break anonymity. A cryptographer has access to two of the coins, and so has more information.

By symmetry of the system, we have only to consider cryptographer 0. In this case, there is extra information consisting of the $look.0$ events; so the only hidden events are the $look.1$ and the $look.2$ events. We aim to establish anonymity for the set $pays.1, pays.2$.

If the $look.i$ events are completely invisible to $CRYPT0$ then hiding is most suitable, and the appropriate check is

$$MEAL \setminus \{look.1, look.2\} \sqsubseteq f_{p12}^{-1}(f_{p12}(MEAL \setminus \{look.1, look.2\}))$$

where $f_{p12}(pays.1) = f_{p12}(pays.2) = \alpha$.

On the other hand, if the cryptographer can see when the other cryptographers are looking at a coin, then renaming abstraction is more suitable. In this case we use the renaming function

$$f_{l12}(look.i.j.x) = \begin{array}{ll} look.i.j & \text{if } i = 1 \text{ or } i = 2 \\ look.i.j.x & \text{otherwise} \end{array}$$

to rename only $look.1$ and $look.2$.

The check required in this case is

$$f_{l12}(MEAL) \sqsubseteq f_{p12}^{-1}(f_{p12}(f_{l12}(MEAL)))$$

Again, in both cases, FDR confirms that the relationship holds: that the protocol does provide anonymity for each cryptographer against the others.

A double-headed coin If the system contains a double-headed coin, then the situation is subtly changed. Although $CRYPT0$ still has access to the same information, it is within the context of a slightly altered system description, and anonymity may thereby be compromised.

The double headed coin is described by $HEADS(i)$: it can only provide heads. We will consider the situation where it could be any of the three coins. In this case the description of the coins becomes

$$\begin{aligned} COINS' = \ & HEADS(0) \ ||| \ COIN(1) \ ||| \ COIN(2) \\ & \sqcap \ COIN(0) \ ||| \ HEADS(1) \ ||| \ COIN(2) \\ & \sqcap \ COIN(0) \ ||| \ COIN(1) \ ||| \ HEADS(2) \end{aligned}$$

The behaviour of the cryptographers remains unaltered, but the description of the meal must change to reflect the changed description of the coins:

$$MEAL' = ((CRYPTS \,\|[\,look\,]\|\, COINS')\,\|[\,pays, notpays\,]\|\, MASTER) \setminus notpays$$

Checking this system for anonymity with respect to $\{pays.1, pays.2\}$ against cryptographer 0 we check

$$MEAL \setminus \{look.1, look.2\} \sqsubseteq f_{p12}^{-1}(f_{p12}(MEAL \setminus \{look.1, look.2\}))$$

Applying FDR to this description reveals that the refinement relation fails to hold. FDR's debugging facilities provide a witness trace: one which is possible for the right hand side but not for the left.

The trace obtained is $tr = \langle pays.1, out.2.agree, look.0.0.tails, look.0.1.tails\rangle$.

This trace is not possible for the system for the following reason: if two coins have both been observed with *tails*, then the knowledge that one of the three coins must read *heads* allows the deduction (provided it is known that the coin is biased) that the third coin $COIN2$ must be the double-headed one. Since $out.2.agree$ has been observed, and it is also known that the two coins seen by $CRYPT2$ read differently, this sequence cannot follow the event $pays.1$.

On the other hand, the events observed by $CRYPT0$ are possible if the initial event was $pays.2$, since then the protocol dictates that $CRYPT2$ should announce *agree* if the coins disagree. In other words, the sequence of events $\langle pays.2, out.2.agree, look.0.0.tails, look.0.1.tails\rangle$ is a possible trace of the process $MEAL \setminus \{look.1, look.2\}$. For this reason the trace tr above is possible for the right-hand process.

This illustrates the way in which the feedback from the FDR debugger may be used to gain an understanding of why anonymity does not hold. The messages seen by cryptographer 0 are possible when one of the other cryptographers is paying, but not when the other one is. So there are situations where cryptographer 0 can identify who is paying. In this case it is possible when both visible coins read *tails*. This allows the deduction that the third coin reads *heads*, which means that the coins both sides of each of the other cryptographers are known, enabling cryptographer 0 to tell whether each *agree* or *disagree* declaration is appropriate.

All the FDR checks in this section took about 5 seconds on a sparc 5.

Four cryptographers The situation extends naturally to four cryptographers, and verification that anonymity for any cryptographer against any one of the others is easily established.

A new situation of interest arises when there are four cryptographers: the possibilities of anonymity in the case where two of the participants share their information.

The description alters in the obvious way:

$$MASTER = (\bigsqcap_{i:CRYPTNAMES} pays.i \to notpays.((i+1) \bmod 4)$$
$$\to notpays.((i+2) \bmod 4)$$
$$\to notpays.((i+3) \bmod 4) \to STOP)$$
$$\sqcap notpays.0 \to notpays.1 \to notpays.2 \to notpays.3 \to STOP$$

$$CRYPT(i) = notpays.i \to look.i.i?x \to look.i.((i+1) \bmod 4)?y \to$$
$$(\textbf{if } (x = y) \textbf{ then } (out.i.agree \to STOP)$$
$$\textbf{else } (out.i.disagree \to STOP))$$
$$\Box \; (pays.i \to look.i.i?x \to look.i.((i+1) \bmod 4)?y \to$$
$$(\textbf{if } (x = y) \textbf{ then } out.i.disagree \to STOP$$
$$\textbf{else } out.i.agree \to STOP))$$

$$COIN(i) = HEADS(i) \sqcap TAILS(i)$$
$$HEADS(i) = look.i.i!heads \to HEADS(i)$$
$$\Box \; look.((i-1) \bmod 4).i!heads \to HEADS(i)$$
$$TAILS(i) = look.i.i!tails \to TAILS(i)$$
$$\Box \; look.((i-1) \bmod 4).i!tails \to TAILS(i)$$

$$CRYPTS = CRYPT(0) \;|||\; CRYPT(1) \;|||\; CRYPT(2) \;|||\; CRYPT(3)$$
$$COINS = COIN(0) \;|||\; COIN(1) \;|||\; COIN(2) \;|||\; COIN(3)$$

$$MEAL = ((CRYPTS \;[\![\, look \,]\!]\; COINS) \;[\![\, pays, notpays \,]\!]\; MASTER) \setminus notpays$$

Consider first the possibility of two adjacent cryptographers pooling their information. Without loss of generality we may consider them to be cryptographers 0 and 1.

In this case, the information available to these cryptographers is given by the set $out \cup look.0 \cup look.1$, and we require anonymity for $\{pays.2, pays.3\}$.

In this case the following check is appropriate:

$$MEAL \setminus \{look.2, look.3\} \sqsubseteq f_{p23}^{-1}(f_{p23}(MEAL \setminus \{look.2, look.3\}))$$

where $f_{p23}(pays.2) = f_{p23}(pays.3) = \alpha$.

FDR confirms that the check indeed holds. This check took approximately 35 seconds on a sparc 5.

The other possibility is that opposite cryptographers pool their information. In this case we will assume that they are cryptographers 0 and 2.

In this case, the information available to these cryptographers is $out \cup look.0 \cup look.2$, and we require anonymity for $\{pays.1, pays.3\}$.

The following check is performed:

$$MEAL \setminus \{look.1, look.3\} \sqsubseteq f_{p13}^{-1}(f_{p13}(MEAL \setminus \{look.1, look.3\}))$$

where $f_{p13}(pays.1) = f_{p13}(pays.3) = \alpha$.

In this case FDR establishes that the check fails, (also in approximately 35 seconds) and provides a witness trace, possible for the right hand process but not for the left:

$$\langle pays.1, out.3.disagree, look.2.2.tails, look.2.3.tails, look.0.0.tails \rangle$$

The information obtained by $look.2.3.tails$ and $look.0.0.tails$ is that the two coins adjacent to $CRYPT3$ both read $tails$. Hence it is not possible to have observed $out.3.disagree$ following $pays.1$, since if cryptographer 3 is not paying then the declaration should match the readings on the coins.

However, such observations as have been made by cryptographers 0 and 2 are possible following an occurrence of $pays.3$. Hence they are able to distinguish the events $pays.1$ and $pays.3$ and hence to deprive cryptographer 3 of anonymity.

6 Discussion

This paper has proposed a formal CSP definition of anonymity and has illustrated its use with the example of the dining cryptographers. The availability of the FDR model-checking tool [FSEL94] for CSP means that anonymity properties can be checked for systems in a mechanical fashion. Furthermore, in cases where anonymity fails, the CSP analysis provides useful feedback as to the particular behaviour of the system which violates the anonymity requirement. Use of a small example such as the dining cryptographers acts as a feasibility study for the approach and tests the definition against our general understanding of anonymity. We intend next to apply this approach to larger systems and to real-world anonymity protocols.

This notion of anonymity is appropriate for situations where every anonymous event is entirely independent of every other such event, as might be the case in cash-transactions. But there are some situations where this requirement is too strong, such as anonymous voting protocols. Even if anonymity is required for the identity of the voter, it must still be ensured that different votes such as $a_1.v_1$ and $a_2.v_2$ are generated by different agents. Hence two different votes are not entirely independent, since a_1 and a_2 must be distinct. Such a voting system would fail our definition above, which requires that each of two votes could independently have originated from the same agent: that the trace $\langle a_3.v_1, a_3.v_2 \rangle$ should be possible. It appears likely that subtly different definitions of anonymity will be required for different situations depending on the particular requirements. The formalisation of these definitions will allow the distinctions to be understood explicitly, and will facilitate the correct choice. The authors are currently exploring further notions of anonymity, and their relationship to the definition of this paper.

Treatments of anonymity often include an analysis of the probabilistic behaviour of the system. For example, in [Wai90] the scheme is proven to have the property that the conditional probability for an input vector given the observed output vector is the same as the a priori probability for that input vector: in other words the output vector provides no additional information about the probabilities associated with the inputs. This paper has not considered probability, focusing instead on simple possibilities. This identifies anonymity for an agent with the *possibility*, however unlikely, that other agents could equally have performed the same event. In this analysis, if a set of biased coins was used where each had a 99% chance of landing *heads*, then any cryptographer *may* have be paying given any particular outputs, but it is much more likely in the case of two *agree* calls that the one who called *disagree* is actually the one who is paying: the conditional probability given the outputs is not the same as the a priori probability.

It seems likely that the use of probabilistic CSP [Sei92, Low93] could directly address this issue. This would allow the association of probability values with particular traces. It may be the case that the same definition of anonymity will extend directly to probabilistic models for CSP: that $f_A^{-1}(f_A(P)) = P$. In a probabilistic model this would mean that the identification of different events should not make any difference to the probabilities associated with each of those event. The definition captures the idea that it is not possible to tell the difference between the outcomes of a number for different events. What is meant precisely by 'telling the difference' is defined by the CSP model being used. In the traces model it simply means that all resulting processes should have the same traces; a model with probabilities will also require that resulting probabilistic behaviours should also be the same.

7 Acknowledgements

Thanks are due to Peter Ryan for posing the dining cryptographers as a challenge for anonymity, and for his comments; to Birgit Pzitzmann for a thorough reading and detailed comments; and also to Irfan Zakiuddin, Dieter Gollmann, Bill Roscoe, Gavin Lowe, and Michael Goldsmith for other comments on various stages of this work. We are also grateful to the anonymous referees for their reviews and suggestions.

The authors are grateful to the DRA and to Peter Ryan for funding this research.

References

[Cha85]   D. Chaum, *Security without Identification: Card Computers to make Big Brother Obsolete*, CACM 28(10), 1985.

[Cha88]   D. Chaum, *The dining cryptographers problem: unconditional sender and recipient untraceability*, J. Cryptology (1), 1988.

[FSEL94] Formal Systems (Europe) Ltd, *Failures Divergences Refinement User Manual and Tutorial*, 1994.

[Hoa85]   C.A.R. Hoare, *Communicating Sequential Processes*, Prentice-Hall, 1985.

[Low93]   G. Lowe, *Probabilities and priorities in timed CSP*, D.Phil thesis, Oxford, 1993.

[PfW94]   B. Pfitzmann and M. Waidner, *A general framework for formal notions of "secure" system*, Hildesheimer Informatik-Berichte 11/94, Institut für Informatik, Universität Hildesheim, 1994.

[Ros94]   A.W. Roscoe, *CSP and determinism in security modelling*, Submitted for publication, 1994.

[Sch96]   S.A. Schneider, *Security properties and CSP*, IEEE Symposium on Security and Privacy, 1996.

[Sei92]   K. Seidel, *Probabilistic Communicating Processes*, D.Phil Thesis, Oxford, 1992.

[Wai90]   M. Waidner, *Unconditional sender and recipient untraceability in spite of active attacks*, Eurocrypt'89, LNCS 434, Springer, 1990.

Formal Semantics for Authentication Logics

Gabriele Wedel[1]* and Volker Kessler[2]

[1] RWTH Aachen, Math. Grundlagen der Informatik, Ahornstr. 55, D-52074 Aachen
[2] Siemens AG, Corporate Research and Development, ZFE T SN 3, D-81730 Munich
Volker.Kessler@zfe.siemens.de

Abstract. We present a new BAN-like logic and a new formal semantics for logics of authentication. The main focus of this paper is on the foundation of this logic by a possible-worlds semantics. The logic was designed for implementation in the tool AUTLOG and is able to handle most kinds of protocols used in practice. The underlying logic is a K45-logic, including negation. We replace the critical idealization step by changing the set of premises. The formal semantics enables us to detect flaws in previous logics. We apply the logic to a new authentication protocol designed for UMTS.

Key Words. Formal verification, logic of authentication, cryptographic protocols, key management.

1 Motivation

Seven years ago Burrows, Abadi and Needham published their well-known BAN-logic [2] in order to analyze cryptographic protocols. In the meantime, BAN-logic has become the most widely used formal method in the analysis of cryptographic protocols despite its well-known limitations. So, obviously, people find this method a useful one to apply.

Still, so far there has been no complete logical foundation for the underlying concept. The problem is that people while applying the BAN-logic introduce new rules in order to handle the specific features of the investigated protocols. Unfortunately, it often happens that although each rule might seem reasonable alone in isolation the combination of the rules leads to unforeseen and unwanted effects which contradicts the underlying meaning, cf. Sect. 6. Therefore, a proof of the soundness of the logic is absolutely vital.

A first approach was taken by Abadi-Tuttle (AT-logic) [1]. Their idea was to give an independent formal semantics for the calculus of the BAN-logic. Actually, their use of the possible-worlds interpretation gave much insight into what is really happening during the analysis. Unfortunately, the AT-logic has two deficiences. First, the calculus of the AT-logic is not strong enough to handle all the protocols developed in security systems. For example, it is a common practice to digitally sign a hash value of a document rather than the document itself. But hash functions do not fit into the AT-logic.

---

* Work on this thesis was sponsored by Siemens AG.

Second, their possible-worlds semantics is not exactly compatible with the logic: the issue is the correct semantics of a formula like *P believes P sees M*. The intuitive meaning is that *P* reads a message *M* which he can verify to be *M* and distinguish from all other messages. Therefore *P* must comprehend the full structure of *M*. The AT-logic is not able to express conditions for comprehendability. The message-meaning rule (A11 in [1]) leads to a formula *P believes P sees M* and is thus an essential part of the concept but cannot be proved to be sound. Abadi and Tuttle have noticed this problem, but they have not yet published a solution to it.

A first solution to this problem was given by Syverson and van Oorschot (SvO) in [9]. They combine several extensions of the BAN-logic into one logic, and prove that this SvO-logic is sound on the basis of a suitable possible-worlds semantics. However, the SvO-logic is not sufficient for practical purposes because it is not able to handle partly comprehendable messages.

Independent from our activities, Syverson and van Oorschot continued working on this subject. In [10] they introduced a symbol '*' in the syntax in order to label incomprehendable submessages. However, they give no formal semantics to these new formulae, and their calculus is not strong enough to compute the comprehended submessages. These messages must be determined during the idealization step and added to the premises.

Our approach marks possibly incomprehensible messages and derives the comprehended submessages by analyzing the properties of the used functions. We give a formal semantics which enables us to prove the soundness of our logic and to decide whether a given rule is valid or not. By applying our model interpretation we found incorrect rules in BAN[2], GNY [6], AT [1], and a former version of AUTLOG [7].

The most criticized point in BAN-logic is the so-called idealization step because of its vagueness and ambiguity. We decided to replace the idealization of messages by additional premises. The way a message is interpreted by the receiver is described in the premises. Consequently, formulae are no longer allowed to be part of messages. This leads to a clear distinction between the pure protocol, i.e. what is actually transmitted, and the assumptions which must hold so that the protocol can work.

Furthermore, we introduce negation in the BAN-logic which gives a clear solution of the symmetry problem and thus reflection attacks can be handled. The applicability of the logic is demonstrated by an example.

2 Syntax

Messages. First of all we introduce the language of our logic. Our goal was to deal with the essential properties of a wide variety of cryptographic tools by introducing a minimum of different names. The so-called set of basic items $\Sigma = \mathcal{P} \cup \mathcal{M}_0 \cup \mathcal{K} \cup \mathcal{F}$ consists of

- a set of agents $\mathcal{P} = \{P, Q, S, T, ...\}$, who communicate with each other,
- a set of public key schemes $\mathcal{K} = \{K_p, K_q, ...\}$,

- a set of basic messages and shared keys $\mathcal{M}_0 = \{M, N, data, K_{pq}, ...\}$, and
- a set of computable functions $\mathcal{F} = \{enc, h, \sigma\}$.

A public key scheme K consists of a private component K^- and a public component K^+ and can be used for signature/verification, encryption/decryption, and key agreement. The symbol h denotes all hash functions including message authentication codes and σ denotes signatures without message recovery. $enc(K, M) = \{M\}_K$ denotes both encryption of a message M with K (symmetric or asymmetric encryption) and a signature with message recovery (e.g. RSA-signature, Rabin-signature). The main issue for messages denoted by $\{M\}_K$ is that cleartext M can be derived from $\{M\}_K$ under knowledge of the inverse key K^{-1} (which is the corresponding component for public key schemes and equal to K in the symmetric case).

For any function $F \in \mathcal{F}$, $F(M)$ denotes the *structure* of the message computed by F on M. Even if the *values* of two different computations $F(M)$ and $G(N)$ are the same the *messages* $F(M)$ and $G(N)$ are considered as different because the identifier of a message always includes the way it has been computed.

These basic items can be put together to more complex messages. The set of messages $\mathcal{M}$ consists of

- the names of agents and basic messages in $\mathcal{P} \cup \mathcal{M}_0$,
- the components K^- and K^+ of the public key schemes $K \in \mathcal{K}$,
- lists of messages $(M_1, ..., M_n)$ with all $M_i \in \mathcal{M}$,
- computed messages $F(M)$ for $F \in \mathcal{F}$ and $M \in \mathcal{M}$, and
- derived keys $\alpha(\{K_p, K_q\})$ for key agreement key schemes $K_p, K_q \in \mathcal{K}$.

A derived key $\alpha(\{K_p, K_q\})$ (e.g. Diffie-Hellman key) can be computed either by K_p^- and K_q^+ or by K_q^- and K_p^+. Since both ways lead to the same shared key we chose a common notation for both and separated α from $\mathcal{F}$.

Localized Messages. An important problem is how to get information about the inner structure of a message. An agent receives the *value* of a computation and has to verify the expected structure of the messsage. Let M_P denote a message M in the view of P. We call such a message *localized towards P*. P does not necessarily understand M_P. Especially, we have to consider the case that an agent may only be able to verify parts of this structure. For example, P receives a list including a cryptogram and a hash value: P sees $(\{X\}_K, h(M))$. Now assume that P cannot decrypt the ciphertext but knows M. We can express his comprehension by the formula P believes P sees $(\{X\}_K, h(M))_P$ which is equivalent to P believes P sees $((\{X\}_K)_P, h(M))$ under the described conditions. The latter cannot be further reduced because P does not comprehend $\{X\}_K$.

Let $\mathcal{M}_\mathcal{P}$ be the *set of generalized messages*. This set is built similar to $\mathcal{M}$ with the additional feature being closed under localization, i.e. $\mathcal{M}_\mathcal{P}$ consists of

- the agents and basic messsages in $\mathcal{P} \cup \mathcal{M}_0$,
- the components K^- and K^+ of key schemes $K \in \mathcal{K}$,
- lists of generalized messages $(M_1, ..., M_n)$ with all $M_i \in \mathcal{M}_\mathcal{P}$,
- computed messages $F(M)$ with $F \in \mathcal{F}, M \in \mathcal{M}_\mathcal{P}$,
- derived keys $\alpha(\{K_p, K_q\})$ for key schemes $K_p, K_q \in \mathcal{K}$, and

- localized messages M_P for agents $P \in \mathcal{P}$ and messages $M \in \mathcal{M_P}$.

In contrast to other BAN-logics we do not allow any formulae as messages.

Formulae. The set of formulae of our logic, Φ, consists of the following formulae (with messages $M, N \in \mathcal{M_P}$, agents $P, Q \in \mathcal{P}$, and formulae $\varphi, \psi \in \Phi$):

$P \overset{K}{\leftrightarrow} Q$ for keys $K \in \mathcal{M}$ [3],

$\epsilon \overset{K}{\leftrightarrow} Q$ for asymmetric encryption key schemes $K \in \mathcal{K}$,

$\sigma \overset{K}{\leftrightarrow} Q$ for signature key schemes $K \in \mathcal{K}$,

$\alpha \overset{K}{\leftrightarrow} Q$ for key agreement key schemes $K \in \mathcal{K}$.

$fresh(M)$: Message M has been created in the current protocol run.

$good_F(M)$: $M \in \mathcal{M_P}$ is suitable for key derivation with the function $F \in \mathcal{F}$.

$M \equiv N$: The concept of equivalence of generalized messages is necessary in order to axiomize the computing of the comprehendable submessages in a localized submessage M'_P of M.

$P\ sees\ M$: Agent P was able to read M as a submessage of a received message.

$P\ said\ M$: Agent P has sent the message M and has been conscious of sending it at that time.

$P\ says\ M$: Agent P has sent the message M knowingly and recently.

$P\ has\ M$: P knows message M and can use it for further computations.

$P\ recognizes\ M$: Either P has reason to believe that M is not a random string but willingly constructed or that M is a random string already known to P.

$P\ controls\ \varphi$: P is able to decide whether φ is correct or not.

$P\ believes\ \varphi$: P has strong evidence that φ is correct as far as P can understand the messages in φ, that means except the localized submessages.

$\neg\varphi, \varphi \wedge \psi$ negation and conjunction.

It may surprise that we drop formulae from the set of messages. Idealization, i.e. attaching formulae to messages whenever this formula is necessary to describe the meaning of a certain message, seems to be one of the main issues in BAN-Logic. But this process is widely criticized because it is quite arbitrary, scarcely formalized, and it complicates the interpretation of a successful analysis. We do not need this sort of idealization.

Instead of attaching a formula φ to a message M (e.g. substituting a key K by the formula $A \overset{K}{\leftrightarrow} B$) we leave the message transactions unchanged and add another protocol assumption, e.g. $B\ believes\ (A\ says\ K \longrightarrow A\ believes\ A \overset{K}{\leftrightarrow} B)$. Together with "$B\ believes\ A\ says\ K$" this will lead to "$B\ believes\ A\ believes\ A \overset{K}{\leftrightarrow} B$" by application of the rationality rule (axiom K in modal logic). An expression like that one was substituted in the AT-logic [1] by "$B\ believes\ A\ says\ A \overset{K}{\leftrightarrow} B$" for two reasons. First, the meaning of a formula "$B\ believes\ A\ believes\ ...$" was not clear and, second, the axiom $P\ said\ M \wedge fresh(M) \longrightarrow P\ believes\ M$ is obviously not valid in general. But, now the se-

---

[3] Any message $K \in \mathcal{M}$ can be used in the formula $P \overset{K}{\leftrightarrow} Q$.

mantics are clarified and *B believes* (*A says M* $\longrightarrow$ *A believes* φ) is formulated as an *assumption* for this protocol, and not as a general rule.

The main issue we have to check in order to derive *B believes A believes* φ is whether *B* does really comprehend the message *M*.

3 Formal Semantics

We need to define a formal semantics in order to prove soundness. First we concentrate on the non-modal formulae, then we give a semantics for the modal formulae *P believes* ϕ. We have to design models which simulate the run of a protocol. Such models have already been given in [1, 9, 10]. They have to be modified for our purposes.

3.1 The Model

Runs. A run r can be thought as an infinite chain of states starting at some time $k_r \leq 0$ in the past. The point 0 describes the starting point of the current protocol run and divides past and present. A state can be changed by one of the following actions:

$send_P(M, Q)$: P sends message M to agent Q.

$receive_P(M)$: P reads a message which has been sent before. Since we assume an open environment the message could have been meant for another agent.

$generate_P(M)$: P generates a new message. This action does not stand for computing new messages from old messages but for creating new basic items like random strings.

$name_P(M, N)$: P gives a new basic name $N \in \Sigma$ to a received message M. Thereby he ignores any possible structure of M. We introduce this action in order to formalize P's understanding of the inner structure of a compounded message.

Without restriction we can assume that only one action takes places at a certain state. The action at time k in run r is denoted by $H^{(r,k)}$. Thus a run is given by an infinite chain of actions $(H^{(r,k)})_{k \geq k_r}$. An action can change the knowledge base of an agent, including all messages which P can use - either generated or received messages:

Definition 1. For a given sequence of actions $r = (H^{(r,k)})_{k \geq k_r}$ we define the *knowledge base* $S_P^{(r,k)}$ of agent P at time $k \geq k_r$ as a set of all messages which P knows:

$$S_P^{(r,k)} \stackrel{\text{def}}{=} \{M \mid \exists k', N : \quad k_r \leq k' \leq k \land$$
$$H^{(r,k')} \in \{generate_P(M), receive_P(M), name_P(N, M)\} \}$$

Of course, P can use the elements of $S_P^{(r,k)}$ for further computations, so that his knowledge increases. This is described by the set $\overline{S}$:

Definition 2. $\overline{S}$ is defined as the smallest set including S and
- each list $(M_1, ..., M_n)$ if $M_1, ..., M_n \in \overline{S}$,
- each component M_i if $(M_1, ..., M_n) \in \overline{S}$,
- each computation $F(X)$ for $F \in \mathcal{F}$ if $X \in \overline{S}$,
- each derived key $\alpha(\{K_p, K_q\})$ if $K_p^-, K_q^+ \in \overline{S}$, and
- each cleartext M if $\{M\}_K, K^{-1} \in \overline{S}$.

Now we can formally describe a run:

Definition 3. A *run* $r = (H^{(r,k)})_{k \geq k_r}$ is a sequence of actions

$$H^{(r,k)} \in \{send_P(M, Q), receive_P(M), generate_P(M), name_P(M, N)\}$$

with $M, N \in \mathcal{M}, P, Q \in \mathcal{P}$ and obeying the following conditions:

1. Only computable texts can be sent:

$$H^{(r,k)} = send_P(M, Q) \Longrightarrow M \in \overline{S_P^{(r,k)}}.$$

2. Only sent messages can be received:

$$H^{(r,k)} = receive_P(M) \Longrightarrow \exists k' < k, Q \in \mathcal{P}: \quad H^{(r,k')} = send_Q(M, S)$$

3. Only basic items can be generated:

$$H^{(r,k)} = generate_P(M) \Longrightarrow M \in \Sigma.$$

4. Only known messages can be named with basic names:

$$H^{(r,k)} = name_P(M, N) \Longrightarrow M \in \overline{S_P^{(r,k)}} \wedge N \in \Sigma.$$

Finally we can fix a certain moment $k \geq k_r$ in a run and obtain *points* (r, k) which are suitable as models for non-modal formulae. But first we have to investigate which parts of a message are comprehensible with respect to a given knowledge base.

The Function *sight*. The central concept of our logic lies in deriving information from received messages. Therefore, we have to focus on the question of how much information an agent can get out of a certain message. For example, consider the case where an agent P sees a cryptogram $\{M\}_K$. If P does not know the decryption key K^{-1}, he will not know anything about the structure of this message: it could be either a ciphertext, or a hash value, or simply a random string.

To describe the information which P can derive from a message it is sufficient to replace all unreadable, i.e. not verifiable, submessages by a certain symbol '*' representing a bitstring whose meaning or structure is not specified. We obtain such a projection by introducing a function $sight_P^{(r,k)}$ which maps each message M to a message over an extended set of basic messages $\mathcal{M}_0 \cup \{*\}$ which has to be carefully defined for every kind of message.

A ciphertext $\{M\}_K$ can be recognized as a ciphertext if it can be decrypted with the decryption key K^{-1} and the result M allows the conclusion that the correct decryption key has been used. Therefore it is sufficient if the result does not look like randomly, i.e. it must contain something recognizable:

$$sight_P^{(r,k)}(\{M\}_K) := \begin{cases} \left\{ sight_P^{(r,k)}(M) \right\}_K, & \text{if } K^{-1} \in \overline{S_P^{(r,k)}}, \ sight_P^{(r,k)}(M) \neq *, \\ *, & \text{else.} \end{cases}$$

Hash values can only be verified by applying the hash function again, not by inverting the hash function. Therefore the hashed value must be known:

$$sight_P^{(r,k)}(h(M)) := \begin{cases} h(sight_P^{(r,k)}(M)), & \text{if } M \in \overline{S_P^{(r,k)}}, \\ *, & \text{else.} \end{cases}$$

Signatures without message recovery $\sigma(K^-, M)$ must be handled separately. In order to verify them, you have to know M and the public parameter K^+:

$$sight_P^{(r,k)}(\sigma(K^-, M)) := \begin{cases} \sigma(K^-, sight_P^{(r,k)}(M)), & \text{if } K^+, M \in \overline{S_P^{(r,k)}}, \\ *, & \text{else.} \end{cases}$$

Key agreement keys can be verified by using one of the necessary key pairs:

$$sight_P^{(r,k)}(\alpha(\{K_q, K_r\})) := \begin{cases} \alpha(\{K_q, K_r\}), & \text{if } K_q^-, K_r^+ \in \overline{S_P^{(r,k)}}, \\ *, & \text{else.} \end{cases}$$

Concerning lists we assume that there exists information about the format of the list *if* at least one component of the list is recognizable:

$$sight_P^{(r,k)}((M_1, ..., M_n)) := \begin{cases} (sight_P^{(r,k)}(M_1), ..., sight_P^{(r,k)}(M_n)), \\ \quad \text{if } \exists i \in \{1...n\} \text{ with } sight_P^{(r,k)}(M_i) \neq *, \\ *, \quad \text{else.} \end{cases}$$

A basic item is recognizable if either it has been generated by the agent himself or the agent has read it anywhere and uses it as a basic item. Note that in the latter case he cannot be sure that it really is a basic item. The receiver might think that a given number is completely random, whereas it is actually the hash value of a contract about a new vacuum cleaner! For $N \in \Sigma$ we define:

$$sight_P^{(r,k)}(N) := \begin{cases} N, \text{if } \exists k' \leq k : H^{(r,k')} \in \{generate_P(N), name_P(M, N)\}, \\ *, \text{else.} \end{cases}$$

What agent P can recognize in a message localized towards Q depends on what Q can recognize in the message:

$$sight_P^{(r,k)}(X_Q) := sight_P^{(r,k)}(sight_Q^{(r,k)}(X)).$$

And finally, P cannot recognize anything in a hidden message:

$$sight_P^{(r,k)}(*) := *.$$

Instantiation. For the semantics for the non-modal formulae we must link "real" messages in $\mathcal{M}$ with generalized messages in $\mathcal{M}_P$. We call a message $M \in \mathcal{M}$ an *instance* $M \preceq X$ of a generalized message X iff M and X are identical except for all localized submessages in X. Formally:

- Every message in $\mathcal{M}$ is an instance of itself:

$$\forall M \in \mathcal{M} \qquad M \preceq M.$$

- If M is an instance of X, then $F(M)$ is an instance of $F(X)$ as well:

$$M \preceq X \quad \Rightarrow \quad F(M) \preceq F(X).$$

- A list is an instance of a localized list iff all corresponding components are instances of a localized list:

$$(\forall i \in \{1, ..., n\} \quad M_i \preceq X_i) \quad \Leftrightarrow \quad (M_1, ..., M_n) \preceq (X_1, ..., X_n).$$

- Let $X \in \mathcal{M}_P$. Then each message M is an instance of the localized message X_P :

$$\forall X \in \mathcal{M}_P \, \forall M \in \mathcal{M} \qquad M \preceq X_P.$$

It follows directly that the only instance of a message $M \in \mathcal{M}$ is M itself.

3.2 Semantics for the non-modal formulae

Now we can fix the semantics of all non-modal formulae relative to a point (r, k). These semantics are quite straightforward and some of them are known from [1, 9, 10], but they have to be generalized to extended formulae possibly containing localized messages.

The semantics for negation and conjunction are classical:

$$(r, k) \models \neg \varphi \quad \overset{\text{def}}{\Longleftrightarrow} \quad not \, (r, k) \models \varphi,$$
$$(r, k) \models \varphi \wedge \psi \quad \overset{\text{def}}{\Longleftrightarrow} \quad (r, k) \models \varphi \, and \, (r, k) \models \psi.$$

P has X. P possesses a message iff one of its instances is computable from his knowledge base:

$$(r, k) \models P \, has \, X \quad \overset{\text{def}}{\Longleftrightarrow} \quad \exists M \preceq X \text{ with } M \in \overline{S_P^{(r,k)}}.$$

P sees M. P sees a message M iff he is able to compute it as a submessage of a received message. Let $seensub_S(M)$ be the smallest set containing M itself, containing each component M_i if it contains the list $(M_1, ..., M_n)$, and containing the deciphered text M if it contains the cryptogram $\{M\}_K$ and K^{-1} is an element of $\overline{S}$, i.e. $seensub_S(M)$ is the closure of M under projection and decryption.

$$(r, k) \models P \, sees \, X \quad \overset{\text{def}}{\Longleftrightarrow} \quad \exists M \preceq X \, \exists k' \leq k \, \exists N \in \mathcal{M} :$$
$$H^{(r,k')} = receive_P(N) \text{ and } M \in seensub_{S_P^{(r,k)}}(N).$$

P said M (resp. **P says M**). P has sent the (sub)message M once (respectively in the current run). The problem is that P might have forwarded some message not knowing the content of it. The idea is to make P "responsible" only for all those submessages he could have known. This depends, of course, on P's knowledge in the state when P sent M. These submessages are given by the following set:

Let $\text{saidsubs}(M)$ be the smallest set including M itself, and containing each component M_i if it contains $(M_1, ..., M_n)$, containing the decrypted text M, if it contains the cryptogram $\{M\}_K$ and $K^{-1} \in \overline{S}$, containing the preimage X if it contains $F(X)$ and $X \in \overline{S}$. Thus we get:

$$(r, k) \models P \text{ said } X \stackrel{\text{def}}{\Longleftrightarrow} \exists M \preceq X \, \exists k' \leq k \, \exists N \in \mathcal{M}:$$
$$H^{(r,k')} = send_P(N, Q) \text{ and } M \in \text{saidsub}_{S_P^{(r,k')}}(N),$$

$$(r, k) \models P \text{ says } X \stackrel{\text{def}}{\Longleftrightarrow} \exists M \preceq X \, \exists k' \in \{0, ..., k\} \, \exists N \in \mathcal{M}:$$
$$H^{(r,k')} = send_P(N, Q) \text{ and } M \in \text{saidsub}_{S_P^{(r,k')}}(N).$$

P recognizes M. This means that there is something within M known by P. It is either redundancy with respect to P's knowledge or M is a random number already known by P. Defining a formal semantics is straightforward and does not need any new concepts in our formal model:

$$(r, k) \models P \text{ recognizes } X \stackrel{\text{def}}{\Longleftrightarrow} sight_P^{(r,k)}(X) \neq *.$$

In section 6 we will compare our concept of recognizability with the GNY-concept [6, p.246].

P controls φ. P is competent in judging φ. It is sufficient and realistic to define this condition to hold only at the actual point:

$$(r, k) \models P \text{ controls } \varphi \stackrel{\text{def}}{\Longleftrightarrow} \text{If } (r, k) \models P \text{ believes } \varphi \text{ then } (r, k) \models \varphi.$$

Note that our definition has to be different from AT and SvO because we do not allow formulae as messages.

fresh(M). M has not been used before the current run has started. Let submsgs (M) be the set of all syntactic submessages of M. (For example, if $M = F(N)$, then N is a syntactical submessage of M, etc.) A generalized message shall be *fresh* if every instance is fresh (so there is no doubt about its freshness):

$$(r, k) \models fresh(X) \stackrel{\text{def}}{\Longleftrightarrow} \forall M \preceq X:$$
$$M \notin \bigcup \{ \text{submsgs}(N) \mid \exists k \leq 0: \quad H^{(r,k)} = send_P(N) \}$$

Since keys are elements of $\mathcal{M}$ they do not contain localized submessages:

$P \overset{K}{\leftrightarrow} Q$. K is a good shared key if it is only used by P and Q:

$$(r, k) \models P \overset{K}{\leftrightarrow} Q \overset{\text{def}}{\Longleftrightarrow} \forall k' \leq k : \text{If } (r, k') \models R \text{ said } F(K, M) \text{ then}$$
$$(r, k') \models R \text{ sees } F(K, M) \text{ or } R \in \{P, Q\}.$$

$\epsilon \overset{K}{\mapsto} P$. K is a good public encryption key for P in the sense that only P does use the corresponding secret key K^- for decryption. Similar to [9, p.19] we define:

$$(r, k) \models \epsilon \overset{K}{\mapsto} P \overset{\text{def}}{\Longleftrightarrow} \forall k' \leq k : (\forall X : (r, k') \models Q \text{ sees } \{X\}_{K+} \Rightarrow (r, k') \models Q \text{ sees } X)$$
$$\Rightarrow Q = P.$$

$\sigma \overset{K}{\mapsto} P$. P's signature key should only be used by P:

$$(r, k) \models \sigma \overset{K}{\mapsto} P \overset{\text{def}}{\Longleftrightarrow} \forall k' \leq k : \text{If } (r, k') \models Q \text{ said } F(K^-, M) \text{ then}$$
$$Q = P \text{ or } (r, k') \models Q \text{ sees } F(K^-, M).$$

$\alpha \overset{K}{\mapsto} P$. Key agreement keys are difficult to handle. We refer to [9, p.20]:

$$(r, k) \models \alpha \overset{K}{\mapsto} P \overset{\text{def}}{\Longleftrightarrow}$$

There exists a second key-agreement-scheme K_q of agent Q building a good key together with K_p:

$$\exists Q, K_q \quad (r, k) \models P \overset{\alpha(\{K_p, K_q\})}{\longleftarrow} Q,$$

whereas for all agents S and their key schemes K_s it is the case that if $(r, k) \not\models P \overset{\alpha(\{K_p, K_s\})}{\longleftarrow} S$ then there is no agent R being able to derive a good shared key for R and S using K_s:

$$\forall R, K_r \quad (r, k) \not\models R \overset{\alpha(\{K_r, K_s\})}{\longleftarrow} S.$$

$good_F(X)$. This formula is used for key derivation parameters ([4]):

$$(r, k) \models good_F(X) \overset{\text{def}}{\Longleftrightarrow} \forall M \preceq X \ \forall k' \leq k \text{ and for all keys } K:$$
$$\text{If } (r, k') \models P \overset{K}{\leftrightarrow} Q \text{ then } (r, k') \models P \overset{F(K, M)}{\longleftarrow} Q.$$

This definition leads back to the semantics for good shared keys. The essential condition for M being a good parameter for key derivation is that for all good secret keys K for P and Q neither P nor Q gives away the message $F(K, M)$, so nobody except P and Q can know about it.

$\mathbf{X} \equiv \mathbf{Y}$. Two generalized messages are called equivalent iff they are identical after substituting each localized subformula X_P by $sight_P^{(r,k)}(X)$. Therefore we introduce the function $sight^{(r,k)}$ replacing each localized submessage N_P by $sight_P^{(r,k)}(N) \in \mathcal{M}^*$.

$$(r,k) \models X \equiv Y \quad \overset{\text{def}}{\Longleftrightarrow} \quad sight^{(r,k)}(X) = sight^{(r,k)}(Y).$$

3.3 Semantics for the Modal Formulae

The basic idea is to construct a model consisting of a set of *possible worlds* for the non-modal formulae:

$$W = \{(r,k) \mid r \text{ is a run and } k \geq k_r\}.$$

The agents stay in one of these worlds but they do not know which one because the agents only realize parts of their reality letting a set of worlds seem possible. In order to formalize this, we have to fix a possibility relation $\sim_P \subset W \times W$ for each agent. $w \sim_P w'$ should be the case iff agent P staying in world w keeps w' as possible. This is the case if P cannot distinguish between w and w'. Now we say that 'P believes that φ is true' means that φ is true in all worlds P considers possible.

The main issue is to define such a possibility relation $\sim_P$. The question is how much an agent realizes about the point (r,k) at which he is a member.

First, each agent has some assumptions like the existence of good keys or confidential key servers etc. These assumptions restrict his set of possible worlds. In order to model this formally we have to fix a subset $W_P \subset W$ of "good-natured" worlds obeying all these assumptions. The only restriction we make on this set in our formal model is that a "bad-natured" world cannot become "good-natured" by adding an action:

$$k \geq k_r \text{ and } (r,k) \notin W_P \quad \Rightarrow \quad (r,k+1) \notin W_P.$$

Second, we have to extract all information about (r,k) of which P is aware and which helps P to distinguish his real world from others. Therefore, we restrict the "*global history*" of all actions until moment k to the "*local history*" consisting of all those actions P has performed himself considering the chronological order: let $\mathcal{H}_P^{(r,k)}$ be the sequence $(H^{(r,k_0)}, \ldots, H^{(r,k_n)})$, $H^{(r,k_i)} \in \{send_P(M,Q), receive_P(M), generate_P(N), name_P(M,N)\}$, with $Q \in \mathcal{P}$, $M \in \mathcal{M}$, $N \in \Sigma$ of all actions $H^{(r,k')}$, $k_r \leq k' \leq k$, performed by P himself.

In addition, we have to restrict the local history to all the information of which P is aware. Therefore, we extend the definition of $sight_P^{(r,k)}$ to sequences of actions in the canonical manner by replacing all messages M by $sight_P^{(r,k)}(M)$. A point (r',k') shall be possible for P in (r,k) if (r',k') belongs to the good-natured worlds and if P cannot distinguish between (r,k) and (r',k'):

Definition 4.
$$(r,k) \sim_P (r',k') \quad \overset{\text{def}}{\Longleftrightarrow} \quad (r',k') \in W_P \wedge sight_P^{(r,k)}(\mathcal{H}_P^{(r,k)}) = sight_P^{(r',k')}(\mathcal{H}_P^{(r',k')}).$$

Definition 5. P believes that ϕ is true iff it is true in every possibly true world:

$$(W, (W_P)_{P \in \mathcal{P}}) \models_{(r,k)} P \text{ believes } \phi \overset{\text{def}}{\Longleftrightarrow}$$
$$\forall r', k' \quad (r,k) \sim_P (r', k') \implies (W, (W_P)_{P \in \mathcal{P}}) \models_{(r',k')} \phi.$$

For non-modal formulae the expression $(W, (W_P)_{P \in \mathcal{P}}) \models_{(r',k')} \phi$ is the same as $(r', k') \models \phi$. If the system $(W_P)_{P \in \mathcal{P}}$ is fixed $(W, (W_P)_{P \in \mathcal{P}}) \models_{(r,k)} P \text{ believes } \phi$ will be abbreviated by $(r, k) \models P \text{ believes } \phi$.

Let $\mathcal{AUT}$ consist of all structures $(W, (W_P)_{P \in \mathcal{P}})$ with $W_P \subset W$ for all $P \in \mathcal{P}$. Then every world of every structure satisfies the well-known axioms

K (Rationality Rule) $P \text{ believes } (\varphi \to \psi) \longrightarrow (P \text{ believes } \varphi \to P \text{ believes } \psi),$

4 (Positive Introspection) $P \text{ believes } \varphi \longrightarrow P \text{ believes } P \text{ believes } \varphi,$

5 (Negative Introspection) $\neg P \text{ believes } \varphi \longrightarrow P \text{ believes } \neg P \text{ believes } \varphi.$

characterizing our modal logic as a K45-logic ([3]). This logic corresponds to models with transitive and euclidian possibility relation.

It can happen that these structures are not serial: if the assumptions of agent P defining the set W_P are not consistent with the information P has about his real world (r, k), then there is no world he considers possible. In this case the antecedent in Definition 5 is never true which implies that $(r, k) \models P \text{ believes } \varphi$ holds for all formulae φ. This result does not mean that the logic is inconsistent, it simply means that the so-called axiom D: $P \text{ believes } \varphi \longrightarrow \neg P \text{ believes } \neg \varphi$ does not hold.

3.4 Stability

Since we allow negation our logic is not monotone. According to their semantical definition the formulae *has*, *sees*, *said*, *says*, *recognizes*, and *fresh* are stable, i.e. $(r, t) \models \varphi$ implies $(r, t+1) \models \varphi$. Our restriction on "good-natured" worlds (sect. 3.3) makes sure that formulae like $P \text{ believes } \varphi$ with a stable formula φ are also stable.

According to the chosen definition the instable formulae are *controls*, $P \overset{K}{\leftrightarrow} Q$, $\overset{K}{\mapsto} P$, *good*, and some negated formulae $\neg \varphi$. In the practical analysis of a protocol, these instable formulae only occur as initial beliefs, i.e. they are within the scope of a *believe*-operator and are stated as an intial assumption (cf. sect. 8).

So, whenever a possibly instable formula is applied during a derivation after the receipt of a message, one has to check if this initial belief is still justified. For example, a belief like $A \text{ believes } \neg A \text{ said } \{M\}_K$ might be reasonable during the first two protocol steps but it might be in contradiction to the third message where A actually does send $\{M\}_K$.

4 Calculus

The symbol F represents any function in $\mathcal{F} = \{enc, \sigma, h\}$ and H is a one way function out of $\{h, \sigma\}$. X, X_i, Y, Z represent generalized messages in $\mathcal{M}_\mathcal{P}$ whereas M, M_i, K, K_p, K_q belong to the message set $\mathcal{M}$. P and Q represent agents in $\mathcal{P}$ and φ, ψ are formulae in Φ. $(K^+)^{-1} / (K^-)^{-1}$ stand for the corresponding inverse keys K^- / K^+. For symmetric cryptosystems the decryption key K^{-1} equals the encryption key K.

Inference Rules.

MP If φ and $(\varphi \rightarrow \psi)$ then ψ

M If φ is a theorem then P believes φ is a theorem.

A theorem is a formula which can be derived from axioms alone.
   The axioms are all instances of tautologies of propositional calculus and the following axiom schemas:

Modalities.

K P believes $\varphi \wedge P$ believes $(\varphi \rightarrow \psi) \longrightarrow P$ believes ψ

4 P believes $\varphi \longrightarrow P$ believes P believes φ

5 $\neg P$ believes $\varphi \longrightarrow P$ believes $\neg P$ believes φ

Jurisdiction. If P controls φ and believes that φ is true then it is true indeed:

J $(P$ controls $\varphi \wedge P$ believes $\varphi) \longrightarrow \varphi$

Possession.

H1 P sees $X \longrightarrow P$ has X

H2 P has $X_1 \wedge ... \wedge P$ has $X_n \longrightarrow P$ has $(X_1, ..., X_n)$

H3 P has $X \longrightarrow P$ has $F(X)$

H4 R has $K_p^- \wedge R$ has $K_q^+ \longrightarrow R$ has $\alpha(\{K_p, K_q\})$

Recognizability. A message is recognizable if any component is recognizable or if it can be verified by a specific computation:

R1 P recognizes $X_i \longrightarrow P$ recognizes $(X_1, ..., X_n)$

R2 P recognizes $X \wedge P$ has $K^{-1} \longrightarrow P$ recognizes $enc(K, X)$

R3 P has $M \longrightarrow P$ recognizes $H(M)$

R4 P has $(K^+, M) \longrightarrow P$ recognizes $\sigma(K^-, M)$

R5 R has $K_p^- \wedge R$ has $K_q^+ \longrightarrow R$ recognizes $\alpha(\{K_p, K_q\})$

Freshness. A message is fresh if any component having been used to compute it is fresh:

F1 $fresh(X_i) \longrightarrow fresh((X_1, ..., X_n))$

F2 $fresh(X) \longrightarrow fresh(F(X))$

F3 $fresh(K_p) \longrightarrow fresh(\alpha(\{K_p, K_q\}))$

Seeing.

SE1 $P\,sees\,(X_1, ..., X_n) \longrightarrow P\,sees\,X_i$

SE2 $P\,sees\,enc(K, X) \land P\,has\,K^{-1} \longrightarrow P\,sees\,X$

Saying.

NV $P\,said\,X \land fresh(X) \longrightarrow P\,says\,X$

SA1 $P\,said\,(X_1, ..., X_n) \longrightarrow P\,said\,X_i$

SA2 $P\,says\,(X_1, ..., X_n) \longrightarrow P\,says\,X_i$

Suppose P said a hash value $h(X)$. In order to conclude that P also said X we must exclude the case that P has forwarded $h(X)$ without knowing about its structure. One possibility is to introduce a notation for forwarded messages as it was done in [1]. But this implies that we have to decide during the idealization process which message is *expected* to be forwarded, thus excluding the possibility that an intruder might transmit a stolen hash value without knowing the content. So we have to suppose that P must have computed $h(X)$ himself:

SA3 $P\,said\,h(X) \land \neg P\,sees\,h(X) \longrightarrow P\,said\,X$

SA4 $P\,says\,h(X) \land \neg P\,sees\,h(X) \longrightarrow P\,says\,X$

Authentication and Key Confirmation. There is a general problem in using secret keys: If P sharing a secret key K with Q receives a cryptogram $\{M\}_K$ he has to exclude himself as originator in order to protect against a reflexion attack. AT and SvO suggest to use a special notation naming the originator. The disadvantage is that this notation was included in the idealization process and that it has no counterpart in the message. Setting this field leaves open the question of how P can exclude the case that he has encrypted M himself. We think that it is preferable to set out all assumptions about the protocol explicitly and to use no more notation than necessary. Therefore we choose the following authentication rules:

A1 $R\,sees\,F(K, X) \land P\overset{K}{\leftrightarrow}Q \land \neg P\,said\,F(K, X) \longrightarrow Q\,said\,(K, X)$

A2 $R\,sees\,F(K^-, X) \land \sigma\overset{K}{\leftrightarrow}Q \longrightarrow Q\,said\,(K^-, X)$

Comprehension. In order to compute the comprehended submessages of a received message we have to compute the localized message:

C $P \; sees \; M \wedge M_P \equiv Y \; \longrightarrow \; P \; believes \; P \; sees \; Y$

We assume that the formats of any sent lists are available and that it is sufficient to recognize any component in order to find the correct format:

C1 $P \; recognizes \; X_i \; \longrightarrow \; (X_1, ..., X_n)_P \equiv ((X_1)_P, ..., (X_n)_P)$

Decrypting a cryptogram and recognizing the deciphered text is enough evidence to comprehend the structure of a cryptogram:

C2 $P \; recognizes \; X \wedge P \; has \; K^{-1} \; \longrightarrow \; (enc(K, X))_P \equiv enc(K, X_P)$

Whoever knows M is able to verify the one-way computation $H(M)$:

C3 $P \; has \; M \; \longrightarrow \; H(M)_P \equiv H(M_P)$

C4 $P \; has \; K_q^- \wedge P \; has \; K_r^+ \; \longrightarrow \; \alpha(\{K_q, K_r\})_P \equiv \alpha(\{K_q, K_r\})$

Signatures without message recovery can be verified by using the contents and the corresponding public key:

C5 $P \; has \; (K^+, M) \; \longrightarrow \; \sigma(K^-, M)_P \equiv \sigma(K^-, M_P)$

Equivalences. The following group of axioms allows to compute the comprehended submessages of any seen message:

E1 $X \equiv X$

E2 $X \equiv Y \wedge Y \equiv Z \; \longrightarrow \; X \equiv Z$

E3 $X \equiv Y \; \longrightarrow \; F(X) \equiv F(Y)$

E4 $X_1 \equiv Y_1 \wedge ... \wedge X_n \equiv Y_n \; \longrightarrow \; (X_1, ..., X_n) \equiv (Y_1, ..., Y_n)$

Key Derivation.
Symmetry property of shared keys:

S $P \overset{K}{\leftrightarrow} Q \; \longrightarrow \; Q \overset{K}{\leftrightarrow} P$

Applying a shared key K and a suitable key derivation parameter M for the key derivation function F yields a new good shared key $F(K, M)$:

KD $P \overset{K}{\leftrightarrow} Q \wedge good_F(M) \; \longrightarrow \; P \overset{F(K, M)}{\longleftrightarrow} Q$

Key agreement:

KA $\alpha \overset{K_p}{\mapsto} P \wedge \alpha \overset{K_q}{\mapsto} Q \; \longrightarrow \; P \overset{\alpha(\{K_p, K_q\})}{\longleftrightarrow} Q$

     We did not try to find a complete axiomatisation because our goal is to find a tool as small as possible for analysing protocols whose soundness can be proven.

5 Proof of Correctness

Theorem 1. *Every derivable formula is valid in $\mathcal{AUT}$.*

It is sufficient to show that all axioms are valid in $\mathcal{AUT}$ and that the rules transfer valid formulae into valid formulae. A formula is called to be *valid* in $\mathcal{AUT}$ iff it is valid in every world of every structure in $\mathcal{AUT}$. Therefore we fix some $(\mathcal{W}, (\mathcal{W}_P)_{P \in \mathcal{P}}) \in \mathcal{AUT}$ and $(r, k) \in \mathcal{W}$.

Most axioms follow directly from the definitions in section 3. Soundness of **MP**, **M**, **K**, **4**, and **5** follows easily from the properties of $\mathcal{AUT}$.

Soundness of **H1** can be proven by an easy induction on the structure of $seensub_{S_P^{(r,k)}}(X)$. A proof of **A1** and **A2** is similar to the proof in [9, p.8]. The most interesting innovation is Axiom

C $P\, sees\, M \wedge M_P \equiv X \longrightarrow P\, believes\, P\, sees\, X$

In order to prove its soundness we need the following two lemmas:

Lemma 2. *Let X and X' be arbitrary generalized messages satisfying $sight_P^{(r,k)}(X) = sight_P^{(r',k')}(X')$ and S resp. S' be abbreviations for the knowledge bases $S_P^{(r,k)}$ resp. $S_P^{(r',k')}$. For all submessages $M \in seensub_S(X)$ there exists a $M' \in seensub_{S'}(X')$ satisfying $sight_P^{(r',k')}(M') = sight_P^{(r,k)}(M)$.*

Lemma 3. *Let $(r, k), (r', k') \in \mathcal{W}$ be two points, $M \in \mathcal{M}$ a message and $X \in \mathcal{M}_P$ a generalized message:*

$$sight^{(r',k')}(M_P) = sight^{(r,k)}(X) \quad \Rightarrow \quad M \preceq X.$$

Proof (Soundness of Axiom C). Suppose $(r, k) \models P\, sees\, M \wedge M_P \equiv X$. By definition there exists a time $k^* \leq k$ so that $H^{(r,k^*)} = receive_P(N)$ and $M \in seensub_{S_P^{(r,k)}}(N)$. Let (r', k') be an arbitrary point satisfying $(r, k) \sim_P (r', k')$. We have to show that $(r', k') \models P\, sees\, X$. By definition there exists an action $H^{(r',k'')}$ so that

$$sight_P^{(r',k')}(H^{(r',k'')}) = sight_P^{(r,k)}(H^{(r,k^*)}) = receive_P(sight_P^{(r,k)}(N)).$$

Therefore $H^{(r',k'')} = receive_P(N')$ and $sight_P^{(r,k)}(N) = sight_P^{(r',k')}(N')$. Lemma 2 shows the existence of $M' \in seensub_{S_P^{(r',k')}}(N')$ satisfying $sight_P^{(r',k')}(M') = sight_P^{(r,k)}(M)$. In order to prove $(r', k') \models P\, sees\, X$ we have to show the existence of an instance $M'' \preceq X$, so that $(r', k') \models P\, sees\, M''$. By the assumption $(r, k) \models M_P \equiv X$ it is $sight^{(r,k)}(X) = sight^{(r,k)}(M_P) = sight_P^{(r,k)}(M) = sight_P^{(r,k)}(M')$. By Lemma 3 we can conclude $M' \preceq X$ and because of $(r', k') \models P\, sees\, M'$ this completes the proof. $\square$

Proof (Lemma 2). The proof is an induction on the structure of $\text{seensub}_S(X)$. We restrict to the case of a ciphertext $C = enc(K, M) \in \text{seensub}_S(X)$ satisfying the lemma, $K^{-1} \in \overline{S}$ and, thus, $M \in \text{seensub}_S(X)$. We have to show that also M satisfies the lemma.

Because C satisfies the lemma, there exists $C' \in \text{seensub}_{S'}(X')$ such that $sight_P^{(r',k')}(C') = sight_P^{(r,k)}(C)$. First we consider the case that $sight_P^{(r,k)}(M) \neq *$. Thus we get

$$sight_P^{(r',k')}(C') = sight_P^{(r,k)}(enc(K, M)) = enc(K, sight_P^{(r,k)}(M)).$$

Thus C' must be a cryptogram $C' = enc(K', M')$ satisfying

$$sight_P^{(r',k')}(C') = enc(K', sight_P^{(r',k')}(M')).$$

It follows $K'^{-1} \in \overline{S'}$ and thus $M' \in \text{seensub}_{S'}(X')$. $sight_P^{(r',k')}(M') = sight_P^{(r,k)}(M)$ completes the case.

Second, let $sight_P^{(r,k)}(M) = *$. Then $M' = C'$ does the job because $sight_P^{(r,k)}(enc(K, M)) = * = sight_P^{(r,k)}(C')$. $\qquad\square$

Lemma 3 can be proved by induction on the complete structure of X by considering the cases $X = Y_P$, $X \in \mathcal{M}$, $X = (X_1, ..., X_n)$, and $X = F(Y)$.

6 Detection of Invalid Axioms

The formal semantics enables us to detect invalid axioms of other logics. It confirms that the axiom A11 of [1], is invalid as already noted by Abadi-Tuttle themselves (cf. [9]). The original message-meaning-rule of BAN [2] is also invalid if it is interpreted according to our semantics.

A further interesting example concerns the recognizability operator of GNY-logic [6]. Because GNY do not give a formal semantics we can only examine whether their axioms satisfy our given semantics. It is easy to see that [4]

R6 $\qquad P\, has\, H(M) \longrightarrow P\, recognizes\, M$

is not valid with respect to our semantical interpretation because $H(M) \in \overline{S_P^{(r,k)}}$ does not imply $sight_P^{(r,k)}(M) \neq *$. At this point it is not clear if the rule is incorrect or if our semantics is inappropiate.

Iterative application of the GNY-axioms P1 : $\quad P\, sees\, M \longrightarrow P\, has\, M$, P4 : $\quad P\, has\, M \longrightarrow P\, has\, H(M)$ and R6 yields that $P\, sees\, M$ will always imply $P\, recognizes\, M$. This implication does not fit to our intuitive meaning of recognition. Therefore we argue that R6 should be omitted. (The issue of GNY-rule R6 was also discussed in [9, 10].)

---

[4] The GNY-Expressions $P \ni M$ and $P \models \phi(M)$ are substituted by $P\, has\, M$ and $P\, recognizes\, M$ respectively.

We note that some axioms of a previous version of AUTLOG [7] are invalid as well, for example the key confirmation rule

$K1$ $P \, sees \, \{M\}_K \wedge P \, believes \, P \overset{K}{\leftrightarrow} Q \wedge P \, believes \, Q \, says \, M$

   $\longrightarrow P \, believes \, Q \, says \, P \overset{K}{\leftrightarrow} Q$

The point is that Q might have sent the cryptogram $\{M\}_K$ in a previous run. Imagine that in the meantime Q has lost confidence in key K but he has again sent the message M in the current run. Then the premises are fulfilled but the conclusion does not hold.

7   AUTLOG

The calculus was designed in order to be implemented in the Siemens tool AUT-LOG which is written in PROLOG. Of course, a formal analysis using a BAN-like logic can still be made by hand within a reasonable amount of time. The main advantage of using an automatized tool like AUTLOG is the correctness of the analysis. Human beings tend to mixture syntactical and semantical reasoning. Therefore one risk of hand-made formal deductions is that rules are applied which are not explicitly stated in the calculus (e.g. [4, p.10]).

Since our logic is designed for automated derivations we have to be more precise about the functions than the SvO-logic is, e.g. the rule 10 of [10] is split up into two rules H2 and H3. Therefore the number of rules of our logic increases the number of SvO-rules.

We note that the new calculus compared to [7] significantly increases the speed of the automated derivations. PROLOG tries to satisfy the goal by looking for candidates using a backward search. Our new calculus has reduced the number of possible candidates.

8   Example

The following protocol was designed as an authentication protocol between network operator, N, and user, U, in a mobile net like UMTS. We follow the description in [8] in order to demonstrate how the prerequisites, the transactions, and the goals are expressed in the formal language.

8.1   Transactions

1. User U generates a random number t and computes his public key agreement key $Ku^+ = g^t$ which he sends to N:

   $U \longrightarrow N: \quad g^t$

2. At this stage N does not know the identity of the sender of the first message. N computes the agreed key $\alpha(\{Kn, Ku\}) = (g^t)^s$. He then generates a random number r which he uses to compute a fresh shared secret key

$K = h1((g^t)^s, r) = h1(\alpha(\{Kn, Ku\}), r)$ by applying the one-way function $h1$. N confirms the possession of K by applying the hash function $h2$. If required N sends encrypted *data* to U.

$$N \longrightarrow U : \quad r, h2(K), \{data\}_K$$

3. Since U knows N's public key agreement key g^s he can compute the key agreement key $\alpha(Ku^-, Kn^+) = (g^s)^t$ and the derived key $K = h1((g^s)^t, r)$. He is thus able to check $h2(K)$ and to read *data*. He now signs the hash value $h3(K, data)$ and thus confirms the possession of K. (Since the field *data* is optional we have to choose $h3 \neq h2$ in order to avoid a simple reflection of $h2(K)$). The possession of K confirms that U has indeed chosen g^t. U encrypts his idenitiy $IMUI$ in order to ensure anonymity.

$$U \longrightarrow N : \{IMUI\}_K, \{\sigma(KU^-; h3(K, data))\}_K$$

4. N decrypts the ciphertexts, gets to know $IMUI$, and can now verify the signature.

8.2 Prerequisites

U generates a random number t which he believes to be fresh, i.e., not used in a run before. He chooses the pair $Ku := (Ku^-, Ku^+) := (t, g^t)$ as a temporary key agreement key.

$$U \text{ has } Ku^- \;(U1) \quad U \text{ believes } fresh(Ku^-)\;(U2) \quad U \text{ believes } \alpha \overset{Ku}{\mapsto} U \;(U3)$$

U has a copy of the public long-term key agreement key $Kn^+ := g^s$ of N and believes that this is the right key

$$U \text{ has } Kn^+ \quad (U4) \qquad U \text{ believes } \alpha \overset{Kn}{\mapsto} N \quad (U5)$$

U is able to convince himself that r is *good* for key derivation.

$$U \text{ believes } good_{h1}(r) \quad (U6)$$

U names the derived key with K. Furthermore he can check that he did not send $h2(K)$ himself.

$$(K)_U \equiv K \quad (U7) \qquad U \text{ believes } \neg U \text{ said } h2(K) \quad (U8)$$

Of course, N has a copy of his key agreement key and believes that this is the right key.

$$N \text{ has } Kn^- \quad (N1) \qquad N \text{ believes } \alpha \overset{Kn}{\mapsto} N \quad (N2)$$

N generates a random number which he believes to be fresh and to be good for key derivation using the hash function $h1$.

$$N \text{ has } r \;(N3) \quad N \text{ believes } fresh(r)\;(N4) \quad N \text{ believes } good_{h1}(r) \;(N5)$$

N has got a copy of U's public verification key KU and believes that this is an authentic copy but he first has to learn $IMUI$ before he knows which key he has to take.

$$N \; sees \; IMUI \; \longrightarrow \; (N \; has \; KU^{+} \wedge N \; believes \; \sigma \overset{KU}{\mapsto} U) \quad (N6)$$

N believes that U has the jurisdiction to choose his own key agreement keys and N believes that if U says $K = h1(\alpha(\{Ku, Kn\}), r)$, then U believes that Ku is U's key agreement key.

$$N \; believes \; U \; controls \; \alpha \overset{Ku}{\mapsto} U \qquad\qquad (N7)$$

$$N \; believes \; (U \; says \; K \; \longrightarrow \; U \; believes \; \alpha \overset{Ku}{\mapsto} U) \quad (N8)$$

N has and comprehends $data$. He names the derived key by K.

$$N \; has \; data \qquad (N9) \qquad N \; recognizes \; data \; (N10)$$

$$(data)_N = data \; (N11) \qquad (K)_N = K \qquad (N12)$$

N believes that the value $h3(K, data)$ was not sent to U, i.e., U has generated this hash value himself. Since $data$ is optional this belief is only justified if $h3(K)$ cannot be computed from the knowledge of $h2(K)$, especially $h2 \neq h3$.

$$N \; believes \; \neg U \; sees \; h3(K, data) \quad (N13)$$

8.3 Goals

According to [8, p2] the protocol is supposed to meet the following goals:

1. Mutual explicit authentication:

$$U \; believes \; N \; says \; X, \quad N \; believes \; U \; says \; X$$

2. Agreement on a shared secret key with mutual implicit key authentication:

$$U \; has \; K, \; N \; has \; K, \; U \; believes \; U \overset{K}{\leftrightarrow} N, \; N \; believes \; N \overset{K}{\leftrightarrow} U$$

3. Mutual key confirmation:

$$U \; believes \; N \; says \; K, \; N \; believes \; U \; says \; K$$

4. Mutual assurance of key freshness:

$$U \; believes \; fresh(K), \; N \; believes \; fresh(K)$$

5. Non-repudiation by U of data sent by U to N, i.e., N has obtained a signature by U on $data$ and N believes that U has recently sent the data:[5]

$$N \; sees \; \sigma(KU^{-}; h3(K, data)), \; N \; believes \; U \; says \; data$$

6. N knows the identity of U:

$$N \; believes \; N \; sees \; IMUI$$

---

[5] A compromise of the private signature key KU^{-} is not taken into account

8.4 Proving the goals

We have listed the numbers of the formulas which lead to the new formula. Since the rules MP and K are applied very often we do not always mention it.

The transactions are written as

$$N \, sees \, Ku^+ \tag{1}$$

$$U \, sees \, (r, h2(K), \{data\}_K) \tag{2}$$

$$N \, sees \, (\{IMUI\}_K, \{\sigma(KU^-; h3(K, data))\}_K) \tag{3}$$

We start looking at U's state.

$$U1, U4 \xrightarrow{H4} U \, has \, \alpha(\{Ku, Kn\}) \tag{4}$$

$$2, 4 \xrightarrow{SE1, H1-H3} \boxed{U \, has \, h1(\alpha(\{Ku, Kn\}), r)} \tag{5}$$

$$U3, U5 \xrightarrow{KA} U \, believes \, U \xleftarrow{\alpha(\{Ku, Kn\})} N \tag{6}$$

$$U6, 6 \xrightarrow{KD} \boxed{U \, believes \, U \xleftarrow{h1(\alpha(\{Ku, Kn\}), r)} N} \tag{7}$$

$$U2 \xrightarrow{F3, F2} \boxed{U \, believes \, fresh(h1(\alpha(\{Ku, Kn\}), r))} \tag{8}$$

Setting $K = h1(\alpha(\{Ku, Kn\}), r))$ and $K^{-1} = K$ we get

$$2 \xrightarrow{SE1} U \, sees \, h2(K) \tag{9}$$

$$5 \xrightarrow{C3} (h2(K)_U) \equiv h2(K_U) \tag{10}$$

$$U7 \xrightarrow{E3} h2(K_U) \equiv h2(K) \tag{11}$$

$$10, 11 \xrightarrow{E2} (h2(K))_U \equiv h2(K) \tag{12}$$

$$9, 12 \xrightarrow{C} U \, believes \, U \, sees \, h2(K) \tag{13}$$

$$U8, 7, 13 \xrightarrow{A1, K} U \, believes \, N \, said \, K \tag{14}$$

$$8, 14 \xrightarrow{NV} \boxed{U \, believes \, N \, says \, K} \tag{15}$$

Since the last statement refers to both goal 1 and goal 3 we have proven that the protocol meets the goals concerning U.

For N we can prove the following:

$$1, N1, N3 \xrightarrow{H4, H3} \boxed{N \, has \, h1(\alpha(\{Kn, Ku\}), r)} \tag{16}$$

$$N4 \xrightarrow{F2, F3} \boxed{N \, believes \, fresh(h1(\alpha(\{Kn, Ku\}), r))} \tag{17}$$

$$3 \xrightarrow{SE1} N \, sees \, \{IMUI\}_K \tag{18}$$

$$16, 18 \xrightarrow{SE2} \boxed{N \, sees \, IMUI} \tag{19}$$

$$N6, 19 \xrightarrow{MP} N \, has \, KU^+ \wedge N \, believes \, \sigma \xmapsto{KU} U \tag{20}$$

$$3, 16 \xrightarrow{SE1, SE2} \boxed{N \, sees \, \sigma(KU^-; h3(K, data))} \tag{21}$$

By iterated applying of the rules for comprehending and equivalence it follows from N9 – N12, 16, and 20

$$\ldots \longrightarrow (h3(K, data))_N \equiv h3(K, data) \tag{22}$$

$$\ldots \longrightarrow \sigma(KU^-; h3(K, data))_N \equiv \sigma(KU^-; h3(K, data)) \tag{23}$$

$$21, 23 \xrightarrow{C} N \text{ believes } N \text{ sees } \sigma(KU^-; h3(K, data)) \tag{24}$$

$$24, 20 \xrightarrow{A2,K} N \text{ believes } U \text{ said } h3(K, data) \tag{25}$$

$$17, 25 \xrightarrow{F2,NV} N \text{ believes } U \text{ says } h3(K, data) \tag{26}$$

$$N13, 26 \xrightarrow{SA4} \boxed{N \text{ believes } U \text{ says } (K, data)} \tag{27}$$

$$N8, 27 \xrightarrow{K} N \text{ believes } U \text{ believes } \alpha \overset{Ku}{\mapsto} U \tag{28}$$

$$N7, 28 \xrightarrow{J} N \text{ believes } \alpha \overset{Ku}{\mapsto} U \tag{29}$$

$$N2, 29 \xrightarrow{KA,K} N \text{ believes } U \overset{\alpha(\{Kn, Ku\})}{\longleftarrow} N \tag{30}$$

$$N5, 30 \xrightarrow{KD,K} \boxed{N \text{ believes } U \overset{h1(\alpha(\{Kn, Ku\}), r)}{\longleftarrow} N} \tag{31}$$

We have thus proven that the protocol meets the goals.

9 Conclusion

We present a logic for the analysis of authentication protocols and give a formal semantics which enables us to prove its soundness.

The logic can handle a wide variety of cryptographic mechanisms using a minimum of notation. The use of negative formulae enables us to deal with hash values without introducing an additional notation for forwarded messages and allows a satisfying solution for the symmetry problem.

The elimination of the formulae out of the idealized messages leads to a clear distinction between the protocol itself and the assumptions about it. A careful examination of all initial assumptions gives a much deeper insight to the real outcome of the analysis and allows the detection of a wide variety of protocol flaws. In addition, this distinction is necessary in order to solve the issues of recognizability, computability, and comprehension.

Acknowledgements. The first author thanks Erich Graedel for the supervision of her diploma thesis. The second author thanks Martin Abadi, Paul Syverson, and Pekka Nikander for fruitful comments they gave to him during the participation at the Coding, Cryptography and Computer Security programme at the Newton Institute, Cambridge. Finally, we thank the anonymous referees for suggestions concerning the presentation.

References

1. M. Abadi, M. Tuttle, "A Semantics for a Logic of Authentication," *Proc. of the ACM Symposium of Principles of Distributed Computing*, 1991, 201-216.

2. M. Burrows, M. Abadi, R. Needham, *A Logic of Authentication*, Report 39 Digital Systems Research Center, Pao Alto, California, 1989.
3. Chellas, *Modal Logic*, Cambridge University Press, Cambridge, England, 1980.
4. L. Chen, D. Gollmann, Y. Han, C. Mitchell, *Formal Verification of a Mutual Authentication Protocol*, Royal Holloway, University of London 3GS3/IREP/ RHUL/032/A(draft), 1995.
5. R. Fagin, J. Halpern, Y. Moses, M. Vardi, *Reasoning about knowledge*, MIT Press, Cambridge, Mass., 1995.
6. L. Gong, R. Needham, R. Yahalom, "Reasoning about Belief in Cryptographic Protocols," *Proc. of the 1990 IEEE Symp. on Research in Security and Privacy*, 234-248.
7. V. Kessler, G. Wedel, "AUTLOG - An Advanced Logic of Authentication," *Proc. of the Computer Security Foundations Workshop VII*, Franconia, IEEE Computer Society Press 1994, 90-99.
8. ETSI SMG/SG/TD 73/95 *Protocols for UMTS Providing Mutual Authentication and Key Establishment Using Asymmetric Techniques.*
9. P. Syverson, P. van Oorschot, "On Unifying Some Cryptographic Protocol Logics", *Proc. of the IEEE Computer Society Symp. on Security and Privacy 1994*, 14-28.
10. P. Syverson, P. van Oorschot, *A Unified Cryptographic Protocol Logic*, Unpublished preprint, March 1996.
11. G. Wedel, *Formale Semantik für Authentifikationslogiken*, Diplomarbeit FB Mathematik der RWTH Aachen, Nov. 1995.

Threat Scenarios as a Means to Formally Develop Secure Systems*

Volkmar Lotz

Siemens AG, Corporate Research and Development, ZFE T SN 3
D–81730 München
e–mail: `Volkmar.Lotz@zfe.siemens.de`

Abstract. We introduce a new method for the formal development of secure systems that closely corresponds to the way secure systems are developed in practice. It is based on FOCUS, a general-purpose approach to the design and verification of distributed, interactive systems. Our method utilizes threat scenarios which are the result of threat identification and risk analysis and model those attacks that are of importance to the system's security. We describe the adversary's behaviour and influence on interaction. Given a suitable system specification, threat scenarios can be derived systematically from that specification. Security is defined as a particular relation on threat scenarios and systems. We show the usefulness of our approach by developing an authentic server component, thereby analysing two simple authentication protocols.
Keywords. Security, Formal Methods, Threat Identification, Risk Analysis, Stream Processing Functions, Authentication, Protocols.

1 Introduction

When developing IT-systems for security critical applications, it is of particular importance to show that the proposed solution maintains security. Formal methods can be used to prove security on a mathematically sound basis, provided an appropriate formalization of security is given. However, there is no general notion of security: for each application, different aspects of security, as confidentiality, authenticity/integrity or availability, may be relevant. Though abstract security policies may be defined, the concrete security requirements are heavily influenced by the kind of attacks that are expected for the given system and the application domain.

Informal approaches that have been shown useful in practice are therefore based on threat identification and risk analysis, where the system and its environment are investigated in detail in order to determine the kind of possible attacks, their probability, and the loss in case of the attack being performed. Thus, critical system components are identified, for which the associated risk cannot be tolerated, leading to application specific security requirements. [HMS93] gives

---

* This work has been carried out at Technische Universität München as part of the author's PhD research.

an overview of typical requirements on several security application domains. As in general systems are not secure by themselves, mechanisms, as for example access control, encryption or authentication protocols ([FFKK93]), have to be implemented to ensure security. It is the the system designer's task to show that a specific set of mechanisms is suitable to meet the security requirements.

A formal method for the development of secure systems that is intended to be supportive in practice should be based on the above considerations. In particular, it should employ a definition of security that is independent of security mechanisms and is therefore suitable to show the effectiveness of a mechanism. It should allow the formalization of individual security notions. Additionally, such a method should offer the opportunity of integrating security analysis and functional system development. This can be achieved by using a general-purpose method for system design and verification.

Methods achieving all these goals are currently not available. Though a lot of formal security models have been proposed and continuously developed during the last 20 years ([BLP73], [GoMe82], [TeWi89], to mention but a few), they, in general, consider specific security policies and concentrate on particular security aspects or even mechanisms. Additionally, the relationship to system implementations is often vague (one of the few exceptions is given by [BLP76]), which may explain, why these models have not been heavily used in commercial practice. Approaches ([BAN89], [Mea94], [Sne95]) dedicated to the formal analysis of certain classes of hard-to-understand mechanisms, namely authentication protocols, are promising, but often employ specification techniques and/or semantics exclusively dedicated to support security analysis and, by their nature, are not suited for the analysis of different security aspects.

In the context of process algebras, CSP in particular, there are approaches going beyond security modelling. Jacob ([Jac90]) uses inference functions describing properties of system traces in order to specify non-interference requirements. Roscoe et.al. ([RWW94]) propose to express non-interference properties as determinism of a certain system abstraction with respect to security classes and user models. In both approaches, security becomes a property of the system itself and corresponence checks with explicit security models are avoided. However, non-interference conditions seem to be too restrictive for certain applications of communication systems, for example, if only authenticity is required. Additionally, since security analysis typically occurs at early development steps, we would like to allow underspecification.

In this paper, we introduce a new formal method for the development of secure systems that is intended to meet all of the requirements mentioned above. Since we are mainly interested in applications of communication systems, we utilize a general-purpose approach to the design and verification of distributed, interactive systems. FOCUS ([BDD+93], [Br95], [BrSt96]) models agents by stream processing functions and is compositional with respect to refinement. In our approach, threat analysis results in the definition of threat scenarios. They are specified in FOCUS and can be easily derived from a system specification. Security analysis is then performed by checking the relationship between threat scenario and system specification. If the security relation holds, the threat scenario can be dropped, and system development proceeds as usual. Because of compositionality, further system refinements are secure with respect to the initial threat scenario.

Section 2 gives a brief overview of the FOCUS method and its basic notions. The properties of the semantic model of FOCUS are exploited in Sect. 3 to define threat scenarios and several notions of security that correspond to different seurity aspects. Using transmission media and typical attacks on them as example, we demonstrate how parameterized threat scenario templates can be defined. The usefulness of our approach is shown by example in Sect. 4, where we analyse two simple protocols based on ISO 9798-2 and ISO 10181-2 with respect to authenticity. The broad spectrum of our approach is indicated by the fact that the analysis of one of the protocols shows that authenticity is achieved at the expense of losing availability if an attack occurs.

2 System Specification and Development with FOCUS

In the following, we give a short introduction to the basic notions of FOCUS. We define the concepts and notations that are used in the remainder of the paper. For further reading we refer to [BDD+93] and [Br95]. The reader is expected to be familiar with set theory. We use N to denote the set of natural numbers, and $\mathsf{B} = \{0, 1\}$ to denote the set of bits. $\mathcal{P}(M)$ denotes the powerset of a set M.

2.1 Streams

In FOCUS, systems are viewed as communicating asynchrounously via named channels. Communication histories of channels are modelled by *streams* of messages, where a stream is defined to be a finite or infinite sequence of messages. Given a set of messages M, we define $M^{\overline{\omega}}$, $M^{\overline{*}}$ and $M^{\overline{\infty}}$ to denote the set of streams, finite streams and infinite streams of messages from M, respectively. We have $M^{\overline{\omega}} = M^{\overline{*}} \cup M^{\overline{\infty}}$.

Streams can be viewed as functions mapping natural numbers to messages. For example, a finite stream $s \in M^{\overline{*}}$ of length $n \in \mathsf{N}$ is an element of the function space $[1..n] \to M$. With dom.s and rng.s we denote the domain and the range, respectively, of a function modelling a stream.

We use $\langle\rangle$ to denote the empty stream, which is the unique finite stream that contains no messages, and $\langle m_1, m_2, \ldots, m_n\rangle$ to denote the finite stream containing the n messages $m_1, m_2, \ldots, m_n$. We utilize a number of operations on streams:

- $s \frown t$ denotes the concatenation of two streams s and t. $s \frown t$ yields the stream that starts with s and proceeds with the elements of t, if s is finite. If $s \in M^{\overline{\infty}}$, we have $s \frown t = s$. We overload the concatenation operator to messages, with $m \frown s$ denoting the result of appending the message m to s.
- $\#s$ denotes the length of a stream s with $\#s = \infty$ if $s \in M^{\overline{\infty}}$ and $\#s = n$ if $s = \langle m_1, \ldots, m_n\rangle$.

- $A\copyright s$ denotes the stream generated from s by filtering away all elements not in A.
- $s.i$ denotes the i-th element of a stream s, if $i \leq \#s$.
- $s \sqsubseteq t$ denotes the prefix relation on streams. We have $s \sqsubseteq t$ if and only if $\exists r \in M^{\bar{\omega}} : s ^\frown r = t$.
- $s|_i$ denotes the prefix of length i of a stream s, if $i \leq \#s$, otherwise it yields s.
- $\mathrm{map}(s, f)$ for a stream s and a function f yields the stream resulting from applying f to all elements of s.
- s^n denotes the n-time iteration of the stream s. We have $s^0 = \langle\rangle$ and $s^{n+1} = s ^\frown s^n$.

Some of the above operators are overloaded to tuples of streams in a straight-forward way. In particular, $\#(s_1, \ldots, s_n)$ yields the length of the shortest stream in $(s_1, \ldots, s_n)$, and $A\copyright(s_1, \ldots, s_n)$ filters each stream of $(s_1, \ldots, s_n)$ with respect to A. We use the operator $(A_1 \times \ldots \times A_n)\copyright(s_1, \ldots, s_n)$ to denote the substream of those $(s_1.i, \ldots, s_n.i)$ that are elements of $A_1 \times \ldots \times A_n$. To select the i-th element of a tuple, we use the projection function Π_i.

2.2 Timed Streams

To model the progress of time, we use so-called *timed streams*. In timed streams, the special symbol $\sqrt{}$ ("tick"), which is not an element of M, occurs. Each occurrence of $\sqrt{}$ denotes that a time unit of a particular length has passed. Messages occurring between two successive ticks are assumed to be communicated within the same time unit. Since time never halts, each infinite timed stream contains infinitely many ocurrences of $\sqrt{}$. By M^ω, M^* and M^∞ we denote the set of timed streams, finite timed streams and infinite timed streams of messages of M, respectively. We have $M^\omega = M^* \cup M^\infty$.

For timed streams, we may use all of the operators defined on (untimed) streams, with ticks interpreted as ordinary messages. Moreover, we use $s\downarrow_j$ to define the least prefix of S that contains j occurrences of $\sqrt{}$. $s\downarrow_j$ therefore describes the history of a channel up to the j-th time unit. Abstraction from time is denoted by $\bar{s}$, where $\bar{s}$ results from s by removing all ocurrences of $\sqrt{}$.

2.3 Stream Processing Functions

FOCUS models deterministic system components by stream processing functions. In order to distinguish channels, stream processing functions usually work on named stream tuples instead of simple stream tuples. We define named stream tuples by assigning names to the input and output channels of a component, and define a mapping $\alpha \in Q \to M^\omega$, provided a set of channel identifiers Q is given. The operators on stream tuples that have been introduced so far are overloaded to named stream tuples, if necessary. In particular, time abstraction is lifted to named stream tuples, and denoted by $\bar{\alpha}$ for a named stream tuple α.

If $Q \cap P = \emptyset$, we define $\alpha \uplus \beta$ to denote the element of $Q \cup P \to M^\omega$ such that $c \in Q \Rightarrow (\alpha \uplus \beta)(c) = \alpha(c)$ and $c \in P \Rightarrow (\alpha \uplus \beta)(c) = \beta(c)$.

Moreover, we use **Q** as a shorthand for $Q \to M^\omega$. In Sects. 3 and 4 we often identify streams and channel names, if this is expected not to cause confusion.

We model a deterministic component C with input channels I and output channels O by a function $\tau \in \mathbf{I} \to \mathbf{O}$ that maps communication histories for the input channels to communication histories for the output channels.

To correctly reflect the behaviour of real-life components, we require for each stream-processing function modelling a component, that its output at any time j is completely determined by its input received so far, which means up to time j. If additionally a possible delay of the component is considered, requiring the output at time $j + 1$ being completely determined by the input up to time j, we call the function *strongly pulse driven*. The requirements on strongly pulse driven functions τ are formally described by

$$\alpha{\downarrow}_j = \beta{\downarrow}_j \Rightarrow \tau(\alpha){\downarrow}_{j+1} = \tau(\beta){\downarrow}_{j+1} .$$

The arrow $\xrightarrow{s}$ is used to model domains of strongly pulse driven functions.

2.4 Composition

Strongly pulse driven functions can be composed using a number of different composition operators. For the outline of our approach, we need sequential composition, parallel composition, and feedback, which are depicted in Fig. 1 below.

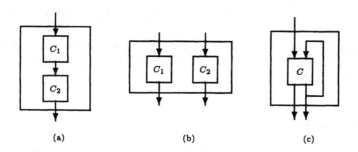

Fig. 1. Composition: (a) sequential, (b) parallel, (c) feedback

Given two strongly pulse driven stream processing functions $\tau_1 \in \mathbf{I}_1 \xrightarrow{s} \mathbf{O}_1, \tau_2 \in \mathbf{I}_2 \xrightarrow{s} \mathbf{O}_2$, we use the operator " $\succ$ " to denote sequential composition, if $O_1 = I_2$, and the operator "$\|$" to denote parallel composition, if $I_1 \cap I_2 = O_1 \cap O_2 = \emptyset$. Formally, we have

$$(\tau_1 \succ \tau_2)(\alpha) \stackrel{\text{def}}{=} \tau_2(\tau_1(\alpha)) ,$$

$$(\tau_1 \| \tau_2)(\alpha) \stackrel{\text{def}}{=} \tau_1(\alpha|_{I_1}) \uplus \tau_2(\alpha|_{I_2}) .$$

where $\alpha|_Y$ denotes the restriction of the named stream tuple α to those channels contained in Y. The functions resulting from sequential and parallel composition of strongly pulse driven stream-processing functions are strongly pulse driven as well ([BrSt96]).

Given $\tau \in \mathbf{I} \xrightarrow{s} \mathbf{O}$ we define feedback by identifying a subset of τ's output channels with a subset of τ's input channels. Let $X \subset O$ and $r \in X \rightarrow I$ be a bijection that associates a subset of τ's input channels with X. We then define $\mu_X(\tau) \in (\mathbf{I} \setminus \mathbf{r(X)}) \rightarrow \mathbf{O}$ by

$$\mu_X(\tau)(\alpha) = \beta \qquad \text{where} \qquad \beta = \tau(\alpha \uplus \beta|_{r(X)}) \ .$$

Because of the properties of strongly pulse driven stream-processing functions, it can be shown that for each α there is a unique β that satisfies the above equation. Moreover, $\mu_X(\tau)$ is itself strongly pulse driven ([BrSt96]).

Network components are modelled by sets of stream processing functions, with this set being a singleton, if the component is deterministic. For a component $C \subseteq \mathbf{I} \xrightarrow{s} \mathbf{O}$ we define the set $C_{i/o}$ of input/output-behaviours by

$$C_{i/o} = \{(\alpha, \beta) \mid \exists \tau \in C : \tau(\alpha) = \beta\}.$$

The composition operators for stream processing functions are lifted uniformly to components. If C, C_1 and C_2 are appropriately defined, we have

$$C_1 \succ C_2 = \{\tau \in \mathbf{I} \xrightarrow{s} \mathbf{O} \mid \forall \alpha : \exists \tau_1 \in C_1, \tau_2 \in C_2 : \tau(\alpha) = (\tau_1 \succ \tau_2)(\alpha)\} \ ,$$
$$C_1 \parallel C_2 = \{\tau_1 \parallel \tau_2 \mid \tau_1 \in C_1 \wedge \tau_2 \in C_2\} \ ,$$
$$\mu_X(C) = \{\tau \mid \forall \alpha \in (\mathbf{I} \setminus \mathbf{r(X)}) : \exists \tau' \in C : \tau(\alpha) = \mu_X.\tau'(\alpha)\} \ .$$

The specific kind of the definitions for sequential composition and feedback is provided in order to achieve full abstractness of the semantic model, see [Br95] and [BrSt96] for details.

2.5 Specifications

FOCUS provides many different specification formats, whose semantics are based on the mathematical model introduced above. For our purposes, we are particularly interested in time-independent (ti) and time-dependent (td) specifications. Let I be a set of input channel names and O be a set of output channel names. The two specification formats are syntactically given by

$$S \equiv (I \triangleright O) \overset{ti}{::} R \ ,$$
$$S \equiv (I \triangleright O) \overset{td}{::} R \ ,$$

where S is the name of the specification, and R is a predicate logic formula with elements of I and O as its only free variables. Semantically, a specification is interpreted to describe the set of strongly pulse driven stream processing functions that "satisfy" R.

To formally define the semantics of a specification, we first define what it means for a named stream tuple to satisfy a predicate: For any named stream tuple $\alpha \in C \to M^\infty$, and formula P, whose free variables are contained in C, we define $\alpha \models P$ to hold iff P evaluates to true when each free variable c in P is interpreted as $\alpha(c)$. We then define the denotation of the time-independent and time-dependent specification format by

$$[\![S]\!] \stackrel{\text{def}}{=} \{\tau \in I \xrightarrow{s} O \,|\, \forall \alpha : \overline{(\alpha \uplus \tau(\alpha))} \models R\} \;,$$
$$[\![S]\!] \stackrel{\text{def}}{=} \{\tau \in I \xrightarrow{s} O \,|\, \forall \alpha : (\alpha \uplus \tau(\alpha)) \models R\} \;,$$

respectively. Note the use of the time abstraction operator for named stream tuples in the first line.

Specifications can be composed using the same composition operators as defined for components. Since specifications describe components, the semantics of composite specifications is straightforward. Composite specifications can be syntactically given in an operator style, using the composition operators, or in a constraint style, using equations on named channels and renaming. Due to its better readability, the constraint style is often preferred in practice.

2.6 Refinement

When formally developing systems, the notion of refinement plays a central role. FOCUS offers a number of refinement techniques ([Br93]), of which only behaviour refinement is of interest for the following exposition. With respect to behaviour refinement, a system defined by a specification T is said to refine a system given by a specification S, if each function modelling a behaviour of T also describes a behaviour of S. If T refines S, we write $S \leadsto T$ and formally define

$$S \leadsto T \equiv [\![T]\!] \subseteq [\![S]\!] \;.$$

In order to prove that T is a refinement of S, it suffices to show that $R_T \Rightarrow R_S$.

3 System Security

3.1 Development of Secure Systems

In practice, the development of secure systems is performed in a stepwise manner. We start with a system specification S_0 which describes a system that, in general, is not secure. S_0 has to be modified by introducing security mechanisms which counter those threats that have been identified as critical. The system S_1 resulting from this modification should be a refinement of S_0, since suitable security mechanisms are expected not to affect the specified system behaviour. Constructing a secure system is an iterative process, since security mechanisms introduce new components and/or data to the system which may themselves be subject to attack and have to be secured by further mechanisms. For example, considering a cryptographic mechanism that relies on secret keys, we need a mechanism to keep these keys confidential. For each iteration, we identify the following activities to be carried out (let S_i be the starting system specification, which will be refined to S_{i+1}):

1. **Threat Identification and Risk Analysis.** This is an application specific task that has to be carried out each time a security analysis is to be performed. Though classes of possible threats can be defined with respect to component types and application domains, the actual assessment of threats and associated risks heavily depends on the given system S_i. For example, if transmission media are considered, the associated risk depends, among others, on whether they are located in a secure or in a public area. Threat identification and risk analysis results in a classification of system components with respect to their criticality, and a description of the attacks that critical components may be subject to. Threat descriptions are concrete in the sense of referring to particular system components, and multiple occurences of the same kind of threat are possible (for example, if there are several communication links that are assumed to be eavesdropped).

2. **Definition of Threat Scenario.** The results of threat identification and risk analysis are used to specify a formal threat scenario B_i, in which critical components are replaced by subsystems that specify the relevant attacks. Thus, B_i models the system behaviour in a situation where all of the relevant attacks occur, which is the worst case with respect to security. Obviously, B_i is not necessarily a refinement of S_i.

3. **Selection or Development of Mechanisms.** During this activity, suitable security mechanisms are selected or developed, where "suitable" means that the mechanisms are able to counter the threats as well as that they satisfy further criteria, including non-technical ones as, for example, cost and performance.

4. **Refinement.** S_i is extended by a specification of the selected mechanisms. We yield a system specification S_{i+1} and, implicitly, a refined threat scenario B_{i+1}. It has to be shown that S_{i+1} is a refinement of S_i.

5. **Security Analysis.** In order to justify the selection of mechanisms in step 3, we have to show that S_{i+1} is secure, which is performed by proving that the security property holds with respect to S_{i+1} and B_{i+1}. The concrete structure of the security property depends on the security policy and the security requirements, see Sect. 3.3 for details. If the proof fails, the selected mechanisms are not appropriate, and steps 3 to 5 have to be repeated.

Starting from S_0, we yield a sequence of system specifications S_1, S_2, ..., S_n. The process is finished with a secure system S_n, if the risk analysis does not identify further threats that have to be countered, or the remaining threats are countered by non-technical mechanisms that are beyond the scope of our approach. Thus, step 1 must always follow step 5, which ensures that new threats resulting from the introduction of mechanisms are always considered. However, it often turns out to be useful to already include such new threats in the construction of B_{i+1}, which, for example, is done in Sect. 4.

Our approach aims at the formal foundation of the development steps described above. However, risk analysis and selection of mechanisms are excluded, since they heavily depend on non-technical arguments and thus are out of reach of formal treatment. Since all of the formal work is performed within the Focus framework, at each time of security development there is a unique relationship to system development according to its functional specification. However, methodological issues of integrated functional and security development are beyond the scope of this paper, and further work will be dedicated to this subject.

3.2 Threat Scenarios

A threat scenario is a modification of a system specification that describes a situation in which the system is attacked by an adversary, according to the results of threat identification and risk analysis. In most application cases, the threat scenario can be derived systematically from the system specification: threat identification and risk analysis are typically performed on the basis of an architectural view of the system, which means that we have a compositional specification as starting point of security considerations. For each of the components, it can then be determined, whether it is likely to be subject to adversary actions. In the derivation of a threat scenario, the critical components will then be replaced by specifications modelling the adversary's influence on them.

Candidates for critical components can often be defined on the basis of an analysis of the application domain and the type of the component, or its role within the system specification. This offers the opportunity of defining templates describing abstract attacks on the component types of interest. Using instantiations of these templates for the modification of critical components identified by risk analysis, application specific threat scenarios can be easily constructed. Note that not necessarily each of the components of a given type has to be replaced, but if risk analysis leads to a specific component of that type being classified as critical, the template can be used.

In distributed communication systems and networks, it is mainly the communication medium rather than the communicating entities (users or computer systems) that are considered to be at risk (imagine logical communication channels being implemented by using public telephone lines). Therefore, in order to perform a risk analysis reasonably, we require the specification to explicitly model media as network agents, using an appropriate level of abstraction. However, this does not seem to cause problems in practice: if the medium is subject to further development, for example if it is going to be implemented by a protocol working on an unreliable physical medium, it will be explicitly specified, otherwise it can be simply modelled by an agent behaving like the identity on its input. In the following, we provide a template for the construction of threat scenarios describing attacks on communication media. Given the results of the threat identification and risk analysis for a particular link of the system to be secured, the template can be easily instantiated, leading to an appropriate threat scenario for the given link. This will be demonstrated in Sect. 4.

Suppose M being a set of arbitrary messages, and MD being the specification of a medium transmitting messages of M, formally defined by

$$\text{MD} \equiv (i : M \triangleright o : M) :: \quad R_{MD} \ ,$$

with R_{MD} being an arbitrary predicate describing the communication behaviour of MD. If risk analysis identifies MD as critical, in the worst case an adversary is able to eavesdrop communication as well as to influence the transmission behaviour of the channel. Such an attack can be modelled by a network as depicted in Fig. 2, which replaces MD in the threat scenario construction. The

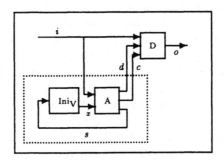

Fig. 2. Threat scenario for communication channels

threat scenario template is based on an explicit model of the adversary, together with the initial information available to her and the set of functions she can use to compute new information. As in [Sne95] and [Mea94], we use an explicit model of the adversary's influence on communication, based on the semantic model of FOCUS: the "data flow component" D specifies how the adversary influences the behaviour of the transmission medium. For example, the adversary may insert or delete messages. Obviously, the specification of D has to take into account properties of the medium MD, leading to D being a function of MD. A formal specification of the threat scenario MD_{Thr}, an instance of which is to replace each specification of a critical medium of the system analysed is given below. For better readability, the specification is given in constraint style.

$$\text{MD}_{\text{Thr}} \equiv (i : M \triangleright o : M) ::$$
$$(o) := \text{D}(\text{MD})(i, d, c), \quad (d, c, s) := \text{A}(i, x), \quad (x) := \text{Ini}_V(s) \ .$$

The specification is basically divided into two parts: D models the influence on communication, and the subnetwork consisting of Ini_V and A (indicated by the dotted box in Fig. 2) describes the adversary's abilities to generate new messages. Let U be a set of values, elements of which the adversary may use to perform her attacks. $V \subseteq U$ represents the set of values that are initially available to the adversary. Each time the adversary eavesdrops a message sent by a client, this set of values is extended according to the contents of this message and the set of functions the adversary may use to compute new values from already known ones. Let $F \subseteq \left(\bigcup_{n \in \mathbb{N}} U^n \to U\right) \times \mathbb{N}$ be a set of functions together with their arities that operate on messages, formally, if $n \in \mathbb{N}$ and $(f, n) \in F$, then $f \in U^n \to U$. The set of new messages C_F the adversary may get by stepwise computation from V using functions from F is then given by

$$C_F(V) = \bigcup_{n \in \mathbb{N}} C_F^N(n, V) \ ,$$

where $C_F^N(0, V) = V$ and $C_F^N(m+1, V) = \{x \in U \mid \exists (f, n) \in F, x_1, \ldots, x_n \in C_F^N(m, V) : x = f(x_1, \ldots, x_n)\}$.

Note that we are only interested in values satisfying the type constraints on MD's interface, since other values do not help the adversary in compromising the system. The formal specification of the components relating to the adversary is given by

$$\text{Ini}_V \equiv (s : \mathcal{P}(U) \triangleright x : \mathcal{P}(U)) \overset{\text{ti}}{::} x = V \frown s \ ,$$

$$A \equiv (i : M, x : \mathcal{P}(U) \triangleright d : M, c : C, s : \mathcal{P}(U)) \overset{\text{ti}}{::}$$
$$\#d = \#x \ \land$$
$$\forall j \in \text{dom}.x :$$
$$\quad d_j \in (x_j \cup \{i_j\}) \ \land$$
$$\quad j \in \text{dom}.i \Rightarrow s_j = C_F(x_j \cup \{i_j\})\}) \ \land$$
$$\quad j \notin \text{dom}.i \Rightarrow s_j = x_j \ .$$

At each point j, x_j contains the set of messages known to the adversary. Whenever she is able to eavesdrop a message from i, the set of messages will be updated according to the functions in F. The adversary may use each of the messages available to influence communication, e.g. by inserting them. Such fraudulent messages issued by the adversary are modeled by d. In some applications, it may turn out to be necessary to explicitly specify the influence of the adversary on the legitimate entity's communication, for example by determining the point of time at which a fraudulent message is inserted. We use c to model this kind of control, where data from a set of controls C are issued. Typically, we have $C = \mathbb{B}$. Within the template, we do not impose further restrictions on c, however, in an instantiation of the template further constraints can be introduced.

Note that, from a technical point of view, the specification could as well have been given by modelling the set of values available to the adversary as an internal state of A, thus saving the component Ini_V. However, we chose the above specification in order to explicate the central role of the adversary's knowledge in the context of security analysis.

In our template for attacks on communication channels, the data flow component D is not further specified, since the adversary's influence on communication is considered to be application specific. However, the syntactical interface of D (legitimate messages on i, fraudulent messages on d, and controls on c) allows all kinds of possible attacks, as for example listed in [Mun93], to be specified. Often, reliability aspects of the medium and specific attack descriptions can be separated, leading to a simple structure of D with respect to its parameter MD:

$$D(MD) \equiv (i, d, c \triangleright o) :: \quad D' \succ MD$$

for some D'. If, for example, the adversary may only insert new messages, without infinitely blocking legitimate messages, but is not able to determine the position where to insert, D' is given by the specification of the fair merge agent in [BDD+93].

This concludes the specification of the threat scenario template for transmission media. Its parameters are given by the adversary's initial set of values V, the set F of functions available, the type of control messages C, and the specification of the data flow component D. In addition, for some applications it may be suitable to further strengthen A. Section 4 shows a sample use of this template.

The kind of adversary model used in the threat scenario specification is close to the approach taken in [Sne95] and [Mea94], where it turned out to be useful for the analysis of cryptographic protocols. Differences occur, however, in the explicit modelling of the adversary's influence on communication, which in our approach can be tailored to the application at hand.

3.3   The Security Property

Given a system specification S and a threat scenario B that has been derived from S, security can be expressed using a particular binary relation R_{Sec} on specifications. If $R_{Sec}(B, S)$ holds, S is said to be secure with respect to the threats represented in B. However, the implications of $R_{Sec}(B, S)$ on the security of a system being implemented according to S depend heavily on the concrete definition of R_{Sec}. In the remainder of this section we want to introduce a number of variants of such a definition, which correspond to different kinds of security notions. Thus, our interpretation of security is split into two parts: a system specific part, which relates to vulnerabilities of the system under development, the specific abilities of an attacker to that system, and the environment of it, being modelled in a threat scenario, and a general part expressing common security requirements, being modelled using a particular security relation.

We start with the definition of the most restrictive type of security, in which adversary interference is expected to have no influence on the behaviour of the system. In this case, the threat scenario must be a refinement of the original system.

Definition 1. A system S with syntactic interface (I,O) is called *absolutely secure* with respect to a threat scenario B, with the same interface, if $R_S(B,S)$ holds, with R_S being defined by $R_S(B,S) \equiv S \rightsquigarrow B$. $\qquad\square$

In practice, absolute security is usually hard to achieve, and sometimes it is even not desired: if there are interactions that are not considered to be security relevant, then an adversary may influence these without compromising security.

If the security requirements on the application at hand are known exactly, we may use only these to define the system's security.

Definition 2. Given a predicate P, a system S with syntactic interface (I,O) is called *P-secure* with respect to a threat scenario B, with the same interface, if $P(B)$ holds. $\qquad\square$

For certain common aspects of security, like integrity, authenticity, confidentiality, or availability, formal definitions can be provided. Using these definitions in a security analysis, the analyst need not formalise particular security requirements, but may only use the definition covering the aspects that are of importance to her application. Since in Sect. 4 we focus on authentication mechanisms, we provide a general definition for authenticity of a system. Similar definitions can be given for the other aspects mentioned.

Definition 3. A system S with syntactic Interface (I,O) is called *authentic* with respect to a threat scenario B, with the same interface, if $R_{Ath}(B,S)$ holds, with R_{Ath} being defined by

$$R_{Ath}(B,S) \equiv \forall f \in I \xrightarrow{s} O :$$
$$f \in [\![B]\!] \Rightarrow \forall x \in I \ \exists h \in B^{\overline{\omega}}, f' \in [\![S]\!] : f'(\mathrm{sel}(x,h)) = f(x) ,$$

where $\forall x \in I, h \in B^{\overline{\omega}} : \mathrm{sel}(x,h) = \Pi_1((M \times 1)\copyright(x,h))$. $\qquad\square$

The above definition states, that, if $(x, f(x))$ is an i/o-behaviour of B, then there is a substream x' of x such that $(x', f(x))$ is an i/o-behaviour of S, with the appropriate substream being selected by an oracle h and the function sel. This means that each output of B is caused by a "legitimate" input, but we do not require the attacked system to respond to all legitimate inputs.

3.4 Security Mechanisms

When threat identification and risk analysis is performed, systems, in general, turn out not to be secure. Therefore, we have to specify particular means, called security mechanisms, that are suited to counter the threats that have been identified as critical. We distinguish between technical mechanisms, which are given by a particular functionality of an IT system, and non-technical mechanisms, which are organisational or physical means located in the system's environment. As an example of non-technical means, take a messenger delivering a secret key, or a door lock preventing an intruder from accessing a computer system located in a particular room. In our approach, we only consider technical mechanisms, since they form a part of the system to be developed and can therefore be treated in the same way as functional requirements. However, assumptions based on non-technical mechanisms may influence the adversary model.

A lot of basic technical mechanisms suited to meet different security requirements have been proposed. [FFKK93] gives a representative overview. In general, for a given security problem, there are several mechanisms that are suited to meet the requirements, differing only with respect to non-functional criteria as performance, cost, and legal issues (patents, licences). Though these criteria may be of major importance to the application, they do not contribute to security analysis as described in the previous sections. Therefore, the selection problem is considered to be out of scope of our approach.

The mechanisms we are particularly interested in, include those based on cryptographic methods. They are based on concepts as common secrets, cryptographic keys, random numbers, nonces, and so on. In our approach, each of these concepts is modelled by a specific data type, where the adversary's abilities on the usage of elements of these data types are restricted. Consider, for example, the set of cryptographic keys and cryptograms in Sect. 4. The model of communication and the semantics of FOCUS allows to benefit from results of approaches specifically dedicated to the description of cryptographic systems, for example [Sne95] or [Mea94].

4 A Sample Development

4.1 A Simple Server

Our example provides the specification of a very simple, idealized server component that is able to receive requests submitted by a client via a transmission medium and to respond to those requests that have been issued by authorized clients by sending results using a different communication channel. Since the main focus of the example is on security analysis of the server, the detailed structure and contents of requests and results are not important. However, if looking for possible applications for servers of this kind, imagine a door lock which is only released upon request, for example by inserting a smart card, or a mobile phone system, in which connect requests are received by a server and, possibly supplied with additional data about the requestor, forwarded to a switching center. We assume that there are several clients using the same request channel, thus each request has to be tagged with the client's identifier. Figure 3 shows an abstract view of the server, consisting of a server component SV and the transmission medium MD. To formally specify the server in FOCUS, let *Id* be a set of identifiers, $L \subseteq Id$ the set containing the identifiers of the authorized clients and *Req*, *Res* represent the set of requests and results, respectively. As

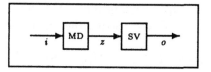

Fig. 3. A simple server

argued above, *Req* and *Res* are not specified in detail. Using the operator style of specification, the server is described by

$$S \equiv (i : Id{\times}Req \rhd o : Res) :: \quad MD \succ SV \ ,$$

with the component specifications given by

$$MD \equiv (i : Id{\times}Req \rhd z : Id{\times}Req) \overset{ti}{::} \quad z = i \ ,$$

$$SV \equiv (z : Id{\times}Req \rhd o : Res) \overset{ti}{::} \quad \#o = \#(L©\mathsf{map}(z, \Pi_1)) \ .$$

Note that we assume an ideal transmission medium, resulting in the component MD being simply the identity on its input channel. This has been chosen in order to keep the simplicity of the example. Section 3.2 outlines how one may deal with more sophisticated media specifications.

SV states that each request of an authorized client, and only those, will be served. Because of the semantic model of time independent specifications in FO-CUS, SV ist quite implicit: from the strong guardedness constraint on functions satisfying SV it follows that requests are served in order of their receipt, and that no responses are issued in advance, anticipating future requests.

4.2 The Threat Scenario

In Sect. 3.2 we stated that each threat scenario is the result of an application specific threat identification and risk analysis, where templates can be used in the construction of the scenario. Since risk analysis heavily depends on non-technical arguments, for example consideration of associated financial loss, it is not completely covered by our method. For our example, we therefore assume that a risk analysis has been carried out, with the supposed result of the adversary being assessed as being able to eavesdrop the transmitted messages, to know about the set of possible and legitimate clients and requests, and to insert fraudulent messages. Additionally, we assume that the adversary inserts at most one fraudulent message between two legitimate messages (note that this requirement is only added to keep the example simple). These assumptions completely describe the adversary's behaviour, particularly she cannot manipulate or delete messages on *i* in our example scenario.

Since MD models a transmission medium as discussed in Sect. 3.2, the template given there can be used to construct the threat scenario B. Thus,

$$B \equiv (i : Id \times Req \rhd o : Res) :: \quad MD_{Thr} \succ SV \ ,$$

with MD_{Thr} as defined in Sect. 3.2, using the message set $M = Id \times Req$. Let $V = M$ and $F = \emptyset$, which states that the adversary knows the complete set of messages that may be transmitted. Moreover, let $C = B$ be the set of control messages. The assumptions on the adversary are modelled by adding the following conjunct to the specification of A in the scenario template MD_{Thr} of Sect. 3.2:

$$\#1 \copyright c = \#d \quad \wedge \quad \exists i,j \in \mathsf{N}, k \in \mathsf{N} \cup \{\infty\}: \quad c = (\langle 0 \rangle^i \frown \langle 1 \rangle \frown \langle 0 \rangle^j)^k \ .$$

The first conjunct states that for each message in d we have a corresponding 1 in c, and the second that c contains no substring s with more than one 1's in a row.

We still have to instantiate the data flow component D of MD_{Thr}. Since we have decided to strengthen the adversary model A, we may use a quite general specification of D, which will be suited for other analyses as well. We define

$$D \equiv (i : M, d : M, c : B \rhd z : M) \overset{ti}{::}$$
$$i \sqsupseteq \Pi_1((M \times 0) \copyright (z, c' \frown 0^\infty)) \quad \wedge \quad d|_n = \Pi_1((M \times 1) \copyright (z, c'))$$

$$\textsf{where} \quad n = \min(\#d, \#1 \copyright c) \quad \wedge \quad c' \sqsubseteq c \quad \wedge \quad \#1 \copyright c' = n \ .$$

Note that D to some extent corresponds to the specification of a merge component, with the oracle partly determined by the control sequence c. Fairness of D depends on the control sequence input: if, and only if, the control sequence allows the insertion of infinitely many messages, transmission of messages of i may be suspended for ever, this fact being reflected by using the prefix relation instead of equality with respect to i, and by extending the control sequence in the first conjunct. On the other hand, given an appropriate control sequence, each of the adversary's messages will indeed be inserted. Potential loss of fairness is intentional, since it does not seem to be reasonable to always assume a fair adversary. The auxiliary values n and c' are introduced to handle cases where the control sequence and the messages sent by the adversary do not fit together, meaning that there are less 1's in c than messages in d or vice versa. However, from our specification of A, we always have appropriate control sequences.

S is not authentic with respect to B, as is shown in the following theorem.

Theorem 4. S *is not authentic w.r.t.* B, *i.e.* $R_{Ath}(B, S)$ *does not hold.*

Proof. Choose $i = \langle \rangle$, $d = \langle (id_0, rq) \rangle$ for some $id_0 \in L$, $rq \in Req$, and $c = \langle 1 \rangle$ as existential witnesses. Then, $(i, (d, c))$ is a possible i/o-behaviour of $\mu(Ini_V \succ A)$. In this case, by the definition of D, we have $z = \langle (id_0, rq) \rangle$, leading to $\#o = 1$

by the definition of SV. Since for all $h \in B^{\overline{\omega}}$, $\text{sel}(h, \langle\rangle) = \langle\rangle$, authenticity of S would require (i, o) to be an i/o-behaviour of S, which is obviously not the case, because for all $f \in [\![S]\!]$, we have $\#x = \#f(x)$. □

4.3 Two Authentication Protocols

In order to specify an authentic server, we have to refine S by introducing an appropriate security mechanism. ISO proposes two variants of a simple challenge-response authentication protocol ([ISO92], [ISO93]) that are considered to be suited for applications like our server. The protocols are based on symmetric cryptoalgorithms and random number generators, and assume that the server and each of the legitimate clients share a secret key. To model cryptographic systems, a value space as for example defined in [Sne95] is suited for our stream based communication model as well.

To describe the cryptographic system used in our example, let K be a set of cryptographic keys, Cr a set of cryptograms, and Ms a set of messages. We have an encryption function $E : K \times (Cr \cup Ms) \to Cr$ and a decryption function $D : K \times (Cr \cup Ms) \to (Cr \cup Ms)$. In symmetric cryptosystems, we have

$$D(k, E(k, x)) = x, \qquad\qquad x \in Ms \cup Cr ,$$
$$E(k, x_1) = E(k, x_2) \Rightarrow x_1 = x_2, \qquad\qquad k \in K, x_1, x_2 \in Ms \cup Cr.$$

Further properties hold with high probability. Since FOCUS, like almost all other approaches to distributed systems design and verification, is not intended to deal with probabilities, we have to approximate them by predicate logic formulæ. A reasonable idealization is to take properties that hold with high probability for granted.

It is considered to be improbable that the adversary constructs cryptograms (by simply guessing or taking arbitrary keys and messages – which in good cryptosystems both are of nearly equal probability) that match cryptograms being issued by legitimate users. We model this fact by

$$E(k_1, x) = E(k_2, x) \Rightarrow k_1 = k_2, \qquad k_1, k_2 \in K, x \in Ms \cup Cr,$$
$$E(k_1, m_1) = E(k_2, m_2) \Rightarrow k_1 = k_2 \wedge m_1 = m_2, \quad k_1, k_2 \in K, m_1, m_2 \in Ms,$$

and assume that the adversary does not exploit the finiteness of the set of cryptograms. Note that the latter formula is modelled to only hold for messages of Ms, and requires that Ms is of considerably less cardinality than Cr.

The protocols also use random numbers. We choose a set R of values from which random numbers are taken. For each stream $r \in R^{\overline{\omega}}$ of random numbers, we at least require that no duplications occur, described by $PRN(r)$, with

$$PRN(r) \equiv \forall j \in \text{dom}.r : r.j \notin \text{rng}.\,(r|_{j-1}) \ .$$

PRN obviously does not completely characterize random numbers, but is sufficient to show authenticity of one of the protocols specified below. We are

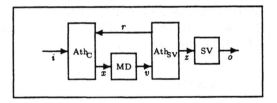

Fig. 4. An authentication mechanism

now ready to specify the authentication protocols. They both share the same structure, as depicted in Fig. 4. Each time a request is received by Ath_{SV}, it issues a challenge on r and proceeds only in the case that the next message received is an appropriate response to the challenge. Otherwise, the request will be ignored. Ath_C is responsible for passing on requests and suitable responses, if challenges are received. The two protocols differ only in the type of challenges (ISO 9798-2: random numbers, ISO 10181-2: encrypted random numbers) and responses (ISO 9798-2: encrypted random numbers, ISO 10181-2: random numbers). For simplicity of the example, we specify a slight abstraction of the ISO-protocols, namely without considering the inclusion of SV's identifier in the response. Thus, we lose protection against reflection attacks, which is, however, of less importance with respect to the demonstration of how our approach works. The refined server is specified by

$$SA_i \equiv (i : Id \times Req \rhd o : Res) :: \quad \mu (\text{Ath}_C^i \succ MD \succ \text{Ath}_{SV}^i) \succ SV \ ,$$

with $i \in \{1, 2\}$ indicating the actual variant of the protocol. MD and SV are specified as in Sect. 4.1. In the component specifications, we do not only describe a single run of the protocol, but also specify how the authentication agents serve multiple requests. For the moment, we assume that Ath_C buffers all incoming challenges.

Each legitimate client shares a secret key with the server, meaning that there is a set $K_0 \subseteq K$ with $K_0 = \{k_{id} | id \in L\}$. For $i = 1$ denoting the variant based on ISO-9798-2, we then have (with $M = Id \times Req$ as in Sect. 4.2)

$$\text{Ath}_C^1 \equiv (i : M, r : R \rhd x : M \cup Cr) \overset{ti}{::}$$
$$\exists\, f_1 \in (M^{\overline{\omega}} \times R^{\overline{\omega}}) \to (M \cup Cr)^{\overline{\omega}}, f_2 \in (Id \times M^{\overline{\omega}} \times R^{\overline{\omega}}) \to (M \cup Cr)^{\overline{\omega}} :$$
$$x = f_1(i, r)$$

where $\forall i \in M^{\overline{\omega}}, r \in R^{\overline{\omega}}, (id, req) \in M, rn \in R:$

$f_1(\langle\rangle, r) = \langle\rangle,$
$id \in L \Rightarrow f_1((id, req)\frown i, r) = (id, req)\frown f_2(id, i, r),$
$id \notin L \Rightarrow f_1((id, req)\frown i, r) = f_1(i, r),$

$f_2(id, i, rn\frown r) = E(k_{id}, rn)\frown f_1(i, r)\ .$

and

$\mathrm{Ath}_{SV}^1 \equiv (v : M \cup Cr \rhd r : R, z : M)\ \overset{\mathrm{ti}}{::}$

$\exists\ f_3 \in (M \cup Cr)^{\overline{\omega}} \to (R^{\overline{\omega}} \times M^{\overline{\omega}}),$
$\quad f_4 \in (Id \times Req \times R \times (M \cup Cr)^{\overline{\omega}}) \to (R^{\overline{\omega}} \times M^{\overline{\omega}}):$
$\quad z = f_3(v, r)\quad \wedge\quad PRN(r)$

where $\forall i \in (M \cup Cr)^{\overline{\omega}}, (id, req) \in M, rn \in R, cr \in M \cup Cr:$

$f_3(\langle\rangle) = (\langle\rangle, \langle\rangle),$
$id \in L \Rightarrow \exists rn \in R : f_3((id, req)\frown v) = (\langle\rangle, rn)\frown f_4(id, req, rn, v),$

$D(k_{id}, cr) = rn \Rightarrow f_4(id, req, rn, cr\frown v) = ((id, req), \langle\rangle)\frown f_3(v),$
$\neg D(k_{id}, cr) = rn \Rightarrow f_4(id, req, rn, cr\frown v) = f_3(v)\ .$

The specification is given in a rather operational style, which corresponds to the way cryptographic protocols are typically presented. Both are underdetermined, which in our case does not matter because of the particular composition of SA_i. If any of the agents is waiting for a response, anything except the response awaited will be rejected, with the agent set back in a state where it waits for new requests.

The specification for the second variant, based on ISO 10181-2, is entirely similar, with the type of challenges and responses exchanged, and the type of channels adjusted.

In order to show that SA_i describes an appropriate security mechanism, we first have to prove that SA_i is a refinement of S.

Theorem 5. *For $i \in \{1, 2\}$, SA_i is a behaviour refinement of S, i.e. for all $f \in M^{\overline{\omega}} \to Req^{\overline{\omega}}$ we have $f \in [\![SA_i]\!] \Rightarrow f \in [\![S]\!]$.*

Proof. We show the theorem only for $i = 1$. The proof for the second variant of the protocol is entirely similar. Since MD describes the identity, with respect to the specification of SV it suffices to show, for all $i \in M^{\overline{\omega}}, f_{\mathrm{Ath_C}} \in [\![\mathrm{Ath_C}]\!], f_{\mathrm{Ath_{SV}}} \in [\![\mathrm{Ath_{SV}}]\!]$, that

$$\mu(f_{\mathrm{Ath_C}} \succ f_{\mathrm{Ath_{SV}}})(i) = L©\mathrm{map}(i, \Pi_1)$$

holds. This is shown by proving, if $(z,r) = (f_{\text{Athc}} \succ f_{\text{Athsv}})(i,r)$ for a fix point r, then $z = L\textcircled{c}\text{map}(i, \Pi_1)$. Using induction on i, this is shown for finite i, and by continuity of the functions involved, for infinite i. The equation above then follows from the definition of feedback.

$i = \langle\rangle$. We have $f_{\text{Athsv}}(f_{\text{Athc}}(\langle\rangle, r)) = (\langle\rangle, r)$.

$i = (id_0, req_0) \frown i'$.

If $id_o \notin L$, we have $(z,r) = f_{\text{Athsv}}(f_{\text{Athc}}(i,r)) = f_{\text{Athsv}}(f_{\text{Athc}}(i',r))$, with the assertion following immediately from the induction hypothesis.

If $id_0 \in L$, we have

$$
\begin{aligned}
(z,r) &= f_{\text{Athsv}}(f_{\text{Athc}}(i,r)) \\
&= f_{\text{Athsv}}((id_0, req_0) \frown f_2(id_0, i', r)) \\
&= (\langle\rangle, rn) \frown f_4(id_0, req_0, rn, f_2(id_0, i', r))
\end{aligned}
$$

for some $rn \in R$. From the fix point property of r, we conclude $r = rn \frown r'$ and further yield

$$
\begin{aligned}
(z,r) &= (\langle\rangle, rn) \frown f_4(id_0, req_0, rn, E(k_{id_0}, rn) \frown f_{\text{Athc}}(i', r')) \\
&= (\langle\rangle, rn) \frown ((id_0, req_0), \langle\rangle) \frown f_{\text{Athsv}}(f_{\text{Athc}}(i', r')) \ .
\end{aligned}
$$

We therefore have r' being a fix point with respect to i', which from the induction hypothesis and $id_0 \in L$ leads to the assertion. $\qquad\square$

Now, the last step remaining in developing an authentic server is to show that SA_i, $i \in \{1,2\}$ indeed satisfies the authenticity definition of Sect. 3.3. Since with the definition of the security mechanism additional channels and new message types have been introduced, it is appropriate to update the threat scenario parameters. For our example, we assume that challenges are transmitted via a secure channel (remember Fig. 4, where the threatened medium is only specified for the request and response channel), but that the adversary knows the set of possible random values R, and thus can guess one of them. In addition, she has some keys available, but not those of the legitimate clients, and may encrypt as well as decrypt. We further assume that the adversary only inserts fake requests and immediately tries to give an appropriate authentication response. The threat scenario instantiation is then given by $V = M \cup R \cup K_A$ for some $K_A \subseteq K \setminus K_0$, $F = \{E, D\}$, D as defined in Sect. 4.2, and A strenghtened by

$$
\begin{aligned}
&\exists h \in B^{\bar\omega}, n \in \mathsf{N} \cup \{\infty\} : h = \langle 0, 1\rangle^n \wedge \text{sel}(h, d) \in Cr^{\bar\omega} \wedge \text{sel}(\bar h, d) \in M^{\bar\omega} \wedge \\
&\exists i, j \in \mathsf{N}, k \in \mathsf{N} \cup \{\infty\} : c = (\langle 0\rangle^{2i} \frown \langle 1, 1\rangle \frown \langle 0\rangle^{2j})^k \ ,
\end{aligned}
$$

with $\bar h$ denoting the bitwise complement of a bitstream h. Note that the basis for this strengthening is the adversary specifcation A of Sect. 3.2, not the one from Sect. 4.2. With this threat scenario instantiation BA_1, we can show

Theorem 6. SA_1 *is authentic w.r.t.* BA_1, *i.e.* $R_{Ath}(\text{SA}_1, \text{BA}_1)$ *holds.*

Proof. It suffices to show that, if $(z,r) = f_{\text{Athsv}}(f_{\text{MD}_{\text{Thr}}}(f_{\text{Ath}_C}(i,r)))$ for $i,z \in M^{\bar{\omega}}, r \in R^{\bar{\omega}}, f_{\text{Ath}_C} \in [\![\text{ Ath}_C]\!], f_{\text{MD}_{\text{Thr}}} \in [\![\text{ MD}_{\text{Thr}}]\!], f_{\text{Athsv}} \in [\![\text{ Athsv }]\!]$, then there is $h \in B^{\bar{\omega}}$ such that

$$z = \text{sel}(h, L\textcircled{c}\text{map}(i, \Pi_1)) \ .$$

Let $j \in \mathsf{N}$ be the highest index with $f_{\text{Ath}_C}((L{\times}Req\textcircled{c}i)|_j, r) \sqsubseteq f_{\text{MD}_{\text{Thr}}}(f_{\text{Ath}_C}(i,r))$, i.e. the adversary for the first time inserts a message after the j-th legitimate request. Since we have $\#r \geq \#i$ for each fix point r, from the definition of Ath_C we can conclude $f_{\text{Ath}_C}((L{\times}Req\textcircled{c}i)|_j, r) = f_{\text{Ath}_C}((L{\times}Req\textcircled{c}i)|_j, r|_j)$. Thus,

$$(z,r) = f_{\text{Athsv}}(f_{\text{MD}_{\text{Thr}}}(f_{\text{Ath}_C}(i,r)))$$
$$= ((L{\times}Req\textcircled{c}i)|_j, r|_j) \frown f_{\text{Athsv}}(v \frown f_{\text{MD}_{\text{Thr}}}(f_{\text{Ath}_C}(i',r'))) \ ,$$

with $i = i|_j \frown i', r = r|_j \frown r'$, and, from the definition of MD_{Thr} which reflects the assumption on the adversary, $v = \langle (id_0, req_0), e \rangle$ for some $id_0 \in L, req_0 \in Req$, and $e \in Cr$. This leads to

$$(z,r) = ((L{\times}Req\textcircled{c}i)|_j, r|_j) \frown (\langle\rangle, rn) \frown f_4(id_0, req_0, rn, e \frown f_{\text{MD}_{\text{Thr}}}(f_{\text{Ath}_C}(i',r')))$$

for some $rn \in R$. We now either have $e = E(k, rn'), k \in K_A \subseteq K \setminus K_0, rn' \in R$, i.e. a cryptogram constructed by the adversary, or $e = E(k_{\Pi_1((L{\times}Req\textcircled{c}i).j')}, r.j')$ for some $j' \leq j$, i.e. a cryptogram eavesdropped by the adversary. From $PRN(r)$ it follows that $rn \notin \text{rng}.r|_j$, thus it follows by the properties of the cryptographic system, that the authentication fails, leading to

$$(z,r) = ((L{\times}Req\textcircled{c}i)|_j, r|_j) \frown (\langle\rangle, rn) \frown f_{\text{Athsv}}(f_{\text{MD}_{\text{Thr}}}(f_{\text{Ath}_C}(i',r'))) \ .$$

By an inductive argument we can the show that each following authentication fails as well (since Ath_C always takes an "old" challenge), leading to

$$(z,r) = ((L{\times}Req\textcircled{c}i)|_j, r) \ ,$$

from which the assertion follows (with $h = \langle 1 \rangle^j \frown \langle 0 \rangle^\infty$). $\quad\square$

SA_2 is not authenthic, if the analoguous threat scenario instantiation BA_2 is considered.

Theorem 7. SA_2 *is not authentic w.r.t.* BA_2, *i.e.* $R_{Ath}(\text{SA}_2, \text{BA}_2)$ *does not hold.*

Proof. Since the set of random values is available to the adversary, she may guess an appropriate response without knowledge of the challenge cryptogram. Take $i = \langle\rangle, r = \langle rn \rangle, d = \langle (id_0, req_0), rn \rangle$, and $c = \langle 1, 1 \rangle$ as existential witnesses. $\quad\square$

SA_2 can only be shown to be authentic, if further restrictions on the adversary behaviour are introduced. For example we may exclude R from the set of values initially available to the adversary, and require that a new challenge cannot be predicted from the eavesdropped ones, which means that for each $r \in R, j \in \mathsf{N}$, there is no function $f \in F$ such that $r.(j+1) = f(r.1, \ldots, r.j)$.

Unfortunately, the proof of theorem 6 shows an unpleasant property of our authentication mechanism: if a fraudulent request is once issued, all forthcoming legitimate requests will be denied, since an additional challenge is issued, and due to the buffering of challenges Ath_C and Ath_{SV} will never synchronize. To avoid this effect in order to increase availability of the system, we need a time dependent specification of Ath_C which ignores all challenges until it has issued a new request. Such an Ath'_C can be specified as follows:

$$Ath'_C \equiv (i : M, r : R \rhd x : M \cup Cr) \stackrel{\text{td}}{::}$$

$$\exists f_1 \in (M^\omega \times R^\omega) \to (M \cup Cr)^\omega, f_2 \in (Id \times M^\omega \times R^\omega) \to (M \cup Cr)^\omega :$$
$$x = \sqrt{}^\frown f_1(i,r)$$

where $\forall i \in M^\omega, r \in R^\omega, (id, req) \in M, rn \in R :$

$$f_1(\sqrt{}^\frown i, \sqrt{}^\frown r) = \sqrt{}^\frown f_1(i,r),$$
$$f_1(\sqrt{}^\frown i, rn^\frown r) = \sqrt{}^\frown f_1(i,r),$$
$$id \in L \Rightarrow f_1((id, req)^\frown i, \sqrt{}^\frown r) = \sqrt{}^\frown (id, req)^\frown f_2(id, i, r),$$
$$id \in L \Rightarrow f_1((id, req)^\frown i, rn^\frown r) = (id, req)^\frown f_2(id, i, r),$$
$$id \notin L \Rightarrow f_1((id, req)^\frown i, \sqrt{}^\frown r) = \sqrt{}^\frown f_1(i, r),$$
$$id \notin L \Rightarrow f_1((id, req)^\frown i, rn^\frown r) = f_1(i, r),$$

$$f_2(id, i, \sqrt{}^\frown r) = \sqrt{}^\frown f_2(id, i, r),$$
$$f_2(id, i, rn^\frown r) = E(k_{id}, rn)^\frown f_1(i, r).$$

With the same proof techniques as employed in the proof of theorem 6, we can show that a server using Ath'_C is authentic as well.

5 Conclusion and Further Work

We have introduced a new approach to the formal development of secure systems that is based on a procedure being established in practice and aims at a mechanism independent security notion, flexibility with respect to security aspects as well as integration of security analysis and development according to the functional requirements on the system. Application specific security requirements, as a result of threat identification and risk analysis, are formally modelled by threat scenarios which specify the anticipated behavior of the adversary, in particular her influence on communication. Security is defined as a relation on threat scenarios and systems.

The main focus of this paper has been to show the basic principles of our approach by conducting a comprehensive sample development of an authentic server. For purposes of presentation, our example has been simplified: we focus exclusively on authentication, provide simple protocols, and restrict the behaviour of the adversary. However, our example is of practical relevance, since the protocols are only slight abstractions of standard protocols ([ISO92], [ISO93]) and the adversary characterization seems to be reasonable for certain application situations (for example, a secure door lock).

The example shows a number of promising results that raise evidence that the approach is well-suited to support the formal development of secure systems in practice. Firstly, with respect to the asumptions on the adversary, we have been able to prove the authenticity of SA_1, and to show that SA_2 is not authentic. Moreover, the construction of the proof of authenticity of SA_1 leads to a revision of the protocol specification: though preserving authenticity, the first specification, which buffers challenges, turns out to lack availability in case of an attack, leading to a time dependent protocol specification SA_1'. Thus, our method turns out to be suitable for the analysis of effects resulting from multiple executions of protocols, because the semantic model guarantees the consideration of the whole lifetime of the system instead of just a single protocol run. Additionally, it offers the opportunity to reason about different security aspects. Formal definitions of several security notions have been given.

Applicability of our method is supported by dividing the security notion in an application specific part (threat scenario) and a general part (security relation). In common applications, threat scenarios may be derived systematically from compositional system specifications, which has been shown for components modelling transmission media in communication systems.

Our approach particularly benefits from choosing FOCUS as the basis of formalization. Since FOCUS is a general purpose formal development method, it offers the opportunity to continue system development from those specifications that result from security analysis. On the other hand, security analysis can be performed at each stage of the system development. Systematic derivation of threat scenarios is supported: information flow to the adversary is modelled by simply adding (logical) channels to the system specification.

However, a lot of work remains to be done: the approach has to be generalized by defining further security relations, corresponding, for example, to confidentiality and availability. Effects of multiple attacks, which may occur if an adversary is able to simultaneously attack several critical components, and of interleaving of protocol runs have to be investigated. To improve practicability, it is important to provide a set of threat scenario templates that can be instantiated for a variety of common threat analysis results, and a set of basic mechanism specifications. The approximation of cryptographic algorithms has to be further improved. A notion of compositionality with respect to different threats and threatened components is desirable.

Even in its initial state, our approach provides significant progress with respect to a formal method that reaches the aims mentioned above. With further work being performed, we will get close to a method that can be profitably applied in practice.

References

[BLP73]   D.E. Bell, L. LaPadula: Secure Computer Systems: Mathematical Foundations (NTIS AD-770 768), A Mathematical Model (NTIS AD-771 543), A Refinement of the Mathematical Model (NTIS AD-780 528), MTR 2547 Vol. I-III, ESD-TR-73-278, Mitre Corporation, Bedford MA, 1973

[BLP76]   D.E. Bell, L. LaPadula: Secure Computer Systems: Unified Exposition and Multics Interpretation, NTIS AD-A023 588, MTR 2997, ESD-TR-75-306, Mitre Corporation, Bedford MA, 1976

[BDD+93]   M. Broy, F. Dederichs, C. Dendorfer, M. Fuchs, T.F. Gritzner, R. Weber: The Design of Distributed Systems – An Introduction to FOCUS – Revised Version, Technical Report TUM-19202-2, Technische Universität München, 1993

[Br93]   M. Broy: (Inter-)Action Refinement: The Easy Way, in: M. Broy (Ed.): Program Design Calculi, NATO ASI Series F, Vol. 118, Springer, 1993

[Br95]   M. Broy: Advanced Component Interface Specification, in: T. Ito, A. Yonezawa (Eds.): Theory and Practice of Parallel Programming, Proceedings TPP '94, Springer LNCS 907, 1995

[BrSt96]   M. Broy, K. Stølen: Interactive System Design, Book Manuscript, 1996

[BAN89]   M. Burrows, M. Abadi, R. Needham: A Logic of Authentication, Report 39, Digital Systems Research Center, Palo Alto, 1989

[FFKK93]   O. Fries, A. Fritsch, V. Kessler, B. Klein (Hrsg.): Sicherheitsmechanismen: Bausteine zur Entwicklung sicherer Systeme, REMO Arbeitsberichte, Oldenbourg Verlag, München 1993 (in German)

[GoMe82]   J.A. Goguen, J. Meseguer: Security Policies and Security Models, Proc. of the IEEE Symposium on Security and Privacy, 1982, pp. 11–20

[HMS93]   S. Herda, S. Mund, A. Steinacker (Hrsg.): Szenarien zur Sicherheit informationstechnischer Systeme, REMO Arbeitsberichte, Oldenbourg Verlag, München 1993 (in German)

[ISO92]   ISO/IEC CD 9798: Information Technology – Security Techniques – Entity Authentication Mechanisms, Part 2: Entity Authentication Using Symmetric Techniques, 1992

[ISO93]   ISO/IEC DIS 10181-2.2: Information Technology – Open Systems Interconnection – Security Framework for Open Systems: Authentication Framework, 1993

[Jac90]   J.L. Jacob: Specifying Security Properties, in: C.A.R. Hoare (ed.): Developments in Concurrency and Communications, Addison-Wesley, 1990

[Mea94]   C. Meadows: The NRL Protocol Analyzer: An Overview, Journal of Logic Programming, Vol. 19, 1994

[Mun93]   S. Mund: Sicherheitsanforderungen – Sicherheitsmaßnahmen, VIS '93 (Herausgeber: P. Horster, G. Weck), Vieweg Verlag, 1993 (in German)

[RWW94]   A.W. Roscoe, J.C.P. Woodcock, L. Wulf: Non-interference through Determinism, in: D. Gollmann: Computer Security – ESORICS '94, Springer LNCS 875, 1994

[Sne95]   E. Snekkenes: Formal Specification and Analysis of Cryptographic Protocols, PhD thesis, 1995

[TeWi89]   P. Terry, S. Wiseman: A 'New' Security Policy Model, Proc. of the IEEE Symposium on Security and Privacy, 1989, pp. 215–228

The Impact of Multilevel Security on Database Buffer Management

Andrew Warner[*], *Qiang Li*[*], *Thomas Keefe*[*], *Shankar Pal*[+]

[*]*Dept. of Computer Science and Engineering*
The Pennsylvania State University
University Park, PA 16801

[+] *Microsoft Corporation*
One Microsoft Way
Redmond, WA 98052

Abstract: Multilevel security introduces new constraints on methods for DBMS buffer management. Design issues include buffer allocation across security levels, secure page replacement, and reader/writer synchronization. We present a client/buffer manager interface with a set of synchronization guarantees that does not delay low writers in the presence of concurrent high readers, an allocation scheme that partitions slots by security level but allows buffers, underutilized at the low level, to be used by subjects at high levels using a technique we call "slot stealing." We also propose a general page replacement algorithm and methods of synchronizing readers and writers that involve varying degrees of page replication. We use simulation to investigate the performance characteristics of the various solutions.

1 Introduction

Databases are typically too large to be held in main memory; therefore, pages of the database must be shuttled between secondary storage and memory for access by transactions. A buffer management system attempts to choose a set of resident pages to minimize physical I/O and maximize throughput. Therefore, the buffer manager must choose carefully the pages maintained in main memory and may need to synchronize conflicting accesses. Multilevel secure DBMSs impose additional requirements on buffer management. It is required that buffer allocation across security levels, page replacement, and reader/writer synchronization be accomplished without allowing illegal information flows. This paper focuses on those restrictions, their implications for buffer management, and techniques for satisfying these restrictions. This work is part of the Secure Transactional Resources - Database System (*-DBS) project. The goal of this project is to develop an experimental prototype multilevel secure database management system. An initial version of the prototype was described in [WARN95].

The rest of this section provides background in multilevel security and database buffering. Section 2 introduces the problems involved in secure DBMS buffering. Section 3 describes how subjects interact with the buffer manager and what guarantees the buffer manager provides to its clients. Section 4 considers page replacement. Section 5 discusses buffer allocation policies. Methods of securely synchronizing readers and writers are considered in Section 6. Section 7 presents a simulation study of the performance of several buffer allocation policies and reader/writer synchronization methods. Finally, Section 8 presents our conclusions and suggests directions for future work.

1.1 Multilevel security

This paper deals with buffer management for database management systems that enforce a military security policy [DOD85]. The military security policy consists of two distinct parts: a *mandatory* and *discretionary* security policy. The mandatory policy controls the flow of information based upon the perceived trustworthiness of an individual. The discretionary security policy controls the flow of information based upon user identity. This work considers mandatory security only.

In systems enforcing multilevel security, elements of information, called *objects*, are assigned security levels called *sensitivity levels* and programs in execution, called *subjects*, are assigned security levels called *classification levels*. The security level of a subject or object P is denoted as *level(P)*. These security levels are partially ordered by the dominates ($\geq$) relation. We refer to the partially ordered set of security levels as the *security poset*. We say a security level is active if there is currently a subject active at that level. We call the security poset restricted to active levels the *active poset*. If two security levels l_1 and l_2 satisfy $l_1 \geq l_2$, we say l_1 *dominates* l_2. Furthermore, if l_1 *dominates* l_2 and $l_1 \neq l_2$, we say l_1 *strictly dominates* l_2. The mandatory security policy allows information to flow from a subject s_1 to another subject s_2 only if the classification level of s_2 dominates the classification level of s_1. The Bell and LaPadula model [BELL87] introduced the following properties to control access in an MLS system:

> **Simple Security Condition**: A subject is allowed read access to an object only if the subject's classification level dominates the object's sensitivity level.

> ***-Property (Star Property)**: A subject is allowed write access to an object only if the object's sensitivity level dominates the subject's classification level.

In addition to the flow of information through direct reads and writes of data objects, information can be transmitted by mechanisms that are not normally used for communications and therefore are not protected by mandatory access controls. These communication paths are known as *covert channels*. The "Orange Book" [DOD85] requires the designers of systems evaluated at class B3 or above to "conduct a thorough search for covert channels and make a determination (either by actual measurement or by engineering estimation) of the maximum bandwidth of each identified channel." At higher levels of assurance, a limit is placed on the maximum bandwidth a covert channel may have.

Any subject with privileges allowing it to violate the *-property is said to be *trusted*. The intention being that the subject was investigated and found to be sufficiently trustworthy to warrant such privileges.

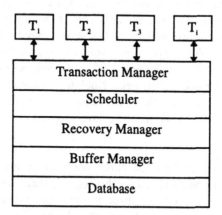

Fig. 1. Database System Architecture

1.2 Database Buffering

This section outlines the basic issues related to database buffer management. For a more detailed discussion the reader is referred to [GRAY93] and [EFFE84]. For the purposes of this paper, the buffer manager occupies the position shown in Figure 1 of the DBMS architecture [BERN87]. Transactions submit operations to the transaction manager which performs any required preprocessing. The scheduler controls the relative order in which these operations are executed. The recovery manager is responsible for transaction commitment and abortion. The buffer manager operates directly on the database which is maintained in non-volatile storage.

We now describe the buffer manager interface. The *pin* operation specifies a page number and access mode (i.e., read or write) indicating whether the data page will be updated or not. The buffer manager locates the data page, reading it in from secondary storage if necessary, and places it in main memory in an unoccupied *buffer slot*. The address of the buffer slot is returned and is used by the requester to access the page. When the requester is finished accessing the page it submits an *unpin* request.

To improve throughput, a buffer manager allows non-conflicting pin requests to proceed concurrently. Two pins conflict if they reference the same page and at least one is a write-pin. A buffer manager cannot allow two conflicting pins to be held on a page at the same time. Therefore, the buffer manager must have some policy for resolving two concurrently requested conflicting pins.

For the purposes of this paper the inputs and outputs of an MLS buffering system are as follows. The inputs are pin/unpin requests by subjects for specific pages and disk I/O responses. The outputs to our buffering system are pin request responses and disk access requests. The pin requests and responses are labeled with the security level of the requesting subject. A disk access may be the result of either a page fault or flushing a dirty page to non-volatile storage. The disk requests and responses are labeled with the security level of the subject that caused the page fault or the subject that modified the page. Noninterference states that an output of our system (pin responses and disk access requests) must not be affected by the inputs of subjects at strictly dominating levels (pin/unpin requests and disk responses).

When a pin request is submitted, the buffer pool is searched. If the page is not found, a buffer slot must be allocated for this page. If there are free slots available to the buffer manager then one of these is used; otherwise, one of the pages currently held in a slot must be replaced. The choice of which page to evict is made following a *page replacement policy*. Typical factors affecting the replacement decision are the time since the last reference to the page, the frequency of references to the page, whether the page is dirty (i.e., the page has been updated but not yet flushed to disk), and whether or not the page is pinned.

The choice of a victim is often made in two stages. First buffers are allocated to groups of transactions or specific purposes. This is known as the buffer slot allocation algorithm [EFFE84]. Second, particular pages are chosen from the appropriate pool following a local replacement policy.

2 Issues Related to Secure Buffering

This section identifies security issues related to database buffer management. We develop a pin/unpin buffering model compatible with security constraints, a secure page replacement policy, methods for synchronizing read-pins and write-pins across levels, and the allocation of buffer slots. We first discuss related work.

In [HU92] a method is presented of eliminating the covert channel due to the interaction between process scheduling and processor caches. The channel relies on timing an access. It takes a long time if it is not cached and it is quick if it is cached. Hu overcomes this by partitioning the security lattice into strictly dominating paths, scheduling processes according to their security level from low to high up one of these paths, and then clearing the cache when a newly scheduled process is strictly dominated by the previous process to execute. This results in a cleared cache only when there is a context switch from a high process to a low process. This approach is not applicable to the secure database buffering problem for two reasons. The first is that typically database systems do not have control over the scheduling of processes and doing so would increase the complexity. The second is that it would increase the amount of I/O done in a workload with many updates. We apply a similar idea in our "page stealing" algorithm as presented later in Section 5.2.2.

If there is no sharing of buffer slots between subjects at different levels then the system cannot adapt to changing workloads as effectively and there is a potential for poor resource utilization. Therefore, we desire a method of allocating buffer slots that allows resource sharing between subjects at different levels without presenting a covert channel.

In a traditional buffering model write-pins guarantee exclusive access to a pinned page. This implies that no other pins may be granted while a write-pin is granted and that a write-pin request is delayed until all current pins are released. In an MLS system this guarantee contradicts security requirements. If a subject is holding a read-pin on a page at a strictly dominated level and a subject requests a write-pin on it, the write-pin cannot be delayed. If it were, a covert channel would result. Therefore, we must develop an MLS buffering model that will make appropriate guarantees to a subject holding a read-pin on a strictly dominated page. Related to this issue is the problem of synchronizing the strictly dominating read-pin in the presence of concurrent write-pins (i.e., the secure readers/writers problem).

A multilevel secure transaction scheduler orders transactions' operations on data elements so that read/write conflicts between security levels are avoided. However, read-pin/write-pin conflicts between security levels accessing the same page may occur for the following reasons. The granularity of the scheduler's data element (e.g. tuples) and the buffer manager's slot size (e.g. pages) may be different. If two or more data elements reside on the same page, the scheduler would allow a high-level read and a low-level write to proceed concurrently resulting in inter-level pin conflict. The low-level write may update data structures common to all tuples on the page, such as a tuple index. If the update is not atomic, the high-level read may retrieve incorrect data. A second potential for inter-level pin conflicts results from shared resources that are not accessed through a secure scheduler, for example B-trees, version chains, and disk allocation bitmaps.

Using a secure buffer manager does not eliminate the need for a secure scheduler. Covert channels not directly attributed to reader/writer synchronization would still exist if a non-secure scheduler was used in conjunction with a secure buffer manager. For example, if a two-phase locking scheduler is used, a high-level transaction could acquire a lock on low-level data and cause low-level transactions to wait until the lock is released before accessing the data.

In [REED79] methods for handling the secure readers/writers problem are presented using event counts. With this method an event counter is checked, work is performed on the data, and the event counter is checked again to determine if the data was modified during the work. In a DBMS, the length of time a pin is held on a page is determined, in part, by the programmer. The buffer model we adopt assumes that the data in a buffer is accessed in place rather than being copied to local storage and accessed there. Thus, the solution presented in [REED79] is not directly applicable as it allows the data to be updated while it is being accessed by the reader. While this is possible, it will require a very careful programming style. In section 6, we suggest algorithms that combine reader/writer synchronization with the maintenance of a stable copy to work from.

In a single-level system, all page references may be used to calculate which resident page is replaced in response to a pin request for a non-resident page. In an MLS system, if a page is replaced based upon references from subject S_1 and the page is referenced in the future by subject S_2, where $level(S_1) \not< level(S_2)$, the pin response delay of S_2 may be affected and introduce a covert channel. The delay arises because the page must be fetched from disk to satisfy the request of S_2. Therefore, in an MLS buffering system, we must ensure that a replacement decision initiated by a pin request on behalf of a subject S_1 does not affect the pin response delay caused by a pin request of subject S_2 if S_2 does not dominate S_1.

3 Basic Model and Policies

This section defines our model and policies for an MLS buffering system. Our model consists of a subject/buffer manager interface and a set of policies. The interface defines how subjects interact with the buffer manager. The policies will define what guarantees the buffer manager will make to the subjects. The policies can be grouped into security policies and consistency/concurrency policies. We also include a section on the use of buffer slots within the buffer manager.

3.1 Interface

Our buffer manager uses a pin/unpin interface where a pin request for *page* has a mode of either *read* or *write*. A subject *sbj* makes a pin request for *page* to a buffer manager of the form pin(*sbj, page, mode*). Subjects make unpin requests of the form unpin(*sbj, page, mode*). The security level of an (un)pin request is denoted as *level*((un)pin(*sbj, page, mode*)). It is assumed that subjects will have at most one outstanding pin on a particular page and that the pin/unpin requests are eventually balanced with respect to a page and subject.

3.2 Access Control Policy

The request (un)pin(*sbj*, *page*, read) may be granted only if *level*(*sbj*)≥*level*(*page*). Otherwise, the request is rejected. The request (un)pin(*sbj*, *page*, write) may be granted only if *level*(*sbj*)=*level*(*page*). Otherwise, the request is rejected. Note that we restrict the *-property that we presented in Section 1.2.

3.3 Synchronization Guarantees

This section describes the concurrency and consistency guarantees made by the buffer manager to its clients. For the following discussion, a pin is considered outstanding if it has been granted, but a subsequent unpin request has not been processed.

While an operation pin(sbj_j, $page_i$, write) is outstanding, no other requests of the form pin(sbj_k, $page_i$, mode) are granted. While a pin(sbj_j, $page_i$, read) request with $level(sbj_j)=level(page_i)$ is outstanding, requests of the form pin(sbj_k, $page_i$, write) will not be granted. However, requests of the form pin(sbj_k, $page_i$, read) may. While a pin(sbj_j, $page_i$, read) request with $level(sbj_j)>level(page_i)$ is outstanding, requests of the form pin(sbj_k, $page_i$, read) and pin(sbj_k, $page_i$, write) may be granted.

A request of the form pin(sbj_j, $page_i$, read) with $level(sbj_j)>level(page_i)$ will pin the state of $page_i$ following the most recent write-unpin on $page_i$. If pin(sbj_k, $page_i$, write) is granted before unpin(sbj_j, $page_i$, read) is submitted, the buffer manager informs the subject sbj_j, in response to unpin(sbj_j, $page_i$, read), that $page_i$ was modified. This allows the subject to redo the work until a successful acknowledgment is obtained.

Alternatively, a buffer manager may guarantee a semantics based correctness criteria. The semantics based correctness is application specific and is based upon the semantics of the data being buffered. The semantic based correctness guarantees are in general weaker than the general guarantees. An example follows. In [WARN95] a prototype multilevel secure database system is presented that uses a multiversion scheduler. As writes occur new versions of data elements are created and timestamps are used to determine which versions are appropriate for a transaction to read. As a result the version a page contains may change over time. Specifically, assume that a version v is initially contained in page p. In time, a new version v' may be placed in page p. An out of date replica of p which still contains version v could be used to access v, even though the page has been updated and the replica is no longer fresh. We can present an old view of a page to a transaction if the old view contains the appropriate version. Semantics based correctness is not considered further in this paper.

3.4 Buffer Allocation

This section describes a framework for buffer allocation policies. First, we need to introduce some notation. The function *map_level* maps buffer slots to security levels. If map_level(*sl*)=*l*, the implication is that slot *sl* is currently allocated to level *l*. This allocation can be static or be redefined in a dynamic fashion.

A buffer slot (*sl*) may only be used to satisfy a write-pin request pin(*sbj*, *page*, write) if *level*(*sbj*)=map_level(*sl*). Because we forbid write-up, this implies *level*(*page*)=*level*(*sbj*)=*level*(*sl*) if *sl* is write-pinned. A buffer slot may be used to satisfy a read-pin pin(*sbj, page*, read) only if *level*(*sbj*)≥map_level(*sl*). If the read rule is violated or if subjects can use strictly dominated slots for write-pin requests, then a page may be readable to non-dominating subjects. If a subject is allowed to use a strictly dominating slot for write-pin requests, then the availability of the slots introduces a covert channel.

4 Replacement

In this section we discuss methods of selecting pages for replacement. A replacement algorithm is described by two components, a page set and a ranking function, which we now define. Let *ref* be an execution history containing pin and unpin requests. The subsequence of *ref* consisting of requests dominated by security level l_i is denoted $ref|_{\leq l_i}$. Let *page_set* be a function mapping a reference history and a set of *m* pages to a set of pages. The result of page_set(*ref*, {$page_1...page_m$}) is the subset of the *m* pages that will be maintained in memory. We refer to the set of pages output by the page_set algorithm as the page set.

Let $<_{ref}$ be a total order over a set of pages. The implication of $page_i<_{ref}page_j$ is that $page_i$ will be replaced before $page_j$ following the history *ref*. This order is referred to as the *ranking*.

The slot containing a page that is resident but not output by the page set algorithm is freed. If a page is needed for replacement at a particular level and there are no free slots, the unpinned, resident page with the highest ranking should be replaced.

The contents of the slots must be the same as if the algorithms had been used with only the dominated reference string in order to satisfy noninterference. Formally the following properties must hold for all levels l_i, and all pages $page_i$ and $page_j$ such that $level(page_i)=level(page_j)=l_i$:

1) page_set(*ref*, {$page_1...page_m$})$|_{\leq l_i}$ = page_set($ref|_{\leq l_i}$, {$page_1...page_m$})$|_{\leq l_i}$; and

2) $page_i >_{ref} page_j$ **iff** $page_i >_{ref|_{\leq li}} page_j$

A good approach to replacement is to have separate instances of the page set and ranking algorithms operating at each security level l_i with its input being the dominated reference strings and operating on the set of pages $\{page_j \mid l_i \geq level(page_j)\}$. The advantage of a buffer manager receiving the dominated reference string, as opposed to just references at its own level, is that it can calculate the set of pages resident at dominated buffer managers. In implementation, a buffer manager can receive only the same level reference string and determine the state of the strictly dominated buffer managers by direct examination of the data structures.

A buffer manager may maintain a page that is output by its own page set algorithm and that of a strictly dominating level. When a page is replaced at the lower level we would like to offer it to the next highest level buffer manager that needs it. Therefore, before such a page is replaced it should be offered to all covering buffer managers where the page is output by the page set algorithm and has a higher rank than at least one page that is currently held in that buffer. It should be noted that a page may be placed in more than one strictly dominating buffer manager due to incomparable security levels.

5 Buffer Slot Allocation

Because buffer managers are partitioned by security level, each running its own instance of the page set and ranking algorithms, we need a method of allocating buffer slots to buffer managers. This allocation can be either static or dynamic.

5.1 Static Allocation

With *static allocation* a fixed number of buffer slots are allocated to a buffer manager and those slots remain under the control of that buffer manager. This implies there must be a buffer manager with allocated buffer slots at each security level in the lattice, whether there are transactions active at that level or not. The advantage of this method is simplicity. The disadvantages are poor performance due to low resource utilization when the workloads differ from the assigned allocation. If the security poset has a large number of inactive security levels, then there will be a large number of unused buffer slots. If a buffer manager's page set size is larger than its allocation then it is in need of slots, if the opposite is true then it has free slots. With static allocation there is no way to distribute free slots to buffer managers in need of slots. For these reasons the static approach is only suitable for systems with relatively static workload distribution across a small number of security levels.

5.2 Dynamic Allocation

If workloads are dynamic, there is an advantage in dynamically allocating buffer slots to subjects. We discuss two types of dynamic allocation. The first we call arbitrary allocation and the second slot stealing.

Arbitrary Allocation.

Arbitrary allocation is characterized by a movement of buffer slots between buffer managers without regard for the security order partial order. As a result, arbitrary allocation can introduce a covert channel. We must therefore regulate this channel.

To accomplish this, at fixed intervals buffer slots are redistributed according to the workload. A security level upon activation must wait until the next fixed allocation time before it is allocated slots. Likewise, as security levels become inactive their resources will be released at the next fixed allocation time. We only allow changes to an allocation to occur in very restricted ways (i.e., the number of possible allocations is small). In this way we can control the covert channel capacity. For example a re-allocation of buffers may occur every 10 seconds at which time we either add or remove 10% of the current allocation.

Slot Stealing.

Arbitrary allocation will adjust for slow changes in workloads at individual security levels, such as changes in the number of clients. In order to adjust to fast changes in workload such as changes in locality we present *slot stealing*. With this method, buffer slots move up and down strictly dominated chains in the active poset. The basic idea is to have buffer managers offer unused buffer slots to strictly dominating buffer managers and then reclaim these buffer slots as the need arises. In particular, buffer slots may be passed to a single strictly dominating buffer manager if the buffer slot is not needed based upon the page set algorithm of the donor.

The movement of buffer slots is complicated when a level has more than one covering level. In order to be secure, the decision as to which covering level can use the buffer slot cannot be based upon the need of the workload at the covering level.

The first approach is to partition the active poset into strictly dominating paths and allow each buffer slot to move up and down a single pre-assigned path. The second approach is to assign probabilities for the next free slot at a particular buffer manager to be offered to each parent. As buffer slots become free they are offered to a strictly dominated buffer manager with these probabilities. This is similar to the method used to allocate the CPU to processes in [HU92].

When a buffer manager's page set size grows beyond the number of resident buffer slots it may either attempt to reclaim a previously offered slot or it may attempt to steal a slot from a strictly dominated buffer manager. In the first case we must ensure that a buffer manager can reclaim a buffer slot from a strictly dominating buffer manager without delay. This implies that the number of buffer slots that are clean and not performing I/O must be as large as the number of slots borrowed. An unpinned, clean buffer slot is returned by the strictly dominating buffer manager.

6 Solutions for the Secure Reader/Writer Problem

This section describes methods to synchronize readers and writers of different levels. The writer must not be delayed due to the high-level read-pin(s), yet the read and write-pins and the associated work must be done to satisfy the properties of Section 3.3. There are two general choices for dealing with this problem. The first choice is to allocate a single buffer for the reader and writer to share. The second choice is to allocate a buffer to the writer and another to the reader. This we call replication. Specifically, if a page is found in more than one buffer slot, sl_i and sl_j where $level(sl_i) > level(sl_j)$, then we say there is *replication*.

If replication is not used then we must have some mechanism to allow the reader to see a stable copy of the page while the write is taking place or abort the work of the reader. Without replication, the buffer managers can hold more distinct pages in a given number of buffer slots. If replication is used, a method of maintaining consistency between the multiple copies is needed. Replication can ease an untrusted implementation, allow distribution more naturally, and can prevent aborts due to reader/writer conflicts.

The remainder of this section presents solutions to these issues. Some of these solutions require specific manipulations of the mapping between virtual memory and physical memory. We assume the ability to modify the mappings between virtual addresses and physical pages. Furthermore, we assume the ability to handle the exception caused by an invalid mapping.

6.1 Non-replicated Approaches

With no replication each dominance chain contains at most one instance of the page. Therefore, conflicting pin requests from different levels are satisfied using the same replica. We must, however, synchronize readers and writers of this replica. Thus, we need some method of notifying the transaction holding a read-pin when the contents of the buffer slot are modified. Following the notification we can abort the transaction holding the read-pin or attempt to redo the partially completed work associated with the page.

A *page*$_i$ is resident at level l_i only if it is not resident at any level strictly dominated by l_i. If a read-pin is requested for *page*$_i$, the buffer slots (sl_j) are searched where level(pin(sbj,*page*$_i$,read))$\geq$level(sl_j)$\geq$level(*page*$_i$). If the page is not found, it is brought into a free buffer slot at the level of the requester and the read-pin is granted. If the page is found, the read-pin is granted once any active write-pin is released. If the page is found at more than one incomparable level then the choice of which slot to access is made arbitrarily.

If a write-pin request is made or if a page is replaced while a strictly dominating read-pin is granted on that page, then the page is invalidated for the high level reader. In this case the subject holding the high level read-pin must be notified, either on the next memory access or as a response to the unpin request, that the slot has been modified. We present two methods of accomplishing this. The first method uses event counts and the second invalidates the memory mapping of the read-pinned slot causing an interrupt on the next memory reference to the slot.

For the first method, event counts are used to indicate when a slot is modified (write-pinned or replaced) as in [REED79]. The subject that requested the read-pin checks the event count before and after doing its work. If the event count has changed, the work is redone from some save point or alternatively the transaction can be aborted if this is not convenient.

The second method is to invalidate the memory mapping of the read-pinner before the contents of the slot are modified, causing a fault during the next memory reference of the read-pin requester. As before, the interrupt handler can attempt to redo the work or simply abort.

6.2 Replication

Replication simplifies synchronization of the readers and writers but introduces a consistency requirement. Here we allow a page to be cached more than once in a strictly dominating path. This allows conflicting read and write-pin operations of different security levels to access their own private replica of the page. This solution introduces a potential for inconsistency between the different replicas of a page. Replication can occur every time a read-pin is requested on a page in a strictly dominated slot (*immediate replication*) or only when a read/write conflict is discovered (*delayed replication*).

Immediate Replication.

For immediate replication, if a read-pin is requested on a strictly dominated page, the response to the read-pin is delayed until there is no outstanding write-pin on the page. At this time the page is loaded into a buffer slot (either fetched from disk or copied from a lower level buffer slot) at the subject's level, and the read-pin is granted. The read-pin requester accesses the page there. If the page is modified (by a low level transaction in a low level slot) and subsequently accessed again at the high-level, the original replica must be invalidated or updated. The page remains in this slot until it is invalidated or replaced, at which time it is freed. We identify four basic approaches to maintaining consistency. They are immediate invalidation, propagation, publishing modifications, and a validation server.

Immediate Invalidation: With immediate invalidation the replicated page is only used for one read-pin and then invalidated. This in effect gives each strictly dominating read-pin a private workspace in which to work. The advantage of this method is its simplicity, low overhead, and ease with which an untrusted implementation can be achieved. The disadvantage is that a page is not used for future pin requests. Thus it may result in less efficient use of buffer slots, more in memory page transfers, and more disk I/O.

Propagation: The second method is to propagate modifications to strictly dominating buffer slots. For every modification of a page, the strictly dominating buffer slots are searched and the corresponding pages are invalidated or updated with the new changes. A trusted implementation of this is straight forward. The disadvantages of an untrusted approach are due to the difficulty of reliable communications in the upward direction [KANG93] and the number of messages needed to be sent (one to each strictly dominated ancestor for each update).

Publishing Modifications: A third method of maintaining consistency is to publish changes in well known places, e.g., an update log in main memory. Buffer managers can check the logs at strictly dominating levels for consistency as needed. An untrusted method for doing this is described below.

Here we assume an untrusted buffer manager at each security level. Each buffer manager maintains, in main memory, a circular queue, of size *queue_size*. The queue contains page numbers of pages that have been write-pinned by a transaction at that security level. The entry is added before the write-pin is granted. Associated with each queue is a queue serial number (*queue_serial*) that is incremented with each insertion. The value *queue_serial* mod *queue_size* gives the location of an entry within the queue where *queue_serial* is the value at the time the entry was made. The value of $\lfloor queue\_serial/queue\_size \rfloor$ gives the number of times the queue has rolled over. We assume that the *queue_serial* counter is large enough that it will never roll over.

We associate with each page in a buffer, a validation time. For each page held in a buffer slot of the same level, its validation time is initialized to infinity. When a valid page is found and loaded into a strictly dominating buffer the validation time is set to the value of the *queue_serial* at the level of the page. When a search for a page is done, the replica with the largest validation time is chosen from all dominated buffers. Once the page is found, it is validated. If the queue has rolled over since the validation time of the page then it is invalid. If the queue has not rolled over since the page's validation time but there is an update to the page in the queue with a smaller validation time then that of the buffer slot, then the page is also invalid. Otherwise the page is valid. If the page is found to be valid then its validation time is updated to the current value of the *queue_serial*. If the page is invalid the page must be retrieved from disk and the validation time updated to the current value of the *queue_serial*.

Pages are validated again just before the release of a high-level read-pin and the pinning subject is notified if the page was modified. This will give the requester the option of redoing the work if necessary.

Validation Server: The last method of maintaining consistency is to use a validation server. Here, a trusted server maintains the pages held by each buffer manager and the outstanding write-pins. The buffer managers can explicitly inform the validation server when a change in the resident set occurs and when write-pins are granted and released. When a write-pin is requested for a page the validation server makes all replicas of that page at strictly dominated buffer slots invalid. Before a buffer manager grants a read-pin on a strictly dominated page, it checks with the validation server to see if the page is valid. If it is not valid the slot holding the page is cleared and freed, and the page is searched for again. If it is valid the read-pin is granted.

Delayed Replication.

For delayed replication a data page is replicated only after a (high) read (low) write conflict has been discovered. If a write-pin request is made for $page_i$ that is held in slot sl_i where level($page_i$)=map_level(sl_i) and pin(sbj,$page_i$,read) is outstanding on slot sl_i where level(sbj)>map_level(sl_i), then before the write-pin is granted $page_i$ is copied into buffer slot sl_j where map_level(sl_j)=level(sbj) and the reader continues using the new copy.

A read (down) pin is delayed until there are no write-pins on the buffer, at which time the address of the strictly dominated buffer slot is returned to the subject. If a write-pin is requested while the read-pin is held, the page is copied to a buffer slot at the high-level, the mapping is changed for the high-level read requester from the low-level slot to the high-level slot, and finally the write-pin is granted. After the read-pin completes, if a copy was done, the high-level buffer slot is freed and invalidated.

The copy on write can introduce a covert channel. The channel is due to the CPU time needed to copy the page from the low buffer to the high buffer (this copy must be done before the write-pin can be granted). To address this, we can delay all write-pin requests by the time required to copy the page, or randomize the delay for granting a write-pin [HU91].

A buffer slot must be available immediately at the high-level. If the page is to be replicated, the high-level buffer manager must have one buffer slot that can be replaced immediately (no pins, clean, and not in the process of doing I/O) for every read down pin held. If one is not available immediately it can fall back to using a non-replicated approach.

Figure 2 summarizes the solutions outlined in this section.

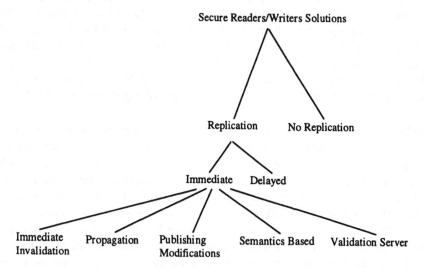

Fig. 2. Secure Reader/Writers Solutions

7 Performance Analysis

The purpose of this analysis is to investigate the performance trade offs between static and dynamic allocation of slots and the three approaches (no replication, delayed replication, and immediate replication) to synchronizing readers and writers.

7.1 Simulation

We have performed an event-based simulation to study the performance implications of the various methods we have proposed for allocation and reader/writer synchronization. The simulator consists of two components, a reference string generator and a buffer manager simulator. There is a separate reference string generated for each active security level. Each reference consists of a page number, a page level, and an arrival time. The database consists of 1000 pages at each security level. For each active security level there are *PS* page sets. Each page set is composed of a set of pages and associated page security levels. The size of each page set is either *fixed* or *uniformly* distributed (*PSD*) with mean *PSM* and variance *PSV*. A reference from security level l_i will read a page at security level l_j where $l_i \geq l_j$ with probability $PR_{i,j}$ and will write a page with probability PW_i. Pages in a page set referencing pages at a different security level are chosen with the distribution *PD*, with corresponding variance *PDV* and mean *PDM*, from the pages in the database at that security level. References are generated by first choosing a page set. The hold time (HT) is the number of references that will be generated from that page set before choosing another. After *HT* references are generated from the page set, the next page set is chosen from all page sets with uniform probability. The HT references may either be randomly chosen from the set of page set pages or be chosen sequentially. This choice is referred to as the micro model. Each reference generated is assigned an arrival time drawn from an exponential distribution with a corresponding mean *ATM*.

The buffer manager simulator is event based, and the only events that cause time to advance are disk I/O, and the arrival of a pin or unpin request. There are BS_i buffer slots at level l_i. The disk I/O requires 60 time units and each pin will be held for a mean of 400 time units with an exponential distribution. The arrival time for each reference is drawn from an exponential distribution with a corresponding mean 2000 time units. Disk I/O requests are serviced on a round-robin basis within a level. If a security level has no request at the beginning of its corresponding round-robin service cycle, no disk I/O is performed. This method of generating disk I/O times is meant to approximate techniques used to eliminate the covert channel associated with disk scheduling. Each execution of the simulation will have an associated slot allocation method (static or dynamic) and a secure reader/writer conflict resolution method (no replication, delayed replication, immediate replication). The working set algorithm [DENN68] is used as the page set algorithm. All pages referenced in the last 2*PSM references are output by the algorithm. We use the LRU replacement policy [GRAY93] as our ranking algorithm. We also simulate a traditional single level buffer manager that uses LRU as its replacement policy but makes decisions based upon the entire reference string. This is used as a performance benchmark for the secure protocols.

7.2 Experiments

Each data point in the following plots is an average over six test runs. Each test run consisted of 40,000 page references. A 90% confidence interval was calculated and plotted for each average of sample points [TRIV82]. The confidence interval is shown as error bars on the graphs. Because the method for finding the confidence interval assumes the data points are normally distributed, the results of each set of test runs was evaluated using the Kolmogorov-Smirnov goodness of fit test [LIND78] and found to be normally distributed with $\alpha=0.05$.

The first experiment investigates the benefits of the dynamic allocation methods presented. The second set of experiments explores the reader/writer conflict resolutions.

Buffer Slot Allocation Methods.

The purpose of this experiment is to investigate the performance improvement provided by the slot stealing buffer allocation method. In this experiment there are two security levels, Low and High. The variance in the page set sizes of both security levels is varied and the total hit rate is measured. The experiment was run for static allocation, slot stealing with a 90%(Low)-10%(High) division of buffer slots, slot stealing with a 50%-50% allocation of buffer slots, and single level (traditional) LRU. Table 1 gives the complete list of parameters used in this experiment.

Parameter	Description	Value	
PS	number of page sets	50	
PSD	page set size distribution	uniform	
PSM	page set size mean	30 pages	
PSV	page set size variance	0,25,50,...,200	
PD	page selection distribution	normal	
PDM	page selection mean	page number 500	
PDV	page selection variance	500	
HT	hold time for a page set	500 references	
micro_model	selection of pages from page set	sequential	
		Low	**High**
PW_i	probability of writing to l_i	0.25	0.25
$PR_{i,LOW}$	probability l_i reading from l_{LOW}	0.75	0.0
$PR_{i,HIGH}$	probability l_i reading from l_{HIGH}	0.0	0.75
BS_i	number of buffer slots at level l_i	35,63	35,7

Table 1. Parameters for the Buffer Slot Allocation Experiment

Figure 4 shows the results of this experiment. With a small variance, all three methods work about the same, all having good hit rates. Each level needs and can get the approximately 30 slots needed to keep the page set resident. The dynamic 90/10 performs the worst because Low slots are taken back during a page set change when the working set sizes are large. As the variance increases the static allocation hit rate drops quickly because when either page set grows beyond the number of slots allocated to that level (35), a page that is contained in the page set must be replaced to allow a new page to be retrieved. Dynamic allocation 50/50 hit rate drops off at a moderate rate. Here, if the Low page set size is below the number of slots allocated to the lower level (35) and the High page set is larger than 35 (at the same time) then the High buffer manager may borrow a slot from the low level, thus increasing the hit rate at the high level. If the reverse is true, no redistribution of slots is possible and no performance benefit is achieved. Because of the 50/50 split we would expect each of the two cases to happen with about equal probability. Dynamic allocation with a 90/10 split shows the best hit rate of the secure algorithms in this experiment, staying close to the standard LRU. Here, anytime the Low page set size is below 63 and the High page set size is above 7, the remainder of the low level's buffer slots may be borrowed by the high level. If this is the case and the sum of the page sets is less than or equal to 70, then each level's buffer manager will have enough slots to keep the entire page set resident. This allocation of buffer slots does allow the low level to "starve" the high level if its page set becomes large (as when changing localities). This is one factor that keeps the hit rate less than unsecure LRU. Unsecure LRU always achieves the best hit rate as is expected. As long as the sum of the page sets sizes are below 70 they will both remain resident.

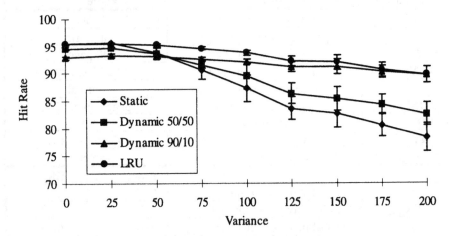

Fig. 4. Buffer Slot Allocation Methods

Secure Readers/Writers Solutions.

The purpose of the next two experiments is to investigate the proposed solutions to the secure readers/writers conflict. The first experiment investigates the way the solutions utilize buffer slots. The second experiment investigates the behavior of the solutions as the inter-level conflict rate increases. Both experiments have two active levels, High and Low. The High hit rate is plotted for delayed and immediate replication. For both experiments the hit rate for no replication and delayed replication were the same and only one was plotted. The aborts caused when no replication is used was also measured and found to be less than 1%.

In the first experiment each level has one page set consisting of 40 pages. The Low workload has a 100% write rate (i.e., every access is a write). The High workload consists of 50% of the accesses are reads of the High level pages and 50% read pages at the Low level. The High and Low page sets share 20 Low pages in common. There are 40 buffer slots allocated to the Low level. This allows all 40 pages in the Low page set to be resident. The number of High buffer slots is varied from 5 to 45. The parameters for this experiment are shown in Table 2.

Figure 5 shows a plot of the High hit rate as the number of High buffers is varied. As the number of buffer slots is increased the hit rate for both delayed and immediate replication increase. For both methods every read to a Low page results in a hit because the Low buffer manager has enough buffer slots to keep all the Low pages resident. This is the reason the Low hit rate is excluded in Figure 5. The delayed replication hit rate reaches a maximum when it has 20 buffer slots. All 20 High pages in the High page set can be maintained in these 20 buffer slots because delayed replication only replicates a page when there is a conflict, and the conflict rate is very low as indicated by the 1% abort rate using no replication. This results in all 20 buffer slots being used almost solely for High pages. The immediate replication hit rate reaches a maximum at 40 buffer slots. This is because a page is replicated on each reference to the Low level. Thus, one slot is needed for each of the High 20 pages and each of the Low 20 pages.

The next experiment measures the hit rate as the inter-level conflict rate increases. The page sets of both levels are the same and static. The conflict is controlled by varying the probability that a high level reference will read down to a low level page. There is a 100% write rate at the low level, 100% read rate at the high level. The complete set of parameters are shown in the Table 3.

Figure 6 shows the results of this experiment. Below a 50% read down percentage delayed replication appears to be better, while above 50% immediate replication is better. Delayed replication works better below 50% because more High than Low pages are in the High page set. These High pages must be maintained in a High buffer slot. When a page is replicated, a High page may have to be replaced. Because Delayed replication only replicates a page during a conflict, it makes better use of the High buffer slots resulting in a higher hit rate for High pages. With read down percentages below 50%, there are more Low than High pages in the High page set. For both methods, the High buffer manager makes good use of the Low buffer slots. However, immediate replication allows a buffer manager to make better use of the High buffer slots. It replicates on every read down and maintains the replicas until they are invalidated by a subsequent write. This results in the High buffer manager maintaining some Low pages that have been replaced at the Low buffer manager. Delayed replication does not have this advantage because it only replicates during a conflict and the page is immediately invalidated. This advantage for immediate replication can only occur when the Low buffer manager does not have enough slots to maintain its page set.

Parameter	Description	Value	
PS	number of page sets	1	
PSD	page set size distribution	uniform	
PSM	page set size mean	40 pages	
PSV	page set size variance	0	
PD	page selection distribution	uniform	
PDM	page selection mean	page number 500	
PDV	page selection variance	40	
HT	hold time for a page set	500 references	
micro_model	selection of pages from page set	random	
		Low	**High**
PW_i	probability of writing to l_i	1.0	0.0
$PR_{i_{LOW}}$	probability l_i reading from l_{LOW}	0.0	0.5
$PR_{i_{HIGH}}$	probability l_i reading from l_{HIGH}	0.0	0.5
BS_i	number of buffer slots at l_i	40	5,10,...,45

Table 2. Parameters for the Reader/Writer Synchronization Experiment #1

8 Conclusions

In this work we have identified issues related to secure database buffering (a secure pinning policy, page allocation, replacement, read/write conflict resolution), presented solutions to these problems, and performed performance analysis for some of these solutions.

Due to security constraints we cannot adopt a traditional pin/unpin buffer policy and still satisfy multilevel security. We have presented a method that presents high level readers with the most recent copy of a buffered low level page while allowing low level writers to proceed unaffected. A method of page replacement was presented that allows traditional replacement algorithms but restricts the reference string to those of dominated references only.

Because of the potentially dynamic nature of transaction workloads we proposed a secure dynamic buffer allocation scheme. The scheme allows high level buffer managers to "steal" slots from strictly dominated buffer managers while still allowing the strictly dominated buffer managers to reclaim the slots at any time.

Parameter	Description	Value	
PS	number of page sets	1	
PSD	page set size distribution	uniform	
PSM	page set size mean	30 pages	
PSV	page set size variance	0 pages	
PD	page selection distribution	uniform	
PDM	page selection mean	page number 500	
PDV	page selection variance	30	
HT	hold time for a page set	500 references	
micro_model	selection of pages from page set	random	
		Low	**High**
PW_i	probability of writing to l_i	1.0	0.0
$PR_{i,LOW}$	probability l_i reading from l_{LOW}	0.0	0.0,0.1,...,1.0
$PR_{i,HIGH}$	probability l_i reading from l_{HIGH}	0.0	1.0,0.9,...,0.0
BS_i	number of buffer slots at level l_i	23	23

Table 3. Parameters for the Reader/Writer Synchronization Experiment #2

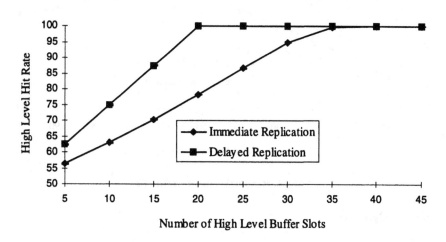

Fig. 5. Reader/Writer Conflict #1

Due to the potentially long pin hold times, the secure reader/writer problem is complicated in database systems. We presented three secure methods to deal with this problem. The first involves aborting high level readers when a conflicting low level write-pin is submitted. The second involves making a copy of the before image of the page for high level read-pinners before a conflicting write-pin is granted. The third method makes a separate copy of the low level page prior to granting high level read-pins.

Through simulation we have shown that the dynamic allocation scheme outperforms static allocation for dynamic workloads. For static workloads static allocation may be attractive due to its low overhead and simplicity. The simulation also has shown that when buffer managers have enough slots to maintain their page set, delayed and no replication outperform immediate replication. Immediate replication can outperform the others when a buffer manager has an excess of buffer slots while a strictly dominated buffer manager has too few. Immediate replication may also present a good alternative when manipulating virtual memory functions as outlined previously are undesirable as in distributed systems.

In the future, we intend to study implementation issues by prototyping a buffer manager on a multilevel secure MACH based platform, i.e., DTOS [SCC95]. In particular we intend to investigate methods of implementing the memory mapping functions required by the delayed replication and the page stealing allocation methods.

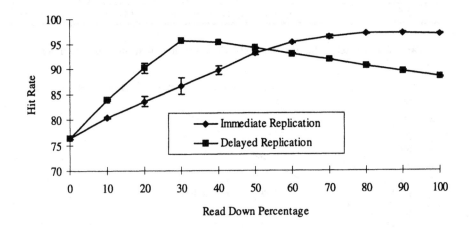

Fig. 6. Reader/Writer Conflict #2

Acknowledgments

This work is supported in part by the U.S. Department of Defense under contract number MDA 904-94-C-6121.

References.

[BELL76]   D.E. Bell and L.J. LaPadula, "Secure Computer Systems: Unified Exposition and Multics Interpretations," Technical Report MTR-2997, Mitre Corp., March 1976.

[BERN87]   P.A. Bernstein, V. Hadzilacos, and N. Goodman, *Concurrency Control and Recovery in Database Systems*, Addison-Wesley Publishing Company, Reading, MA, 1987.

[DENN68]   P.J. Denning, "The Page set Model for Program Behavior," *Communication of the ACM*, November, 1968, pp. 323-333.

[DOD85]   Department of Defense Computer Security Center, *Department of Defense Trusted Computer Systems Evaluation Criteria*, DoD 5200.28-STD, December 1985.

[EFFE84]   W. Effelsberg and T. Haerder, "Principles of Database Buffer Management," *ACM Transactions on Database Systems*, Vol 9, No. 4, December 1984, pp. 560-595.

[GOGU82]   J.A. Goguen and J. Meseguer, "Security Policy and Security Models," *Proceedings of the IEEE Symposium on Security and Privacy*, Oakland, CA, April 1982, pp. 11-20.

[GRAY93]   J. Gray and A. Reuter, *Transaction Processing: Concepts and Techniques*, Morgan Kaufmann Publishers, San Mateo, CA, 1993.

[HAIG87]   J.T. Haigh and W.D. Young, "Extending the Noninterference Version of MLS for SAT," *IEEE Transactions on Software Engineering*, Vol. SE-13, No. 2, February 1987, pp. 141-150.

[HU91]   W. Hu, "Reducing Timing Channels with Fuzzy Time," *Proceedings of the IEEE Symposium on Security and Privacy*, Oakland, CA, 1991, pp. 8-20

[HU92]   W. Hu, "Lattice Scheduling and Covert Channels," *Proceedings of the IEEE Symposium on Security and Privacy*, Oakland, CA, 1992, pp. 52-61

[KANG93]   M.H. Kang and I.S. Moskowitz, "A Pump for Rapid, Reliable, Secure Communication," *Proceedings of the ACM Conference on Computer and Communication Security*, Fairfax, VA, 1993, pp. 119-129.

[LIND78]   B.W. Lindgren, G.W. McElrath, and D.A. Berry, *Introduction to Probability and Statistics*, Macmillan Publishing Co., New York, 1978.

[REED79]   D.P. Reed, and R.K. Kanodia, "Synchronization with Eventcounts and Sequencers," *Communications of the ACM*, Vol. 22, No. 2, Feb. 1979, pp. 115-123.

[SCC95]   *DTOS Users Manual*, Secure Computing Corporation, Roseville, MN, 1995.

[TRIV82]   K.S. Trivedi, *Probability and Statistics with Reliability, Queuing, and Computer Science Applications*, Prentice-Hall, Englewood Cliffs, NY, 1982.

[WARN95]   A.C. Warner and T.F. Keefe, "Version Pool Management in a Multilevel Secure Multiversion Transaction Manager," *Proceedings of the IEEE Symposium on Security and Privacy*, Oakland, CA, pp. 169-181.

Enhancing the Controlled Disclosure
of Sensitive Information

Donald G. Marks, Amihai Motro, and Sushil Jajodia

Department of Information and Software Systems Engineering
George Mason University
Fairfax, VA 22030-4444

Abstract. The so-called "aggregation problem" is addressed, where the issue is how to release only a *limited* part of an information resource, and foil any attacks by users trying to aggregate information beyond the preset limits. The framework is that of relational databases, where sensitive information can be defined flexibly using view definitions. For each such view, the tuples that have already been disclosed are recorded *intensionally* rather than *extensionally*; that is, at each point, sub-view definitions are maintained that describe all the sensitive tuples that have been released to each individual. While our previous work foiled sequences of single-query attacks attempted by individual users, it did not consider multi-query attacks, where a *combination* of queries is used to invade the sensitive information. In this study we enhance our previous solutions to guard the sensitive information against two kinds of multi-query attacks: join attacks, and complement attacks. We then argue that the enhanced algorithm renders the sensitive information immune to attacks.

1   Introduction

In has been observed, that often the release of a limited part of an information resource poses no security risk, but the release of a sufficient part of that resource might pose such risks. This problem of controlled disclosure of sensitive information is known as the *aggregation* problem. In [10] we argued that it is possible to articulate the specific sensitive concepts within a database that should be protected against over-disclosure, and we provided an accounting system to enforce such controlled disclosure. Our methods foil any attempt to attack these predefined secrets either by disguising queries or by surreptitiously accumulating tuples. The accounting methods that we developed to thwart such attempts were shown to be both accurate and economical.

Our previous work tracked continuously the queries attempted by each individual user, but it assumed that each "attack" consisted of a single query at a time; that is, it did not consider attacks through combinations of several

The work of Motro was supported in part by ARPA grant, administered by the Office of Naval Research under Grant No. N0014-92-J-4038. The work of Jajodia was supported in part by NSF Grant No. IRI-9303416.

queries. In this study we enhance our previous solutions to guard the sensitive concepts against two kinds of multi-query attacks: (1) *join attacks*, in which two queries targeting narrower (and therefore unprotected) associations of attributes are joined, to create larger associations that are supposed to be protected: and (2) *complement attacks*, in which a query targeting a larger set of tuples (which embeds the protected tuples, but is itself unprotected) is combined with a query on the unprotected tuples within the larger set (which is unprotected), to derive tuples in the protected set. In addition, we show that the enhanced algorithm prevents any kind of attack on sensitive concepts.

Section 2 summarizes these concepts and methods as developed in [10]. Section 3 describes the multi-query attack strategies, Section 4 shows how these attacks can be foiled, and Section 5 argues that the enhanced algorithm provides concepts with immunity to attacks. Section 6 considers several related considerations, and Section 7 discusses further research problems.

1.1 Related Work

Related work was discussed in [10] and has not changed significantly in the interim. Major studies of interest include [11, 4, 7, 6, 5]. Many of the previous studies suggest terminology and reason from examples to derive specific solutions for specific problems. Recent work on the problem has been meager, with an occasional reference in the more general context of inference problems. For example, Campbell [2] notes that aggregation is a "big security problem" but offers no references to detailed studies, only to approaches that work in some cases. Of course, many of the techniques used in this study have been developed previously for use on other problems. These efforts are noted as appropriate.

Similar problems occur for statistical databases (SDB). In statistical databases users can retrieve various characterizations (such as salaries), but not identities (such as people or institutions). The work of [1] and [9] provide excellent overviews of statistical database security problems. None of the SDB techniques assume that the data is kept in a relational databases, rather the problems are couched in terms of simple tables. Common techniques for controlling disclosure include linear programming and answer size restrictions. Little research has been done on auditing or query sequence control as is addressed here. If the holders of statistical data, such as census bureaus, wish to make data more widely available through on-line access to relational databases, variations of the techniques presented here may have applicability.

Our approach allows a flexible (view-based) definition of the sensitive information, but develops an accurate method for accounting access to such views. The main contribution of [10] was a method to articulate specific sensitive concepts and to account for individual user access to these sensitive concepts. The main contributions of this study is to control alternative ways of determining tuples in these sensitive concepts.

We choose views as our mechanism for articulating more specific sensitive concepts. This was previously proposed by Denning et al. [3] as an access control mechanism, but this is the first application of the technique to the aggregation problem. As queries are also views, we can then check each query to see if it intersects a sensitive view. This intersection is also a view; in fact, it is a sub-view of both the sensitive concept and the query. By maintaining a "history" of these sub-views of the sensitive views and their sizes, we know how many, and which, tuples of each sensitive concept have been accessed. This eliminates the need to maintain a history of the sensitive tuples themselves that have been accessed. The technique integrates the accounting and naming mechanisms of secrets, resulting in an efficient and complete system for tracking access.

1.2 Phonebook Example

The Secret Government Agency (SGA) Phonebook is a common example of the aggregation problem. In this example, the entire phonebook is a classified document and is not available without the appropriate clearance; yet, individual phonebook entries are available to inquiring callers. A simple example of such a phonebook, with scheme *Emp = (Name, Tel, Div, Mail, Bldg, Room)* is shown in Figure 1. The reason that the entire phonebook is classified is because a phonebook provides a way of grouping the *individuals* into *concepts*. In relational database systems tuples are associated together by means of *views*, so each view may be regarded as a concept.

Name	Tel	Div	Mail	Bldg	Room
A. Long	x3333	A	m505	2	307
P. Smith	x1111	B	m303	2	610
E. Brown	x2345	B	m101	1	455
C. Jones	x1234	A	m202	1	307
M. Johnson	x1234	A	m101	3	103
B. Stevenson	x2222	A	m202	1	305
S. Quinn	x2222	C	m606	3	101
R. Helmick	x1234	A	m404	1	307
A. Facey	x1122	C	m505	2	400
S. Sheets	x2345	B	m101	1	455

Fig. 1. The Phonebook example

2 The Model

2.1 Basic Assumptions

The model is mostly unchanged from [10], and we repeat here the assumptions and features that are relevant to this paper. We assume that the sensitive information is a relatively small portion of a relational database. We adopt the usual definition of relational databases, but restrict our attention to databases that are *single* relations, each with a *simple key*, and to *projection-selection* views, where all selections are conjunctions of simple clauses of the form *attribute = value*. We denote the database scheme $R = (A_1, \ldots, A_n)$. The domain D_i of an attribute A_i is the projection of the given instance of R on this attribute. This so-called *active* domain is the finite set of values used for A_i in the database instance. All tuples $t = (t_1, t_2, \ldots, t_n)$ are therefore elements of the set $D_1 \times D_2, \cdots, \times D_n$.

We will define both sensitive information and queries in terms of such selection-projection views. More comprehensive views may be formed by taking complements and unions of views. Databases consisting of several relations may be treated view the Universal Relation formalism [12]. The limitation of selection clauses to the form *attribute = value* is fairly serious, as it prohibits clauses of the form *attribute < value*. While such views may be handled by decomposing them into a set of *attribute = value* views, handling such views satisfactorily is a topic for future research.

2.2   Queries and Concepts

A *query* is a view. Its extension in the present database instance is the *answer* to the query. Queries are defined by users and describe the information they are seeking. A *concept* is also a view. Concepts are defined in the system and describe the information that needs to be protected. Views (queries or concepts) may be syntactically different, but yet describe the same information. Consider the example database scheme *Emp = (Name, Tel, Div, Mail, Bldg. Room)* and the views **select** *Name, Room* **where** *Room=103* and **select** *Name* **where** *Room=103*. Both view definitions are identical, except that the latter view does not project a selection attribute which is projected by the former (*Room*). Nevertheless, because the values of selection attributes are known (in this case, the constant value 103), there is no difference in the information these views describe. Consequently, regardless of their syntax, we shall treat all views as is their projection attributes include all their selection attributes.

2.3   Concept Disclosure

Let U and V be views of database scheme R. U *overlaps* V, if their selection conditions are not contradictory, [1] and U's projection attributes contain V's projection attributes. When U overlaps V, then the extension of U could be processed by another view that will remove the extra attributes. Some of the resulting tuples may be in the extension of V.

Assume that U overlaps V. The *restriction* of V to U, denoted $V \mid U$, is the view obtained from V by appending to its selection condition the selection condition of U. The *exclusion* of U from V, denoted $V \mid \neg U$, is the view obtained

---

[1] The selection conditions of U and V are *contradictory*, if U's selection condition includes the clause $A_i = a$ and V's selection condition includes the clause $A_i = b$, for some attribute A_i and two different constants a and b.

from V by appending to its selection condition the *negation* of the selection condition of U.[2] Obviously, $V = (V \mid U) \cup (V \mid \neg U)$.

Let C be a concept view and let Q be a query view. Q *discloses* C, if Q overlaps C. Intuitively, a query discloses a concept, if its result could be processed by another query, to possibly derive tuples from the protected concept. The disclosure relationship between a query and a concept is illustrated schematically in Figure 2.

As an example, with the previous database scheme, consider this concept

$$C = \pi_{Name,Div,Room}\, \sigma_{(Room=103)\wedge(Div=B)}$$
(names of those in division B and in room 103)

and these three queries

1. $Q_1 = \pi_{Name,Tel,Div,Room}\, \sigma_{(Room=103)\wedge(Div=B)\wedge(Tel=x2345)}$
   (names of those in room 103, in division B, and with telephone x2345)
2. $Q_2 = \pi_{Name,Div,Room}\, \sigma_{Div=B}$
   (names and rooms of those in division B)
3. $Q_3 = \pi_{Name,Div,Room}\, \sigma_{Room=102}$
   (names and divisions of those in room 102)

Q_1 discloses C, because applying the query $\pi_{Name,Div,Room}$ to the result of Q_1 may yield some tuples in C. Q_2 discloses C in its entirety, because applying the query $\sigma_{Room=103}$ to the result of Q_2 yields all the tuples of C. Q_3 does not disclose any tuples of C because their selection conditions are contradictory.

Notice that a concept protects its tuples, but not its sub-tuples; i.e., a query on a *subset* of the concept's projection attributes does not disclose the concept. On the other hand, a query on a *superset* of the attributes would disclose the concept (unless their selection conditions are contradictory).

As mentioned earlier, disclosure control requires that the number of tuples disclosed from a given concept does not exceed a certain predetermined number. For each concept C we define three integer values called *concept total*, *concept threshold* and *concept counter*, and denoted respectively, N, T and D. N denotes the total number of tuples in the extension of this concept, T denotes the maximal number of tuples that may be disclosed from this concept, and D denotes the number of tuples from this concept that have already been disclosed. If $T \geq N$, then the concept is *unrestricted*; we shall assume that none of the concepts are unrestricted. As queries are processed, the database system must keep track of D to ensure that $D \leq T$. The number of tuples in the extension of a view V will be denoted $\|V\|$; e.g., $\|C\| = N$.

[10] described a quick method that determines whether Q discloses C, and then defines the precise sub-view of C that is disclosed by Q. This method was at the basis of several algorithms for controlling the disclosure of sensitive concepts. The main feature of the solution is that tuples that have already been disclosed are recorded *intensionally* rather than *extensionally*; that is, at each point, view definitions are maintained that describe all the concept tuples that have released to each individual.

---

[2] Note that the resulting selection condition is no longer a simple conjunction.

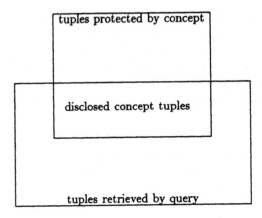

Fig. 2. Disclosure relationships between a query and a concept

3 Attack Strategies

As already noted, an essential principle behind these methods is that a concept protects its tuples, but not its sub-tuples; i.e., a query on a *subset* of the concept's projection attributes is always allowed. The idea is that concepts are designed to protect *minimal associations* of attributes; any lesser associations are assumed to be "harmless". This, however, leaves concepts vulnerable to attacks that attempt to construct additional concept tuples from information that is available freely.

Recall that a concept is a set of projection attributes α and a selection condition ϕ (and α includes the attributes used in ϕ). The obvious way to generate tuples over α that satisfy ϕ is to start with "larger" views, where either the set of attributes contains α and/or the condition does not contradict ϕ, and then use projection and/or selection to generate concept tuples. However, such views are tracked by the algorithms described in [10].

The only other possibility is to generate concept tuples from views in which the set of attributes is *strictly contained* in α and/or the condition *contradicts* ϕ, as such views are not controlled by these algorithms.

Given the sensitive concept

$$C = \textbf{select } \alpha \textbf{ where } \phi$$

two attacks are possible:

1. **Join.** In the join attack two queries are submitted:

$$Q_1 = \textbf{select } \alpha_1 \textbf{ where } \phi_1$$
$$Q_2 = \textbf{select } \alpha_2 \textbf{ where } \phi_2$$

where $\alpha_1 \cup \alpha_2 = \alpha$ and $\alpha_1 \cap \alpha_2$ contains a *key* to C, and ϕ_1 and ϕ_2 are conditions that do not contradict ϕ. Both queries are allowed, because the attribute sets α_1 and α_2 are not protected. Clearly, their natural join $Q_1 \bowtie Q_2$ yields tuples in C.

2. **Complement.** In the complement attack two queries are submitted:

$$Q_1 = \text{select } \alpha' \text{ where } \theta$$
$$Q_2 = \text{select } \alpha \text{ where } \theta \wedge \neg\phi$$

where θ is a condition that is less restrictive than ϕ, and α' is obtained from α, by removing the selection attributes that are no longer necessary, because θ requires less attributes than ϕ. The former query is allowed because α' is not protected; the latter query is allowed because its condition contradicts ϕ. Clearly, their difference $Q_1 - Q_2$ (the complement of Q_2 within Q_1) yields tuples in C.

In both attacks, some additional information was used. In the first attack, it was knowledge of the database scheme and the key attribute. In the second attack, the condition $\neg\phi$ would have to be expressed via specific values that "complement" the values used in ϕ. In both cases, however, the system must assume that such knowledge might be available to the attacker.

As an example, assume the sensitive concept

select *Name* where *Bldg*=1 and *Room*=307

The key to this concept is *Name*.

1. **Join.** Consider the queries

$$Q_1 = \text{select } Name, Tel \text{ where } Bldg=1$$
$$Q_2 = \text{select } Name, Tel \text{ where } Room=307$$

Both would be allowed as neither contains the complete set of the concept's attributes (*Name*, *Bldg*, *Room*). Yet, their natural join "contains" the concept (appropriate selecting and projecting from this join will yield the concept in its entirety).

2. **Complement.** Consider the queries

$$Q_1 = \text{select } Name \text{ where } Bldg=1$$
$$Q_2 = \text{select } Name \text{ where } Bldg=1 \text{ and } Room=305$$
$$Q_3 = \text{select } Name \text{ where } Bldg=1 \text{ and } Room=455$$

The first would be allowed because it does not contain the entire set of the concept's attributes, and the other two because their selection conditions are contradictory with that of the concept. Yet, the difference of the first and the union of the other two corresponds to the concept.

4 Guarding against Attacks

The common element in both attacks was the lack of control over views that ask for a subset of the concept's attributes that contains the key attribute of the concept (Q_1 and Q_2 in the first attack, and Q_1 in the second attack). By extending our control to such views, both kinds of attacks would be foiled.

This extension implies a significant change to the semantics of a sensitive concept: *a concept now protects also all its key projections.* To implement the new semantics, we define a new view relationship.

Let U and V be two views of database scheme R. U *critically overlaps* V, if their selection conditions are not contradictory, and the intersection of their projection attributes contains a *key* of V. When U critically overlaps V, then the extension of U could be processed by a projection that removes the attributes in U but not in V, and possibly generate sub-tuples of tuples in the extension of V, that include its key attribute. The definitions of the restriction $V \mid U$ and the exclusion $V \mid \neg U$ remain unchanged.

We now update the *disclosure* relationship between a query and a concept. Let C be a concept and let Q be a query. Q *discloses* C if Q critically overlaps C. Intuitively, a query discloses a concept if its result could be processed by another query to possibly derive sub-tuples from the protected concept that include its key attribute. The new disclosure relationship between a query and a concept is illustrated schematically in Figure 3.

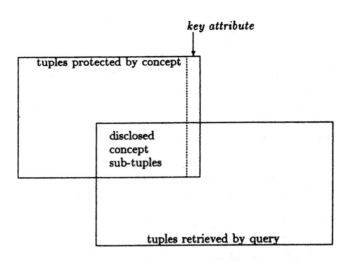

Fig. 3. Disclosure relationships based on critical overlap

By considering queries that target the key of a concept (i.e., critically overlap the concept), as if they "fully" overlap the concept, attacks of the kind described above would be foiled. With this extended definition of disclosure, the earlier disclosure control algorithms are still valid. Figure 4 reproduces such an algorithm.

This algorithm associates with each concept C a *predicate P* that describes the concept tuples that have already been disclosed. P is initialized to *true*. Assume that $Q_1, \ldots, Q_p$ have already been processed when Q_{p+1} is received, and let $\alpha_1, \ldots, \alpha_p$ denote their respective selection conditions. The present value of P would be $\alpha_1 \vee \cdots \vee \alpha_p$. After computing the restriction of C to Q_{p+1} (the tuples in this concept that are disclosed by this query), we exclude from it the view σ_P (the tuples of this concept that have already been disclosed by the previous queries). The tuples in this new query are those that have *not* been delivered already.

The input to this algorithm is a set $C_1, \ldots, C_m$ of protected concepts, each with its associated predicate P_i and counters N_i, T_i and D_i, and the query Q whose selection predicate is α. When it terminates, the value of *permit* indicates whether the answer to Q should be presented to the user or not.

```
Algorithm (disclosure)
permit := true
materialize Q
i := 0
while permit and i < m
do
        i := i + 1
        Mᵢ := 0
        if Q critically overlaps Cᵢ
        then
                Mᵢ := ‖(Cᵢ | Q) | ¬σₚᵢ‖
                if Dᵢ + Mᵢ > Tᵢ
                then
                        permit := false
                        break
                endif
        endif
done
if permit
then
        for i = 1, ... m
        do
                Pᵢ := Pᵢ ∨ α
                Dᵢ := Dᵢ + Mᵢ
        done
endif
```

Fig. 4. Disclosure control algorithm that defeats join and complement attacks

It should be noted that key-containing sub-tuples are counted as if they were full tuples. That is, a query that overlaps a concept and a query that critically overlaps a concept incur the same "cost" to the user, against that concept. However, a user who, in two separate queries, extracts two sub-tuples of the *same* tuple, is only "charged" once!

Note that a query that intersects only with the non-key attributes of a concept, is answered freely, as concepts protect only their key projections. The reason is that such queries cannot be used in any of the attacks described earlier. It should be noted, though, that it might be necessary to consider *near keys* (i.e., concept attributes whose active domains are nearly the size of the concept) as if they were keys.

As an example, consider the previous concept **select** *Name* **where** *Bldg*=1 and *Room*=307, and the join attack and complement attacks specified earlier. In the join attack, both Q_1 and Q_2 critically overlap the concept, and their tuples will be accounted for. Similarly, in the complement attack, Q_2 and Q_3 will be delivered freely, as they do not critically overlap the concept (their selection conditions are contradictory to the concept's), but Q_1, which critically overlaps the concept, will be accounted for. Altogether, these attempts no longer provide any additional opportunities.

5   Immunity to Attacks

In this section we argue that the algorithm presented in Section 4 provides sensitive concepts with immunity to attacks.

Consider a set X of elements and a binary property p, where each $x \in X$ either has or does not have this property p, and assume that we are tasked with finding the subset Y of X of elements that have the property p. It is obvious that Y could be built in only two ways:

1. **Positively**: by starting with $Y = \emptyset$, and then examining every element of X and adding it to Y iff it has p.
2. **Negatively**: by starting with $Y = X$, and then examining every element of X and removing it from Y iff it does not have p.

Transferring this problem to relational databases, we assume a set of unique values, each such value is associated with a non-unique set of values, and an extra value that denotes whether the element has the property. Altogether, an element is now $x = (x_1, \ldots, x_n)$, where x_1 provides the identity of the element (the key), x_n denotes (e.g., using the values 1 and 0) whether the element has the property or not (the condition), and the other values constitute the description of the element. The task is now to isolate elements $x = (x_1, \ldots, x_n)$ such that $x_n = 1$.

In accordance with the previous observation, these elements could be isolated in one of two ways:

1. Positively: $Y = \sigma_{x_n=1}(X)$
2. Negatively: $Y = X - \sigma_{x_n \neq 1}(X)$

Note that the first X in the second formula does not use its x_n values, and the method will still work even when this value is unknown.

Assume now that we are tasked to *prevent* the retrieval of tuples of X that satisfy the condition. Then defeating these two methods of construction is guaranteed to accomplish this task.

Clearly, barring all tuples $(x_1, \ldots, x_n)$, unless they are certain not to satisfy the condition, will defeat both methods of construction, because when X contains only tuples that do not satisfy the condition, both formulas evaluate to the empty set. Thus, to populate the set Y, one needs to construct tuples $(x_1, \ldots, x_n)$ that *might* satisfy the condition.

Intuitively, to populate the set X in the first formula (the positive method) with tuples $(x_1, \ldots, x_n)$ that might satisfy the condition, one may use (1) queries that specify all these attributes (and possibly others) and might satisfy the condition; or (2) queries that specify fewer attributes and might satisfy the condition. Only the former kind of queries was controlled by the earlier model. The latter kind is the source for the join attack. The set X in the first term of the second formula (the negative method) can be populated in similar ways (though x_n need not be retrieved). Once this term is populated, it is combined with the second term to form a complement attack. Hence the two new attack methods, the join and the complement.

Yet, regardless of the specific method, by barring access to any tuple that contains the key x_1, unless it is certain not to satisfy the condition x_n, it is clear that tuples $(x_1, \ldots, x_n)$ that might satisfy the condition would never become available (and Y will remain empty). Queries that contain tuples with the key and might satisfy the condition, were said to critically overlap the concept. This discussion is summarized in the following theorem.

Theorem. Monitoring queries that critically overlap a concept provides complete protection to the concept.

Of course, inference based on other knowledge may still be possible [8], but users will not be able to attack the concept by queries alone.

6 Additional Considerations

6.1 Partial Answers

All our disclosure algorithms behaved similarly, when the size of an answer to a disclosing query exceeds the allotment remaining on a particular concept: such a query is denied in its entirety. This approach maintains the *completeness* of the answers issued; that is, queries are either answered completely, or not answered at all.

At times, it would seem preferable in such situations to deliver the remaining allotment, even if it does not answer the query completely. It should be emphasized that in abandoning completeness, we are violating a basic premise of query answering mechanism, by which all answers must be sound and complete.[3]

Modifying our disclosure algorithms to deliver partial answers is straightforward, though a question that still remains is which tuples to deliver, and whether users should be notified when answers are incomplete.

6.2 Disclosing Key Projections

The enhancements of the controlled disclosure algorithm against attacks offered in Section 4 required new semantics for concepts: concepts protect all their key projections. At times, however, these semantics may be at odds with reality. In our example, consider the sensitive concept select *Name* where *Bldg*=1 and *Room*=307. To protect this concept, in every query that includes *Name*, the number of employees in room 307 of building 1 is noted, and the cumulative number is not allowed to exceed a predetermined threshold. However, this might prove impossible, if, for example, the institution needs to make public its entire list of employees in building 1; i.e., the concept select *Name* where *Bldg*=1. In such a case, the concept becomes vulnerable to complement attacks, via a query on the names of employees in building 1, and queries on the names of employees in building 1 but in rooms other than 307.

Hence, when a key projection of a concept cannot be protected, the concept remains vulnerable to complement attacks. Formally, assume that

$$C = \text{select } \alpha \text{ where } \phi$$

is declared as sensitive, but

$$D = \text{select } \alpha' \text{ where } \theta$$

is disclosed, where θ is a condition that is less restrictive than ϕ, and α' is obtained from α, by removing the selection attributes that are no longer used, because θ requires less attributes than ϕ. In this case D may be combined with the query

$$Q = \text{select } \alpha \text{ where } \theta \wedge \neg\phi$$

to attack C, using the complement strategy $D - Q$.

Our solution in this case is to enlarge the condition of C from ϕ to θ; that is, to replace C with

$$C' = \text{select } \alpha \text{ where } \phi$$

The query Q would then return no tuples, its condition being $\theta \wedge \neg\theta$, and $D - Q$ will return D. In the above example, this would mean changing the sensitive concept to select *Name* where *Bldg*=1.

---

[3] It may be interesting to note, that whereas here we maintain soundness while abandoning completeness, in statistical databases the dual approach has been suggested, in which completeness is maintained while soundness is abandoned. Specifically, complete answers are augmented with fictitious information.

7 Conclusion

In this paper we extended our previous work on the controlled disclosure of sensitive information to foil multi-query attacks, and we argued that the enhanced algorithm prevents any kind of attack on sensitive information. Much work remains to be done and we mention three research problems.

First, we are interested in extending this work to remove the simplifying assumptions that have been made. Chiefly among them are the assumptions of a single relation database, and the limitations on the kind of views that may be used for both concepts and queries.

Second, we have assumed that the databases are "static"; i.e., when considering a sequence of queries by the same user, we assumed that the extensions of concepts do not change via insertions or deletions of tuples. While this may be the nature of statistical databases, a general disclosure control algorithm must account for updates as well (for example, when the tuples previously released are deleted from the database).

This study extended the analysis from sequences of single-query attacks to sequences of multi-query attacks. However, each user continues to maintain an individual "account" with the system. The methods are thus still vulnerable to groups of several users who in collusion aggregate an amount of information that is considered to pose a security risk.

References

1. M. R. Adam and J. C. Wortmann. Security-control methods for statistical databases: a comparative study. *ACM Computing Surveys*, 21(4):515–556, December 1989.
2. J. R. Campbell. A brief database security tutorial. In *Proceedings of 18th National Information System Security Conference* (Baltimore, Maryland, October 10–13), pages 740–757, 1995.
3. D. E. Denning, S. G. Akl, M. Morgenstern, P. G. Neumann, R. R. Schell, and M. Heckman. Views for multilevel database security. In *Proceedings of IEEE Symposium on Security and Privacy,* (Oakland, California), 1986.
4. S. Jajodia. Aggregation and inference problems in multilevel secure systems. In *Proceedings of the 5th Rome Laboratory Data Security Workshop*, 1992.
5. T.Y. Lin. Database, aggregation and security algebra. In *Proceedings of the 4th IFIP Working Conference on Database Security*, September 1990.
6. T.F. Lunt. Aggregation and inference: Facts and fallacies. In *Proceedings of IEEE Symposium on Security and Privacy*, pages 102–109, May 1989.
7. T.F. Lunt and R.A. Whitehurst. The Sea View formal top level specifications. Technical report, Computer Science Laboratory, SRI International, February 1988.
8. D. G. Marks. Inference in MLS databases. *IEEE Transactions on Knowledge and Data Engineering*, 8(1):46–55, February 1996.
9. Z. Michalewicz. Security of a statistical database. In Z. Michalewicz, editor, *Statistical and Scientific Databases*. Ellis Horwood, Chichester, England, 1991.

10. A. Motro, D. G. Marks, and S. Jajodia. Aggregation in relational databases: Controlled disclosure of sensitive information. In *Proceedings of ESORICS-94, Third European Symposium on Research in Computer Security,* (Brighton, UK, November 7-9), Lecture Notes in Computer Science No. 875, pages 431-445. Springer-Verlag, Berlin, Germany, 1994.

11. B. Thuraisingham, editor. *Proceeding of the 3rd RADC Database Security Workshop,* Report MTP 385. Mitre Corp., Bedford, Massachusetts, 1991.

12. J. D. Ullman. *Database and Knowledge-Base Systems, Volume II.* Computer Science Press, Rockville, Maryland, 1989.

Secure Concurrency Control in MLS Databases with Two Versions of Data

Luigi V. Mancini[1] and Indrajit Ray[2]

[1] Dipartimento di Informatica e Scienze dell'Informazione
Università di Genova, Genova, Italy
mancini@disi.unige.it
[2] Center for Secure Information Systems and
Department of Information and Software Systems Engineering
George Mason University, Fairfax, VA 22030
iray@isse.gmu.edu

Abstract. In multilevel secure database systems, higher level transactions are either delayed or aborted when they read lower level data, due to lock conflicts with updating lower level transactions. Multiversion data has been suggested in the literature as a way to prevent lower reading transaction from getting delayed or aborted. In these multiversion protocols transactions that read lower level data are provided older versions of the data and thus low reading and writing operations are allowed to proceed concurrently. However almost all of these algorithms suffer from shortcomings - either they require a potentially unbounded number of versions to be maintained in the system, or they enforce a time limit in which higher level transactions have to complete. Maintaining multiple committed versions adds additional overhead to the system. Moreover, these algorithms always provide older copies of data for reading by higher level transactions which may not be acceptable for certain applications. We propose a secure concurrency control algorithm that is based on a locking strategy and that requires only two versions - one committed and one non-committed version - of data. All read operations, high or low, are performed on the previous committed version while the write operation proceeds on the uncommitted version. Thus no read operation is ever given an outdated copy. Moreover, extra overhead for version management is lesser than the other protocols because almost all transaction management systems maintains a before-image of data for recovery purposes and our scheme takes advantage of this before-image value.

1 Introduction

Transactions are an important programming paradigm for simplifying the development of applications that require concurrent access to shared mutable data. A transaction can be informally defined to be a collection of operations (a program) bracketed by two markers: Begin_Transaction and End_transaction [16]. Transactions provide the ACID properties in a program, which allow the programmer to pay lesser attention to concurrency and failure issues during program development.

While transaction management techniques and algorithms are fairly well understood for traditional database systems, they are much less well understood for multilevel secure (MLS) systems. In these systems, the data and user processes are classified into different (possibly hierarchical) security levels. Access to a data item by a process is allowed only if the access satisfies the following two mandatory access control rules (cf. [3]):

1. a process P can read data item x only if security level of x is lower than or equal to that of P and
2. P can write into x only if x is at the same security level as x.

These restrictions together with the need to avoid *covert timing channels* prevent the lock based concurrency control protocols of classical transaction processing from being used without modification in the MLS environment [5, 15].

A number of secure concurrency control techniques have been proposed in the literature which address the problem of covert timing channels. Some of these works [12, 7] that employ a lock based protocol on single version data, abort a higher level transaction T_i that is reading down, when a lower level updating transaction T_j conflicts with T_i. The drawback of these protocols is that transactions that read down may be subject to starvation. Other works have been proposed that employ time stamp ordering for concurrency control. Amman and Jajodia [2] give two time stamp based algorithms on single version data that yield serializable schedules; however both of them suffer from indefinite delays of higher level transactions.

Some secure versions of commercial database management systems have provided secure concurrency control algorithms; however the algorithms are not always completely satisfactory. For example the algorithm of the Trusted Oracle DBMS [13], based on a combination of two phase locking, timestamp ordering and multiversioning, generate histories that are not always one-copy serializable. As an additional example, Informix-OnLine/Secure DBMS [9, 10] uses an approach in which a low level transaction is granted a write lock on a data item even if a higher level transaction holds a read lock on the same data item. Further the high level transaction is allowed to continue without aborting, thus creating non serializable schedules.

Researchers have also looked into using multiple versions of data for secure concurrency control. In all these works, higher level transactions are given older versions of the data for reading down. Keefe and Tsai [11] propose a scheduler based on multiple versions of data and a priority queue of transactions according to their access classes. This approach is secure and starvation free. However an important drawback of this approach is that a high level transaction is always placed before all active low transactions and as a result it is given much older versions of the low data items than may be acceptable. Moreover maintaining multiple versions of data and accessing them involves additional costs, more so because this method may require a potentially unbounded number of versions.

A second work by Ammann, Jaeckle and Jajodia [1] proposes a concurrency control protocol using two snapshots of the database in addition to the most recently committed version - i.e. three copies of the database. This protocol represents a significant improvement over [11] as it requires a fixed number of versions. The protocol can be naturally implemented using timestamp ordering, although other scheduling algorithms can be used to control the transactions executing at a given security level. However, the algorithm ensures serializability only by enforcing a fixed time limit on each transaction during which the transaction must complete or get aborted.

A more recent work [14] has proposed a locking protocol using two committed versions of data which produces one-copy serializable and strict schedules. In this protocol, higher level transactions read down on an earlier committed version of the data while transactions accessing data at their own level execute on the later committed version. The protocol is free of starvation of higher level transactions because a higher level transaction is never aborted due to a lower level transaction. However, the protocol is too conservative. It imposes a deadline within which transactions must complete if they read data at dominated levels. If they cannot, then such transactions have to be aborted, possibly resulting in indefinite delay of such transactions. Moreover, higher level transactions are always given older versions of the data to read, and this may not be acceptable always.

In this work we propose a lock based secure concurrency control protocol on two versions of data. Unlike [14] we use one committed version of the data and one uncommitted version. Whenever a transaction T_i writes a data item x, it creates a new version of the data. Transactions that read the data item (both higher level transactions and those at the same level as the data item), continue to read the committed version. If a second transaction T_j wants to write x, it has to wait till T_i commits. When T_i commits, the version of x that it wrote, becomes the new committed version. The old committed version is now discarded. Maintaining these two versions of data does not impose any additional cost on the system. A transaction processing system almost always have to maintain a before image information of at least those data items which have been updated by active transactions. This is for recovery purposes in case these updating transactions abort. Using two versions of data for concurrency control thus does not entail any additional cost to data management and hence seems to be useful.

Our locking protocol uses two additional lock modes besides the conventional read and write locks on data items. The current protocol is based on the ideas presented in one of our earlier works [5]. We propose new language primitives which can be used by the sophisticated programmer to support advanced programming paradigms like exception handling, forward recovery and partial rollback within a transaction. Our locking protocol together with these primitives provide secure yet flexible transaction processing in a multilevel secure database system.

The rest of the paper is organized as follows: Section 2 presents the security model for our concurrency control protocol. Section 3 describes the locking protocol while section 4 describes the various locking modes, the lock compatibility matrix and the algorithm for the Lock Manager. Section 5 introduces the language primitives used for transaction processing and gives an algorithm for the transaction manager to implement these primitives. Correctness proof for the locking protocol is provided in Section 6. Finally the paper concludes in Section 7.

2 Security Model

The multi level secure system consists of a set D of data items, a set T of transactions (subjects) which manipulate these data items and a lattice S of security levels, called the *security lattice*, whose elements are ordered by the dominance relation $\preceq$. If two security levels s_i and s_j are ordered in the lattice such that $s_i \preceq s_j$, then s_j *dominates* s_i. A security level s_i is said to be strictly dominated by a security level s_j, denoted as $s_i \prec s_j$ if $s_i \preceq s_j$ and $i \neq j$. Each data item from the set D and every transaction from the set T is assigned a fixed security level.

In order for a transaction T_i to access a data item x, the following two *necessary* conditions must be satisfied:

1. T_i is allowed a read access to data item x only if $L(x) \preceq L(T_i)$. In other words the transaction must be at a security level that dominates the security level of the data item x in order for T_i to read x.
2. T_i is allowed a write access to the data item x only if $L(x) = L(T_i)$. That is, the transaction must be at the same security level as the data item x, if it has to write to x.

Note that the second constraint is the restricted version of the $\star$-property which allows transactions to write to higher levels [3, 6]; the constrained version is desirable for integrity reasons.

3 Overview of the Locking Protocol

We use two versions of the data for transaction processing. Initially all data items in the system has only one version. Transactions that want to read a data item x, reads the only version that is present. When a transaction T_i, wants to write to the data item x, it creates a new version x_i of the data item. Consequently, transaction T_i does not conflict with any other transaction (higher or at the same level) that reads x. If transaction T_j, wants to read x after T_i has written to it but before T_i completes, it reads the older version x of the data item and consequently does not conflict with T_i. One the other hand if T_j wants to write x it has to wait until T_i completes. If the transaction T_i wants to read x after it has created the new version x_i, it reads the version x_i. When T_i completes execution by committing, the old version x is discarded, and all transaction begins accessing the new version x_i. If on the other hand T_i aborts then the version x_i it created, is discarded and transactions continue accessing the old version x.

Note that in the above protocol a read operation on a data item x is allowed to proceed simultaneously with a write on the same data x. The only time this should not be allowed is when the old version of x, that was being used for reading purposes, is discarded and replaced with the latest version. This "version switch" occurs at the commit time of the updating transaction; thus the commit of the updating transaction should be delayed till such time when there is no transaction reading x. However, we cannot delay the commit of the updating transaction if there is a higher level transaction that is reading x. Doing so opens up the same timing covert channel that we have been trying to avoid.

To do all this, the update transaction T_i converts its write locks to *certify* locks - locks that conflicts with both read and write lock - after the last write operation. Since the certify lock conflicts with both read and write locks, this process of upgrading has to wait till such time as conflicting read locks on same data items have been released. The conversion of write locks to certify locks is allowed to proceed even if there are higher level transactions with read lock on lower level data that has been written by the update transaction (We should point out here that to read a lower level data, a higher level transaction acquires a different kind of read lock on the data; we call these locks, signal locks to differentiate from the conventional read locks. Signal locks have different properties than ordinary read locks. We discuss this in more details in the next section.) Finally, note that the upgrading process does not have to wait for conflicting write locks of different update transactions at the same level as such locks cannot exist during the lock conversion time.

To prevent the lock conversion from waiting on high transactions, we adopt the notion of *signals* proposed in [5]. If a write lock on a data item x is converted to a certify lock even when there are high level transactions with lower level read locks (read signal locks) on x, a lock exception arises; the high level transactions with low read locks on x are notified of the lock exceptions by the Lock Manager. The latter sends *signals* to the respective high level transactions to achieve this. Before the high level transactions commit they have to handle all accumulated lock exceptions. We call this process of handling lock exceptions as *servicing signals*.

A high level transaction can service a signal in a number of ways. It can choose to ignore the signal; it can choose to abort if a signal comes. The former way of handling signals result in non-serializable histories, while the latter guarantees serializability but may result in starvation of the higher level transaction. The higher level transaction may opt for servicing the signal in more sophisticated ways than these two. These include performing partial or complete rollback of the transaction with re-execution, or performing some kind of a forward recovery (like re-reading the lower level data and continuing with the execution). Rollback with re-execution guarantees serializability whereas forward recovery achieves weaker notions of correctness which may be useful depending on the application. In our model we allow the sophisticated programmer to decide how a higher level transaction should service signals (if and when required). However, since such a decision affects correctness, the naive programmer is limited to the default behavior that guarantees serializability.

In the following section we describe the different lock modes that we employ and the locking protocol. This is followed by a description of the Lock Manager.

4 Secure Two-version Two Phase Locking Protocol

To support secure concurrency control on two-version data, we extend the conventional two-phase locking protocol to employ four different lock modes. A transaction T_i is required to lock a data item in the proper mode prior to accessing it. The different lock modes are:

Read Lock If T_i wants to read a data item x, at the same security level as T_i, it has to acquire a *read lock* on x.

Signal Lock If T_i wants to read a data item x, at a security level lower than itself, it has to acquire a *signal lock* on x .

Write Lock If T_i wants to write to data item x, which is at its own security level, it has to acquire a *write lock* on x.

Certify Lock When T_i has acquired the last write lock and before it commits, it has to convert all its write locks into *certify locks*.

The lock compatibility matrix given in figure 1 determines how the Lock Manager satisfies lock request by a transaction when there is a lock already in place on the same data item. A "yes" in a cell [i,j] of the lock matrix implies that the requested lock i does not *conflict* with the already granted lock j; a "no" implies that the lock i does conflict with lock j.

Referring to the compatibility matrix we find that a read lock or a signal lock does not conflict with a write lock on the same data item whereas a write lock does conflict with another write lock on the same data item. A read lock conflicts with a certify lock. So does a write lock. Signal locks on the other hand may or may not conflict with certify locks, depending on which is granted first. If a signal lock is requested by a higher level transaction T_i on a lower level data item x, and there is no certify lock already on x, the signal lock is granted; if on the other hand a lower level transaction T_j already has a certify lock on x, T_i has either to wait for T_j to release the certify lock or get aborted. Conversely however, if the lower level transaction T_j requests a certify lock on x when the higher level transaction T_i has a signal lock on x, the certify lock is granted. Such a strategy is necessary because we cannot delay or abort a lower level transaction due to a higher level transaction without opening up a covert channel.

A transaction T_i can write a data item x at its own security level, provided that there is no uncommitted transaction in the system T_j, such that $L(T_j) = L(T_i)$ and T_j writes to x. At some point in the execution of T_i, after it has completed all its write operations but before it commits, the transaction manager (TM) for T_i attempts to convert all the write locks acquired by T_i, into certify locks. This conversion takes place only if no other transaction T_j, at the same level as T_i, holds a read lock on x. Note that at this point T_j cannot be holding a write lock, and hence a certify lock, on x.

Requested \ Granted	Read	Write	Signal	Certify
Read	Yes	Yes	Yes	No
Write	Yes	No	Yes	No
Signal	Yes	Yes	Yes	No
Certify	No	No	Yes	No

Yes = Lock is granted

No = Lock is not granted

Fig. 1. Lock Compatibility Matrix for Two Version Data

The Lock Manager allows the conversion of the write lock to a certify lock even if a higher level transaction T_k holds a signal lock on x. The high level transaction T_k receives a *signal* from the Lock Manager, that identifies the data item x as one with a newer value. As mentioned in Section 3 this signal needs to be *handled* properly before T_k commits. Note that the transaction T_k can receive more than one signal, one corresponding to each of the low data items that T_k has read, and all these signals have to be serviced before T_k can commit. To guarantee serializability, T_k has to perform a *rollback* (partial or complete) and re-execute (some or all) steps. However, our model also allows T_k to abort (serializability guaranteed), or do some *forward recovery* (serializability may not be guaranteed but may produce useful consistency results suitable for the application). The transaction programmer is empowered with making the choice. Using the transaction primitives that we have defined, the transaction programmer can specify within the body of the transaction T_k one or more pieces of code on what to do if such signals need to be serviced. Further, if the programmer is not sure about how to handle these signals, the system implements the default behavior which achieves serializability.

```
LockManager()
loop
Receive(TMₗ,Tᵢ,op,x,mode);
case mode do
    Read / Write / Certify:
        If L(TMₗ) ≠ L(Tᵢ) ≠ L(x) then
            Send(TMₗ,Tᵢ,"lock-illegal");
    Signal:
        If L(TMₗ) ≠ L(Tᵢ) OR L(Tᵢ) ≺ L(x)
            Send(TMₗ,Tᵢ,"lock-illegal");
endcase
case op do
    Lock:
        if mode ≠ Certify then
            If mode does not conflict with other locks that are already set on x
                then SetLock(Tᵢ,x,mode);
                    Send(TMₗ,Tᵢ,"lock-granted");
            else Delay(Tᵢ,x,mode);
        else
            let x₁ ... xₙ be the data items locked in
                write mode by Tᵢ
            for each xᵢ do
                if there is no Tₖ with a read lock on xᵢ then
                    for each Tⱼ that has a signal lock on xᵢ do
                        notify the transaction manager for Tⱼ of a
                            new value for xᵢ;
                else Delay(Tᵢ,xᵢ,Certify);
            Send(TMₗ,Tᵢ,"lock-granted");
    Unlock:
        ReleaseLock(Tᵢ,x,mode);
        Send(TMₗ,Tᵢ,"unlock-ok");
        If there is some transaction Tₖ that had previously
            requested a lock of mode mₖ on x, but was not granted the lock,
            then awake Tₖ;
        SetLock(Tₖ,x,mₖ);
        Send(TM_{L(Tₖ)},Tₖ,"lock-granted");
endcase
forever
```

Fig. 2. Lock Manager Module

4.1 The Lock Manager

The Lock Manager component in our model is made trusted. Its duties are summarized by the algorithm in Figure 2. There is one transaction manager at each security level which is untrusted. The transaction manager at security level l sends a request of the form $(Sender, T_i, op, data - id, mode)$ to the lock manager. Here $Sender$ is the identity of the transaction manager sending the request, T_i is the identifier of the transaction requiring the operation, op is the type of operation (i.e., lock or unlock) requested on the data item $data$-id and $mode$ is the particular lock mode requested. Before setting any lock, the Lock Manager checks if the security level of the transaction manager requesting the operation and the transaction named in the request are same and compatible with the lock mode requested for the data item named.

Delay(T,x,$mode$)	puts the transaction T in waiting for a lock of type $mode$
Receive($From$,T,op,x,$mode$)	returns a operation request from the transaction manager $From$; the operation is op on data x with mode $mode$
Send(To,T,$response$)	sends $response$ to transaction manager To for transaction T
SetLock(T,x,$mode$)	adds to the lock table for transaction T a lock entry of type $mode$ for data x
ReleaseLock(T,x,$mode$)	removes from T's lock table the entry corresponding to the lock of mode $mode$ on x

Fig. 3. Notations used in Figure 2

5 Language Support for Transaction Processing

To support our locking protocol we propose a set of new language primitives. These primitives offer power and flexibility to the experienced programmer to improve performance. At the same time the primitives export a default interface of the locking protocol to the naive programmer so that consistency is guaranteed. Transaction processing is achieved in our model by ten system primitives. Of these, the six basic primitives - Begin_Transaction, End_Transaction, Commit, Abort, Read and Write - or their equivalent are available in almost all transaction processing systems. In addition, we introduce four new primitives. They are:
sl = SaveWork();

Rollback(sl);

Certify;

GetSignal [$sl_1 \rightarrow handler_1$] ... [$sl_n \rightarrow handler_n$];

Among these newly introduced primitives, the first two or their equivalent are available in quite a few sophisticated transactional systems [8]; however their semantics are not exactly the same. All of these primitives can be invoked by the programmer from within a transaction. In addition the programmer has access to the system variable, rollbackCount, that is associated with each instance of a transaction in execution. This variable cannot be modified by the programmer.

Any piece of program code that is bracketed by the basic primitives Begin_Transaction and End_Transaction is termed a transaction and inherits the ACID property of a transaction. The transaction execution is then coordinated by a Transaction Manager (TM) at the security level of the transaction. When the TM executes a Begin_Transaction call corresponding to a transaction T_i, it establishes the local environment for the transaction. This involves initializing all local variables that are used by T_i, including the system variable rollbackCount, initializing a *local instruction list* LW_i, for T_i - which is similar to a transaction log except that it keeps track of all instructions executed by T_i including reads - initializing a second queue for T_i - the signal queue SQ_i to store signals received by T_i -, establishing the default *savepoint* for T_i (the notion of savepoints is explained a little later) and finally appending a start-transaction record to the global transaction log at its security level. After this the TM returns a transaction identifier for T_i to the system and begin execution of the transaction by scheduling its operations.

The End_Transaction primitive signifies the completion (after commit or abort) of the transaction T_i. The transaction manager for T_i, TM, releases all system resources that T_i acquired during its execution and then forgets about T_i. Note that the End_Transaction system call must be preceded by a Commit or Abort primitive. The Commit primitive commits the transaction T_i by writing a commit record in the transaction log. TM, on executing this primitive, makes all of T_i's updates permanent. The Abort primitive on the other hand aborts the transaction T_i and TM discards all of T_i changes to the database. The Read and Write primitives perform the main database item access operation.

The SaveWork() system primitive establishes a savepoint [8] which causes the system to record the current state of processing. Each transaction manager writes a savepoint record on the transaction log, while the run-time support of the programming language saves the current values of any local variables on the volatile memory. SaveWork call returns to the transaction T_i a handle in the form of the identifier sl (called a *signal label*) which can subsequently be used to refer to that savepoint. The transaction can reestablish (return to) any savepoint by invoking a RollBack command and passing to it the signal label of the savepoint that it wants to be restored. Savepoints established at partially consistent states of the application can be used as internal restarts points when problems are encountered subsequently. Depending on the application logic, the transaction programmer can decide to return to the most recent savepoint or to any other savepoint. Note that each savepoint established by a transaction is local to only that transaction.

The RollBack(sl) primitive takes as parameter a signal label sl and restores the state of the system to the state that existed at the time of the establishment of the savepoint sl. The transaction then restarts its execution from the step following the sl = SaveWork() step. More formally, the result of the RollBack(sl) command is the execution of a series of $undo(op_i)$ operations, the *duals* of the operations op_i. The transaction manager performs a rollback by reading the transaction's local instruction list backwards (most-recent-first order). For each operation op_i that precedes RollBack(sl) and up to the command SaveWork() corresponding to the signal label sl (but excluding the SaveWork() command), an $undo(op_i)$ is executed. The effect of an *undo* operation is to release any lock that op_i acquired on a data object, and remove the result of op_i from the system, as if op_i was never executed. Consequently, the data items as well as the local program variables are restored to the state at the savepoint sl. Once that state has been restored, the RollBack(sl) call terminates. The transaction is now ready to re-execute starting from the operation that follows the SaveWork() command. Note that if there is a conditional branching command between the sl = SaveWork() step and the RollBack(sl) step, then a different set of commands may be executed during the re-execution time, than was executed initially before the rollback.

The Certify command is executed by a transaction T_i after it has acquired its last write lock. On execution of this command, the transaction manager sends out a certify lock request for each write lock of T_i. If there is no read lock on the write locked data item x_k, the Lock Manager converts the write lock to certify lock, else delays the lock conversion. The Lock Manager then considers the data items x_k on which T_i holds certify locks, and checks if there is any higher level transaction T_j, not yet committed, that holds a signal lock on x_k. If such a transaction T_j exists, the Lock Manager signals the transaction manager for T_j. When all such higher level transaction managers have been notified, the Lock Manager acknowledges the transaction manager for T_i.

When the transaction manager TM' for the higher level transaction T_j gets signals from the Lock Manager, it locates the savepoint which immediately precedes the read of the data item identified by the signal. For example, if the signal indicates a new value for the data item x, then the signal label sl_j corresponding to the savepoint before the operation $r_j[x]$ is chosen. In this case we say that the signal label sl_j covers the data item x. TM' then associates this signal label with the signal and queues up the signal together with the signal label. Eventually when T_j executes a GetSignal call, TM' services all the signals queued up for T_j. The way to service the signals is specified as a program code in the GetSignal call.

The GetSignal call has two exit points: a standard one which is the next instruction after the GetSignal step and an exceptional continuation which is represented by the expression

$$[sl_1 \rightarrow handler_1], \ldots, [sl_n \rightarrow handler_n]$$

Each sl_i represents a signal label and the corresponding handler represents the code to be executed for this signal label (or to be precise for the signal that corresponds to this signal label).

If there are no signals to be serviced when the GetSignal primitive is executed, the primitive returns with a nil value and the computation continues from the next instruction (i.e. the standard continuation is followed). On the other hand if there is any signal the exceptional continuation is followed. In such a case, suppose the signal is for a low data x. Then the signal label sl_x that covers x in the transaction is passed to the GetSignal primitive and the exceptional continuation represented by the handler $sl_x \rightarrow handler_x$ (if any in the body of the GetSignal) is executed. If there is no such handler the standard continuation is followed. If the handler contains a Rollback(sl_x) call, then the state changes produced after the savepoint sl_x are undone and the transaction is re-executed starting from sl_x. If there are multiple signals to be serviced TM' considers all the signals it has buffered for T_j, and selects one signal to be serviced as follows: It selects the signal label that covers all data items that have been signaled. (i.e., the signal label that precedes all other signal labels that are generated due to "overridden" signal locks).

The default invocation for GetSignal is GetSignal[→ rollback] without specifying any signal label. When any signal is received this default GetSignal rollbacks the transaction T_j to the savepoint immediately preceding the oldest read operation among all the low reads performed by T_j, that need to be redone owing to updates by low transactions. If no savepoint has been explicitly established in the transaction then it rollbacks to the default savepoint coinciding with the Begin_Transaction. It should be noted that the GetSignal call is non-blocking, i.e. the call does not wait for the arrival of a signal. If a signal is already available, it is serviced, otherwise no action is taken.

5.1 Transaction Manager Module

We employ a transaction manager for each security level. The transaction manager for security level l is responsible for the proper execution of the transactions at its level. Whenever a transaction manager receives a transaction T_i, it initiates two concurrent threads the TransactionRunTimeSupport$_i$ and the SignalReceiver$_i$. The former thread is responsible for executing the operations of the transaction while the latter thread is responsible for managing the signals received by the transaction manager from the Lock Manager corresponding to T_i. For each active transaction T_i the transaction manager maintains two queues SQ_i (the signal queue) and LW_i (the operation queue). Figure 4 gives the algorithm for the transaction manager. The transaction manager also have several other submodules (for example for recovery purposes etc.) which we do not consider in the figure.

6 Correctness of the Locking Algorithm

To guarantee consistency, the transaction programmer has to implement a *well-formed transaction*. A transaction is well-formed in our model if it satisfies the following criteria:

1. The transaction acquires an appropriate lock on a data item before accessing it.
2. The transaction eventually releases all locks that it acquired before it completes.
3. The transaction cannot acquire a lock after it has released any lock unless the release of locks occur due to the execution of a RollBack primitive.
4. The transaction executes a Certify command after its last write operation.
5. The transaction executes a GetSignal command after the last operation that required it to acquire any lock, Moreover, the execution of the GetSignal primitive should follow the execution of the Certify command.
6. The GetSignal call should contain a handler for any signal that may be potentially be returned and each handler should specify a RollBack to the appropriate signal label. In short the handler should be $sl_x →$ RollBack(sl_x) and all low read data items should be covered.

TransactionManager$_l$()
```
/* h is a translation function that converts the read / write */
/* operations on a data items into operations on the appropriate */
/* version of the data item *
for each active transaction T_i at level l do
create queue SQ_i; /* queue for signals for Lock Manager */
create queue LW_i; /* queue for operations executed by T_i */
  .
  .
  .
cobegin
  .
  .
  .
thread TransactionRunTimeSupport_i()
    AppendToQueue(LW_i,CurrentInstruction);
    case CurrentInstruction of
        Begin_Transaction:
            perform initialization function and
            establish the default savepoint;
        End_Transaction:
            free resources assigned for T_i and exit
        Read(x):
            if L(x) = L(T_i) then
                if h(r(x)) = r(x_i) then
                    /* reading the version it has written */
                    /* which is already write locked */
                    execute read[x_i]
                else                    /* reading a version x_j */
                    wait(LockManager,T_i,lock,x,read)
                    /* wait till read lock is granted */
                    execute read[x_j] /* read an old version */
                else                    /* lower level read */
                    wait(LockManager,T_i,lock,x,signal)
                    execute read[x_j]
        Write(x):
            wait(LockManager,T_i,lock,x,write)
            execute write[x_i] /* create a new version */          SaveWork:
            sl_x ← system generated unique savepoint identifier
            AppendToQueue(LW_i,sl_x)
            return(sl_x)
        RollBack(sl_x):
            rollback transaction up to the savepoint denoted by sl_x in LW_i
        Certify:
            let y_1 ... y_n be the data items
            write locked by T_i
            for each y_i do
                wait(LockManager,T_i,lock,y_i,certify)
        GetSignal:
            AppendToQueue(SQ_i,GetSignalMark)
                /* put a marker in the queue SQ_i to indicate */
                /* that only those signals in the queue before */
                /* and up to the marker will be serviced */
                find the oldest low read operation read[x] from
                    the queue SQ_i among all the signaled low
                    read operations.
                choose the signal label sl_x immediately preceding
                    read[x] in LW_i
                execute handler code corresponding to sl_x
```

Fig. 4. Transaction Manager Module (continued on next page)

```
        Commit:
            for all data items yᵢ written by Tᵢ
                discard old version yⱼ
                make new version yᵢ the only version
            endfor
            for all data items zᵢ locked by Tᵢ
                wait(LockManager,Tᵢ,unlock,zᵢ,mode)
        Abort:
            for all data items yᵢ written by Tᵢ
                discard new version yᵢ
            for all data items zᵢ locked by Tᵢ
                wait(LockManager,Tᵢ,unlock,zᵢ,mode)
    endcase
    ⋮

thread SignalReceiverᵢ()
    loop
        receive a signal from Lock Manager corresponding to
            a low read data item x
        AppendToQueue(SQᵢ,x)
    forever
    ⋮

coend
    ⋮

endfor
```

Fig. 4. Transaction Manager Module (continued from previous page)

AppendToQueue($Queue - name, Item$)	Insert $Item$ at the end of the queue $Queue$
Wait(LockManager,$T_i,op,x,op - mode$)	Send a message to LockManager. The message includes the transaction identifier T_i of the current transaction, the operation op requested of the LockManager, the identifier of the data item x on which to perform the operation and the operation mode $op - mode$

Fig. 5. Notations used in Figure 4

Note that the naive programmer can be spared the burden of ensuring a well-formed transaction by making the execution of the Certify and GetSignal commands in the required order, a part of the commit operation and by letting the invocation of the GetSignal command be the default invocation.

In the following we prove that a multilevel two-version data history consisting of well-formed transactions is serializable. To do this we follow the approach of [4] i.e., show that the serialization graph for the two-version data history is acyclic.

The interleaving of a set of transactions when they execute concurrently is modeled by a *history* [4]. A history consisting of transactions at different security levels is called a *multilevel history*. In the following discussions we will be using the term history to refer to a multilevel history. Also we will use the following notations:

- The read of a data item x by a transaction T_i is given as $r_i[x]$. The corresponding write operation is given by $w_i[x]$.
- The Certify command in transaction T_i is given as ct_i and the GetSignal command is denoted by gs_i. If the GetSignal command returns a signal label sl_x, it is denoted as $gs_i(sl_x)$. If a GetSignal call does not return any signal, this is designated as $gs_i(nil)$
- The Commit operation is denoted by c_i.

A read operation presented to the scheduler is converted by a suitable *translation function*, h, into a read operation on an appropriate version of the data item. More precisely the translation function h is such that

1. $h(w_i[x]) = w_i[x_i]$
2. if $w_i[x] <_i r_i[x]$ then $h(r_i[x]) = r_i[x_i]$
3. if $w_i[x] \notin T_i$ or $r_i[x] <_i w_i[x]$ then $h(r_i[x]) = r_i[x_j]$ for some j.

We define a *complete two version history* as follows:

Definition 1. A *complete two-version (2V) history* H over a set of transactions $T = \{T_1, \ldots, T_n\}$ is a partial order with ordering relation $<_H$ where

1. $H = h(\cup_{i=1}^n T_i)$ for some translation function h;
2. $<_H \supseteq \cup_i^n <_i$;
3. for each T_i and all operations p_i, q_i if $p_i <_i q_i$, then $h(p_i) <_H h(q_i)$;
4. for any two conflicting operations $p,q \in H$, either $p <_H q$ or vice versa.
5. if $h(r_j[x]) = r_j[x_i]$, then $w_i[x_i] <_H r_j[x_i]$;
6. if $w_i[x] <_i r_i[x]$, then $h(r_i[x]) = r_i[x_i]$ and
7. if $h(r_j[x]) = r_j[x_i]$, $i \neq j$, and $c_j \in H$, then $c_i <_H c_j$.

Henceforth by a two-version history we will assume a complete two-version history. Some more definitions required for our proof follows:

Definition 2. A 2V history H over a set of transactions $T = \{T_1, \ldots, T_n\}$ is *serial* if H is a totally ordered 2V history such that for any pair of transactions T_i, $T_j \in T$, either all of T_i's operations precede all of T_j's, or vice versa.

Definition 3. Given a two-version history H over a set of transactions T, transaction $T_i \in T$ *reads-x-from* transaction $T_j \in T$ if $r_i[x_j] \in H$.

Definition 4. A serial 2V history H is *one-copy serial* if whenever T_i reads-x-from T_j, either $i = j$ or T_j is the last transaction preceding T_i in H, that writes into x.

Note that a serial 2V history H_s can never contain a GetSignal such that the GetSignal generates a rollback computation. This is solely because there is no interleaving of the transactions in the history. In other words only $gs(nil)$ can be in H_s. However, in general, 2V histories may contain such GetSignal operations as generating rollback computations. Consequently, it is not appropriate to proclaim the equivalence of a 2V history with any serial 2V history. On the other hand, a rollback computation in effect does not modify the file system. This leads us to the notion of a *rollback-free projection* of a 2V history H. Informally, given a 2V history H, the rollback-free projection of H is the 2V history obtained from H by deleting all the operations that were undone due to the rollback command.

Definition 5. The *rollback-free projection* $R(H)$ of a 2V history H is a restriction of the partial order $(H, <_H)$, such that

1. $R(H) \in H$, that is, the operations in $R(H)$ are from the set of operations in H and operate on the same versions of data items;
2. if op_i, $sw_i(sl)$ and $rb_i(sl) \in H$ such that $sw_i(sl) <_H op_i <_H rb_i(sl)$, then both $rb_i(sl), op_i \notin R(H)$;
3. any $op_i \in H$ not excluded by 2 above is included in $R(H)$;
4. for all $op_i, op_j \in R(H)$, $op_i <_{R(H)} op_j$ iff $op_i <_H op_j$.

Definition 6. Two 2V histories H and H' are said to be *equivalent* and denoted by $H \equiv H'$, if

1. H and H' are over the same set of transactions T ;
2. both H and H' have the same set of operations and
3. H and H' have the same reads-from relationships.

Definition 7. A 2V history H over a set of transactions T is *one-copy serializable* if there exists a one copy serial 2V history H' over T, such that H' is equivalent to the rollback free projection $R(H)$ of H.

Definition 8. Given a 2V history H over a set of transactions T, if x is a data item operated upon by one or more transactions in T, then a *version order* for x is a total order for all versions of x in H. The version order is denoted by $\ll$ and if version x_i of x precedes version x_j in the version order, we write $x_i \ll x_j$.

Definition 9. Suppose that $R(H)$ is the rollback free projection of a 2V history H, over a set of transaction T and that there is some version order $\ll$ for each item x operated on by transaction $T_i \in T$. A two-version serialization graph for $R(H)$ *2VSG(R(H))* is a directed graph such that

- Nodes of *2VSG(R(H))* are transactions in T.
- There is directed edge $T_i \to T_j$, $i \neq j$, in *2VSG(R(H))* whenever $r_j[x_i] \in R(H)$.
- For each $r_k[x_j]$ and $w_i[x_i]$ in $R(H)$, there is a *version-order edge* $T_i \to T_j$ if $x_i \ll x_j$; otherwise there is a version order edge $T_k \to T_i$.

With the above definitions of a version order and 2V serialization graph, it can be readily shown as in [4] that

Theorem 10. *If $R(H)$, the rollback free projection of a 2V history, H over a set of transaction T, has an acyclic 2V serialization graph 2VSG(R(H)), then $R(H)$ is one-copy serializable and so is H.*

Before we show the correctness of our locking protocol, we summarize the properties of 2V histories consisting of well-formed transactions.

1. For every $T_i \in R(H)$, the Certify operation of T_i, ct_i, follows all of T_i's write operations and precedes T_i's commit.
2. For every $T_i \in R(H)$ the GetSignal operation, gs_i, follows the last lock operation of T_i and precedes T_i's commit. Also gs_i follows ct_i.
3. For every $r_k[x_j]$ in $R(H)$, if $j \neq k$, then $c_j <_{R(H)} r_k[x_j]$; otherwise $w_k[x_k] <_{R(H} r_k[x_k]$.
4. For every $w_k[x_k]$ and $r_k[x_j] \in R(H)$, if $w_k[x_k] <_{R(H)} r_k[x_j]$, then $j = k$.
5. If $r_k[x_j]$ and $w_i[x_i]$ are in $R(H)$, then either $ct_i <_{R(H)} r_k[x_j] <_{R(H)} gs_j$ or $r_k[x_j] <_R (H) gs_j <_R (H) ct_i$. The reason for this property is as follows. Each transaction T_i that writes x must obtain a certify lock on x before it commits. Consequently, for each transaction T_k, at the same security level s as T_i that reads x, either T_i must delay its certification until T_k has been certified, or else T_k must wait till such time as T_i has released its Certify lock on x before it can set its read lock on x. If T_k is at a security level s' higher than that of T_i, then there is no need for T_i to delay its certification. Rather, T_k is signaled and it has to re-acquire a Signal lock on x to re-read x. Note that by the lock-compatibility matrix of 1 T_k has to wait for such time as T_i has released the Certify lock on x, to re-acquire a Signal lock on x.
6. For every $w_i[x_i]$ and $w_j[x_j]$, either $ct_i <_{R(H)} ct_j$ or $ct_j <_{R(H)} ct_i$. In other words the certification of every two transactions that write the same data item are atomic with respect to each other.

Lemma 11. *For every $r_k[x_j]$ and $w_i[x_i]$, where i,j and k are all distinct, if $ct_i <_{R(H)} r_k[x_j]$, then $ct_i <_{R(H)} ct_j$ else if $r_k[x_j] <_{R(H)} ct_i$, then $ct_k <_{R(H)} ct_i$.*

Proof. Since both transactions T_i and T_j write to the same data item x, they have to be at the same security level s (say). With transaction T_k then there can be two cases viz: security label s' of T_k is strictly higher than those of T_i or T_j, i.e. $s \prec s'$ or security level of T_k is the same as those of T_i or T_j, i.e., $s' = s$. We will consider each of these cases in turn:

1. $\underline{s' = s}$ Since $r_k[x_j] \in R(H)$ we must have $c_j <_{R(H)} r_k[x_j]$. Also since T_k reads-x-from T_j, T_j must have been the last transaction before T_k that writes to x. Hence if T_i is to write to x, (judging by $w_i[x_i] \in R(H)$), then either $w_i[x_i] <_{R(H)} w_j[x_j] <_{R(H)} r_k[x_j]$ or $r_k[x_j] <_{R(H)} w_i[x_i]$. Now,
   (a) if $ct_i <_{R(H)} r_k[x_j]$, this means that $w_i[x_i] <_{R(H)} w_j[x_j] <_{R(H)} r_k[x_j]$. Hence from the properties of histories of well-formed transactions we have $ct_i <_{R(H)} ct_j$, else
   (b) if $r_k[x_j] <_{R(H)} ct_i$, then T_i can have a Certify lock on x only after T_k have released the read lock on x. Thus $c_k <_{R(H)} ct_i$ (because T_k releases its read lock at commit time and $ct_k <_{R(H)} c_k$) and hence $ct_k <_{R(H)} ct_i$.
2. $\underline{s \prec s'}$ As in the previous case T_k reads-x-from T_k and we can have either $w_i[x_i] <_{R(H)} w_j[x_j] <_{R(H)} r_k[x_j]$ or $r_k[x_j] <_{R(H)} w_i[x_i]$. Now,

(a) if $ct_i <_{R(H)} r_k[x_j]$, then reasoning as in item 1(a) above we have $ct_i <_{R(H)} ct_j$, else

(b) if $r_k[x_j] <_{R(H)} ct_i$, then if T_k is not yet committed when T_i issues a Certify command, $r_k[x_j]$ will be undone and has to be redone. In order for T_k to redo the read of x, it has to acquire a Signal lock on x, and this can be done only after T_i has committed. This reasoning leads us to conclude if $r_k[x_j] \in R(H)$, then T_k must commit before T_i issues the certify command otherwise at best we can have $r_k[x_i] \in R(H)$. Hence $ct_k <_{R(H)} ct_i$.

Hence the proof.

Lemma 12. *Given two well-formed transactions T_i and T_j, if there is an edge $T_i \to T_j$ in $2VSG(R(H))$ then $gs_i <_{R(H)} gs_j$.*

Proof. The edge $T_i \to T_j$ occurs in $R(H)$ in two ways viz.:

1. if T_j reads-x-from T_i, i.e., $r_j[x_i] \in R(H)$
2. if $r_k[x_j]$ and $w_i[x_i]$ are in $R(H)$ and $x_i \ll x_j$.

Note that if the edge $T_i \to T_j$ exists in $R(H)$ owing to reason (1) above, then T_j cannot be at a security level lower than T_i. It can only be at a equal or higher security level. T_i and T_j cannot be at incomparable security level because of the fact that they both operate on the same data item x and T_i's operation is a write.

1. If T_i and T_j are at the same security level, then the read operation $r_j[x_i]$ has to be delayed till after the Certify lock held on x by T_i has been released, i.e., till after the commit of T_i. Also since each transaction is well formed we have $r_j[x_i] <_{R(H)} gs_j$. Thus we have $ct_i <_{R(H)} gs_i <_{R(H)} c_i <_{R(H)} r_j[x_i] <_{R(H)} gs_j$.
2. If T_j is at a security level higher than that of T_i the same reasoning as the above holds.

On the other hand if the edge $T_i \to T_j$ is a version order edge which occurs due to some other transaction T_k, then T_i and T_j have to be at the same security level (they both write to x), and T_k can either be at the same security level as either T_i or T_j or has to be at a higher security level.

1. If T_k is at the same security level as either T_i or T_j then from lemma 11 we must have either $ct_i <_{R(H)} ct_j$ or $ct_k <_{R(H)} ct_i$. Now since $x_i \ll x_j$ and $r_k[x_j] \in R(H)$ we cannot have $ct_k <_{R(H)} ct_i$. Again since T_i and T_j both write to x, one of them can issue a Certify command only after the commit of the other. Thus owing to these two reasons we must have the following $ct_i <_{R(H)} gs_i <_{R(H)} c_i <_{R(H)} ct_j <_{R(H)} gs_j <_{R(H)} c_j$.
2. If T_k is at a higher security level than both T_i and T_j then also the same reasoning as in above holds

Thus finally we have $gs_i <_{R(H)} gs_j$.

Theorem 13. *A 2V history consisting solely of well-formed transactions is one-copy serializable (1SR).*

Proof. By definition of one-copy serializable histories, the rollback-free projection $R(H)$ of the history H need only be considered. We will show that the serialization graph for $R(H)$, $2VSG(R(H))$ does not contain any cycle.

By lemma 12 we have already shown that the edges in $2VSG(R(H))$ are in GetSignal order, i.e., if $T_i \to T_j$ in $2VSG(R(H))$, then $gs_i <_{R(H)} gs_j$. If $2VSG(R(H))$ is to contain a cycle of the form $T_1 \to T_2 \to \ldots \to T_n \to T_1$, then we must have $gs_1 <_{R(H)} gs_2 <_{R(H)} \cdots <_{R(H)} gs_{n-1} <_{R(H)} gs_n <_{R(H)} gs_1$.

Clearly this is a contradiction.

That is $2VSG(R(H))$ is acyclic and hence our proof.

7 Conclusions

We have proposed a secure lock based concurrency control protocol that uses two versions of the data - one a committed version while the other a non-committed version. All read operations proceed on the committed version while the write operation proceeds on the uncommitted version.

Almost all transaction processing mechanisms maintain before image information (i.e. the last committed version) of at least those data items which have been updated by active transactions (i.e. the current non-committed version) for recovery purposes in case these updating transactions abort. Thus using these two versions of data for concurrency control does not entail any additional cost to data management and hence seems to be useful. Version management is thus cheaper than that in [11] or [1]. Moreover unlike [1] or [14] we do not impose any deadline within which transactions must complete if they read data at dominated levels. Last but not the least, as all read operations - high or low - are performed on the most recent committed version, none is ever given an outdated copy (as in some of the multi-version protocols).

The advanced transaction mechanism that we have proposed allows the sophisticated programmer to have more control over the concurrency control protocol. With the help of our transaction control primitives the advanced programmer can incorporate advanced programming paradigms like exception handling, partial rollback and forward recovery within the transaction framework. This enables him to achieve correctness criteria less stringent than serializability if a particular application allows it while at the same time guarantee serializability if so required.

References

1. P. Ammann, F. Jaeckle, and S. Jajodia. Concurrency Control in Secure Multi-Level Databases Via a Two-Snapshot Algorithm. *Journal of Computer Security*, 3(3):87–113, 1995.

2. P. Ammann and S. Jajodia. A Timestamp Ordering Algorithm for Secure, Single-Version Multilevel Databases. In C. E. Landwehr, editor, *Database Security, V: Status and Prospects*, pages 191–202. Elsevier Science Publishers B. V. (North-Holland), 1992.

3. D.E. Bell and L.J. LaPadula. Secure computer systems: Unified exposition and multics interpretation,. Technical Report MTR-2997, The Mitre Corp., Burlington Road, Bedford, MA 01730, USA, March 1976.

4. P. A. Bernstein, V. Hadzilacos, and N. Goodman. *Concurrency Control and Recovery in Database Systems*. Addison-Wesley Publishing Company, Reading, MA, 1987.

5. E. Bertino, S. Jajodia, L. V. Mancini, and I. Ray. Advanced Transaction Processing in Multilevel Secure File Stores. *IEEE Transactions on Knowledge and Data Engineering*, 1996. To appear.

6. D. E. Denning. *Cryptography and Data Security*. Addison-Wesley, Reading, MA, 1982.

7. A.R. Downing, I.B. Greenberg, and T.F. Lunt. Issues in Distributed Database Security. In *Proceedings of the Fifth Annual Computer Security Applications Conference*, pages 196–203, Tucson, AZ., December 1989.

8. J. Gray and A. Reuter. *Transaction Processing: Concepts and Tecniques*. Morgan Kaufmann Publishers, San Francisco, CA, 1993.

9. Informix Software, Inc., Menlo Park, CA. *Informix-Online/Secure Administrator's Guide*, April 1993.

10. Informix Software, Inc., Menlo Park, CA. *Informix-Online/Secure Security Features User's Guide*, April 1993.

11. T. F. Keefe and W. T. Tsai. Multiversion Concurrency Control for Multilevel Secure Database Systems. In *Proceedings of the IEEE Symposium on Research in Security and Privacy*, pages 369–383, Oakland, California, May 1990.

12. J. McDermott and S. Jajodia. Orange Locking: Channel-Free Database Concurrency Control Via Locking. In B.M. Thuraisingham and C.E. Landwehr, editors, *Database Security, VI: Status and Prospects*, pages 267–284. Elsevier Science Publishers B.V. (North Holland), Amsterdam, 1993.

13. Oracle Corp., Redwood City, CA. *Trusted Oracle Administrator's Guide*, 1992.

14. S. Pal. A Locking Protocol for Multilevel Secure Databases using Two Committed Versions. In *Proceedings of the 10th. Annual Conference on Computer Assurance, COMPASS 95*, pages 197–210, June 1995.

15. I. Ray, E. Bertino, S. Jajodia, and L. V. Mancini. An Advanced Commit Protocol for MLS Distributed Database Systems. In *Proceedings of 3rd ACM Conference on Computer and Communications Security*, New Delhi, India, March 1996.

16. A.Z. Spector. Distributed Transaction Processing Facilities. In Sape Mullender, editor, *Distributed Systems*, pages 191–214. ACM Press Frontier Series, Addison-Wesley Publishing Company, 1989.

Panel session: **Authors' Rights and Copyright protection**

Panelists: Gerard Eizenberg (ONERA-CERT)
Dominique Gonthier (European Commission)
Alistair Kelman (Copyright Barrister)
Jean-Jacques Quisquater (UCL)

The potential world-wide distribution of electronic documents through networks is generating both commercial enthusiasm and anxiety. Aiming wide markets, the authors, producers, publishers and distributors are concerned with fair payments for their contributions.

There are various reasons to restrict the distribution of the electronic works. First, quite different customs and legal contexts exist, even within Europe. A wide dialogue and some harmonisation are requested to make possible the distribution of works. The intensity of present diplomatic initiatives related to that issue is well known. Second, the existence of cost effective technical solutions is not sufficient: the legal acceptance to use and trade them is necessary. With respect to cryptology, this condition is not yet easy to satisfy. Third, appropriate technology must be developed.

The new technology must satisfy many challenging requirements, including:

- the availability of efficient digital payment systems,
- to control the copies of electronic documents, while making their usages convenient and consistent with widespread equipments (the end-user is not always trusted to respect the copy restrictions),
- to avoid the flood of proprietary solutions that could not interoperate
- to respect all the Authors' Rights.

The panelists come from quite different areas, but all these areas are strongly involved in the protection of the Authors' Rights and of the Copyright: the Law and legal context, the European Commission policy and Computer Security. As a framework of the panel session, here are some questions submitted to the panelists and to the attendance:

- Applications of the Computer and Communication Security (CCS) Technology in the Electronic Copyright Management Systems (ECMS): requested security properties, relative importance, examples,
- Give the existing CCS technology appropriate answers to the requirements? If not, are there questions specifically addressed to the searchers in CCS?
- Borders between ECMS and digital payment systems,
- Interoperability of the ECMSs,
- Main existing initiatives in the ECMS area.

The attendance is invited to widen that list and the answers.

Modelling a Public-Key Infrastructure

Ueli Maurer[1]

Department of Computer Science
Swiss Federal Institute of Technology (ETH)
CH-8092 Zürich, Switzerland

Abstract. A global public-key infrastructure (PKI), components of which are emerging in the near future, is a prerequisite for security in distributed systems and for electronic commerce. The purpose of this paper is to propose an approach to modelling and reasoning about a PKI from a user Alice's point of view. Her view, from which she draws conclusions about the authenticity of other entities' public keys and possibly about the trustworthiness of other entities, consists of statements about which public keys she believes to be authentic and which entities she believes to be trustworthy, as well as a collection of certificates and recommendations obtained or retrieved from the PKI. The model takes into account recommendations for the trustworthiness of entities. Furthermore, it includes confidence values for statements and can exploit arbitrary certification structures containing multiple intersecting certification paths to achieve a higher confidence value than for any single certification path. Confidence values are measured on a continuous scale between 0 and 1 and, in contrast to previous work in this area, are interpreted as probabilities in a well-defined random experiment.

Key words. Distributed system security, key management, public-key certification, cryptography, trust, recommendations, probabilistic logic.

1 Introduction

A global public-key infrastructure (PKI) is a prerequisite for security in large networks and distributed systems, and for electronic commerce. While the basic mechanism of public-key certification is well-understood, the problem of building a large distributed PKI is not. The purpose of this paper is to complement previous work on practical ad-hoc approaches to building a PKI by suggesting a precise model of a user's view of a PKI.

In our context, a PKI consists of the entire, generally heterogeneous, set of components that can be involved in issuing, storing, and/or distributing certificates. A PKI can be seen as a distributed database of public-key certificates and further information (e.g. revocation lists, recommendations, etc.). It provides

---

[1] E-mail: maurer@inf.ethz.ch
WWW: http://www.inf.ethz.ch/department/TI/um/group.html

mechanisms for entities to retrieve and possibly also to add information to the PKI. Typically, an entity Alice can retrieve another entity Bob's public key together with evidence of its authenticity. On the other hand, a user can possibly also contribute to building the infrastructure by certifying other entities' public keys or by issuing recommendations. Such certificates and recommendations can be used by entities who trust Alice but are useless for other entities.

In this paper we are not concerned with distributed database and software aspects of a PKI, i.e., we do not consider the problem of how a user Alice can obtain the necessary certificates to authenticate another user Bob's public key. We rather analyse what kind of procedure Alice could use for deriving conclusions, once she has obtained the necessary information. Of course, these two phases need not be independent; Alice (or her system) may initiate a second phase of collecting evidence when realizing that it needs more information for deriving a certain conclusion. In an implementation, collecting evidence can be based on a number of different mechanisms: accessing an official certificate service, retrieval from the certificate databases distributed over the Internet, or an automated negotiation process between Alice's and Bob's systems by which Bob's system provides the necessary certificates or links to certificates needed by Alice's system.

Whether given information constitutes sufficient evidence for Alice for the authenticity of Bob's public key depends on various parameters to be set by Alice, including her assumptions about the trustworthiness of certificate-issuing entities, the authenticity of certain public keys stored in her own data base, and the security requirements of the particular application in which the public key is going to be used.

In a simple model of public-key certification, a user Alice uses a path (or chain) of certificates where each public key is certified by the previous entity in the path, and where she has specified the first public key as authentic and all intermediate entities as trustworthy. Such a simple model can be insufficient for various reasons. First, in a realistic scenario, it should be possible to assign confidence parameters[1] (for instance between 0 and 1) to statements about authenticity and trust. Second, it should be possible to take into account multiple certification paths which, in general, are not independent but can rather be intersecting paths in a possibly complex directed acyclic graph of certificates. Third, trust is often based on recommendations. For instance, Alice may trust an entity T she does not know because it has been recommended as trustworthy by one or several other entities that Alice trusts.

In our model, conclusions about whether a given public key is sufficiently authenticated to be used in a particular application, are derived from Alice's view. Her view consists of statements about which public keys she believes initially to be authentic and which entities she believes initially to be trustworthy, and a collection of certificates and recommendations obtained or retrieved from the PKI. The model takes into account confidence values for statements

---

[1] We use the term confidence parameter and confidence value when it is assigned by the entities or derived within the model, respectively.

and can exploit arbitrary certification structures containing multiple intersecting certification paths in order to achieve a higher confidence value than for any single certification path. Confidence values are measured on a continuous scale between 0 and 1 and are interpreted as probabilities in a well-defined random experiment. One of the contributions of the paper is the possibility for integrating recommendations into the model and for reasoning about trust.

The paper draws its motivation from various sources, including Phil Zimmermann's Pretty Good Privacy (PGP) software [27] and previous work on public-key management [26],[1],[3],[19],[6],[18],[2],[25].

There seems to be an inherent trade-off between the efficiency of an implementation of a model on one hand, and the expressive power of the model and the precision of the semantics on the other hand. One particular problem encountered in the literature is that ad-hoc rules for calculating a confidence value from other confidence values are based on probability-theoretic arguments, despite the fact that no random experiment can be specified in which these probabilities are well-defined.

The emphasis of this paper is on precision rather than efficiency. In order to be used efficiently in a large PKI the model might have to be simplified accordingly. A second restriction of our model is that certificate revocation is not yet included. The solution of both these problems is the subject of future research.

The paper is organised as follows. In Section 2 we discuss various aspects of public-key certification, trust, recommendations and the problems involved in defining a model for a public-key infrastructure. Section 3 presents a deterministic model without confidence values, and this model is extended in Section 4 to a probabilistic model incorporating confidence values which are interpreted as probabilities of events in a random experiment. In Section 5 a few open problems and directions for future research are mentioned.

2 Preliminaries

2.1 Cryptography

Cryptographic techniques (e.g., see [21]), in particular public-key cryptosystems and digital signature schemes [7],[20], are of fundamental importance in distributed systems security and electronic commerce. Two typical applications are key management (e.g., the generation of a secret key shared by two entities not sharing a secret key initially, which can be used to set up a secure connection between them) and the generation and verification of digital signatures, for instance on a digital contract, a purchase order, or an email message.

One of the major advantages of public-key cryptographic techniques, compared to conventional cryptographic techniques, is their asymmetry: while only an entity knowing an appropriate secret key can perform a certain operation (e.g. decrypt or sign a message), everyone knowing the corresponding public key can perform a corresponding operation (e.g. encrypt a message or verify a signature).

A public key of an entity or user Bob[2] is completely useless for a user (say Alice) unless she can convince herself that it is authentic, i.e., that it was indeed generated by Bob and therefore that only he knows the corresponding secret key. One of the major problems in public-key management is therefore to provide mechanisms allowing an entity to obtain or retrieve another entity's public key together with evidence of its authenticity.

The authenticity of a public key can either be verified by invoking a non-cryptographic authentication mechanism, for instance by exchanging a hash value of the public key over the phone (assuming that the speaker can be identified on the phone), or by using public-key certificates described in the following section.

2.2 Public-key certification

A public-key certificate is a digital signature, issued by an entity or authority, for a message stating that a certain public key belongs to a certain entity[3]. Alice can use a certificate issued by an entity X for user Bob if and only if the following two conditions are satisfied:

1. Alice knows the public key of X (for verifying the certificate) and is convinced of its *authenticity*.
2. Alice *trusts* X to be honest and to correctly authenticate the owner of a public key before signing it.

If Alice does not know an authentic copy of X's public key, the first condition can be satisfied by using a certificate for X's public key issued by another entity Y. This process can be iterated, thus making use of a chain of certificates. However, Alice can use such a chain of certificates if and only if she trusts every entity in the chain between her and Bob [14].[4]

Public-key certification can be organised in a number of different ways. Among the proposed structures are hierarchical or semi-hierarchical ones (e.g. CCITT X.509 [28], Privacy Enhanced Mail [29]) and distributed approaches as suggested by Phil Zimmermann [27].[5] Various types of certification structures are emerging independently. They will coexist and together form a global PKI. Government organisations will install a mostly hierarchical infrastructure as a service to the society, large organisations will typically build their own hierarchical infrastructure within the organisation, business communities (e.g. the

---

[2] In this paper we will most often refer to the users Alice and Bob, but the reader should keep in mind that they need not be persons. Their role could be played by an arbitrary entity, for example a server, an application programs, an IP-layer encryption mechanism, a trusted component of an operating system, or a personal token like a chipcard.

[3] A certificate generally contains further information, for instance the date of signing, the expiration date, or the application context for which it is valid.

[4] In PGP, such intermediate entities trusted by Alice are called introducers.

[5] We refer to [23] for a discussion of public-key certification in the context of network security.

banking world) can build a structure for use between organisations of that community, and individual people may become part of a global web according to Zimmermann's "grass roots" approach in which each person takes a share of the responsibility. A given user or system can retrieve, use and combine certificates from arbitrary substructures.

One can expect the growth of a global PKI in the near future, in which arbitrary entities can issue certificates, resulting in a web of certificates that can be represented as a directed graph whose vertices are the entities and where an edge from X to Y means that X has certified Y's public key. It can be expected that some if not most public keys will be certified by several certification authorities and/or users, hence allowing users to select the certificate(s) most suited for their purpose. In consequence, such a web of certificates is likely to be a very large and highly distributed information system.

2.3   Trust and recommendations

Propagating authenticity of public keys by certificates is quite straight-forward. In contrast, it is less obvious how trust should be established and propagated, i.e., how a "web of trust" should be created.[6]

In most previously proposed approaches, including PGP, the propagation of trust is not considered within the model. In PGP, for example, a user can specify which users he or she trusts but the system does not derive any conclusions about the trustworthiness of entities. Such decisions are left completely to the users and are hence dealt with outside of the model.

Recommendations are of fundamental importance in our society because it is impossible to know personally all the people one has to rely on. Such recommendations can be implicit or explicit. The fact that one generally trusts a policeman is an example of an implicit recommendation while a letter of recommendation for a job application is explicit. Yahalom et al. [26] have proposed a public-key management model which includes explicit recommendations. This model was extended in [1]. The model proposed in this paper extends the previous work on explicit recommendations.

A recommendation can be thought of as a signed statement about the trustworthiness of another entity and is similar to a certificate. In contrast to certificates, recommendations can be sensitive information and should sometimes be treated confidentially. This is one of the reasons why PGP does not make use of recommendations. However, confidentiality of recommendations can be implemented by proper encryption and access control mechanisms and is not considered further in this paper.

Including recommendations in public-key certification does not imply that a user loses control over which recommendations can securely be used in her context. To the contrary, a user can specify precisely a policy according to which recommendation are to be used.

---

[6] In the literature, the term "web of trust" is often somewhat misleadingly used to refer to a web of certificates.

Recommendations are more complicated than certificates. There exist several levels of trust and recommendations in the context of public-key certification. A recommendation of the first level is for someone to be trustworthy for the certification of public keys. A recommendation of the second level is for an entity to be trustworthy in recommending other entities for certification. Generally, a recommendation of the i-th level is for an entity to be trustworthy in giving recommendations of level $i-1$. In a certain sense, a certificate can be interpreted as a special type of recommendation of level 0.

Trust is a resource that fades out very quickly along a path of recommendations. A reasonable system would therefore probably use only a small number of levels of recommendations.

2.4 Confidence valuation and using multiple certification paths

No authentication process is perfect, and nobody is completely trustworthy. As pointed out by Phil Zimmermann in [27], trust in a person can range from marginal to fully trusted, and in fact all intermediate degrees of trust are possible. Similarly, the security of an authentication procedure can range from marginal to fully secure. It is therefore natural to increase the confidence in the authenticity of a public key by verifying several different certificate chains for the same public key (see also [1]). Similarly, several independent recommendations can be combined to obtain a stronger combined recommendation. One way of using confidence parameters is for implementing gradual expiration of certificates, by letting the confidence parameter decrease with time.

In order to be able to combine and exploit several independent certification paths or recommendations it is necessary to measure confidence.[7] It appears natural to use a scale from 0 to 1, where 0 stands for no confidence and 1 stands for complete confidence, and to interpret these values as probabilities. However, defining such a random experiment is non-trivial because all the confidence parameters must be interpreted as probabilities of well-defined events of the *same* random experiment. Otherwise, the meaning of probabilities is undefined. For previously proposed approaches (e.g. [1],[27]) no such random experiment can be defined.

Combining the confidence values of independent parallel certification paths into a higher confidence value for the authenticity of the certified public key could perhaps appear to be quite straight-forward [1]. However, certification graphs are generally more complex because the individual paths intersect. This problem is addressed in Section 4 where the probabilistic model is introduced.

2.5 Dependencies between parameters

One of the major problems in reasoning with uncertain information are dependencies between different pieces of input information. There are two types of

---

[7] For example, PGP allows the assignment of a confidence parameter to the trustworthiness of an introducer, but it does not consider confidence parameters for the authenticity of public keys. The scale for measuring trust contains four possible values: unknown, marginally trusted, fully trusted, and ultimately trusted.

dependencies to be considered in a PKI. Structural dependencies were mentioned in the previous section. For example, if two different certification paths contain the same certificate, then they are obviously not independent. A PKI model must take into account that when this certificate is false for some reason, then both certification paths fail simultaneously.

The second type of dependency are correlations between entities and is more difficult to capture in a model. For example, if two entities belong to the same organisation, their trustworthiness may not be independent. In consequence, two disjoint certification paths each containing one of these entities are not independent. One of the major problems with modelling such dependencies is that, in its most general form, the size of a specification of dependencies is exponential in the number of entities. Therefore every scenario considered in practice is bound to be a special case of some type. Nevertheless, our model allows in principle to take into account arbitrary dependencies.

2.6 Security policies

One can distinguish between (at least) two types of security policies that can be involved in distributed system security: (1) policies that specify how entities and organisations should behave when participating in the development of the PKI and (2) the individual users' policies used for deriving conclusions from the available information.

Several policies of the first type can coexist. Such a policy could specify how confidence parameters should be assigned to certificates and recommendations. For example, it could state that authentication based on speaker identification on a telephone line should be assigned a confidence parameter of at most 0.95 whereas authentication based on the verification of a passport could be assigned an arbitrary confidence level.

A user's security policy (second type) could specify the required confidence levels for certain actions and could specify a maximal confidence level (e.g. 0.9) to be used with recommendations. For example, Alice might be satisfied with a confidence value of 0.3 for verifying Bob's invitation to his birthday party, but she would probably require a very high confidence value for the authenticity of the public key she uses for checking the signature on an important digital contract.

2.7 Requirements for a model of a public-key infrastructure

Three goals of defining a model of a public-key infrastructure are:

- to provide a framework (syntax) for expressing statements and security policies.
- to give precise meaning (semantics) to parameters.
- to provide rules and procedures for analysing a particular scenario and for deriving conclusions.

Some of the requirements for such a model are listed below.

- *Generality and expressive power.* The model should capture all aspects of public-key certification, including trust, recommendations, confidence values for trust and authenticity of public keys, multiple certification paths, the revocation of public keys, and dependencies between parameters.
- *Precise Semantics.* The parameters of the model should have a clear interpretation. In particular, when probabilities are used, it should be possible to interpret all confidence values as probabilities of events in a single (overall) random experiment.
- *Evaluation order independence.* The derived conclusions should be independent of the order in which rules are applied or, at least, the order of applying rules should be uniquely specified. Certification or recommendation cycles should not lead to instable feedback in the application of evaluation rules.
- *Efficient implementation.* The model should be suitable for an efficient implementation, i.e., the algorithms for deriving conclusions should be efficient.
- *Scalability.* It should be possible to treat entity populations of arbitrary size, to easily update the parameters when new entities are included in a view, and to implement policies of significant complexity.
- *Easy usability.* The specification of the parameters should be intuitive and the model should be easy to work with.

Clearly, some of these requirements are conflicting. In particular, expressive power and generality are in conflict with efficient implementation and easy usability. It appears impossible to satisfy both types of requirements perfectly, and the focus of Section 4 of this paper is biased towards generality and expressive power. Any completely general model will probably have to be simplified to be used in practice, but such a simplification should be made in full awareness of the restrictions it implies on the general model.

3   A deterministic model for public-key certification, trust and recommendations

We briefly sketch the basic ideas behind our deterministic model that is based on a special type of logic. The syntax is very simple: the propositions or formulas (referred to as *statements* in our context) are simple expressions that take one of four different forms (see Definition 3.1). For example, $Aut_{A,B}$ denotes the statement that, from A(lice)'s point of view, her copy of Bob's public key is authentic. The syntax contains no Boolean operators ($\land$, $\lor$, $\neg$) or quantifiers ($\exists$, $\forall$).

The semantics is based on two inference rules (for authenticity and trust) for deriving statements from sets of statements. The axioms are a set of statements (certificates, recommendations and initial authenticity and trust assignments) considered true by Alice, and the set of axioms is called Alice's initial view. In contrast to classical propositional logic [16], the truth values assigned to statements are not true and false, but *valid* and *invalid*. A statement is valid (in Alice's view) if and only if it can be derived from the axioms (her initial view). An invalid statement is not necessarily false (in a normal sense), but if it is true, then Alice has no evidence of this fact. Alice's derived view is the set of statements derivable from the axioms.

Before defining the model more formally, let us review Alice's procedure for establishing the authenticity of (say) Bob's public key, i.e., the validity of the statement $Aut_{A,B}$. Alice builds her initial view (the set of axioms) by collecting statements that can be relevant in the context of authenticating Bob's public key. There are two categories of statements, namely those provided by other entities (by making them accessible through the PKI) and retrieved by Alice from the PKI[8] (certificates and recommendations), and those specified by Alice as part of her belief (authenticity of certain public keys, trust in certain entities). Each of these categories consists of two types of statements, one referring to the authenticity of public keys and one referring to the trustworthiness of entities, resulting in a total number of four types of statements.

Such statements will in figures be depicted as edges (solid or dashed) in a directed graph in which the vertices correspond to entities. The graph represents the web of certificates, trust and recommendations available to Alice. Authenticity and certificates are represented by solid edges and trust and recommendations by dashed edges. There are several levels of trust and recommendations (as explained in Section 2.3 and below), and dashed edges are labelled with the corresponding level. This is summarised in Definitions 3.1 and 3.2.

Definition 3.1. *Statements* are of one of the following forms:

- *Authenticity of public keys.* $Aut_{A,X}$ denotes Alice's belief that a particular public key P_X is authentic (i.e., belongs to entity X) and is represented graphically as an edge from A to X: $A \longrightarrow X$.
- *Trust.* $Trust_{A,X,1}$ denotes Alice's belief that a particular entity X is trustworthy for issuing certificates. Similarly, her belief that X is trustworthy for issuing recommendations of level $i-1$ is denoted by $Trust_{A,X,i}$. The symbol is a dashed edge from A to X labelled with the trust level: $A \dashrightarrow^{i} X$.
- *Certificates.* $Cert_{X,Y}$ denotes the fact that Alice holds a certificate for Y's public key (allegedly)[9] issued and signed by entity X. The symbol is an edge from X to Y: $X \longrightarrow Y$.
- *Recommendations.* $Rec_{X,Y,i}$ denotes the fact that Alice holds a recommendation of level i for entity Y (allegedly) issued and signed by entity X. The symbol is a dashed edge from X to Y labelled with i: $X \dashrightarrow^{i} Y$.

Alice's *initial view*, denoted $View_A$, is a set of statements.

As the symbols suggest, authenticity could be interpreted as a special type of certification (i.e., signed by Alice's own secret key which is ultimately trusted).

---

[8] By "retrieving from the PKI" we mean any method of obtaining certificates or recommendations, for instance by accessing a certificate server or by asking the owner of a certificate to provide it.

[9] We use the word "alleged" because without verification, there exists no evidence that the certificate was indeed issued by the claimed entity.

Similarly, trust could be interpreted as a special type of recommendation signed by Alice (see also remark 3 at the end of this section). We will not use this simplified notation.

Let us now describe the inference rules of our model, i.e., what it means to derive statements from other statements. The conclusions derived by Alice within the model are statements of one of the first two types of Definition 3.1. In all our examples, the ultimate goal will be to derive the statement $Aut_{A,B}$, namely that in Alice's view her copy of Bob's public key is authentic.

Definition 3.2. A statement is *valid* if and only if it is either contained in $View_A$ or if it can be derived from $View_A$ by applications of the following two inference rules:

$$\forall X,Y: \quad Aut_{A,X},\ Trust_{A,X,1},\ Cert_{X,Y} \vdash Aut_{A,Y} \tag{1}$$

and

$$\forall X,Y,i \geq 1: \quad Aut_{A,X},\ Trust_{A,X,i+1},\ Rec_{X,Y,i} \vdash Trust_{A,Y,i}. \tag{2}$$

For a finite set S of statements, $\overline{S}$ denotes the closure of S under applications of the inference rules (1) and (2), i.e., the set of statements derivable from S. Alice's *derived view* is the set $\overline{View_A}$ of statement derivable from her initial view $View_A$. A statement S is hence valid if and only if $S \in \overline{View_A}$, and invalid otherwise.

The first rule is for deriving statements about the authenticity of public keys. It states that Alice can derive the authenticity of a certified public key for user Y (denoted $Aut_{A,Y}$) if for some entity X who has certified Y's public key (denoted $Cert_{X,Y}$) she can derive the authenticity of X's public key (denoted $Aut_{A,X}$) and trust of level 1 into entity X (denoted $Trust_{A,X,1}$).

The second rule is for deriving statements about trust. It states that for all $i \geq 1$, if Alice has trust of level $i+1$ in X (denoted $Trust_{A,X,i+1}$) then she accepts a recommendation from X of level i for another entity Y (denoted $Rec_{X,Y,i}$), provided that she believes that her copy of X's public key is authentic (denoted $Aut_{A,X}$).

We will assume throughout the paper that trust and recommendations of level i imply trust and recommendations of lower levels, i.e.,

$$\forall X,Y,1 \leq k < i: \quad Trust_{A,X,i} \vdash Trust_{A,X,k} \tag{3}$$

and

$$\forall X,Y,1 \leq k < i: \quad Rec_{X,Y,i} \vdash Rec_{X,Y,k}. \tag{4}$$

These rules, which are not part of the model, appear to be intuitive, but they are not essential for the model. For instance, it seems to make no sense to specify trust of levels 1 and 3 (but not 2) in a certain entity.

Note that an initial view $View_A$ need not necessarily be minimal in the sense that a statement S cannot be derived from the remaining set of statements, $View_A - \{S\}$. We now explain the model by a number of simple examples.

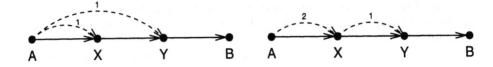

Figure 1.

Example 3.3. Consider a chain of certificates shown in Figure 1 (left). Alice has specified her copy of X's public key as authentic ($Aut_{A,X}$). Her view also contains two certificates: a certificate for Y (allegedly) issued by X ($Cert_{X,Y}$) and a certificate for B allegedly issued by Y ($Cert_{Y,B}$). Furthermore, Alice trusts both X and Y to correctly certify public keys. More formally, we have

$$View_A = \{Aut_{A,X},\ Cert_{X,Y},\ Cert_{Y,B},\ Trust_{A,X,1},\ Trust_{A,Y,1}\}$$

and the statement $Aut_{A,B}$ can be derived by two applications of rule (1):

$$Aut_{A,X},\ Trust_{A,X,1},\ Cert_{X,Y} \vdash Aut_{A,Y}$$
$$Aut_{A,Y},\ Trust_{A,Y,1},\ Cert_{Y,B} \vdash Aut_{A,B}.$$

Hence we have

$$\overline{View_A} = View_A \cup \{Aut_{A,Y},\ Aut_{A,B}\}.$$

Example 3.4. The scenario of Figure 1 (right) shows the same chains of certificates, but Alice does not trust Y initially. However, she trusts X of level 2 ($Trust_{A,X,2}$) and is hence willing to accept recommendations of the first level from X. The statement $Aut_{A,B}$ can be derived in a similar way as described in Example 3.3, but the statement $Trust_{A,Y,1}$ is not contained in Alice's view and must therefore be derived:

$$Aut_{A,X},\ Trust_{A,X,2},\ Rec_{X,Y,1} \vdash Trust_{A,Y,1}$$
$$Aut_{A,X},\ Trust_{A,X,1},\ Cert_{X,Y} \vdash Aut_{A,Y}$$
$$Aut_{A,Y},\ Trust_{A,Y,1},\ Cert_{Y,B} \vdash Aut_{A,B}$$

Example 3.5. A slightly more complicated scenario is shown in Figure 2 (left). The derivation of $Aut_{A,B}$ is achieved by the following steps:

$$Aut_{A,X},\ Trust_{A,X,1},\ Cert_{X,Y} \vdash Aut_{A,Y}$$
$$Aut_{A,X},\ Trust_{A,X,1},\ Cert_{X,Z} \vdash Aut_{A,Z}$$
$$Aut_{A,W},\ Trust_{A,W,3},\ Rec_{W,Z,2} \vdash Trust_{A,Z,2}$$
$$Aut_{A,Z},\ Trust_{A,Z,2},\ Rec_{Z,Y,1} \vdash Trust_{A,Y,1}$$
$$Aut_{A,Y},\ Trust_{A,Y,1},\ Cert_{Y,B} \vdash Aut_{A,B}$$

In this example we have

$$View_A = \{Aut_{A,X},\ Aut_{A,W},\ Cert_{X,Y},\ Cert_{X,Z},\ Cert_{Y,B},\ Trust_{A,X,1},$$
$$Trust_{A,W,3},\ Rec_{W,Z,2},\ Rec_{Z,Y,1}\}$$

and

$$\overline{View_A} = View_A \cup \{Aut_{A,Y},\ Aut_{A,Z},\ Aut_{A,B},\ Trust_{A,Z,2},\ Trust_{A,Y,1}\}.$$

In general, the derived view $\overline{View_A}$ contains more statements than necessary for deriving $Aut_{A,B}$. Hence it is often unnecessary to determine $\overline{View_A}$ completely.

The previous example illustrates that recommendations and certificates can be issued independently. An entity can even recommend an entity whose public key it does not know. For example, W has issued a recommendation for Z without certifying Z's public key. While issuing a certificate requires an authenticated copy of the public key to be certified, a recommendation can be issued without prior exchange of information with the entity that is being recommended.

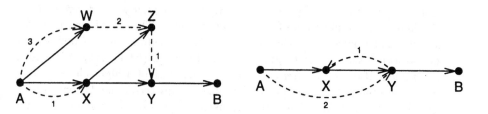

Figure 2.

Example 3.6. Consider the simple scenario of Figure 2 (right). Alice has trust of level 2 in Y and Y has issued a recommendation for X. It may appear that Alice can make use of this recommendation to use the certificate $Cert_{X,Y}$ for deriving $Aut_{A,Y}$. However, the derivation of $Aut_{A,Y}$ should be impossible because if X is dishonest (which is consistent with Alice's view), he can generate fake certificates $Cert_{X,Y}$ and $Cert_{Y,B}$ and a fake recommendation $Rec_{Y,X,1}$ without Y being involved or aware of the attack. The reader can verify that indeed neither the statement $Aut_{A,Y}$ nor the statement $Aut_{A,B}$ can be derived from

$$View_A = \{Aut_{A,X},\ Cert_{X,Y},\ Cert_{Y,B},\ Trust_{A,Y,2},\ Rec_{Y,X,1},\}$$

and in fact we have $\overline{View_A} = View_A$.

In a typical application, if $Aut_{A,B}$ cannot be derived, Alice (or her system) could try to enlarge the initial view $View_A$ by retrieving more certificates and recommendations from the PKI, by specifying further entities as trustworthy, and/or by directly authenticating some of the public keys (e.g. by checking a hashed value of the public key during a telephone call).

In a model without recommendations (e.g. PGP), and hence assuming that (1) is the only inference rule, a result of [3], [14] and [19] can be restated as follows. The proof is straight-forward and is omitted.

Theorem 3.7. *If Alice's initial view ($View_A$) contains no recommendations, then $Aut_{A,B}$ can be derived if and only if there exists a complete chain of certificates from Alice to Bob and Alice trusts every intermediate entity with respect to certification. Formally, we have $Aut_{A,B} \in \overline{View_A}$ if and only if either $Aut_{A,B} \in View_A$ or for some $k \geq 1$ there exist $X_1, \ldots, X_k$ such that $View_A$ contains Aut_{A,X_1}, $Cert_{X_j,X_{j+1}}$ for $j = 1, \ldots, k-1$, $Cert_{X_k,B}$ and $Trust_{A,X_j,1}$ for $j = 1, \ldots, k$.*

Remarks.

1. Entities should not certify public keys whose authenticity was derived within the model (by application of the inference rules). This could lead to undesirable hidden effects for other entities if the individual entities' policies are not known. Assume for example that in Figure 1 (left) entity X's level-1 recommendation for Y ($Rec_{X,Y,1}$) is a consequence of a higher-level recommendation but that Alice's policy is to discard any recommendations of level greater than 1. If Alice knew that X used a high-level recommendation for deriving $Rec_{X,Y,1}$, Alice would have to discard this statement.

2. The above notation could be simplified by the syntactic conventions that authenticity is equivalent to trust of level 0 and that the certification of a public key corresponds to a recommendation of level 0. Together with the simplification mentioned earlier, one could summarise the four types of statements into one category of statements denoted by $S_{X,Y,i}$, where $S_{A,X,0}$, $S_{A,X,i}$, $S_{X,Y,0}$ and $S_{X,Y,i}$ stand for $Aut_{A,X}$, $Trust_{A,X,i}$, $Cert_{X,Y}$ and $Rec_{X,Y,i}$, respectively, for all $i \geq 1$. For such a simplified notation the two rules (1) and (2) can be summarised in a single inference rule:

$$\forall X, Y, i \geq 0: \quad S_{A,X,0}, \; S_{A,X,i+1}, \; S_{X,Y,i} \vdash S_{A,Y,i}$$

3. A number of approaches based on logic for reasoning about security have previously been proposed [4],[10],[24],[5], but they are not directly applicable in our context. Other papers describing calculi of trust and authenticity are [3],[18],[19] and [14], but they do not consider recommendations nor confidence values.

4 Confidence valuation: a model based on probabilistic logic

In a realistic scenario, the statements used in the derivation of a certain conclusion are never completely certain. Trust in a person can vary from marginal to complete, and the authenticity of a given public key may depend on the method used for checking the authenticity. It appears natural to measure the confidence in the validity of a statement on a continuous scale between 0 and 1 and, if possible, to interpret the value in some sense as the probability that the statement is correct. The goal of this section is to present a formal model in which the confidence values of all statements can be interpreted as probabilities in a well-defined random experiment (or probability structure).

One can distinguish different approaches to integrating probabilities into a deterministic model based on inference rules.

- Perhaps a natural approach (see for instance [1]) appears to be to incorporate confidence values into the inference rules, i.e., to use rules that specify the degree of confidence of a conclusion as a function of the confidence values of the preconditions of the rule. However, in such an approach the confidence values of derivable statements will generally depend on the order in which the rules are applied. Moreover, certification and recommendation cycles can lead to an undesirable amplification of confidence, and it appears impossible to model dependencies between the confidence values for different statements. Furthermore, it appears very difficult (if not impossible) to describe the meaning of such derivations, i.e. to describe a random experiment in which the confidence values can be interpreted as probabilities of naturally defined events.
- The second approach, which we have chosen for this paper, preserves the convenience of deterministic inference rules, but considers the initial view to be uncertain (i.e., a random variable). More precisely, we assume a probability distribution over the possible initial views, and the confidence value of a statement is defined as the probability that it can be derived from the initial view.

4.1 Reasoning with uncertain information

Reasoning with uncertain information is an important research area in artificial intelligence. Several approaches and models have been proposed and some of them have been used in the implementation of expert systems. We discuss very briefly some of the issues that have been considered and refer to [8], [12] and [17] for further references to the literature.

A view often taken in probability theoretic approaches to reasoning with uncertain information is that the sample space of the probability structure is a set of *possible worlds* and that the real world corresponds to one of these worlds, each with a certain probability. The probability that a statement is true is the total probability of all worlds in which the statement is true. Possible worlds differ in the axioms, and they can even differ in the set of inference rules that are applicable in the world (e.g., see [5]). A natural requirement is that when all probabilities are either 0 or 1, then the model coincides with a natural deterministic model. As in most papers on probabilistic logic, we assume that the inference rules (of Definition 3.2) are universally applicable in all worlds but that the set of statements assumed by Alice to be valid (i.e., the axioms contained in her initial view) are different in different worlds. Probabilistic logic has previously been applied in the analysis of security protocols in [5].

One potential problem with the described approach is that not all sets of worlds need be measurable according to the probability measure[10]. Several researchers have investigated solutions to this problem, and Fagin and Halpern have even intentionally defined structures containing non-measurable sets.

A very interesting problem (e.g., see [8]), which is not considered in this paper, is for given specified probabilities of statements to compute the admissible intervals of probabilities for the other statements, i.e., to determine the extreme values of these probabilities that are attainable for a probability measure consistent with the given probabilities. A term sometimes used in this context is belief functions.

4.2 The probabilistic model of a PKI

In the probabilistic model (see definition below) we replace the view in the deterministic model by a probability distribution over a finite set of possible views, i.e., by a random variable taking as values deterministic views. Note that for a finite sample space S, the events are all the subsets of S, and a probability measure is specified completely by assigning probabilities to all the sample points. The probability of an event is the sum of the probabilities of the sample points it contains.

Definition 4.1. Let S_A be the set of statements (of the forms $Aut_{A,\cdot}$, $Trust_{A,\cdot,\cdot}$, $Cert_{\cdot,\cdot}$ and $Rec_{\cdot,\cdot,\cdot}$) that Alice considers as possible elements of her initial view[11]. The sample space of the random experiment (i.e., the set of possible worlds considered by Alice) is the power set[12] of S_A, denoted by 2^{S_A}. Alice's *probabilistic initial view* is a pair $[S_A, P]$ where $P : 2^{S_A} \to \mathbb{R}^+$ is a probability function on the sample space 2^{S_A}, which naturally extends to a probability measure for all

---

[10] A probability structure is a triple $(S, \mathcal{X}, P)$ consisting of the sample space S, a σ-algebra $\mathcal{X}$ of subsets of S (i.e., a set of subsets of S containing S and closed under complementation and countable union, but not necessarily consisting of all subsets of S), and a probability measure P assigning a non-negative probability to every element of $\mathcal{X}$ such that the probability of a union of disjoint sets is the sum of their probabilities and $P(S) = 1$.

[11] In the probabilistic model, $S \in S_A$ does not necessarily imply that the statement S is valid, but rather that it is valid with some probability. In our examples, S_A consists of the statements represented by edges in the figures.

[12] the set of subsets

events (i.e., sets of subsets of $\mathcal{S}_A$)[13]. Alice's view $View_A$ now denotes the random variable associated with P, i.e., the random variable that takes on as values the subsets of $\mathcal{S}_A$ with the corresponding probabilities.

Note that this definition of $View_A$ is consistent with that given in Section 3 if one assigns probability 1 to one particular initial view. The events in our random experiment are the subsets of the sample space, i.e., the $2^{2^{|\mathcal{S}_A|}}$ sets of subsets of $\mathcal{S}_A$. Let $\mathcal{V}$ be a subset of $\mathcal{S}_A$. Then $P(\mathcal{V})$ and $P(View_A = \mathcal{V})$ denote the same probability, namely the probability of the elementary event (sample point) $\mathcal{V}$. The event $\mathcal{V} \subseteq View_A$ (which is an abbreviation of $\{\mathcal{U} \subseteq \mathcal{S}_A : \mathcal{V} \subseteq \mathcal{U}\}$), whose probability is denoted by $P(\mathcal{V} \subseteq View_A)$, consists of those subsets of $\mathcal{S}_A$ that contain $\mathcal{V}$.

Because $View_A$ is a random variable taking as values sets of statements, so is $\overline{View_A}$, which takes on as values subsets of $\overline{\mathcal{S}_A}$. For a given statement S in $\mathcal{S}_A$ or derivable from $\mathcal{S}_A$, we can consider the event that S can be derived from $View_A$, i.e., the event $S \in \overline{View_A}$. This event consists of those subsets of $\mathcal{S}_A$ (i.e. of those elementary events) from which S can be derived, and its probability is hence the sum of the probabilities of these subsets. Statements not derivable from $\mathcal{S}_A$ correspond to the empty event (probability 0). Later we will characterize the event $S \in \overline{View_A}$ by the union of events of the form $\mathcal{V}_i \subseteq View_A$, where the $\mathcal{V}_i$ are subsets of $\mathcal{S}_A$ from which S can be derived. This is summarised in the following definition.

Definition 4.2. The *confidence value* of a statement $S \in \overline{\mathcal{S}_A}$, denoted $conf(S)$, is the probability that it can be derived from $\mathcal{S}_A$, i.e., it is

$$conf(S) = P(S \in \overline{View_A}) = \sum_{\mathcal{V} \subseteq \mathcal{S}_A:\, S \in \overline{\mathcal{V}}} P(\mathcal{V}).$$

This model allows to specify arbitrary dependencies between the statements in $\mathcal{S}_A$, by specifying an appropriate probability measure P. For example, the trustworthiness of two entities X and Y belonging to the same organisation could be modelled to be correlated[14].

While such dependencies can be specified by an appropriate choice of P, it is important to notice that dependencies due to intersecting certification paths are captured by the model itself, as are the dependencies due to the fact that certificates and/or recommendations issued by a single entity, if they fail, are likely to fail simultaneously. In fact, capturing such dependencies is one of the major purposes of introducing our model.

---

[13] In the following we will use P to denote both the probability function (with $2^{|\mathcal{S}_A|}$ arguments) as well as the implied probability measure (which formally is a function with $2^{2^{|\mathcal{S}_A|}}$ arguments), and we will use the term probability measure for both.

[14] If they are perfectly correlated, this would imply that the probability measure P is 0 for all subsets of $\mathcal{S}_A$ containing $Trust_{A,X,1}$ but not $Trust_{A,Y,1}$ (or vice versa).

4.3 Independent initial confidence parameters

The probability measure P can be specified by specifying its value for the $2^{|S_A|}$ sample points. The probability of an event is the sum of the probabilities of the corresponding sample points. We will therefore later only specify P for all sample points (subsets of S_A.

In its most general form, a probabilistic view can be intractably complex, and in a realistic scenario one can only consider measures P that can be specified by a reasonable number of parameters. Note that this potential complexity is inherent to the problem and is not due to the choice of our model.

An interesting and often natural restriction for the measure P is to assume that the confidence parameters initially assigned to all the statements in Alice's initial view S_A (i.e., the edges in the graph) are independent. Let $p(S)$ be the confidence parameter assigned initially by Alice to the statement $S \in S_A$.

When S_A is minimal in the sense that no statement $S \in S_A$ can be derived from the remaining set of statements, $S_A - \{S\}$, then we have $conf(S) = p(S)$ for all S. However, S_A is not minimal in general. For instance, in example 4.6 (Figure 4, right), the statement $Aut_{A,Y}$ is in S_A but it can also be derived from the statements $Aut_{A,X}$, $Cert_{X,Y}$ and $Trust_{A,X,1}$. For statements S that can be derived from $S_A - \{S\}$, we generally have $conf(S) > p(S)$: $conf(S)$ is the sum of $p(S)$ and the total probability of all subsets of $S_A - \{S\}$ from which S can be derived. (This is why we refer to $p(S)$ as the initial confidence parameter and to $conf(S)$ as the confidence value.)

It should be mentioned again that our model does not require an independence assumption, but for the sake of simplicity all the examples considered below are based on it. However, there is one exception: according to (3) and (4) we assume that trust and recommendations of levels higher than 1 imply trust and recommendations, respectively, of all lower levels. (The only example involving recommendations, and hence to which the previous comment applies, is example 4.8.)

We are interested in computing the probability that particular subsets, usually minimal[15] subsets from which $Aut_{A,B}$ can be derived, are contained in the initial view $View_A$. When no trust and recommendation statements of levels greater than 1 are in S_A, then the probability that a subset V of S_A is a subset of Alice's initial view $View_A$ is the product of the $p(S)$, where S ranges over the set V. In order to take into account the rules (3) and (4), we must consider only the highest level of trust and recommendation statements (for fixed entities involved) and delete those implied by (3) and (4). Let V^* be the resulting reduced set of statement. Hence we have

$$P(V \subseteq View_A) = \prod_{S \in V^*} p(S) \tag{5}$$

if V is consistent with (3) and (4), and $P(V \subseteq View_A) = 0$ otherwise. Note again

---

[15] In the following, *minimal* means that when one statement is deleted from the set, then $Aut_{A,B}$ cannot be derived.

that when no trust and recommendation statements of levels greater than 1 are in S_A, then $V^* = V$.

The reader should not be confused by the fact that $V \subset V'$ implies $P(V \subseteq View_A) \geq P(V' \subseteq View_A)$. Note that S_A is *not* the sample space, and neither S_A nor the empty set correspond to the certain event. Although this will generally not be needed, we describe how the probability of an elementary event, $P(V)$, can be computed for the case where there are no trust and recommendation statements of levels greater than 1:

$$P(V) = P(View_A = V) = \prod_{S \in V} p(S) \cdot \prod_{S \notin V} (1 - p(S)).$$

In the general case, $P(V)$ is defined similarly.

4.4 Implementation aspects and examples

The figures corresponding to the examples should be interpreted as follows: S_A consists of the statements represented by the edges (dashed or solid) in the graph. Every edge is labelled with the probability $p(S)$ that Alice assigns initially to the statement S represented by the edge. Remember that $conf(S) > p(S)$ is possible.

Consider the problem of computing the confidence value for the statement $Aut_{A,B}$ (or for any other statement derivable from Alice view). Applying the formula given in Definition 4.2 would require the explicit computation of all the subsets of S_A from which $Aut_{A,B}$ can be derived, and adding up their probabilities. This requires an exponential number of steps.

A generally much more efficient algorithm is obtained by determining all the minimal subsets, $V_1, \ldots, V_k$, from which $Aut_{A,B}$ can be derived. They correspond to certification paths from A to B together with the corresponding trust verification statements (which can of course also contain other certification paths). The event that $Aut_{A,B}$ can be derived consists of all the subsets of S_A containing at least one of these minimal sets, i.e., it is the union of the events $V_i \subseteq View_A$ for $i = 1, \ldots, k$:

$$conf(Aut_{A,B}) = P(\bigvee_{i-1}^{k} (V_i \subseteq View_A)).$$

According to the inclusion-exclusion principle, the probability of the union of k events can be computed by taking the sum of their probabilities, subtracting the probabilities of all $\binom{k}{2}$ events resulting from intersecting[16] 2 events, adding

---

[16] It may at first appear counter-intuitive that the intersection of the two events $V_i \subseteq View_A$ and $V_j \subseteq View_A$ is the event $(V_i \cup V_j) \subseteq View_A$, involving the union of the two sets V_i and V_j. However, understanding this fact is a key to understanding our probabilistic model.

the probabilities of all $\binom{k}{3}$ events resulting from intersecting 3 events, etc. This gives

$$\text{conf}(Aut_{A,B}) = \sum_{i=1}^{k} P(\mathcal{V}_i \subseteq View_A)$$
$$- \sum_{1 \leq i_1 < i_2 \leq k} P((\mathcal{V}_{i_1} \cup \mathcal{V}_{i_2}) \subseteq View_A)$$
$$+ \sum_{1 \leq i_1 < i_2 < i_3 \leq k} P((\mathcal{V}_{i_1} \cup \mathcal{V}_{i_2} \cup \mathcal{V}_{i_3}) \subseteq View_A)$$
$$- \cdots$$

The complexity of computing the confidence value for a statement is on the order of $2^{\min(|\mathcal{S}_A|, k)}$, where k is the number of minimal subsets of $\mathcal{S}_A$ from which the statement can be derived.

The numerical values we have chosen in the following examples are probably smaller than what they would be in a real-life example, but they illustrate better the effect of parallel certification paths, recommendations, etc.

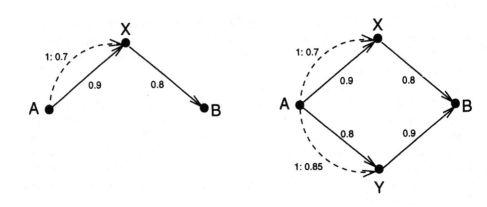

Figure 3.

Example 4.3. A simple example is shown in Figure 3 (left). Alice has assigned confidence parameters 0.9 and 0.7 to the statements $Aut_{A,X}$ and $Trust_{A,X,1}$, respectively. Entity X has assigned confidence parameter 0.8 to the authenticity of B's public key and this confidence parameter is included in the certificate $Cert_{X,B}$. The statement $Aut_{A,B}$ can be derived from

$$\mathcal{S}_A = \{Aut_{A,X}, Trust_{A,X,1}, Cert_{X,B}\}$$

but from no proper subset of S_A. Therefore its confidence value is the product of the three confidence parameters:

$$\begin{aligned}
conf(Aut_{A,B}) &= P(S_A \subseteq View_A) = P(View_A = S_A) \\
&= p(Aut_{A,X}) \cdot p(Trust_{A,X,1}) \cdot p(Cert_{X,B}) \\
&= 0.9 \cdot 0.7 \cdot 0.8 = 0.504.
\end{aligned}$$

Example 4.4. A slightly more complicated example is shown in Figure 3 (right). We have

$$S_A = \{Aut_{A,X}, \; Aut_{A,Y}, \; Trust_{A,X,1}, \; Trust_{A,Y,1}, \; Cert_{X,B}, \; Cert_{Y,B}\}$$

and the statement $Aut_{A,B}$ can be derived from any subset of S_A containing either the minimal set

$$\mathcal{V}_1 = \{Aut_{A,X}, Trust_{A,X,1}, Cert_{X,B}\}$$

or the minimal set

$$\mathcal{V}_2 = \{Aut_{A,Y}, Trust_{A,Y,1}, Cert_{Y,B}\}.$$

We have

$$\begin{aligned}
P(\mathcal{V}_1 \subseteq View_A) &= p(Aut_{A,X}) \cdot p(Trust_{A,X,1}) \cdot p(Cert_{X,B}) \\
&= 0.9 \cdot 0.7 \cdot 0.8 = 0.504
\end{aligned}$$

and

$$\begin{aligned}
P(\mathcal{V}_2 \subseteq View_A) &= p(Aut_{A,Y}) \cdot p(Trust_{A,Y,1}) \cdot p(Cert_{Y,B}) \\
&= 0.8 \cdot 0.85 \cdot 0.9 = 0.612.
\end{aligned}$$

Because the sets $\mathcal{V}_1$ and $\mathcal{V}_2$ are disjoint we have

$$P((\mathcal{V}_1 \cup \mathcal{V}_2) \subseteq View_A) = P(\mathcal{V}_1 \subseteq View_A) \cdot P(\mathcal{V}_2 \subseteq View_A)$$

and hence

$$\begin{aligned}
conf(Aut_{A,B}) &= P((\mathcal{V}_1 \subseteq View_A) \vee (\mathcal{V}_2 \subseteq View_A)) \\
&= P(\mathcal{V}_1 \subseteq View_A) + P(\mathcal{V}_2 \subseteq View_A) - P((\mathcal{V}_1 \cup \mathcal{V}_2) \subseteq View_A) \\
&= 0.504 + 0.612 - 0.504 \cdot 0.612 = 0.8076.
\end{aligned}$$

Example 4.5. The previous example could be treated intuitively (cf. [1]) by the simple observation that the two paths $A - X - B$ and $A - Y - B$ are independent. Consider now the situation of Figure 4 (left), which is obtained from the previous example by replacing B by a new entity Z who has certified B's public key and is trusted by Alice. In other words, we have

$$\begin{aligned}
S_A = \{&Aut_{A,X}, Aut_{A,Y}, Trust_{A,X,1}, Trust_{A,Y,1}, Trust_{A,Z,1}, Cert_{X,Z}, \\
&Cert_{Y,Z}, Cert_{Z,B}\}.
\end{aligned}$$

In this example, the two paths $A - X - Z - B$ and $A - Y - Z - B$ are not independent. Nevertheless, the computation of $conf(Aut_{A,B})$ is intuitive. $Aut_{A,B}$ can be derived from $View_A$ if it contains $Trust_{A,Z,1}$ and $Cert_{Z,B}$ and if $Aut_{A,Z}$ can be derived. The latter condition is equivalent to the condition that $Aut_{A,B}$ can be derived in the previous example. $conf(Aut_{A,Z})$ is hence equal to $conf(Aut_{A,B})$ in the previous example and we have

$$conf(Aut_{A,B}) = conf(Aut_{A,Z}) \cdot p(Trust_{A,Z,}) \cdot p(Cert_{Z,B})$$
$$= 0.8076 \cdot 0.7 \cdot 0.95 = 0.537.$$

Although there are two certification paths from A to B, the confidence value is low because the two paths intersect in the vertex Z and the edge $Z - B$.

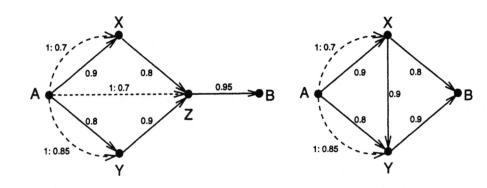

Figure 4.

Example 4.6. The example of Figure 4 (right) is more involved because the three different certification paths $A - Y - B$, $A - X - Y - B$ and $A - X - B$ overlap in a more complicated manner. The calculation of $conf(Aut_{A,B})$ is therefore more complex, and this is the first example that cannot be treated in an intuitive manner. We have

$$S_A = \{Aut_{A,X}, \; Aut_{A,Y}, \; Trust_{A,X,1}, \; Trust_{A,Y,1}, \; Cert_{X,B}, \; Cert_{Y,B}, \; Cert_{X,Y}\}$$

and the statement $Aut_{A,B}$ can be derived from $View_A$ if and only if it contains as a subset one of the following sets:

$$V_1 = \{Aut_{A,X}, \; Trust_{A,X,1}, \; Cert_{X,B}\},$$
$$V_2 = \{Aut_{A,Y}, \; Trust_{A,Y,1}, \; Cert_{Y,B}\},$$
$$V_3 = \{Aut_{A,X}, \; Trust_{A,X,1}, \; Trust_{A,Y,1}, \; Cert_{X,Y}, \; Cert_{Y,B}\}.$$

Considered as an event in our random experiment, the statement $Aut_{A,B}$ thus corresponds to the set of subsets of S_A which contain at least one of these sets. The probability of this event can be computed by the exclusion-inclusion principle as

$$
\begin{aligned}
conf(Aut_{A,B}) &= P((\mathcal{V}_1 \subseteq View_A) \vee (\mathcal{V}_2 \subseteq View_A) \vee (\mathcal{V}_3 \subseteq View_A)) \\
&= P(\mathcal{V}_1 \subseteq View_A) + P(\mathcal{V}_2 \subseteq View_A) + P(\mathcal{V}_3 \subseteq View_A) \\
&\quad - P((\mathcal{V}_1 \cup \mathcal{V}_2) \subseteq View_A) - P((\mathcal{V}_1 \cup \mathcal{V}_3) \subseteq View_A) \\
&\quad - P((\mathcal{V}_2 \cup \mathcal{V}_3) \subseteq View_A) + P((\mathcal{V}_1 \cup \mathcal{V}_2 \cup \mathcal{V}_3) \subseteq View_A) \\
&= 0.825
\end{aligned}
$$

This number is obtained by observing that $\mathcal{V}_1 \cup \mathcal{V}_2 = S_A - \{Cert_{X,Y}\}$, $\mathcal{V}_1 \cup \mathcal{V}_3 = S_A - \{Cert_{X,B}\}$, $\mathcal{V}_2 \cup \mathcal{V}_3 = S_A - \{Aut_{A,Y}\}$ and $\mathcal{V}_1 \cup \mathcal{V}_2 \cup \mathcal{V}_3 = S_A$ and applying (5) to compute the probabilities that these sets are contained in $View_A$. Alternatively, but in this case less efficiently, $conf(Aut_{A,B})$ could be computed by determining for each of the $2^7 = 128$ subsets of S_A whether $Aut_{A,B}$ can be derived, and adding these probabilities. Note that in this example we have $conf(Aut_{A,Y}) = 0.89 > p(Aut_{A,Y}) = 0.8$.

Example 4.7. The example of Figure 5 (left) illustrates a new problem, namely certification cycles, which is quite likely to occur in a large-scale practical scenario and is easily handled by our model. Here the four minimal certification paths are $A - X - B$, $A - Y - B$, $A - X - Y - B$ and $A - Y - X - B$. They correspond to the minimal sets $\mathcal{V}_1$, $\mathcal{V}_2$ and $\mathcal{V}_3$ of the previous example plus the additional set

$$
\mathcal{V}_4 = \{Aut_{A,Y}, Trust_{A,X,1}, Trust_{A,Y,1}, Cert_{Y,X}, Cert_{X,B}\}.
$$

The confidence level of $Aut_{A,B}$ results in $conf(Aut_{A,B}) = 0.8276$. Note that, as could be expected, the additional certificate $Cert_{Y,X}$ improves the confidence value for $Aut_{A,B}$ only marginally.

Example 4.8. For the first time in this section we now consider a recommendation by extending the previous example with the statements $Trust_{A,Y,2}$ and $Rec_{Y,X,1}$ where $p(Trust_{A,Y,2}) = 0.7$ and $p(Rec_{Y,X,1}) = 0.9$ (see Figure 5, right side). Note, however, that the statements $Trust_{A,Y,1}$ and $Trust_{A,Y,2}$ are not independent because $Trust_{A,Y,2}$ implies $Trust_{A,Y,1}$. The confidence value of $Aut_{A,B}$ is $conf(Aut_{A,B}) = 0.838$ which is a noticeable improvement over example 4.7.

4.5 A discussion of the examples

Let us briefly summarise the examples. The confidence values we have chosen may appear to be quite low, but they illustrate our points more clearly than values close to 1.

Except for example 4.5, the set of statements of the examples of this section (examples 4.3, 4.4, 4.6, 4.7, and 4.8) increases monotonically. As a consequence,

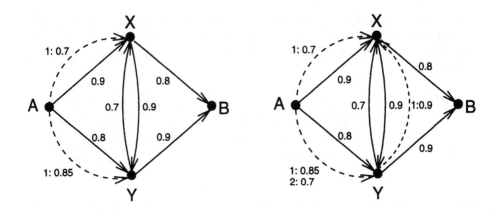

Figure 5.

the confidence value of $Aut_{A,B}$ increases monotonically. This appears to be a desirable property of a model that does not contain "negative" statements such as revocations. The single certification path of example 4.3 gives a confidence value of only 0.504. By adding a parallel path (example 4.4), the value is increased to 0.8076. Adding a further certificate $Cert_{X,Y}$ increases the value to 0.825 whereas the certificate $Cert_{Y,X}$ only adds marginally to the confidence value (0.827). The recommendation $Rec_{Y,X,1}$ increases the confidence value to 0.838.

The most significant increase of confidence in $Aut_{A,B}$ is achieved by introducing an independent certification path. In contrast, all subsequent improvements appear to be rather insignificant because no additional independent entities are involved and the minimal subsets from which $Aut_{A,B}$ can be derived overlap significantly. Our model gives a natural explanation of this fact. The confidence values would increase more significantly if a third independent certification path were introduced. For example, introducing a third path $A - Z - B$ in example 4.4, namely the additional statements $Aut_{A,Z}$, $Trust_{A,Z,1}$ and $Cert_{Z,B}$ (with confidence parameters 0.8 each), would increase $conf(Aut_{A,B})$ to 0.906, and a further such independent path would increase it to more than 0.95. This illustrates the importance of independent certification paths.

4.6 Efficiency considerations

For very large views with many certification paths (or, more precisely, with many minimal subsets of S_A from which $Aut_{A,B}$ can be derived) this described algorithm is infeasible. The examples illustrate that certain minimal subsets can be discarded without much effect on the confidence value of $Aut_{A,B}$. Hence one can efficiently obtain a good approximation to the confidence value which is guaranteed to be pessimistic, i.e. on the "safe side".

For this purpose, it may be useful to perform a sensitivity analysis to find those minimal subsets with small marginal impact on the confidence value of $Aut_{A,B}$. This is suggested as a problem for future research.

As mentioned in Section 4.3, Alice's probabilistic view must, in any realistic application, be specified by a rather small number of parameters. This means that only a small number of dependencies can be modelled. A reasonable simplification is achieved by specifying the (infinite) list of parameters $p(Trust_{A,X,i})$, for $i = 1, 2, \ldots$, as a function of only one parameter α. For instance, one could define

$$p(Trust_{A,X,i}) = \alpha^i$$

for some $\alpha < 1$.

5 Concluding remarks and open problems

We have proposed a deterministic and a probabilistic model for a user's view of a public-key infrastructure. They include recommendations and confidence parameters for statements. It appears likely to the author that recommendations in the context of a PKI will in future implementations be made explicit. It is perhaps less clear whether confidence parameters will ever be used widely, but in a sufficiently user-friendly and error-tolerant implementation this appears quite possible. One of the applications of using confidence parameters could be for letting certificates expire gradually rather than sharply on a particular date. This could be achieved by letting the confidence parameter decrease with time.

For any model of public-key certification there is an inherent trade-off between the levels of details of a particular scenario that can be captured and the complexity of its specification and analysis. Important open research problems are the design of efficient algorithms and simplifications of the model that result in confidence values with guaranteed accuracy.

An interesting but non-trivial problem, which is the subject of ongoing research, is to incorporate public-key revocation into the model. It must be specified who can revoke a public key. In order to make false revocations unlikely it is perhaps useful to specify for each public key a list of entities authorised to revoke the public key.

A drawback of our model is that users must assign precise confidence parameters to the statements available to them. An interesting extension could be to allow an incomplete specification of the parameters of the model, for instance by specifying intervals rather than exact values for the probabilities, or by only partially specifying the dependencies between the parameters. The goal of such an approach would be to derive upper and lower bounds on the confidence values of statements that are consistent with the partial specification.

Acknowledgements

I would like to thank Jan Camenisch, Germano Caronni, Martin Hirt, Jean-Marc Piveteau and Markus Stadler for interesting discussions, and the anonymous referees for several suggestions for improving the paper. The comments from Joachim Biskup and Dieter Gollmann have been particularly useful. Martin Hirt provided help with the figures and programs for computing confidence values. I am also grateful for the generous hospitality of the Isaac Newton Institute for Mathematical Sciences at the University of Cambridge, where part of this paper was written.

References

1. T. Beth, M. Borcherding and B. Klein, Valuation of trust in open systems, *Computer Security - ESORICS '94*, D. Gollmann (Ed.), Lecture Notes in Computer Science, Berlin: Springer-Verlag, 1994, vol. 875, pp. 3–18.
2. A. Birell, B. Lampson, R. Needham and M. Schroeder, A global authentication service without global trust, *Proc. IEEE Symposium on Research in Security and Privacy*, 1986, pp. 223–230.
3. C. Boyd, Security architectures using formal methods, *IEEE Journal on Selected Areas in Communications*, vol. 11, no. 5, 1993, pp. 694–701.
4. M. Burrows, M. Abadi and R. Needham, A logic of authentication, *ACM Transactions on Computer Systems*, vol. 8, no. 1, 1990, pp. 18–36.
5. E. A. Campbell, R. Safavi-Naini and P. A. Pleasants, Partial belief and probabilistic reasoning in the analysis of secure protocols, *Proc. The Computer Security Foundations Workshop V*, IEEE Computer Society Press, 1992, pp. 84–91.
6. S. Chokhani, Towards a national public-key infrastructure, *IEEE Communications Magazine*, vol. 32, no. 9, 1994, pp. 70–74.
7. W. Diffie and M. E. Hellman, New directions in cryptography, *IEEE Transactions on Information Theory*, vol. 22, no. 6, 1976, pp. 644–654.
8. R. Fagin and J. Y. Halpern, Uncertainty, belief, and probability, *Proc. of the Eleventh International Joint Conference on Artificial Intelligence*, August 1989, vol. 2, pp. 1161–1167.
9. W. Feller, *An Introduction to Probability Theory and its Applications*, third ed., vol. 1, New York, NY: Wiley, 1968.
10. J. Glasgow, G. MacEwen and P. Panangaden, A logic for reasoning about security, *ACM Transactions on Computer Systems*, vol. 10, no. 3, 1992, pp. 226–264.
11. V. D. Gligor, S.-W. Luan and J. N. Pato, On inter-realm authentication in large distributed systems, *Proc. IEEE Conference on security and privacy*, 1992, pp. 2–17.
12. T. Hailperin, Probability logic, *Notre Dame Journal of Formal Logic*, vol. 25, no. 3, July 1984, pp. 198–212.
13. B. Lampson, M. Abadi, M. Burrows and E. Wobber, Authentication in distributed systems: theory and practice, Proc. 13th ACM Symp. on Operating Systems Principles, 1991, pp. 165–182.
14. U. M. Maurer and P. E. Schmid, A calculus for secure channel establishment in open networks, *Proc. 1994 European Symposium on Research in Computer Security (ESORICS' 94)*, D. Gollmann (Ed.), Lecture Notes in Computer Science, Berlin: Springer-Verlag, 1994, vol. 875, pp. 175–192.
15. R. Molva, G. Tsudik, E. Van Herreweghen and S. Zatti, KryptoKnight Authentication and Key Distribution System, *Proc. 1992 European Symposium on Research in Computer Security (ESORICS 92)*, Y. Deswarte, G. Eizenberg, J.-J. Quisquater (Eds.), Lecture Notes in Computer Science, Berlin: Springer-Verlag, 1992, vol. 648, pp. 155–174.

16. A. Nerode and R. A. Shore, *Logic for Applications*, Springer Verlag, 1993.
17. N. J. Nilsson, Probabilistic logic, *Artificial Intelligence*, vol. 28, no. 1, 1986, pp. 71–86.
18. C. H. Papadimitriou, V. Rangan, M. Sideri, "Designing Secure Communication Protocols from Trust Specifications", *Algorithmica*, 1994, pp. 485-499.
19. P. V. Rangan, An axiomatic theory of trust in secure communication protocols, *Computers & Security*, vol. 11, 1992, pp. 163-172.
20. R. L. Rivest, A. Shamir, and L. Adleman, A method for obtaining digital signatures and public-key cryptosystems, *Communications of the ACM*, vol. 21, no. 2, 1978, pp. 120-126.
21. B. Schneier, *Applied Cryptography*, 2nd edition, John Wiley & Sons, Inc., New York, 1996.
22. J. G. Steiner, B.C. Neuman and J.I. Schiller, Kerberos: An authentication service for open network systems, Proceedings of *Winter USENIX 1988*, Dallas, Texas.
23. W. Stallings, *Network and Internetwork Security*, Englewood Cliffs, NJ: Prentice Hall, 1995.
24. P. Syverson and C. Meadows, A logical language for specifying cryptographic protocols requirements, *Proc. IEEE Conf. on Research in Security and Privacy*, 1993, pp. 165-180.
25. J. J. Tardo and K. Alagappan, SPX: Global authentication using public key certificates, *Proc. IEEE Conf. on Research in Security and Privacy*, 1991, pp. 232-244.
26. R. Yahalom, B. Klein and T. Beth, Trust relationships in secure systems – a distributed authentication perspective, *Proc. IEEE Conf. on Research in Security and Privacy*, 1993, pp. 150-164.
27. P. Zimmermann, PGP User's Guide, vol. I and II, Version 2.6, May 22, 1994.
28. ISO/IEC International Standard 9594-8, Information technology – open systems interconnection – the directory, Part 8: Authentication framework, 1990.
29. Privacy enhanced mail (PEM), Internet Request for Comments (RFC) 1421-1424.

Analyzing the Needham-Schroeder Public Key Protocol: A Comparison of Two Approaches

Catherine A. Meadows

Code 5543
Center for High Assurance Computer Systems
Naval Research Laboratory
Washington DC, 20375
meadows@itd.nrl.navy.mil

Abstract. In this paper we contrast the use of the NRL Protocol Analyzer and Gavin Lowe's use of the model checker FDR [8] to analyze the Needham-Schroeder public key protocol. This is used as a basis for comparing and contrasting the two systems and to point out possible future directions for research.

Most early work in the automated analysis of cryptographic protocols concentrated on building special-purpose tools, such as the NRL Protocol Analyzer [5, 10], the Interrogator [11, 5], and Longley and Rigby's protocol analysis tool [6]. Although some work existed on the application of existing tools, such as Kemmerer's use of Ina Jo [5], this was not an approach followed by many. Some of this early concentration on special-purpose tools may have been a result of the belief that cryptographic protocols had certain unique properties that would make them more amenable to analysis by a tool using special-purpose models and algorithms. This was certainly the belief that motivated much of the development of the NRL Protocol Analyzer. But, as research has progressed in this area, and people are becoming more and more comfortable with the techniques and assumptions that are needed to analyze cryptographic protocols, more researchers are exploring ways in which existing formal methods tools can be applied to the problem of either assuring a cryptographic protocol's correctness or finding a flaw if it exists. Thus, for example the theorem prover HOL has been used by Snekkenes in [13] for stating and proving properties of cryptographic protocols.

At this point, it makes sense to ask the question: what comparisons can we make between these two ways of approaching the problem? Clearly, some of the advantages of using an existing system is its greater power and maturity, while the advantages of using one's own is that it can be tailored to the problem at hand, giving better assistance for solving the problems of interest. Thus, we might expect existing systems to provide the most help in solving the parts of the problem that most resemble other problems, and a special purpose system to provide the most help in solving the parts of the problem that are unique or at least unusual. But one cannot tell exactly how these things will balance out until some experience has been gained in applying both types of systems to the problem.

In this paper we try to at least begin to answer these questions by comparing the use of two different tools to analyze the same protocol, the Needham-Schroeder public-key authentication protocol [12]. One of these tools, the NRL Protocol Analyzer, is a special-purpose tool for analyzing cryptographic protocols. The other, FDR [2], is a model checker that tests whether CSP programs satsify their specifications. We will use the results of this analysis to provide a basis for the comparison of these two tools. Although this itself will not be enough to provide a comparison of the use of special-purpose versus general tools, it can be used as a basis for further work by others looking at the same problem.

The history of the use of these two tools to analyze the protocol is as follows. The FDR tool was used first by Lowe to find a triangular attack on the protocol [7, 8]. This attack was new; as a matter of fact the protocol had previously been "proven" correct in [1]. The NRL Protocol Analyzer was then used by us to reproduce the same attack, as well as to find some new attacks. [1]

The remainder of this paper is structured as follows. Section 2 contains a description of the Needham-Schroeder public-key protocol (from now on referred to as the Needham-Schroeder protocol, not to be confused with their more famous private-key protocol), and some of the attacks that were found. In Section 3 we present a brief account of FDR and Lowe's analysis of the Needham-Schroeder protocol; a more complete account can be found in [8]. In Section 4 we describe the NRL Protocol Analyzer and show how it was used to analyze the protocol. In Section 5 we compare the two approaches. Section 6 concludes the paper.

1   The Needham-Schroeder Public-Key Protocol

The Needham-Schroeder protocol uses public keys to achieve authentication between two parties. The protocol involves an initiator A, a responder B, and a server S. It proceeds as follows.

1. $A \to S : B$
   A requests B's public key from S.
2. $S \to A : \{K_B, B\}_{K_S^{-1}}$
   S sends B's public key and name to A, signed with its digital signature. A checks the signature and B's name.
3. $A \to B: \{R_A, A\}_{K_B}$
   A sends a nonce R_A, together with A's name to B, encrypted with B's public key. B decrypts to get A's name and nonce.
4. $B \to S: A$
   B requests A's public key from S.

---

[1] The fact that these attacks were not found by FDR does not necessarily point out a limitation in that system or in Lowe's approach; it is simply the result of the fact that we and Lowe made slightly different assumptions about primitives used by the protocol, and that Lowe analyzed a fragment, not the entire protocol.

5. $S \rightarrow B$: $\{K_A, A\}_{K_S^{-1}}$
   S sends B A's public key. B checks the signature and A's name.
6. $B \rightarrow A$: $\{R_A, R_B\}_{K_A}$
   B generates a nonce R_B and sends it together with R_A to A, encrypted with K_A. A decrypts the message. If it finds R_A, it assumes that this is a message from B in response to its original message.
7. $A \rightarrow B$: $\{R_B\}_{K_B}$
   A encrypts R_B with K_B and sends it to B. B decrypts the message. If it finds R_B, it assumes that this is a message from A in response to its original message.

The reasoning behind this protocol is straightforward. When A gets the message $\{R_A, R_B\}_{K_A}$, it assumes that, since B received the message encrypted under its public key, and B has no reason to reveal R_A, only B knows R_A, and thus the message must be from B in response to the message $\{R_A, A\}_{K_B}$. Likewise, when B receives $\{R_B\}_{K_B}$, it reasons that only A knows R_B, and so A must have sent the message in response to the message $\{R_A, R_B\}_{K_A}$. In other words, R_A and R_B serve not only as nonces, but as authenticators. Indeed, in [1] Burrows, Abadi, and Needham suggest that they be used as authenticators in subsequent communication. [2] As we will see below, this could have dangerous consequences.

The above argument appears in more rigorous form in [1] where Burrows, Abadi, and Needham use the logic of authentication set forth in that paper to prove that the protocol is correct. However, since their logic relies upon the assumption that principals to not divulge secrets, it misses the following attack discovered by Lowe [7], which relies on a participant's willingness to divulge a secret nonce. [3] Following Lowe, we leave off the initial distribution of public keys. This attack involves four parties: A, B, and an intruder I. We use the notation I_X to mean I impersonating X. I without a subscript refers to the intruder acting as itself.

3. $A \rightarrow I$: $\{R_A, A\}_{K_I}$
   A initiates communication with I.
3'. $I_A \rightarrow B$: $\{R_A, A\}_{K_B}$
   I initiates communication with B, using R_A.
6'. $B \rightarrow A$: $\{R_A, R_B\}_{K_A}$
   B responds to A. A decrypts and finds R_A.
7. $A \rightarrow I$: $\{R_B\}_{K_I}$
   Thinking that the previous message is a response from I, A responds in kind. I decrypts R_B and can now use it to impersonate A to B.
7'. $I_A \rightarrow B$: $\{R_B\}_{K_B}$
   I completes the protocol with B.

If R_A and R_B are used as authenticators subsequent communication, I now has the ability to impersonate A to B for the rest of the session, although I cannot

[2] This is in contrast to the original Needham-Schroeder paper [12], which suggests that authentication be supplied by digital signatures.
[3] For a more complete discussion of the relationship between the attack and Burrows', Abadi's and Needham's proof of correctness, see [3].

read B's messages. Even if digital signatures are used for subsequent authentication instead, and I cannot impersonate A, I has still managed to get A and B in an inconsistent state in which B thinks that A has initiated communication with it when in fact it has not.

Both Burrows, Abadi, and Needham, and Lowe assume that principals can distinguish between types; that it is not possible, for example, to confuse a name with a nonce, or either with a key. Although this is an assumption that is usually considered easy to ensure by proper formatting, it is nevertheless sometimes useful to see what can happen if types are confused. If nothing else, this can at least point out the places in which unambiguous formatting is vital to security.

The following attack, found using the NRL Protocol Analyzer, makes use of the key distribution as well as the authentication phase of the protocol, and relies upon a confusion between nonces and names.

3. $I_A \rightarrow B : \{R_I, A\}_{K_B}$

4. $B \rightarrow S : A$

5. $S \rightarrow A: \{K_A, A\}_{K_S^{-1}}$

6. $B \rightarrow A: \{R_I, R_B\}_{K_A}$

    I intecepts this message.

3'. $I_{R_B} \rightarrow A: \{R_I, R_B\}_{K_A}$

    I sends the intercepted message to A as the initiator of the protocol, with R_B as the name field.

4'. $A \rightarrow S : R_B$

    A sends the "name" R_B to S in order to get its public key.

7. $I_A \rightarrow B: \{R_B\}_{K_B}$

    I now has the information it needs to impersonate A to B. It encrypts R_B with K_B and sends it to B.

If nonces are used in authenticators during the session, then I can impersonate A to B throughout the session as well.

2 Lowe's Analysis of the Needham-Schroeder Protocol

Lowe specified the Needham-Schroeder protocol in CSP [4], and then used the FDR model checker to search for attacks. FDR works by checking whether or not one CSP specification is a refinement of another. There are several different notions of CSP refinement, of increasing order of complexity. The simplest notion of refinement, usually used for proving safety properties, is the traces model, which is the one used by Lowe. This says that process A refines process B if the traces of A are a subset of the traces of B. If B is a specification of a safety property describing what traces of a system are allowable, and A is a specification of a program, then clearly A satisfies the safety property B if A refines B. FDR checks whether or not one CSP process is a refinement of another in this sense by building up sequences of possible traces for both processes and checking at each stage whether or not the subset property is violated. If it is, it returns the first trace it finds (which will also be the shortest) that violates this property.

Briefly, the specification of the protocol itself consists of three communication events that describe the three authentication messages between A and B. The existence of sets of initiators, responders, public keys, and nonces are assumed. Three channels were specified, the standard *comm*, and two new channels, *fake* and *intercept*, which reflect the intruder's ability to both produce and read messages. Processes are defined for initiators and responders, that describe how they send messages and how they react to received messages. The initiator process begins with a user requesting that process to connect with a responder. Renamings can be applied to the processes to reflect the fact that messages can be intercepted or faked. Thus, if *Msg* is a message sent by the process, then *comm.Msg* can be replaced by *intercept.Msg*; if it is a message received, then *comm.Msg* can be replaced by *fake.Msg*.

Each initiator and responder process is indexed by a name and a nonce. Thus we can think of an initiator or reponder process as corresponding to a single local execution of the protocol. Multiple interleaved executions of a protocol can be represented by interleaving multiple initiator and responder processes. Thus the number of executions in a simulation of the protocol can be limited by limiting the number and type of responder and initiator process.

Finally, a definition of the intruder is given, which describes how it can intercept and fake messages, and how it builds up its knowledge. This is the most complex part of the specification, since each action available to the intruder, who is assumed to be capable of any operation, must be specified separately. The state of the intruder is parametrized by the messages it has been unable to decrypt, and the set of nonces that it has learned. Since the nonces are the only secret information passed in the protocol, this set can be thought of as corresponding to the set of decrypted messages plus any nonces the intruder knows initially (that is, those it generates itself).

After this protocol was specified, the FDR model checker was used on a specification consisting of one initiator process, one responder process, and one intruder process. This meant that FDR only generated traces consisting of at most one local execution of the protocol for initiator and responder. This was sufficient to find the triangular attack on the Needham-Schroeder protocol, however, since this requires only one initiator process and one responder process; the initiator process interacting with the intruder as respondent, and the respondent process interacting with the intruder impersonating the initiator process.

Two specifications of desirable properties of the protocol, one from the point of view of the initiator, and one from the point of view of the responder, were given. The specification *AUTH_RESP* says that an initiator should only accept a responder as authenticated if the responder is attempting to respond to the initiator. The specification *AUTH_INIT* says that a responder should only accept an initiator as authenticated only the user playing the role of the initiator is actually trying to communicate with the responder. FDR was used to determine whether all the traces of the protocol satisfied these two properties. It found no counterexamples to *AUTH_RESP*, but it found the triangular attack when it checked *AUTH_INIT*.

When a flaw is found in a protocol, the next thing to do is fix it. Lowe's suggested fix was to replace the message $\{R_A, R_B\}_{K_A}$ with $\{R_A, R_B, B\}_{K_A}$, so that the originator of the message was not ambiguous. In this way an intruder could not replay B's message as his own. FDR was run on the new protocol using the $AUTH\_INIT$ and $AUTH\_RESP$ specification, and no attacks were found.

But the failure of FDR to find attacks does not mean that the protocol is proven secure, since the protocol specification involved a very limited number of protocol executions. Thus there is still the possibility that there could exist attacks that depend on the interleaving of more executions. Since a model checker cannot verify any properties involving an unbounded number of executions, it alone cannot guarantee security of a protocol. Thus Lowe also performed a hand proof is of a theorem that states, in the case of the fixed Needham-Schroeder protocol, that if no attack can be found involving one initiator and one responder, then the protocol is secure. We will not present this proof in detail, but we note that it hinges upon some key lemmas concerning the circumstances under which the intruder can produce and learn words. The first concerns conditions under which messages containing a nonce can be produced by the intruder, and the second concerns the conditions under which the intruder can respond to a nonce challenge by a principal.

3 The NRL Protocol Analyzer Analysis of the Needham-Schroeder Protocol

3.1 Overview of the NRL Protocol Analyzer

As in Lowe's CSP specification of the Needham-Schroeder protocol, the NRL Protocol Analyzer makes the assumption that principals communicate over a network controlled by a hostile intruder who can read, modify, and destroy traffic, and also perform some operations, such as encryption, that are available to legitimate participants in the protocol. The means by which this network model is realized differ in some aspects, however.

In the NRL Protocol Analyzer, actions of legitimate principals are specified by the user as state transitions. Input to the transitions are values of local state variables and messages received by the principal, the latter assumed to have been generated or passed on by the intruder, and output are the new values of local state variables and messages sent by the principal, the latter which are subject to interception and modification by the intruder. The means by which the intruder can modify messages are specified by having the specification writer indicate which operations are performable by the intruder, and what words the intruder may be assumed to know initially. Some operations, such as list concatenation and deconcatenation, are always assumed to be performable by the intruder.

In NRL Protocol Analyzer specifications, local state variables and transitions are indexed by four things: the name of the principal involved, an identifier for the local execution, the step of the protocol it corresponds to, and the principal's local time. The last we have found redundant, and may eliminate in future versions. Principal names, local execution identifiers, and times are all indicated by variables, which may have an unlimited, even infinite, number of instantiations. If we choose a particular instantiation of principal name and local execution identifier, we see that the set of transitions relevant to a particular role in the protocol corresponds to one of Lowe's CSP processes, where for Lowe the local execution identifier is the nonce generated by a principal for that local execution. The main difference between the Protocol Analyzer and FDR specifications, however, is that for FDR one specifies a finite number of such processes, while the Protocol Analyzer assumes that an unbounded number of runs and principals are possible, since variables in a specification can have an infinite number of possible instantiations. It also allows for odd boundary conditions such as the case in which the same principal plays the role of both initiator and responder; this can be done by instantiating the names of the principals playing these roles to the same term. This possibility of attacks under such conditions will be explored automatically by the Protocol Analyzer unless the user explicitly states that they should not be considered.

The Protocol Analyzer also differs from FDR and other model checkers in that, instead of working forwards from an initial state, it works backwords from a final state. The user of the Analyzer uses it to prove a security property by specifying an insecure state in terms of words known by the intruder, values of local state variables, and sequences of events that have or have not occurred. The Analyzer gives a complete description of all states that can immediately precede that state, followed by a complete description of all states that can immediately precede those, and so forth. Since the search space the Analyzer deals with is infinite, the user is given a number of means of pruning the search space to a manageable size. These include:

1. **Inductive proof of unreachability of infinite classes of states by use of formal languages.** The Analyzer can be used to prove that if the intruder learns a member of the language, then it must have already known a word from that language. The Analyzer in its most recent form can be used to generate languages as well as prove them unreachable.

2. **Remembering conditions on reachability of states.** If a state description has been proved unreachable, or only reachable if the variables in that state description have been instantiated to certain values, the Analyzer can remember that fact and apply it the next time that state description is encountered in a search.

3. **Querying subsets of state descriptions.** When a state description is found by the Analyzer, the user has the option of telling the Analyzer to look for some subset of that state description. For example, given a state description in which the intruder knows two words W and V, the user can ask the Analyzer how to find the state in which the intruder knows V. This is a good strategy, for example, if the user suspects that it is easy to show that the state in which the intruder knows V is unreachable. The Analyzer also has several different sets of search-pruning heuristics built in which the user can specify; these will then be applied automatically. For example, it can be directed to choose to query a state variable or word only if it

contains a term that appeared in the original top-level query. Thus, if the user begins by asking how to find a state in which the intruder knows V, and the Analyzer finds that this can be done if the intruder knows K_A and $\{V\}_{K_A}$, the Analyzer will only look for $\{V\}_{K_A}$, since K_A does not appear in the original query.

Note that these techniques take the place of the theorems Lowe used to narrow his search space to that generated by two processes. Note also that the ability to query a subset of a state description may generate a false attack; the portion of the description that is queried may be reachable, while the entire state is not. Thus any attack produced by the Analyzer when this technique is used must be handchecked to determine whether or not it is a valid one.

Once the various lemmas have been proved, it is possible to use the Analyzer to perform a search. Each time a state is generated in its backwards search, it is checked against each of the lemmas to determine whether or not it is unreachable. If it is, the state is discarded. If it is not, the state is kept, and the Analyzer tries to determine how that state could have been reached. The Analyzer keeps a record of all paths generated, and lets the user know which paths begin in unreachable or initial states. The user can ask the Analyzer to display any path generated.

3.2 The NRL Protocol Analyzer Specification of the Needham-Schroeder Protocol

Our specification of the Needham-Schroeder protocol was written before we had seen Lowe's specification, so there are some important differences. First of all, we specified the request for and distribution of public keys. Secondly, we considered the possibility that old nonces might be compromised. To this end we included a transition that states how a nonce can be compromised any time after it is generated; we specified a "dummy" principal whose sole occupation is to deliver nonces to the intruder.

Finally, we made somewhat different assumptions about principals' ability to distinguish between different types of messages. The Protocol Analyzer always makes the assumption that principals, when asked to retrieve the head of a concatenated list, will always choose the correct word; that is, they will not pick a smaller chunk of the word, or the first two words in the list, for example. However, it makes no other assumptions, except for what the specification writer tells it to assume. Thus we can specify cases in which principals can or cannot tell different types of words from each other.

In our specification we originally started out by making no assumptions about recognizability except for those that are built into the Analyzer. This resulted in searches that failed to terminate, since the Analyzer kept on generating paths that contained local state variables containing longer and longer words. Thus we gave principals the ability to recognize when a message contained the appropriate amount of words. We also gave principals the ability to recognize whether a word was a public key. This seemed reasonable since some formatting of a public key is necessary in order for it to be usable; for RSA, for example, a user needs to know which is the modulus and which is the exponent. Finally, we gave the server the ability to recognize names, since the server could tell whether or not something was a name by determining whether or not there was a public key associated with it, and we gave the initiator the ability to recognize the name of the principal it was trying to initiate a conversation with. However, when a principal was expecting a nonce, or the responder received what purported to be a name of an initiator, we specified no ability to recognize that a word of this type was what was actually received.

3.3 The Analysis

We analyzed four different versions of the Needham-Schroeder protocol. The first was the original version of the protocol, with the assumptions about typing that we mentioned in the previous section. The second was Lowe's fix of the protocol. The third was the fix with the assumption added that the responder could recognize when a word was not a name. The last was a specification as close to Lowe's specification of the fixed protocol as possible, for purposes of comparison. In this specification we left out the key distribution phase, and we also left out the assumption that nonces could be compromised. All our analyses took place using SWIProlog 2.1.14 running on a Sparc 20 running SunOS 5.4.

In all our analyses except one, we kept track of two statistics: the amount of time a search took, and the number of states that were generated during the search. By "state generated" we mean a state the Analyzer generated in the course of a search that was not immediately rejected as unreachable. This means that the correlation between the time a search took and states generated was not very tight, since some searches may generate more unreachable states than others, even if the number of states that had not been proved unreachable was the same. We also note that times could vary considerably given the load on the system; however we still include them because they help give a relative idea of how long the Protocol Analyzer performed on various problems.

We began by asking the Analyzer how to reach two final states: one in which the initiator of a protocol had accepted a nonce as coming from an honest responder, and one in which a responder had accepted a nonce as coming from an honest initiator. These did generate the attacks described at the beginning of this paper, as well as legitimate runs of the protocol. We also found the following attack:

The protocol proceeds normally in the first six steps:

1. $A \rightarrow S: B$
2. $S \rightarrow A: \{K_B, B\}_{K_S^{-1}}$
3. $A \rightarrow B: \{R_A, A\}_{K_B}$
4. $B \rightarrow S: A$
5. $S \rightarrow B: \{K_A, A\}_{K_S^{-1}}$
6. $B \rightarrow A: \{R_A, R_B\}_{K_A}$

At this point, I intercepts the message and sends it to A, as the first message in the authentication coming to A from some other party.

3'. $I \to A : \{R_A, R_B\}_{K_A}$

A decrypts the message, and, thinking that R_B is some party initiating communications, sends off a request to S for its public key.

4'. $A \to S: R_B$

Now I can learn R_B and impersonate A to B, causing B to think A has successfully responded to it:

7. $I_A \to B: \{R_B\}_{K_B}$

We did not attempt to perform an exhaustive search in this case.

Then, in order to better compare our work with Lowe's we tried asking the Analyzer the same or similar questions that Lowe asked FDR. Note that the attack we just mentioned above did not appear in these cases, since although B accepted R_B as from A when it had not been sent by A, A had in fact initiated the conversation.

In each case, we asked the Analyzer how two states could be found. The first, corresponding to Lowe's $AUTH\_RESP$, was a state in which an initiator A would accept a nonce R_B as coming from an honest responder B in response to a request containing R_A when:

1. B had not sent R_B to A in response to R_A, and;
2. R_A had not been compromised.

The second condition was necessary because the Needham-Schroeder protocol (or any other) could trivially be compromised if a secret was compromised during the session in which was generated.

The other state, corresponding to Lowe's $AUTH\_INIT$, was a state in which a responder B accepted a nonce R_A as coming from an honest initiator A to which it had responded with R_B when:

1. A had not initiated a session with B using R_A, and;
2. R_B had not been compromised.

We began by running the Analyzer on the second state. In this case, we were able to generate Lowe's attack and another. This attack, like the one on the initiator we presented earlier, relies upon a confusion between names and nonces.

We also found a number of minor variations on Lowe's and the above attack.

Unfortunately, we were not able to complete an exhaustive search in this case. The Analyzer state space exploded when it was well into its search, and this overwhelmed the resources of our system. However, this had an interesting result. After we finished the analysis of the other protocols, we returned to this case and attempted to complete the search by examining the unreachable states produced in the original search and using the results to suggest new lemmas to be proved about unreachability of states. We were still not successful in completing the search, but we proved similar lemmas for the other versions of the protocol, and found that we had reduced the number of states produced considerably. In most cases we reduced the amount of time taken by a proof too, although the reduction was not as dramatic. This is probably because the time taken up in checking each of the lemmas made up for some of the time saved in checking fewer states.

Our search on the state in which the initiator is fooled went much more smoothly, and completed in about half an hour with no manual intervention, generating 155 states. The Analyzer found the following rather quaint attack, in which the initiator can be fooled if it is trying to talk to itself:

1. $A \rightarrow S : A$
2. $S \rightarrow A : \{K_A, A\}_{K_S^{-1}}$
3. $A \rightarrow A : \{R_A, A\}_{K_A}$

This is intercepted by I, who sends the following to A as responder, impersonating A as initiator.

6. $I_A \rightarrow A: \{R_A, A\}_{K_A}$

A as initiator checks for R_A, and believes that it has successfully responded to itself. It will now assume that the second field is a nonce, encrypt that field under K_A, and send the result to itself.

Again, this "attack" depends upon A's confusing messages containing names with messages containing nonces.

We next ran the Protocol Analyzer on Lowe's fix to the Needham-Schroeder protocol, but did not make the assumption that principals could distinguish between names and nonces. Verification of the protocol from the point of view of the responder (Lowe's $AUTH\_INIT$) could now be done completely automatically, and took a little under an hour, generating 689 states. Verification of the protocol from the point of view of the initiator (Lowe's $AUTH\_RESP$) took only about three and a half minutes, generating 66 states. In our second try using the additional lemmas we had proved, $AUTH\_INIT$ took 50 minutes generating 360 states, and $AUTH\_RESP$ took three minutes generating 34 states. Moreover, we were able to prove that the protocol was now sound with respect to these properties. No attacks were found in the exhaustive search. This is not surprising. First of all, Lowe's attack is prevented because the second message can no longer be passed off as coming from another user. Secondly, the various type of confusion attacks are prevented because, even though principals can not distinquish between a name and a nonce, they can distingish between different types of messages. One is an encrypted string containing one word, one contains two, and one contains three.

We next ran the Protocol Analyzer on the fixed protocol with typing built in. This did not change the results, but the verification was somewhat faster. Verification of soundness from the responder's point of view ($AUTH\_INIT$) took about forty-five minutes, generating 612 states, while verification from the initiator's point of view ($AUTH\_RESP$) took about two and a half minutes, generating 60 states. Using the additional lemmas, $AUTH\_INIT$ took 38 minutes generating 276 states, while $AUTH\_RESP$ took 2 minutes generating 26 states. Note that the ability to distinguish nonces from names did not give us much a benefit here, probably because principals already had the ability to distinguish between different types of messages.

Finally, for the purposes of comparison, we ran the Protocol Analyzer on a version of the protocol that corresponded more closely with Lowe's, leaving off request for and distribution of public keys and the compromise of old nonces. For this protocol, verification of *AUTH_RESP* took under two minutes and generated 57 states, while the verification of *AUTH_INIT* showed even more marked improvement, taking about four and a half minutes and generating 128 states. Using the additional lemmas, *AUTH_RESP* took one minute 45 seconds and generated 32 states, while *AUTH_INIT* took six minutes to generate 75 states. In contrast, the FDR analysis took about thirty seconds each running on a Pentium PC for *AUTH_RESP* and *AUTH_INIT*, most of the time being spent on compiling the process definitions, and generated 251 states for each check [9]. In order to get a feel for how the two tools would perform on the same platform, we also used the Analyzer and FDR to analyze their respective protocol specifications on a Sparc 10 on which we had a copy of FDR. In this case the Analyzer took about four times as long as FDR, so FDR's lead was maintained.

4   Comparision Between the NRL Protocol Analyzer and Lowe's Analysis Method

There are a number of similarities between the NRL Protocol Analyzer analysis and Lowe's. Both model the protocol in terms of processes communicating across a channel controlled by a hostile intruder who can modify, intercept and destroy messages. Both deal with a possibly infinite state space by proving results showing that if an attack takes place it must do so within a finite state space, and then searching that space exhaustively. However, the way in both the search and the proofs are conducted are very different.

With the Protocol Analyzer, the user first uses the tool to generate a number of lemmas that identify a number of states as unreachable, and others that are only reachable if certain conditions are satisfied. The user then specifies an insecure final state, and the Analyzer searches backwards. Each time it encounters a state, it tests it against each of the conditions on unreachability stated by the lemmas. If the state satisfies one of these it is discarded. This means, that, every time a state is generated, it must be subjected to a number of tests. This is an inefficient way of searching, especially towards the end of an analysis when the number of lemmas is large. Thus it is not surprising that the Analyzer is much worse at searching through a large number of states than FDR, or any other model checker, for that matter. There is also the drawback that the user never really knows when the Analyzer has proved enough lemmas, except when a search has successfully completed. Thus the usual strategy is to generate a set of standard lemmas, try a search, see where it blows up, generate some more lemmas, and try a search again.

Lowe's analysis proceeded in a very different way. First, it was proved that the fixed Needham-Schroeder protocol was only vulnerable if an attack could be produced within a certain easily defined search space. Then a specification which generated exactly that search space was searched using FDR. This made for a much for efficient search than that done by the Protocol Analyzer. On the other hand, the proof, which was somewhat complex, was informal and manual. Although the NRL Protocol Analyzer results give independent confirmation that no errors or hidden assumptions were made, this has not always been the case with hand analyses of cryptographic protocols. It is easy to let one's intuition about what should happen get in the way of one's perception of what is actually going on. An automated proof mechanism, which is not burdened by intuition, can often be at an advantage here. Finally, it also appears that the the lemma-proving capability of the Analyzer, if used carefully, can be used to generate a search space that is much smaller than that that would be searched by a model checker. Thus, our analysis of Lowe's fix of the Needham-Schroeder protocol generated 128 and 57 states for the two goals, while Lowe's analysis generated 251 states for each one. The model checker's more efficient search mechanism, however, more than makes up for any potential disadvantages in search time arising from this difference.

One marked difference between the Analzyer and FDR was the fact that the amount of time used to verify $AUTH\_INIT$ and $AUTH\_RESP$ differed greatly for the Analyzer but was the same for FDR. This is because the Analyzer works backwards from a specified final state, and the protocol terminates earlier for the initiator than the receiver. On the other hand, FDR works forwards from an initial state, and thus generates the same state space no matter what property is being verified. We can see how this property of the Analyzer could be useful in analyzing large-scale protocols. Such protocols generally consist of a number of smaller protocols interacting together. If the protocol is well-designed, this interaction should be minimal, and searching backwards from a specified final state should only require examination of a part of the possible state space. Thus, the Analyzer could be well-positioned to explore the security of such protocols.

In summary, it would appear that the Analyzer is better at proving than searching, while Lowe's analysis, at least in its present state, is better at searching that proving. However, Lowe's proofs have the advantage that they are directed to a particular goal, namely, proving that one needs to check only a previously defined finite search space. Thus no trial and error is involved. This suggests a possible direction for Analyzer proofs. Presently lemmas are generated according to rules of thumb, and proved blindly until the user is satisfied, by trial and error, that the Analyzer can complete its search. But it might be possible to indicate a large but finite search space, and see if the Analyzer can used to prove that an exhaustive search of that space is enough to verify a protocol's security.

If it is possible to direct the Analyzer's lemmas in such a way, this suggests a possible way of combining the Analyzer with a model checker. The Analyzer, with its built-in proof techniques specific to cryptographic protocols, could be used to narrow the original infinite search space to a finite one. A model checker could then be used to search the finite space. This would allow us to obtain the benefits of both technologies.

5 Conclusion

In this paper we compared the usefulness of the NRL Protocol Analyzer and model checkers to cryptographic protocol analysis by studying the application of the Analyzer and the model checker FDR to the same protocol. We found the two tools to be somewhat complementary. FDR was very good at exploring a finite state space quickly, but needed outside assistance to prove that exploring a finite state space was sufficient to prove security of a protocol. The Analyzer was considerably slower in exploring state spaces, but could be used to generate a finite state space and prove that exploring it was sufficient for proof of security. This in turn led to considerations of possible directions for future research in which the best parts of the two technologies could be combined.

6 Acknowledgements

I would like to thank Bill Roscoe for suggesting that I apply the NRL Protocol Analyzer to the Needham-Schroeder public key protocol, and Gavin Lowe for useful discussions on his use of FDR to analyze that protocol.

References

1. Michael Burrows, Martín Abadi, and Roger Needham. A Logic of Authentication. *ACM Transactions in Computer Systems*, 8(1):18–36, February 1990.
2. Formal Systems (Europe) Ltd. *Failures Divergence Refinement Users Manual and Tutorial, Version 1.4*, January 1994.
3. Dieter Gollmann. What do We Mean by Entity Authentication? In *Proceedings of the 1996 IEEE Computer Society Symposium on Security and Privacy*, pages 55–61. IEEE Computer Society Press, Los Alamitos, California, 1996.
4. C. A. R. Hoare. *Communicating Sequential Processes*. Prentice Hall, 1985.
5. Richard Kemmerer, Catherine Meadows, and Jonathan Millen. Three Systems for Cryptographic Protocol Analysis. *Journal of Cryptology*, 7(2), 1994.
6. D. Longley and S. Rigby. An Automatic Search for Security Flaws in Key Management Schemes. *Computers and Security*, 11(1):75–90, 1992.
7. Gavin Lowe. An attack on the Needham-Schroeder public key protocol. *Information Processing Letters*, 56:131–133, 1995.
8. Gavin Lowe. Breaking and fixing the Needham-Schroeder public-key protocol using CSP and FDR. In *Proceedings of TACAS*. Springer Verlag, 1996.
9. Gavin Lowe. personal communication, Feb. 1996.
10. Catherine Meadows. The NRL Protocol Analyzer: An overview. *Journal of Logic Programming*, 26(2):113–131, February 1996.
11. J. K. Millen, S. C. Clark, and S. B. Freedman. The Interrogator: Protocol Security Analysis. *IEEE Transactions on Software Engineering*, SE-13(2), 1987.
12. R. M. Needham and M. D. Schroeder. Using Encryption for Authentication in Large Networks of Computers. *Communications of the ACM*, 21(12):993–999, December 1978.
13. Einar Snekkenes. *Formal Specification and Analysis of Cryptographic Protocols*. PhD thesis, University of Oslo, May 1995.

Author Index

Springer-Verlag
and the Environment

We at Springer-Verlag firmly believe that an international science publisher has a special obligation to the environment, and our corporate policies consistently reflect this conviction.

We also expect our business partners – paper mills, printers, packaging manufacturers, etc. – to commit themselves to using environmentally friendly materials and production processes.

The paper in this book is made from low- or no-chlorine pulp and is acid free, in conformance with international standards for paper permanency.

Lecture Notes in Computer Science

For information about Vols. 1–1081

please contact your bookseller or Springer-Verlag

Vol. 1116: J. Hall (Ed.), Management of Telecommunication Systems and Services. XXI, 229 pages. 1996.

Vol. 1117: A. Ferreira, J. Rolim, Y. Saad, T. Yang (Eds.), Parallel Algorithms for Irregularly Structured Problems. Proceedings, 1996. IX, 358 pages. 1996.

Vol. 1118: E.C. Freuder (Ed.), Principles and Practice of Constraint Programming — CP 96. Proceedings, 1996. XIX, 574 pages. 1996.

Vol. 1119: U. Montanari, V. Sassone (Eds.), CONCUR '96: Concurrency Theory. Proceedings, 1996. XII, 751 pages. 1996.

Vol. 1120: M. Deza. R. Euler, I. Manoussakis (Eds.), Combinatorics and Computer Science. Proceedings, 1995. IX, 415 pages. 1996.

Vol. 1121: P. Perner, P. Wang, A. Rosenfeld (Eds.), Advances in Structural and Syntactical Pattern Recognition. Proceedings, 1996. X, 393 pages. 1996.

Vol. 1122: H. Cohen (Ed.), Algorithmic Number Theory. Proceedings, 1996. IX, 405 pages. 1996.

Vol. 1123: L. Bougé, P. Fraigniaud, A. Mignotte, Y. Robert (Eds.), Euro-Par'96. Parallel Processing. Proceedings, 1996, Vol. I. XXXIII, 842 pages. 1996.

Vol. 1124: L. Bougé, P. Fraigniaud, A. Mignotte, Y. Robert (Eds.), Euro-Par'96. Parallel Processing. Proceedings, 1996, Vol. II. XXXIII, 926 pages. 1996.

Vol. 1125: J. von Wright, J. Grundy, J. Harrison (Eds.), Theorem Proving in Higher Order Logics. Proceedings, 1996. VIII, 447 pages. 1996.

Vol. 1126: J.J. Alferes, L. Moniz Pereira, E. Orlowska (Eds.), Logics in Artificial Intelligence. Proceedings, 1996. IX, 417 pages. 1996. (Subseries LNAI).

Vol. 1127: L. Böszörményi (Ed.), Parallel Computation. Proceedings, 1996. XI, 235 pages. 1996.

Vol. 1128: J. Calmet, C. Limongelli (Eds.), Design and Implementation of Symbolic Computation Systems. Proceedings, 1996. IX, 356 pages. 1996.

Vol. 1129: J. Launchbury, E. Meijer, T. Sheard (Eds.), Advanced Functional Programming. Proceedings, 1996. VII, 238 pages. 1996.

Vol. 1130: M. Haveraaen, O. Owe, O.-J. Dahl (Eds.), Recent Trends in Data Type Specification. Proceedings, 1995. VIII, 551 pages. 1996.

Vol. 1131: K.H. Höhne, R. Kikinis (Eds.), Visualization in Biomedical Computing. Proceedings, 1996. XII, 610 pages. 1996.

Vol. 1132: G.-R. Perrin, A. Darte (Eds.), The Data Parallel Programming Model. XV, 284 pages. 1996.

Vol. 1133: J.-Y. Chouinard, P. Fortier, T.A. Gulliver (Eds.), Information Theory and Applications II. Proceedings, 1995. XII, 309 pages. 1996.

Vol. 1134: R. Wagner, H. Thoma (Eds.), Database and Expert Systems Applications. Proceedings, 1996. XV, 921 pages. 1996.

Vol. 1135: B. Jonsson, J. Parrow (Eds.), Formal Techniques in Real-Time and Fault-Tolerant Systems. Proceedings, 1996. X, 479 pages. 1996.

Vol. 1136: J. Diaz, M. Serna (Eds.), Algorithms – ESA '96. Proceedings, 1996. XII, 566 pages. 1996.

Vol. 1137: G. Görz, S. Hölldobler (Eds.), KI-96: Advances in Artificial Intelligence. Proceedings, 1996. XI, 387 pages. 1996. (Subseries LNAI).

Vol. 1138: J. Calmet, J.A. Campbell, J. Pfalzgraf (Eds.), Artificial Intelligence and Symbolic Mathematical Computation. Proceedings, 1996. VIII, 381 pages. 1996.

Vol. 1139: M. Hanus, M. Rogriguez-Artalejo (Eds.), Algebraic and Logic Programming. Proceedings, 1996. VIII, 345 pages. 1996.

Vol. 1140: H. Kuchen, S. Doaitse Swierstra (Eds.), Programming Languages: Implementations, Logics, and Programs. Proceedings, 1996. XI, 479 pages. 1996.

Vol. 1141: H.-M. Voigt, W. Ebeling, I. Rechenberg, H.-P. Schwefel (Eds.), Parallel Problem Solving from Nature – PPSN IV. Proceedings, 1996. XVII, 1.050 pages. 1996.

Vol. 1142: R.W. Hartenstein, M. Glesner (Eds.), Field-Programmable Logic. Proceedings, 1996. X, 432 pages. 1996.

Vol. 1143: T.C. Fogarty (Ed.), Evolutionary Computing. Proceedings, 1996. VIII, 305 pages. 1996.

Vol. 1144: J. Ponce, A. Zisserman, M. Hebert (Eds.), Object Representation in Computer Vision. Proceedings, 1996. VIII, 403 pages. 1996.

Vol. 1145: R. Cousot, D.A. Schmidt (Eds.), Static Analysis. Proceedings, 1996. IX, 389 pages. 1996.

Vol. 1146: E. Bertino, H. Kurth, G. Martella, E. Montolivo (Eds.), Computer Security – ESORICS 96. Proceedings, 1996. X, 365 pages. 1996.

Vol. 1147: L. Miclet, C. de la Higuera (Eds.), Grammatical Inference: Learning Syntax from Sentences. Proceedings, 1996. VIII, 327 pages. 1996. (Subseries LNAI).

Vol. 1148: M.C. Lin, D. Manocha (Eds.), Applied Computational Geometry. Proceedings, 1996. VIII, 223 pages. 1996.

Vol. 1149: C. Montangero (Ed.), Software Process Technology. Proceedings, 1996. IX, 291 pages. 1996.

Vol. 1150: A. Hlawiczka, J.G. Silva, L. Simoncini (Eds.), Dependable Computing – EDCC-2. Proceedings, 1996. XVI, 440 pages. 1996.

Vol. 1151: Ö. Babaoğlu, K. Marzullo (Eds.), Distributed Algorithms. Proceedings, 1996. VIII, 381 pages. 1996.

Vol. 1153: E. Burke, P. Ross (Eds.), Practice and Theory of Automated Timetabling. Proceedings, 1995. XIII, 381 pages. 1996.

Vol. 1154: D. Pedreschi, C. Zaniolo (Eds.), Logic in Databases. Proceedings, 1996. X, 497 pages. 1996.

Vol. 1155: J. Roberts, U. Mocci, J. Virtamo (Eds.), Broadbank Network Teletraffic. XXII, 584 pages. 1996.

Vol. 1156: A. Bode, J. Dongarra, T. Ludwig, V. Sunderam (Eds.), Parallel Virtual Machine – EuroPVM '96. Proceedings, 1996. XIV, 362 pages. 1996.

Vol. 1157: B. Thalheim (Ed.), Entity-Relationship Approach – ER '96. Proceedings, 1996. XII, 489 pages. 1996.

Vol. 1158: S. Berardi, M. Coppo (Eds.), Types for Proofs and Programs. Proceedings, 1995. X, 296 pages. 1996.